DICHO Y HECHO

DICHO Y HECHO

BEGINNING SPANISH

THIRD EDITION

LAILA M. DAWSON
University of Richmond

ALBERT C. DAWSON
University of Richmond

Illustrations by
G. B. McINTOSH

WILEY

JOHN WILEY & SONS
New York ▪ Chichester ▪ Brisbane ▪ Toronto ▪ Singapore

To Eric and Sheila

Library of Congress Cataloging in Publication Data:

Dawson, Laila M., 1943–
  Dicho y hecho : beginning Spanish.

  Albert C. Dawson's name appears first on the
earlier edition.
  Includes index.
  Summary: A textbook for first-year Spanish students which emphasizes communication and
provides a cultural exploration of the Hispanic world.
  1. Spanish language—Textbooks for foreign speakers—English. 2. Spanish language—Grammer—1950–   . [1. Spanish language—Grammar]

I. Dawson, Albert C., 1939–
II. McIntosh, G. B., ill. III. Title.
PC4129.E5D38 1989   468.2'421   88-20784
ISBN 0-471-63136-1

Printed in the United States of America

10 9 8 7 6

PREFACE

Dicho y Hecho offers to you:

—A student-oriented, classroom-tested text that in its first two editions constantly brought praise from students for its clarity, practicality, and ease of use;

—A carefully organized textbook structure that is built around key topics and concepts, which provide a unified, progressive, and integrated approach to learning Spanish;

—A text that is crafted with the goal of creating in the classroom an environment of lively and varied application through:

1. Vocabulary that becomes active by means of multiple and progressive phases of application, ranging from identification in the introductory drawings to personal expression and situational conversations in the *Actividades*;

2. Exercises designed to maximize opportunity for direct interaction between student and teacher with student texts closed;

3. A creative array of exercises and application activities presented to maintain a good pace and rhythm to classroom activity by varying interaction—teacher to student, student to student (pairing), and in small groups;

4. Step-by-step confidence-building techniques that move the student from controlled to creative response and ultimately to self-expression within the context of a particular theme or idea;

5. A visual component that uses a cast of identifiable characters to allow the student to relate and react to situations, actions, and conditions reflecting the theme, vocabulary, and structures of each chapter;

—A clear, uncomplicated introduction to the Hispanic world—its geography, its history, its cultural distinctiveness, the expression of its people;

—A philosophical premise and goals in keeping with the guidelines for proficiency as developed by the American Council on the Teaching of Foreign Languages and the Educational Testing Service.

PROGRAM ■

Dicho y Hecho is a *complete* first-year language program composed of:

—The main textbook of fourteen chapters (including the unique visual component entitled *Integración visual*);
—A workbook/laboratory manual composed of *Integración: ejercicios escritos* designed to practice writing and translation skills, and to reinforce classroom activity, and *Integración: manual de laboratorio* with a format for the tape program that offers the student practice and reinforcement of the vocabulary and grammar of each chapter (including exercises based on the small illustrations) and practice in auditory comprehension;
—Accompanying tapes;
—Accompanying transparencies;
—*Annotated Instructor's Edition* with suggestions for presentation and reinforcement of material, script to accompany the *Integración visual* section, a sample syllabus, and sample tests;
—An extensive component of *Intensive Exercises* for use in small-group drill/ practice sessions.

CHAPTER FEATURES ■

Each chapter is introduced by an overview that includes the goals for communication and the areas of cultural exploration.

Vocabulario: Each unit of vocabulary, topically organized and presented in a context, is based on a theme applicable to the student's life and to "survival" situations in the Spanish-speaking world. In each chapter a drawing related to the theme of the chapter introduces the unit of vocabulary. Introductory exercises practice vocabulary through (1) use of the illustration, (2) application of the vocabulary to areas of personal and general reference, and (3) word association and definition exercises. Vocabulary is also practiced and reinforced through (4) contextual use in the *Conversación*, (5) exercises based on grammar presented in each chapter, (6) creative application in the *Actividades*, and ultimately through (7) the visual component, *Integración visual*.

Conversación: The purpose of the *Conversaciones* is to provide a concise, practical context for application of the vocabulary and introduction to the grammar. (Items related to the vocabulary/grammar of the chapter are printed in boldface.) These short situational dialogues, designed for oral practice, follow the same topical themes as the accompanying vocabulary. *Conversa-*

ciones are followed by a brief exercise (to check retention of content orally) and/or by an *Actividad* designed to create ''on-the-spot'' situations in the classroom for immediate creative, contextual application of the vocabulary.

Estructura: Students first observe grammatical structures in a context through sample sentences, then study the concise explanations (in English) that follow. Each grammatical structure is presented in its most commonly used form without complex ramifications. Related grammatical structures are progressively presented (rather than being fragmented throughout the text) and are consistently reintroduced through practice in subsequent chapters.

Ejercicios: Each segment of grammar is followed by exercises that primarily develop the students' oral/aural proficiency skills. Grammar exercises are fast-moving, contextual (based on a core idea, theme, or situation) and within each grammatical structure progress from controlled response to open-ended creative expression. Ample opportunity is provided for student interaction in pairs, especially through the **Tú y yo** series. Exercises are designed to be used with textbooks closed (with the exception of the **Tú y yo** series) and in Spanish, as all instructions beyond the first half of Chapter 1 are given in the target language.

Actividades: Interspersed throughout the chapter, *Actividades* provide students the opportunity to apply the vocabulary and grammar creatively in particular situations. *Actividades* include situational mini-dramas (both prepared and spontaneous), oral activities and presentations, compositions, mime, and so on. Students are thus able to work in small groups, in pairs, and individually.

Realia: Sayings, advertisements, road signs, and so on, strategically located within each chapter, provide additional cultural insights and are thematically tied to vocabulary and grammar.

Panorama cultural: Reading selections fall into three categories. Chapters 1 through 4 present an introductory overview of the Hispanic world (''*El mundo hispano*,'' ''*La familia hispana*,'' ''*La comida hispana*,'' ''*La vida hispana*''). Chapters 5 through 12 present brief historical-geographic-cultural synopses of the major Spanish-speaking areas of the world including, in some instances, ''*testimonios*'' from individuals who live there. Chapters 13 and 14 provide travel-oriented readings (taken from magazines and brochures) involving the student imaginatively in travel experiences to and in a foreign country.

Integración visual: This unique component following the *Panorama cultural* of each chapter is an integral part of the classroom experience. Used most effectively in the form of transparencies (available through John Wiley & Sons), it encourages an open, communicative atmosphere between student and teacher. All illustrations and accompanying script (found in the *Annotated Instructor's Edition*) are specifically designed to enhance the learning, practice, and reinforcement of the vocabulary and grammar of each chapter and offer an exciting, unique opportunity for teaching, learning, testing.

Repaso de vocabulario activo: At the end of each chapter the active vocabulary (without translations) is presented in a checklist alphabetized by parts of speech.

Autoexamen y Repaso: Review exercises at the end of each chapter may be used by students individually or in groups as an excellent study aid for tests. They provide a brief overview of the vocabulary and structures of the chapter. The last section of each set of review exercises (beginning with Capítulo 3) practices grammatical structures from previous chapters. An Answer Key for the review exercises is in Appendix II.

Reference Tools: At the end of the text are the following reference tools: paradigms of regular, stem-changing, orthographic changing, and irregular verbs; answers to review exercises; Spanish-English, English-Spanish vocabularies (active vocabulary labeled by chapter); and the index.

¡Que les sirva bien, y que gocen de la experiencia!

Laila M. Dawson
Albert C. Dawson

ACKNOWLEDGMENTS

We would like to extend a very personal and warm expression of acknowledgment to our artist Gail McIntosh for her extraordinary illustrations, which bring to the text a unique artistic dimension.

We wish to express our sincere appreciation to our colleagues and friends in the Department of Modern Foreign Languages of the University of Richmond, especially Humberto Cardounel, Robert A. MacDonald, and Rose Marie Marcone, for their support and valued suggestions. A special debt of gratitude is also owed to Elena Sánchez-Olea, José (Pepe) Hernández, Carlos Berguido, Adelina Cid Reborido, Víctor Martell Matus, Guillermo Trujillo Molina, Teófilo Schenker, Lourdes Cardounel, and Judith Buchanan for their assistance in providing information for the sections entitled *Panorama Cultural*. For their assistance in manuscript preparation, we thank Betty Gunter, Jacqueline Moenssens, and Scott Thompson.

For their indispensable observations and insights we thank the following reviewers: Renée Andrade, Mt. San Antonio College; Nelson G. Arana, University of South Dakota; Margaret E. Beeson, Kansas State University; C. Maurice Cherry, Furman University; Neil Devereaux, Angelo State University; Allan Dyer, Eastern Montana College; Charlene R. Flanagan, University of Pennsylvania and St. Joseph's University; John W. Griggs, Glendale Community College; Leonora Guinazzo, Portland Community College; Cristina Lambert, County College of Morris; Viva Lynn, Utah State University; Sivya Molins, Community College of Philadelphia; Jaime Padilla, Kirkwood Community College; Edgardo J. Pantigoso, Northeastern Illinois University; Alicia Ramos, University of Missouri-St. Louis; William H. Roberts, Austin Community College; Gerald R. St. Martin, Salisbury State College; Judith L. Shrum, Virginia Polytechnic Institute and State University; and Claudia Sternberg, San Antonio College. To Ron Nelson, Foreign Language Editor, John Wiley & Sons, and Elizabeth Hovinen, Map and Book Editor, we are deeply grateful for their key roles in the development and final publication of *Dicho y Hecho* and for their continuous support.

LMD
ACD

CONTENTS

CAPÍTULO 5   123

CAPÍTULO 6   155

CAPÍTULO 7   185

■ PRONUNCIATION ■

LA PRONUNCIACIÓN THE SOUNDS OF SPANISH ■

NOTE: The contents of this section are recorded on a separate tape labeled **La pronunciación.**

I. A *sampling of Spanish you already know*

Can you give the Spanish pronunciation of these Spanish/English words?

patio	burro	fiesta	siesta	amigo	taco	adiós	loco
marihuana	matador	tequila	hacienda	adobe	vista		
rodeo	Vega	Pinto	El Dorado	Del Monte	Fresca		
Toro	Colorado	Nevada	California	Florida	Arizona		
San Francisco	Los Ángeles	Amarillo	San Antonio	Las Vegas			
Río Grande	Linda	Teresa	María	Dolores	Margarita		

II. Cognates: *a sampling of words identical or similar in Spanish and in English*

Practice the pronunciation of the following cognates.

hospital	hotel	teléfono	rancho	chocolate	dentista
doctor	general	presidente	millonario	piano	tractor
animal	mosquito	elefante	inteligente	estúpido	
ignorante	famoso	honesto	popular	importante	inferior
superior	extraordinario	interesante	romántico	fantástico	
ridículo	sentimental	terrible	responsable	pesimista	
optimista	idealista	realista	generoso	independiente	
tímido	dinámico	invitar	visitar	comunicar	preferir

III. Vocales
Vowels

Unlike English vowels, each Spanish vowel has only one basic sound, even though there may be slight variations created by its position within a word or phrase. Spanish vowels are short and clipped, never drawn out.

Listen carefully and repeat each sound as it is pronounced. (The English equivalents in italics are only approximations.)

a	*bah*	**ama, fama, lana, mapa, lata**
e	*Betty, let*	**nene, bebe, leche, fe, ese**
i	*bikini*	**mi, si, sin, fin, Fifi**
o	*more*	**loco, coco, toco, foco, mono**
u	*flu*	**tu, su, Tulum, Lulú**

EJERCICIO 1

Repeat the following children's verse, focusing on the vowel sounds.

a   e   i   o   u
Arbolito del Perú
Yo me llamo _____.
¿Cómo te llamas tú?

EJERCICIO 2

Repeat the following sounds, and then pronounce them on your own, gradually increasing your speed.

ama	eme	imi	omo	umu
aba	ebe	ibi	obo	ubu
ala	ele	ili	olo	ulu
afa	efe	ifi	ofo	ufu

EJERCICIO 3

Pronounce the following words, concentrating on the vowel emphasized.

a	patio	taco	fantástico		**o**	famoso	Dolores	rosa
e	Teresa	teléfono	médico		**u**	estúpido	pluma	uno
i	Linda	ridículo	disco					

IV. Diptongos
Diphthongs

> DEFINITION: In Spanish, a diphthong is a combination of two vowels, at least one of which is an unaccented **i** or **u**.

Diphthongs are pronounced as a single syllable.

bien   cuidado   agua

Strong   Weak
a   i
e   u
o

EJERCICIO 4

Pronounce the vowel combinations as found in the following sounds and words.

ai	aire	baile	**iu**	triunfo	viuda
au	auto	Laura	**oi**	oigo	heroico
ei	seis	veinte	**ua**	cuatro	Guatemala
eu	Europa	seudo	**ue**	bueno	Venezuela
ia	piano	Diana	**ui**	Luisa	ruina
ie	fiesta	diez	**uo**	cuota	mutuo
io	adiós	idiota			

V. Consonantes problemáticas
Problem consonants

b The consonants **b** and **v** are identical in pronunciation. Initial **b** and **v** (and after **m** and **n**) are pronounced like the English *b* in *boy*.

bueno   bien   vista   violeta   sombrero

In other positions they are pronounced less explosively.

lobo   favor   jueves   adobe

c In Spanish America, **c** before **e** or **i** has the English *s* sound as in *sister*.

cero   cinco   gracias   centro

In most regions of Spain **c** before **e** or **i** is pronounced with a *th* sound as in *thanks*.

cero   cinco   gracias   centro

Before **a**, **o**, **u**, or consonants **c** has the English *k* sound as in *cat*.

como   cama   clase   criminal

d At the beginning of a phrase or sentence (after a pause), or after **n** or **l**, **d** is pronounced like a slightly softened English **d**.

día   dos   cuando   caldo

In other positions, particularly between vowels and at the end of a word, **d** has a slight *th* sound as in *this*.

médico   todo   Santo Domingo   sed

g Before **e** or **i**, **g** has the English *h* sound as in *help*.

generoso   inteligente   gitano   mágico

In other positions (except between vowels where it is slightly softened) it is hard as in *goat*.

gracias   gusto   tango   amigo

In the combinations **gue** and **gui**, **u** is silent as in *guest*.

guitarra   guerra   guía

h Silent as in *honest*.

hotel   hospital   honor   alcohol

j Approximates the pronounced *h* sound of English as in *help*.

jueves   jardín   junio   ejercicio

ll Approximates the English *y* sound as in *yes*.

> **llamar   calle   silla   llevar**

ñ Has the sound of *ny* as in *canyon*.   ~ = tilde

> **señor   niño   mañana   año**

q Occurs only in the combinations **que** and **qui**, which have a silent **u**.

> **que   chiquita   queso   quince**

r If not initial, **r** approximates the sound of *tt* as in *Betty likes butter better* or *dd* as in *Eddy*.

> **tres   tarea   escriba   oración**

rr Has a trilled sound as in mimicking a motorcycle; initial **r** has the same sound.

> **perro   pizarra   roto   Rodolfo**

Try the following verse:
> Erre con erre cigarro
> erre con erre barril.
> Rápido corren los carros
> carros del ferrocarril.

x Before most consonants **x** has an *s* sound.

> **extra   sexto   experiencia**

Between two vowels **x** has a *ks* sound.

> **examen   existir   taxi**

(A common exception is found in the words **México** and **mexicano** which, although written with an **x**, are pronounced with a Spanish **j**.)

z In Spanish America **z** is pronounced the same as *s*.

> **zapato   Arizona   paz   lápiz**

In most regions of Spain **z** is pronounced with a *th* sound as in *thanks*.

> **zapato   Arizona   paz   lápiz**

EJERCICIO 5

Practice the following consonants.

ca	que	qui	co	cu		lla	lle	lli	llo	llu
ca	ce	ci	co	cu		ña	ñe	ñi	ño	ñu
ga	gue	gui	go	gu		va	ve	vi	vo	vu
ga	ge	gi	go	gu		ba	be	bi	bo	bu
ha	he	hi	ho	hu		za	ze	zi	zo	zu
ja	je	ji	jo	ju		sa	se	si	so	su

VI. El alfabeto
The alphabet

The letters and their names in Spanish are:

a (a)	**f** (efe)	**k** (ka)	**ñ** (eñe)	**rr** (erre)	**w** (ve doble)
b (be)	**g** (ge)	**l** (ele)	**o** (o)	**s** (ese)	(uve doble)
c (ce)	**h** (hache)	**ll** (elle)	**p** (pe)	**t** (te)	**x** (equis)
ch (che)	**i** (i)	**m** (eme)	**q** (cu)	**u** (u)	**y** (i griega)
d (de)	**j** (jota)	**n** (ene)	**r** (ere)	**v** (ve) (uve)	**z** (zeta)
e (e)					

EJERCICIO 6

Spell the following words using the Spanish alphabet.

1. rancho
2. general
3. hotel
4. señorita
5. ejercicio
6. yo
7. Amarillo
8. quince
9. terrible
10. examen
11. voz
12. gusto

VII. Acentuación
Accents and stress

A. In Spanish if a word has a written accent mark (called in Spanish **acento**), the accented syllable is stressed.

tímido   di**ná**mico   ri**dí**culo

B. In words without a written accent the following rules apply.

✳ 1. The next to the last syllable is stressed if the word ends in a vowel or **n** or **s**.

patio   a**do**be   re**pi**tan   **lu**nes

✳ 2. The last syllable is stressed if the word ends in a consonant other than **n** or **s**.

ani**mal**   doc**tor**   liber**tad**

EJERCICIO 7

Pronounce the following words, stressing the correct syllable.

1. pro/fe/sor
2. den/tis/ta
3. es/tú/pi/do
4. ge/ne/ral
5. pre/si/den/te
6. u/ni/ver/si/dad
7. vi/si/tar
8. per/so/nal
9. te/lé/fo/no
10. lla/mo
11. ro/mán/ti/co
12. cla/se

■CAPÍTULO■

1

Goals for communication
- Greeting, meeting, saying good-bye
- Working in the classroom environment
- Identifying and describing people and things
- Counting and expressing time

Cultural exploration
- The Spanish language
- The Hispanic world

SALUDOS Y EXPRESIONES COMUNES ■
GREETINGS AND COMMON EXPRESSIONS

Presentaciones Getting acquainted

ESTUDIANTE	#1	**¿Cómo se llama usted?** (formal)
		(¿Cómo te llamas?) (informal)
	#2	**Me llamo . . .** (name).
	#1	**Permítame presentar a** (name).
	#2	**Mucho gusto.**
	#3	**El gusto es mío.**
STUDENT	#1	*What is your name?* (formal)
		(What's your name?) (informal)
	#2	*My name is* (name).
	#1	*Allow me to introduce* (name).
	#2	*Very pleased to meet you.*
	#3	*The pleasure is mine.*

¿Cómo te llamas?
Estudiantes en Cali,
Colombia.

Saludos 1 (formal) *Greetings*

1 **Buenos días, (señorita).**	*Good morning, Miss.*
(Buenas tardes), (señora).	*(Good afternoon), (Ma'am, Mrs.).*
(Buenas noches), (señor).	*(Good evening, night), (Sir, Mr.).*
2 **Muy buenos. ¿Cómo está usted?**	*Good morning. How are you?*
(Muy buenas.)	*(Good afternoon, evening.)*
1 **Muy bien, gracias. ¿Y usted?**	*Very well, thanks. And you?*
(Excelente.)	*(Fantastic, excellent.)*
(Regular, así así)	*(Fair, so-so.)*
2 **Bien, gracias.**	*Fine, thanks.*

Saludos 2 (informal)

1 **Hola,** (name).	*Hello, hi, (name).*
2 **Hola,** (name). **¿Cómo estás?**	*Hello, hi, (name). How are you?*
(¿Cómo te va?)	*(How's it going?)*
(¿Qué tal?)	*(How's it going?)*

¡Saludos! Guadalajara,
México.

1 Bien, ¿y tú?	*Fine, and you?*
2 Bastante bien, gracias. ¿Qué hay de nuevo?	*Well enough, thanks. What's new?*
1 Nada de particular.	*Nothing much.*

Expresiones de cortesía *Expressions of courtesy*

1 Hágame el favor de abrir la puerta.	*Do me the favor of opening the door.*
(Por favor, abra la puerta.)	*(Please open the door.)*
2 Con mucho gusto.	*With pleasure (gladly).*
1 Muchas gracias, señor (señorita, señora).	*Thank you (many thanks), Sir (Miss, Ma'am).*
2 De nada.	*You are welcome.*
(No hay de qué.)	*(You are welcome.)*

Sí, por favor.	*Yes, please.*
No, gracias.	*No, thank you.*
Perdón.	*Pardon me, excuse me (to get someone's attention or to seek forgiveness).*
Con permiso.	*Pardon me, excuse me (to seek permission to pass by someone or to leave).*

Despedida *Departure*

Adiós. *Good-bye.*
Hasta luego. *See you later.*
Hasta mañana. *See you tomorrow.*

> NOTE: In Spanish there are two different forms of address depending upon the degree of formality or informality that exists between the persons speaking.

¿Cómo está usted? ⎫
¿Y usted? ⎬ Used in formal situations.
¿Cómo se llama usted? ⎭ Last-name-basis relationships.

¿Cómo estás? ⎫
¿Qué tal? ⎪ Used in informal situations.
¿Y tú? ⎬ First-name-basis relationships
¿Cómo te llamas? ⎭ (classmates, peers, children, etc.).

EJERCICIO 1 ¿Cómo se llama usted?

Get acquainted with at least five of your classmates and your instructor by first getting their attention and then learning their names.

Modelos **Perdón, ¿Cómo se llama usted? (Me llamo. . . .)**
Perdón, ¿Cómo te llamas? (Me llamo. . . .)

EJERCICIO 2 Las presentaciones

Following the model, take turns introducing a colleague to at least four other classmates and to the instructor. Each party should respond to the greeting and introduction as appropriate.

Modelo (Introduction) **Buenos días (buenas tardes, noches),** (*name*).
Permítame presentar a (*name*).
(Response to introduction) **Mucho gusto.**
(Followup to response) **El gusto es mío.**

EJERCICIO 3 ¿Sí, por favor *o* no, gracias?

You are at the home of a Spanish-speaking friend for a meal. When your host asks

¿Desea usted . . . ? (*Do you want, desire . . . ?*) how do you respond?

Modelo ¿Desea usted un yogur?
No, gracias. (o)
Sí, por favor . . . ¡muchas gracias!

1. ¿Desea usted rosbif?
2. ¿Desea usted coliflor?

3. ¿Desea usted tacos?
4. ¿Desea usted espárragos?
5. ¿Desea usted ensalada?
6. ¿Desea usted espinacas (*spinach*)?
7. ¿Desea usted vino (*wine*)?
8. ¿Desea usted tequila?
9. ¿Desea usted un chocolate?
10. ¿Desea usted un cigarrillo?
    y, . . . ¿Desea usted una
    "A" en español?

EJERCICIO 4 Saludos y expresiones

Give a logical response to each greeting, question, or expression.

1. Buenos días.
2. Buenas tardes.
3. ¿Cómo se llama usted?
4. ¿Cómo está usted?
5. Permítame presentar a (*name*).
6. Mucho gusto.
7. ¿Qué tal?
8. ¿Qué hay de nuevo?
9. Hágame el favor de abrir la puerta.
10. Muchas gracias.
11. Adiós.

EJERCICIO 5 ¿Qué dice usted? (*What do you say?*)

   Modelo   . . . cuando (*when*) usted necesita pasar enfrente de una per-
            sona en la cafetería.
            Con permiso.

¿Qué dice usted?
            when
1. . . . cuando una persona famosa entra en la clase de español.
2. . . . cuando un amigo entra en la clase de español.
3. . . . cuando el (la) profesor(a) entra en la clase de español.
4. . . . cuando usted necesita interrumpir una conversación.
5. . . . cuando usted necesita salir (*to leave*).
6. . . . cuando usted necesita la atención del profesor.
7. . . . cuando usted necesita pasar enfrente de una persona.
8. . . . cuando usted hace (*make*) un error muy grande.
9. . . . cuando usted recibe un cheque grande de su mamá o papá.

ACTIVIDAD Saludos

You and a classmate create a dialog that might take place on the first day of classes. Use as many greetings and expressions as possible.

VOCABULARIO EN LA CLASE DE ESPAÑOL ▪

la **clase de español**	*Spanish class*	el **lápiz**	*pencil*
el **profesor**	*professor, teacher (m.)*	la **pluma**	*pen*
		el **bolígrafo**	*ballpoint pen*
la **profesora**	*professor, teacher (f.)*	el **libro**	*book*
		la **lección**	*lesson*
el **estudiante, alumno**	*student (m.)*	la **página**	*page*
la **estudiante, alumna**	*student (f.)*	el **ejercicio**	*exercise*
la **puerta**	*door*	la **oración**	*sentence*
la **ventana**	*window*	la **palabra**	*word*
la **pizarra**	*blackboard*	la **pregunta**	*question*
la **tiza**	*chalk*	la **respuesta**	*answer*
la **silla**	*chair*	el **cuaderno**	*notebook*
la **mesa**	*table*	el **papel**	*paper*
el **escritorio**	*desk*	la **tarea**	*homework*
el **pupitre**	*desk (school)*	el **examen**	*exam, test*
		la **nota**	*grade*

¡Vamos a la clase! Buenos Aires, Argentina.

Instrucciones

abra	*open* (singular command—to one person)
abran	*open* (plural command—to more than one person)
cierre(n)	*close*
complete(n)	*complete*
conteste(n)	*answer*
escriba(n)	*write*

voise loud or tall

estudie(n)	*study*
lea(n)	*read*
en voz alta	*aloud*
repita(n)	*repeat*
siénte(n)se	*sit down*
traduzca(n)	*translate*
pase(n) a	*go to*

EJERCICIO 6   Asociación

¿Qué palabra(s) asocia usted con cada (each) una de las siguientes (following) referencias?

Modelo la respuesta
la pregunta

1. la pizarra
2. la pluma
3. el examen
4. la profesora
5. la puerta
6. la mesa
7. la pregunta
8. el libro
9. el cuaderno
10. el escritorio

EJERCICIO 7   Las instrucciones

Usted es el(la) profesor(a). Complete las instrucciones.

Modelo Pase a . . .
Pase a la pizarra.

1. Abra . . .
2. Estudie . . .
3. Traduzca . . .
4. Repita . . .
5. Complete . . .
6. Cierre . . .
7. Lea . . .
8. Escriba con (*with*) . . .
9. Conteste . . .
10. Siéntese en . . .

Modelo el libro
Lea el libro.

11. la ventana
12. el ejercicio
13. la pregunta
14. la pizarra
15. la lección
16. la oración
17. en la silla

✳ CONVERSACIÓN

*Hoy es el primer día de **clases** en la universidad. Susana y Pepe son **estudiantes**.*

SUSANA	¡Hola, Pepe!
	¿Vas a la **clase de español**?
PEPE	Sí. ¿Sabes quién es el **profesor**?
SUSANA	Es la[1] **señora** Gómez.
PEPE	¡Qué bueno! Ella es **cubana** y es una profesora **magnífica**.
SUSANA	¿Ya tienes los **libros de español**?
PEPE	No. Voy a la librería esta tarde para comprar **libros, cuadernos, lápices.** . . .
SUSANA	Oye, **¿qué hora es?**
PEPE	¡Ay! **Son las diez.** ¡Vámonos!

NOTE 1:   In Spanish the definite article (**el**—masculine or **la**—feminine) is used with titles when the person is not addressed directly.

Today is the first day of classes at the university. Susan and Pepe are students.

SUSAN	*Hi, Pepe! Are you going to Spanish class?*
PEPE	*Yes. Do you know who the professor is?*
SUSAN	*It's Mrs. Gomez.*
PEPE	*Great! She is Cuban, and she is a marvelous teacher.*
SUSAN	*Do you already have your Spanish books?*
PEPE	*No. I'm going to the bookstore this afternoon to buy books, notebooks, pencils.* . . .
SUSAN	*Listen, what time is it?*
PEPE	*Oh! It's ten o'clock. Let's go!*

En mi opinión, profesor Gómez . . . Buenos Aires, Argentina.

PREGUNTAS

Conteste en español en oraciones completas.

1. ¿Va Pepe a la clase de historia? No, Pepe va a la clase de español.
2. ¿Cómo se llama la profesora? La profesora se llama Señora Gómez.
3. ¿De qué (*of what*) nacionalidad es la profesora? Ella es cubana.
4. ¿Es la señora Gómez una profesora buena o es una profesora terrible? Ella es una profesora buena.
5. ¿Tiene Pepe los libros de español? No, Pepe no tiene los libros de español.
6. ¿Qué hora es? What hour is it? Son las diez.

ESTRUCTURA ■

I. Artículos y nombres
Articles and nouns

A. Los artículos en el singular

Definite and indefinite articles in Spanish are either masculine or feminine, depending on the noun with which they are used.

1. **El alumno** es excelente.
   La alumna es excelente.

> **Artículos definidos en el singular: el** (masculino) = *the*
> **la** (femenino) = *the*

2. **Un alumno** está (*is*) en la clase.
   Una alumna está en la clase.

> **Artículos indefinidos en el singular: un** (m.) = *a, an*
> **una** (f.) = *a, an*

B. Los nombres en el singular

All nouns in Spanish, even those referring to nonliving things, are either masculine or feminine.

1. **El padre** (*father*) necesita **un libro**.
   El alumno necesita **un cuaderno**.

> Most nouns that end in **o** and nouns referring to male beings are masculine.

2. **Una mujer** (*woman*) entra en **la librería**.
   La señorita necesita **una pluma**.

> Most nouns that end in **a** and nouns referring to female beings are feminine.

3. Traduzca **la conversación**.
   Lea **la oración**.

> Nouns that end in **(c)ión** are feminine.

4. **El lápiz** está en **el pupitre**.
   La clase tiene **un examen** por (*in*) **la tarde**.

All other nouns must be memorized as masculine or feminine. Always study vocabulary by saying the article with the noun.

dad + tad are feminine.

EJERCICIO 8   ¡Estudien!

Usted es el (la) profesor(a). Indique lo que (*what*) *los estudiantes necesitan estudiar. Use el artículo definido* **el** *o* **la**.

   Modelo   vocabulario
            Estudien el vocabulario.

Estudien . . .

1.	lección *la*	5.	oración *la*	9.	examen *el*
2.	respuesta *la*	6.	página *la*	10.	libro *el*
3.	pregunta *la*	7.	conversación *la*	11.	tarea *la*
4.	ejercicio *el*	8.	diálogo *el*		

EJERCICIO 9   ¿Qué es?

Identifique la palabra usando (*using*) *el artículo indefinido.*

   Modelo   silla
            Es una silla.

1.	mesa *una*	5.	cuaderno *un*	9.	ventana *una*
2.	escritorio *un*	6.	lápiz *un*	10.	puerta *una*
3.	pupitre *un*	7.	libro ~~una~~ *un*	11.	observación *una*
4.	bolígrafo *un*	8.	examen *un*	12.	insecto *un*

La alumna y el alumno
conversan de sus clases.
Veracruz, México.

C. Los artículos en el plural

Observe the definite and indefinite plural articles in these sample sentences.

Los alumnos son mexicanos.   **Las profesoras** son bolivianas.
Unos alumnos son argentinos.   **Unas profesoras** son españolas.

> **Artículos definidos en el plural: los** (m.) = *the*
> **las** (f.) = *the*

> **Artículos indefinidos en el plural: unos** (m.) = *some*
> **unas** (f.) = *some*

D. Los nombres en el plural

Compare the formation of the plural nouns in the following sample sentences
(1 and 2).

1. **Los ejercicios** están (*are*) en la página diez.
   Las preguntas están en la pizarra.
   Los estudiantes están el la clase.

   > Nouns ending in a vowel add **-s** to form the plural.

2. **Los profesores** están en la clase.
   Las oraciones están en la pizarra.
   Los lápices están en el escritorio. (*Note spelling change of z to c.*)

   > Nouns ending in a consonant add **-es** to form the plural.

EJERCICIO 10   ¿Qué necesita? (*What do you need?*)

No necesito uno. Necesito muchos. Cambie (change) *la palabra al plural.*

   Modelo   el libro
            Necesito los libros.

Necesito . . .   los exámenes

1. el cuaderno	4. la respuesta	7. el bolígrafo	10. el papel
2. el examen	5. el lápiz	8. la nota	11. la lección
3. la pregunta	6. la pluma	9. la oración	12. la tarea

II. Los adjetivos
Adjectives

Adjectives in Spanish agree in gender (masculine or feminine) and number (singular or plural) with the nouns they modify.

A. Los adjetivos en el singular

Observe the adjectives as they modify masculine and feminine nouns.

1. Carlos es **honesto**.
   Teresa es **honesta**.
   Carlos es un alumno **extraordinario**.
   Teresa es una alumna **extraordinaria**.
   George es un alumno **americano**.
   Susan es una alumna **americana**.

> Adjectives ending in **-o** change the **-o** to **-a** to agree with a feminine singular noun.

2. Carlos es **inteligente**.
   Teresa es **inteligente**.
   Carlos es un alumno **superior**.
   Teresa es una alumna **superior**.

Adjectives ending in **-e** or a consonant, except those of nationality, remain unchanged in gender (masculine or feminine).

3. Roberto es **español**.
   Lolita es **española**.
   Pedro es **portugués**.
   Inés es **portuguesa**.

Adjectives of nationality that end in a consonant add an **-a** for the feminine singular form. Adjectives of nationality are not capitalized in Spanish.

NOTE: An accent on the final vowel of the masculine form is omitted in the feminine: **portuguesa.**

Feminine:
ends in a, change to a
ends in consonant add a.

VOCABULARIO

americano(a)	American	**alemán(a)**	German
chino(a)	Chinese	**español(a)**	Spanish
italiano(a)	Italian	**francés(a)**	French
mexicano(a)	Mexican	**inglés(a)**	English
ruso(a)	Russian	**japonés(a)**	Japanese
		portugués(a)	Portuguese

NOTE: **Alemán, chino, español, inglés, italiano, japonés, portugués,** and **ruso** in the masculine form also function as the name of the language. Note that they are not capitalized.

B. Los adjetivos en el plural

Observe how the plural form of the adjective agrees with the noun it modifies.

Pepe es **romántico**. Lupe es **sentimental**.
Pepe y Pancho son **románticos**. Lupe y Paco son **sentimentales**.
Alicia es **inteligente**. Charles es **inglés**.
Alicia y Ana son **inteligentes**. Charles y Diana son **ingleses**.*

To form the plural, adjectives ending in a vowel add **-s** and those ending in a consonant add **-es**.

*NOTE: When an adjective modifies both a masculine and a feminine noun, the masculine plural form of the adjective is used.

C. Posición de los adjetivos

Observe the position of the adjectives in Spanish in contrast with English.

Felipe es un **estudiante responsable**.	*Philip is a responsible student.*
Lupe es una **persona dinámica**.	*Lupe is a dynamic person.*
Eva y Rita son **alumnas alemanas**.	*Eva and Rita are German students.*

In Spanish descriptive adjectives most commonly *follow* the noun.

EJERCICIO 11   Él y ella (He *and she*)

Él y ella son similares.

Modelo   Él es honesto.
Ella es honesta también (*also*).

1. Él es extraordinario.
2. Él es romántico.
3. Él es sincero.
4. Él es generoso.
5. Él es artístico.
6. Él es inteligente.
7. Él es excelente.
8. Él es importante.
9. Él es popular.
10. Él es sentimental.
11. Él es mexicano.
12. Él es español.
13. Él es inglés.
14. Él es alemán.
15. Él es ruso.

EJERCICIO 12   El señor y la señora Lorca

¿Qué tipo de profesores son?

Modelo   magnífico
El señor Lorca es un profesor magnífico.
La señora Lorca es una profesora magnífica.

1. fantástico
2. responsable
3. dinámico
4. inteligente
5. disciplinado
6. interesante
7. paciente

EJERCICIO 13   ¿Cómo son? (*What are they like?*)

Conteste según el modelo.

Modelo   Diego es honesto, ¿verdad? (*right? true?*)
Sí, es (*he is*) **honesto.**
¿Y Pepe y Paco?
Sí, son (*they are*) **honestos también** (*also*).

1. Diego es modesto, ¿verdad?
   ¿y Lola?
   ¿y Lupe y Linda?
   ¿y Pepe y Paco?

2. Lola es sincera, ¿verdad?
   ¿y Diego?
   ¿y Lupe y Linda?
   ¿y Pepe y Paco?

(handwritten in left margin: Go over again.)

3. Diego es excepcional, ¿verdad?   4. Pepe es español, ¿verdad?
   ¿y Lola?   ¿y Linda?
   ¿y Lupe y Linda?   ¿y Linda y Lola?
   ¿y Pepe y Paco?   ¿y Paco y Diego?

III. Puntuación y posición de palabras
Punctuation and word order

A. Puntuación

¿Cómo se llama la profesora?
¡Ah! ¡Ella es magnífica!

In questions and exclamations, written Spanish uses an inverted question mark at the beginning of questions and an inverted exclamation point at the beginning of exclamations, as well as the expected punctuation at the end.

Names of punctuation marks in Spanish include:

el **signo de interrogación**	¿ . . . ?	*question mark*
el **signo de admiración**	¡ . . . !	*exclamation point*
el **punto**	.	*period*
los **dos puntos**	:	*colon*
la **coma**	,	*comma*
el **punto y coma**	;	*semicolon*
el **paréntesis**	(. . .)	*parenthesis*

B. Posición de palabras en preguntas

Compare the position of the subject in relation to the verb in the following questions and statements.

¿Cómo está **el profesor**? **El profesor** está bien.
¿Es **el señor Lema** italiano? **La señora Lema** es francesa.

> In questions the subject most commonly follows the verb.

C. Posición de palabras en oraciones negativas

Observe the position of **no** in relation to the verb.

Carlos **no es** inteligente.
¿Es Carlos generoso? **No**, Carlos **no es** generoso.

> In negative statements, **no** is placed before the verb. In answering a question with a negative statement, the **no** is repeated.

EJERCICIO 14   ¿Cómo es usted? (*What are you like?*)

Conteste afirmativa o negativamente.

Modelo   ¿Es usted ambicioso(a)?
Sí, soy (*I am*) **ambicioso(a)**.
No, no soy ambicioso(a).

1. ¿Es usted sentimental?
2. ¿Es usted romántico(a)?
3. ¿Es usted cruel?
4. ¿Es usted ridículo(a)?
5. ¿Es usted artístico(a)?
6. ¿Es usted generoso(a)?
7. ¿Es usted sensacional?
8. ¿Es usted ignorante?
9. ¿Es usted terrible?
10. ¿Es usted alemán(a)?
11. ¿Es usted inglés(a)?
12. ¿Es usted chino(a)?

IV. Días de la semana
Days of the week

¿Qué día es hoy?	What day is it today? ¿ or ¿Cuál es la Fecha? Date
lunes	*Monday*
martes	*Tuesday*
miércoles	*Wednesday*
jueves	*Thursday*
viernes	*Friday*
sábado	*Saturday*
domingo	*Sunday*
el fin de semana	*weekend*

La semana tiene **5** vuelos a **EUROPA** por Aeroméxico

Lunes, martes, miércoles, jueves y viernes a las 12:00 horas en punto.

NOTE 1: The days of the week are generally not capitalized in Spanish.

NOTE 2: The definite article **el** or **los** is used with the day of the week to indicate *on*.

el lunes *on Monday*   **los miércoles** *on Wednesdays*

EJERCICIO 15 *¿Qué día es?*

A. Conteste las preguntas según el modelo.

> Modelo Si (*if*) hoy es lunes, ¿qué día es mañana (*tomorrow*)?
> **Mañana es martes.**

1. Si hoy es miércoles, ¿qué día es mañana?
2. Si hoy es viernes, ¿qué día es mañana?
3. Si hoy es domingo, ¿qué día es mañana?
4. Si hoy es martes, ¿qué día es mañana?
5. Si hoy es jueves, ¿qué día es mañana?
6. Si hoy es sábado, ¿qué día es mañana?

B. Indique:

1. Su (*your*) día favorito.
2. Su día menos (*least*) favorito.
3. Un día bueno para (*for*) fiestas.
4. Un día bueno para ir (*to go*) a la catedral, a la iglesia (*church*), a la sinagoga, etc.
5. Los días de la clase de español.
6. Los días de NO ir a la clase de español.
7. Los días del fin de semana.

V. Números 0–29
Numbers

cero	0	diez y seis (dieciséis)	16
uno	1	diez y siete (diecisiete)	17
dos	2	diez y ocho (dieciocho)	18
tres	3	diez y nueve (diecinueve)	19
cuatro	4	veinte	20
cinco	5	veinte y uno (veintiuno)	21
seis	6	veinte y dos (veintidós)	22
siete	7	veinte y tres (veintitrés)	23
ocho	8	veinte y cuatro (veinticuatro)	24
nueve	9	veinte y cinco (veinticinco)	25
diez	10	veinte y seis (veintiséis)	26
once	11	veinte y siete (veintisiete)	27
doce	12	veinte y ocho (veintiocho)	28
trece	13	veinte y nueve (ventinueve)	29
catorce	14		
quince	15		

EJERCICIO 16 Vamos a practicar. (*Let's practice.*)

1. Vamos a contar (*Let's count*):
   a. de cero a veinte y ocho—0, 2, 4, 6, . . .
   b. de uno a veinte y nueve—1, 3, 5, . . .
2. Mi número de teléfono es. . . .
3. Matemáticas
   (*Plus* is **y** or **más**; *minus* is **menos**; *equals* is **son**.)

3	6	7	8	10	20	28	21	26	18
+4	+6	+4	+5	+9	−5	−2	−5	−12	−17

VI. La hora
Telling time

la hora	*the hour, the time*
¿Qué hora es?	*What time is it?*
¿A qué hora?	*At what time?*
cuarto	*a quarter*
media	*half*
de la mañana	A.M. (*in the morning*)
de la tarde	P.M. (*in the afternoon*) 12:00 pm - 7:00 pm
de la noche	P.M. (*in the evening, at night*) 7:00 - 12:00 pm
Es el mediodía.	*It's noon.*
Es la medianoche.	*It's midnight.*

¿Qué hora es?
Son las diez y media de la noche.
No, son las once menos veinte.

Study the following clocks.

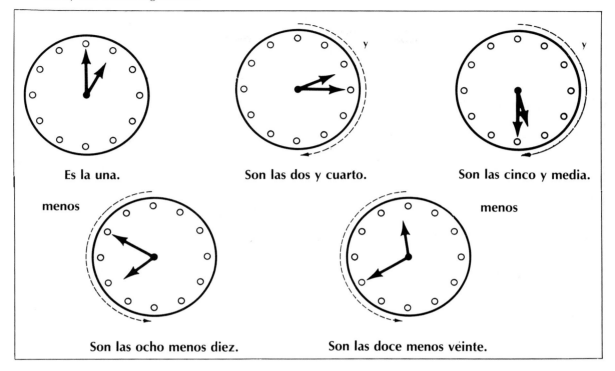

Es la una.　　　　Son las dos y cuarto.　　　　Son las cinco y media.

Son las ocho menos diez.　　　　Son las doce menos veinte.

The most common structure for telling time in Spanish is:

$$\text{Son (es) + las (la) + (hora)} \quad \begin{matrix} \mathbf{y} \\ \mathbf{menos} \end{matrix} \quad \text{(minutos)}$$

During the first thirty minutes after the hour, give the hour just past plus (**y**) the number of minutes. After thirty minutes, give the next hour less (**menos**) the number of minutes to go before the coming hour.

¿Qué hora es? Bogotá, Colombia.

NOTE: To indicate *at what time* an event occurs use:

$$a + las\ (la) + (hora)\ \genfrac{}{}{0pt}{}{y}{menos}\ (minutos)$$

¿A qué hora es el examen?
Es **a las diez menos cuarto de la mañana.**

EJERCICIO 17   ¿Qué hora es?

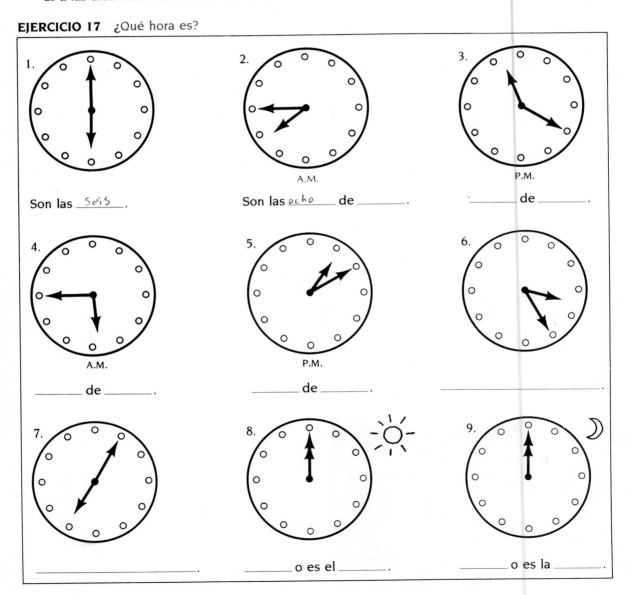

Son las ___*seis*___ .

Son las _*ocho*_ de _____ .

_____ de _____ .

_____ de _____ .

_____ de _____ .

_____ .

_____ .

_____ o es el _____ .

_____ o es la _____ .

EJERCICIO 18   ¿A qué hora?

Pregúntele a un(a) estudiante a qué hora es el programa, la clase, etc.; escuche la respuesta. (Ask a student at what time the program, the class, etc., is; listen to the response.

> Modelo   el programa/9:00
> (pregunta) **¿A qué hora es el programa?**
> (respuesta) **Es a las nueve.**

1. la clase/10:00
2. el concierto/7:00
3. la excursión/2:30

4. el examen/10:15
5. la fiesta/8:45

PANORAMA CULTURAL ▪

Nación	Población (aproximada)	Nacionalidad
México	82,000,000	mexicano
Guatemala	8,600,000	guatemalteco
El Salvador	5,300,000	salvadoreño
Honduras	4,800,000	hondureño
Nicaragua	3,300,000	nicaragüense
Costa Rica	2,800,000	costarricense
Panamá	2,300,000	panameño
Cuba	10,200,000	cubano
La República Dominicana	7,000,000	dominicano
Puerto Rico	3,300,000	puertorriqueño
Colombia	31,000,000	colombiano
Venezuela	18,300,000	venezolano
El Ecuador	10,000,000	ecuatoriano
El Perú	20,700,000	peruano
Chile	12,400,000	chileno
Bolivia	6,300,000	boliviano
El Paraguay	4,300,000	paraguayo
La Argentina	31,100,000	argentino
El Uruguay	3,000,000	uruguayo
España	40,000,000	español
	306,700,000	

Helpful hints for reading in Spanish:

1. Read the entire passage quickly to get a general idea of content.
2. Then read each paragraph for details, checking the glossed words

El Mundo Hispáno

ANDORRA
ESPAÑA
ISLAS BALEARES
ISLAS CANARIAS
MÉXICO
CUBA
REPÚBLICA DOMINICANA
GUATEMALA
HONDURAS
PUERTO RICO
EL SALVADOR
NICARAGUA
VENEZUELA
COSTA RICA
PANAMÁ
COLOMBIA
ECUADOR
PERÚ
BOLIVIA
CHILE
PARAGUAY
URUGUAY
ARGENTINA

0   500
KILÓMETROS

and guessing the meaning of new words within the context of the sentence.

3. Use the dictionary as little as possible, and only for words that you feel are essential to understanding the content.

4. Select important words and phrases from each paragraph to be used as keys for reconstructing essential ideas from the reading selection.

La *lengua* española y el *mundo* hispano*

language/world

La lengua española es una de las cinco lenguas *más* importantes del mundo.
¿*Por qué? Porque* es la lengua nacional de unos veinte *países*. *Más de trescientos*
millones de personas *hablan* español. Se habla español en España, en México, en seis naciones de la América Central, en tres islas de las Antillas
(Cuba, Puerto Rico y la República Dominicana) y en nueve naciones de la
América del Sur. ¿*Sabe* usted que el español es la segunda lengua más hablada en los *Estados Unidos* de América? Unos veinte millones de habitantes
estadounidenses hablan español.

most
*why/because/countries/
more than three hundred/
speak*

*do you know
United States*

El español es una lengua romance porque su origen, *como* el francés, el
italiano, el portugués y *otras* lenguas, es el latín. *Pero* el español *de* país *a*
país *tiene* variaciones de pronunciación y de vocabulario, como el inglés de
Inglaterra es diferente *del de* los Estados Unidos o del de Australia.

*like
other/but/from/to
has
England/that of*

Las personas de habla española representan una población muy diversa:
de origen español, indio, mestizo (combinación de indio y español), negro e
inmigrantes europeos de varios países (principalmente Italia, Alemania y
Portugal).

Cada país del mundo hispano, *desde* España *hasta* los países de la América Latina, tiene un carácter especial y una personalidad distinta, *por su gente*,
por su historia y por su posición geográfica.

*each/from/to
because of/people*

Es fascinante explorar *este* mundo hispano, un mundo extraordinaria-
mente *bello* e interesante. La lengua española *va a ser nuestro* vehículo. ¡Buen
viaje!

*this
beautiful/is going to be our
trip*

¿CUÁNTO RECUERDA USTED?   (How much do you remember?)

Complete las oraciones en la columna A con las conclusiones en la columna B.

A

1. El español es una de las cinco lenguas . . .
2. El origen del español es . . .
3. El español es . . .
4. Las personas que hablan es- pañol representan . . .
5. El español es la lengua nacional . . .
6. Mestizo significa . . .
7. Las tres islas de las Antillas donde se habla español son . . .
8. El español es la segunda lengua más hablada . . .
9. El español tiene variaciones . . .
10. Cada país del mundo hispano tiene . . .

B

a. . . . una lengua romance.
b. . . . en los Estados Unidos de América.
c. . . . más importantes del mundo.
d. . . . Cuba, Puerto Rico y la República Dominicana.
e. . . . el latín.
f. . . . una combinación de in- dio y español.
g. . . . de unos veinte países.
h. . . . un carácter especial.
i. . . . de pronunciación y de vocabulario.
j. . . . una población muy diversa.

*****Hispano**, used as an adjective, describes all that pertains or relates to Spain and the nations of Spanish America.

INTEGRACIÓN VISUAL: Capítulo 1

EJERCICIO 1.1 Vocabulario e instrucciones para la clase

Ejemplo   Lea _____.
Lea el libro.

 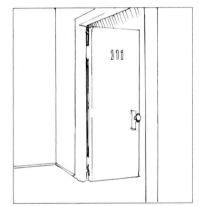 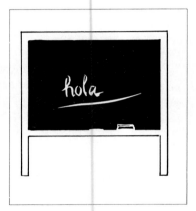

  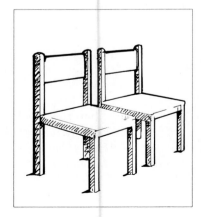

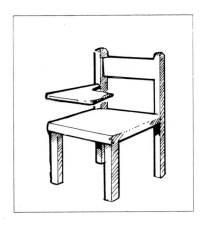

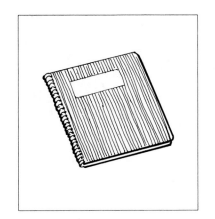

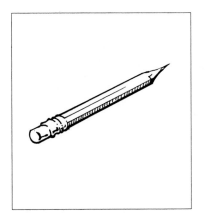

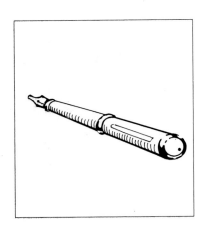

EJERCICIO 1.2   La hora

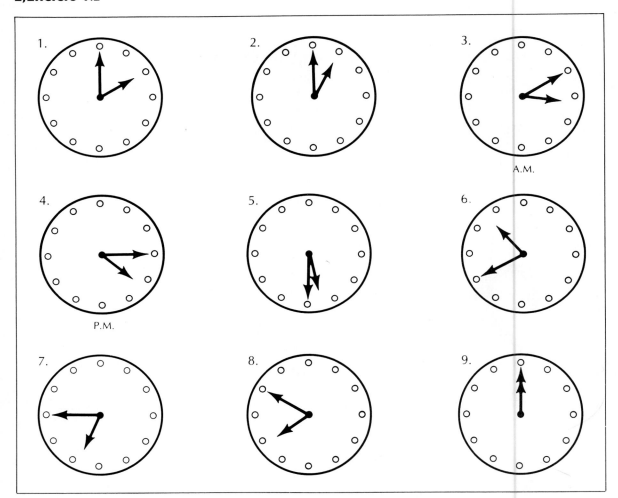

REPASO DE VOCABULARIO ACTIVO ▪

Saludos y expresiones comunes

Buenos días, señorita (señora, señor).
  Muy buenos.
Buenas tardes. Muy buenas.
Buenas noches. Muy buenas.
Hola.
¿Cómo se llama usted? ¿Cómo te llamas?

Me llamo . . . (name).
¿Cómo está usted? ¿Cómo estás?
¿Cómo te va? ¿Qué tal?
Muy bien, gracias.
Bastante bien, gracias.
Excelente.

Regular. Así, así.
¿Y usted? ¿Y tú?
¿Qué hay de nuevo?
Nada de particular.
Permítame presentar a . . . (name).
Mucho gusto.
El gusto es mío.
Hágame el favor de. . . .
Por favor. . . .
Con mucho gusto.

Muchas gracias.
De nada. No hay de qué.
Sí, por favor.
No, gracias.
Perdón.
Con permiso.
Adiós.
Hasta luego.
Hasta mañana.

En la clase de español

la **alumna**	el **escritorio**	la **mesa**	la **pizarra**	el **pupitre**
el **alumno**	el (la) **estudiante**	la **nota**	la **pluma**	la **respuesta**
el **bolígrafo**	el **examen**	la **oración**	la **pregunta**	la **silla**
la **clase de español**	el **lápiz**	la **página**	el **profesor**	la **tarea**
el **cuaderno**	la **lección**	la **palabra**	la **profesora**	la **tiza**
el **ejercicio**	el **libro**	el **papel**	la **puerta**	la **ventana**

abra(n)	conteste(n)	estudie(n)	pase(n) a	siénte(n)se
cierre(n)	escriba(n)	lea(n) . . . en voz alta	repita(n)	traduzca(n)
complete(n)				

Las nacionalidades

alemán(a)	**chino(a)**	**francés(a)**	**mexicano(a)**
americano(a)	**español(a)**	**italiano(a)**	**ruso(a)**

Días de la semana

¿Qué día es hoy?	**miércoles**	**sábado**
lunes	**jueves**	**domingo**
martes	**viernes**	**el fin de semana**

Números

cero	ocho	diez y seis
uno	nueve	diez y siete
dos	diez	diez y ocho
tres	once	diez y nueve
cuatro	doce	veinte
cinco	trece	veinte y uno . . .
seis	catorce	
siete	quince	

La hora

¿Qué hora es?	**media**	**de la noche**
¿A qué hora?	**de la mañana**	**Es el mediodía.**
cuarto	**de la tarde**	**Es la medianoche.**

Artículos

el	los	un	unos
la	las	una	unas

AUTOEXAMEN Y REPASO #1 ▓

I. Saludos y expresiones comunes

Indique el saludo, la pregunta o la expresión de cortesía que corresponde a la palabra indicada.

Modelo   buenos
Buenos días. Muy buenos.

1. buenas
2. llamas
3. llama
4. está
5. nuevo
6. nada
7. bien
8. presentar
9. gusto
10. hágame
11. muchas
12. qué
13. luego

II. Vocabulario e instrucciones

A. *¿Qué palabras asocia usted con cada una de las siguientes referencias?*

1. la tiza
2. el lápiz
3. el/la estudiante
4. la ventana
5. la silla
6. la respuesta
7. el ejercicio
8. la nota
9. el papel
10. el pupitre

B. *¿Qué instrucciones para la clase (**abra, cierre,** etc.) asocia usted con las siguientes palabras?*

1. la puerta
2. la tarea
3. a la mesa
4. las preguntas
5. las respuestas
6. el vocabulario

III. Artículos, nombres y adjetivos

A. *¿Cómo es la persona femenina?*

Modelo   El profesor es magnífico.
La profesora es magnífica.

1. El alumno es americano.
2. El señor Linares es español.
3. El estudiante es inteligente.
4. El señor Gómez es un profesor superior.

B. *¿Cómo son las personas?*

Modelo   Juan es popular. (Juan y Felipe)
Juan y Felipe son populares.

1. La profesora es inglesa. (las profesoras)
2. El estudiante es alemán. (los estudiantes)
3. Ana es sentimental. (Ana y Lupe)
4. La clase es interesante. (las clases)

IV. Posición de palabras en oraciones negativas

Indique que la información no es correcta. Cambie a la forma negativa.

1. Los libros son interesantes.
2. El profesor es ridículo.
3. La pregunta es importante.
4. Andrés es un alumno extraordinario.

V. Números; días de la semana

Complete.

1. dos, cuatro, seis, _____, _____, _____, _____, _____, _____, veinte.
2. uno, tres, cinco, _____, _____, _____, _____, _____, _____, diez y nueve.
3. lunes, martes, _____, _____, _____, _____, domingo.

VI. La hora

¿Qué hora es?

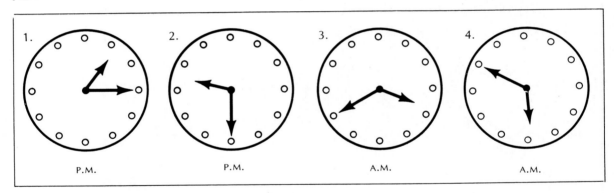

VII. Repaso general

A. *Conteste.*

1. ¿ Cómo te llamas?
2. ¿ Cómo estás?
3. ¿ Qué hay de nuevo?
4. ¿ Qué día es hoy?
5. ¿ Qué hora es?
6. ¿ Es la clase fantástica?

B. *Traduzca al español.*

1. At what time is the exam?
2. It is at 2:20 P.M.
3. What is the teacher's name?
4. Her name is Mrs. Pérez.
5. Mrs. Pérez is a very good professor.
6. The students in the Spanish class are not American. They are English.

NOTE: The answer key to the AUTOEXAMEN Y REPASO can be found in *Appendix II.*

EL SEÑOR Y   ANDRÉS Y JULIA   ANTONIO Y ELISA
LA SEÑORA TORRES   ANA   TEO
ELENA   JUANITO

■CAPÍTULO■

2

Goals for communication
- Talking about the family
- Identifying characteristics and conditions
- Expressing where we are going

Cultural exploration
- The Hispanic family
- Family names

VOCABULARIO LA FAMILIA

Tres generaciones de **la familia** son: *family*

el **abuelo**	*grandfather*	la **hija**	*daughter*
la **abuela**	*grandmother*	el **hermano**	*brother*
el **esposo**	*husband*	la **hermana**	*sister*
la **esposa**	*wife*	el **nene**	*baby* (m.)
el **padre**	*father*	la **nena**	*baby* (f.)
la **madre**	*mother*	el **bebé**	*baby* (m. or f.)
los **padres**	*parents*	el **nieto**	*grandson*
el **hijo**	*son*	la **nieta**	*granddaughter*

Otros **parientes** son: *relatives*

el **tío**	*uncle*	el **primo**	*cousin* (m.)
la **tía**	*aunt*	la **prima**	*cousin* (f.)
el **sobrino**	*nephew*	el **hombre**	*man*
la **sobrina**	*niece*	la **mujer**	*woman*

el **niño**	child (m.)	el **amigo**	friend (m.)
la **niña**	child (f.)	la **amiga**	friend (f.)
el **muchacho**, **chico**	boy	el **novio**	boyfriend
la **muchacha**, **chica**	girl	la **novia**	girlfriend

Algunas profesiones:

el **abogado**	lawyer (m.)	la **enfermera**	nurse (f.)
la **abogada**	lawyer (f.)	el **hombre de negocios**	businessman
el **médico**	doctor (m.)	la **mujer de negocios**	businesswoman
la **médica**	doctor (f.)	el **ingeniero**	engineer (m.)
el **enfermero**	nurse (m.)	la **ingeniera**	engineer (f.)

Otras palabras útiles:

la **casa**	house, home
el **coche**, **carro**, **auto**	car
el **perro**	dog
hay[1]	there is, there are

NOTE 1:   **Hay** derives from the irregular auxiliary verb **haber**, to have, and denotes existence, not location.

¿**Hay** un médico aquí?   Is there a doctor here?
Sí, **hay** un médico y una enfermera aquí.   Yes, there are a doctor and
                                                        a nurse here.

NOTE 2:   In a group that includes both males and females the masculine form predominates.

los **hermanos**   the brothers and sisters
los **hijos**   the sons and daughters

NOTE 3:   In Spanish the definite article is placed before a noun used in a general or abstract sense.

Los **abogados** son ingeniosos.   Lawyers (in general) are ingenious.

refrán (saying): **De tal padre, tal hijo.**

EJERCICIO I   La familia

Conteste en español en oraciones completas según el dibujo (according to the drawing) de la familia.

Modelo   ¿Cómo se llama el padre?
          El padre se llama Andrés.

La familia hispana se
mantiene muy unida.
Bogotá, Colombia.

1. ¿Cómo se llama la madre? ¿y la nena?
2. ¿Cómo se llama el hijo?
3. ¿Cómo se llama la hija?
4. ¿Cómo se llama el tío?
5. ¿Cómo se llama la tía?
6. ¿Cómo se llama el abuelo?
7. ¿Cómo se llama la abuela?
8. ¿Cómo se llama el perro?
9. ¿Es la casa colonial o (or) contemporánea?
10. ¿Hay un coche en el dibujo?

EJERCICIO 2 Las relaciones

Exprese la relación entre (between) *las personas según el dibujo.*

   Modelo   Elena/Juanito
         Elena es la hermana de (of) **Juanito.**

1. Julia/la nena
2. Andrés/Julia
3. el señor Torres/Juanito
4. Elena/la señora Torres
5. Elisa/Juanito
6. Juanito/Julia
7. Andrés y Julia/Elena
8. Juanito/Elena

EJERCICIO 3   Identificación

Dé varios nombres que identifican más a la persona. (Give several nouns that further identify the person.)

> Modelo   el abuelo
> **el hombre, el esposo, el padre**

1. la abuela
2. el tío
3. la madre

4. el hijo
5. la prima

EJERCICIO 4   ¿Hay un profesional aquí (*here*)?

Usted busca (are looking for) *un profesional. Haga dos preguntas con cada* (each) *combinación de palabras según el modelo.*

> Modelo   enfermero/responsable
> **¿Hay un enfermero responsable aquí?**
> **¿Hay una enfermera responsable aquí?**

1. abogado/honesto
2. médico/competente
3. ingeniero/famoso
4. hombre de negocios/ambicioso
5. profesora/bilingüe

CONVERSACIÓN ▩

Juan Hidalgo **es** *un estudiante mexicano.* **Es** *de Monterrey, una ciudad grande y moderna que* **está** *situada en el norte de México. Juan* **está** *visitando una clase de español en los Estados Unidos.*

LINDA   ¿Dónde **está** tu familia, Juan?
JUAN   En este momento **están** de vacaciones en Acapulco.
TERESA   ¿Cómo **es** tu **padre**?
JUAN   Pues, **es** un hombre alto, muy **simpático,** y de profesión **es médico.**
DANIEL   ¿Y tu **madre**?
JUAN   Mi **madre es bonita, morena** y muy **inteligente. Es** una **profesora** de arqueología.
MARÍA   ¿Tienes **hermanos**?
JUAN   Sí. Tengo dos **hermanos** y tres **hermanas. Van a** visitarme en octubre.

Juan Hidalgo is a Mexican student. He is from Monterrey, a large, modern city, which is located in the north of Mexico. Juan is visiting a Spanish class in the United States.

LINDA   *Where is your family, Juan?*
JUAN   *At this moment they are vacationing in Acapulco.*
TERESA   *What is your father like?*
JUAN   *Well, he is a tall, very nice man, and he is a doctor by profession.*
DANIEL   *And your mother?*
JUAN   *My mother is pretty, dark complected, and very intelligent. She is an archeology professor.*
MARÍA   *Do you have any brothers and sisters?*
JUAN   *Yes. I have two brothers and three sisters. They are going to visit me in October.*

PREGUNTAS

Conteste en español en oraciones completas según la conversación (1–6) y personalmente (7–8).

1. ¿Dónde (*where*) está Monterrey?
2. ¿Dónde está Juan Hidalgo?
3. ¿Dónde está la familia de Juan?
4. ¿Cuál (*which*) es la profesión del padre? ¿y de la madre?
5. ¿Cuántos (*how many*) hijos hay en la familia?
6. ¿Quiénes (*who*) van a visitar en octubre?
7. En este momento ¿dónde está su (*your*) familia, (nombre de estudiante)? **Mi** . . .
8. ¿Tiene usted hermanos?

ESTRUCTURA ▓

I. Los pronombres personales
Subject pronouns

The subject pronouns in Spanish are:

yo	*I*	**nosotros(as)**	*we*
tú	*you (familiar, first-name basis)*	**vosotros(as)**	*you (plural, familiar)*
usted	*you (formal, last-name basis)*	**ustedes**	*you (plural, formal)*
él	*he*	**ellos**	*they (m.)*
ella	*she*	**ellas**	*they (f.)*

> NOTE 1: Subject pronouns are most commonly omitted in Spanish when the reference is clear. However, for purposes of clarity, stress, or emphasis they may be used.

> NOTE 2: The **vosotros** form, commonly used in Spain, is rarely heard in Spanish America, where **ustedes** is used instead.

> NOTE 3: **Usted** is often abbreviated to **Ud.** or **Vd. Ustedes** is often abbreviated to **Uds.** or **Vds.** The abbreviated forms are always capitalized.

> NOTE 4: Spanish does not have a subject pronoun equivalent to *it*.

Es mi coche.   *It's my car.*

II. El verbo irregular ser en el presente
The irregular verb ser (to be) in the present tense

You may have observed that Spanish has two verbs meaning *to be*.

La profesora **es** española.	*The professor is Spanish.*
Los alumnos **son** inteligentes.	*The students are intelligent.*
¿Dónde **está** tu familia?	*Where is your family?*
¿Cómo **está** usted?	*How are you?*

These verbs (**ser** and **estar**) are not interchangeable. Each verb will be presented and practiced individually. Then their contrasting uses will be explained.

   Ser is an irregular verb (it does not follow a set pattern of conjugation) and thus must be learned separately. Study the forms of the present tense of the verb **ser** and the sample sentences.

ser *to be*

yo **soy**	*I am*	(Yo) **soy** americano(a).
tú **eres**	*you are*	¿**Eres** (tú) español?
usted **es**	*you are*	¿**Es** (usted) inglés?
él **es**	*he is*	(Él) **es** médico.
ella **es**	*she is*	(Ella) **es** abogada.
nosotros(as) **somos**	*we are*	(Nosotros) **somos** estudiantes.
vosotros(as) **sois**	*you are*	¿**Sois** (vosotros) amigos de él?
ustedes **son**	*you are*	¿**Son** (ustedes) de México?
ellos **son**	*they are*	(Ellos) **son** muy inteligentes.
ellas **son**	*they are*	(Ellas) **son** extraordinarias.

EJERCICIO 5 Características muy positivas

A. *Afirme las descripciones añadiendo* (adding) *un pronombre personal para indicar énfasis.*

> Modelo Es honesto.
> **Él es honesto.** (o)
> **Usted es honesto.**

1. Soy fantástico(a).
2. Eres artístico(a).
3. Es sentimental.
4. Son magníficos.
5. Son extraordinarias.
6. Somos excepcionales.
7. Sois disciplinados.
8. Es sincera.

B. *Indique cómo son las personas usando la forma correcta del verbo* **ser**.

> Modelo él/honesto
> **Es honesto.**

1. yo/inteligente
2. nosotros/simpáticos
3. él/responsable
4. tú/modesto
5. ustedes/admirables
6. ella/bonita
7. ellos/pacientes
8. vosotros/dinámicos
9. usted/generoso
10. ellas/muy positivas

VOCABULARIO In Chapter 1 and up to this point in Chapter 2 you have used, with the verb ser, descriptive adjectives that are similar to their English counterparts. Here are some other adjectives that are commonly used with ser.

gordo(a)	*fat*	**débil**	*weak*
delgado(a)	*slender*	**grande**	*large, big*
flaco(a)	*skinny*	**pequeño(a)**	*small, little*
alto(a)	*tall, high*	**moreno(a)**	*brunette*
bajo(a)	*short, low*	**rubio(a)**	*blonde*
fuerte	*strong*	**malo(a)**	*bad*

¡Que fantástico es ser
jóvenes y novios!
Buenos Aires,
Argentina.

hermoso(a)	*beautiful*	**amable**	*kind, nice, amiable*
bonito(a)	*pretty*	**simpático(a)**	*nice (persons)*
guapo(a)	*handsome,*	**antipático(a)**	*disagreeable, unpleasant*
	good-looking		*(persons)*
feo(a)	*ugly*	**divertido(a)**	*amusing, funny*
viejo(a)	*old*	**serio(a)**	*serious*
joven	*young*	**difícil**	*difficult*
nuevo(a)	*new*	**fácil**	*easy*
rico(a)	*rich*		
pobre	*poor*	**muy**	*very (adverb)*
inteligente	*intelligent*	**y**	*and (conjunction)*
tonto(a)	*dumb, silly*	**o**	*or (conjunction)*
bueno(a)	*good*	**pero**	*but (conjunction)*

NOTE 1: The adjectives **bueno** and **malo** may be placed before a noun.
If the noun is masculine singular, **bueno** and **malo** become **buen**
and **mal**.

Es un **buen** muchacho.   No es un **mal** abogado.

NOTE 2: **Y** changes to **e** when followed by **i** or **hi** but not when followed
by the diphthong **hie**.

Carlos es guapo **e** inteligente.

NOTE 3: **O** changes to **u** before an **o** or **ho**.

¿Hay setenta **u** ochenta personas en la clase?

EJERCICIO 6   Al contrario

Indique en forma afirmativa cómo es la persona (y su casa, etc.) según el modelo.

> Modelo   No es gordo.
> **Es flaco.** (o) **Es delgado.**

1. No es antipático.
2. No es tonto.
3. No es bajo.
4. No es débil.
5. No es feo.

6. No es rubio.
7. No es viejo.
8. No es rico.
9. Su (*his*) casa no es grande.
10. Su coche no es nuevo.

EJERCICIO 7   Descripción

Describa a las personas y los objetos usando adjetivos apropiados.

A. Características

> Modelo   Nosotros somos . . .
> Nosotros somos **inteligentes y jóvenes.**

1. Yo soy . . .
2. Mi (*my*) padre es . . .
3. Mi madre es . . .
4. Mi hermano(a) es . . .
5. Mi novio(a) es . . .
6. Mis amigos son . . .
7. Los médicos (en general) son . . .
8. Mi profesor(a) de español es . . .
9. Mis (*my*) clases son . . .

B. Nacionalidades

> Modelo   La princesa Diana es . . .
> La princesa Diana es **inglesa.**

1. La cámara Yashica es . . .
2. El coche VW es . . .
3. Los Beatles son . . .
4. Los coches Peugeot y Renault son . . .
5. Los coches Honda y Toyota son . . .
6. Los autores Pushkin y Dostoyevski son . . .

EJERCICIO 8   ¿Cómo es?

Para indicar la información correcta, conteste en español en oraciones completas.

> Modelos   ¿Es usted americano(a)?
> **Sí, soy americano(a).** (o) **No, no soy americano(a).**
> ¿Son ustedes jóvenes?
> **Sí, somos jóvenes.** (o) **No, no somos jóvenes.**

1. ¿Es usted una persona muy amable?
2. ¿Es usted guapo(a)?
3. ¿Es usted muy serio(a)?
4. ¿Es usted fuerte?
5. ¿Es usted muy rico(a)?
6. ¿Es usted tonto(a)?
7. ¿Son ustedes muy inteligentes?
8. ¿Son ustedes alumnos muy buenos?
9. ¿Son ustedes muy simpáticos?
10. ¿Son ustedes jóvenes?
11. ¿Es el (la) profesor(a) joven?
12. ¿Es la clase de español fácil? ¿divertida?

III. El verbo irregular estar en el presente
The irregular verb estar (to be) in the present tense
Study the forms of the present tense of the verb **estar** and the sample sentences.

estar *to be*

yo **estoy**	*I am*	(Yo) **estoy** en la universidad.	
tú **estás**	*you are*	¿**Estás** (tú) en España?	
usted **está**	*you are*	¿**Está** (usted) en Miami?	(places)
él **está**	*he is*	(Él) **está** en Acapulco.	
ella **está**	*she is*	(Ella) **está** en Puerto Rico.	
nosotros(as) **estamos**	*we are*	(Nosotros) **estamos** bien.	
vosotros(as) **estáis**	*you are*	¿**Estáis** (vosotros) contentos?	(how you feel) temporarily
ustedes **están**	*you are*	¿**Están** (ustedes) mal?	
ellos **están**	*they are*	(Ellos) **están** muy pálidos.	
ellas **están**	*they are*	(Ellas) **están** en el hospital.	

EJERCICIO 9   ¿Dónde están?

A. *Indique a sus padres dónde usted y sus amigos están.*

Modelo yo/la ciudad
   Estoy en la ciudad.

1. yo/en Washington
2. nosotros/en un hotel bueno
3. mi amigo Luis/en la catedral
4. mis amigos Pablo y José/en un restaurante
5. Lola y Linda/en el museo Smithsonian
6. nosotros/en la capital

B. *Hablando* (speaking) *por teléfono de larga* (long) *distancia haga preguntas a las personas indicadas para saber* (to find out) *dónde están.*

Modelo   tú/San Francisco?
         ¿Estás en San Francisco?

1. ¿tú/Los Ángeles?
2. ¿vosotros/San Diego?
3. ¿ustedes/Monterrey?
4. ¿usted/Santa Bárbara
5. ¿tú/San Antonio?
6. ¿ustedes/El Paso?

VOCABULARIO   Words and phrases commonly used with **estar** to be

bien	*well*	**abierto(a)**	*open*
mal	*bad, badly*	**aquí**	*here*
enfermo(a)	*sick*	**allí**	*there*
cansado(a)	*tired*	**en el campo**	*in the country, field*
contento(a)	*happy*	**en la ciudad**	*in the city*
triste	*sad*	**en las montañas**	*in the mountains*
aburrido(a)	*bored*	**en la playa**	*at the beach*
enojado(a)	*angry*	**en la escuela**	*at school*
cerrado(a)	*closed*	**en la universidad**	*at the university*

NOTE: **Bien**, **mal**, **allí**, and **aquí** are adverbs and therefore do not change
to agree with the subject.

EJERCICIO 10   En la clase

Indique la condición de las cosas (things) *y de las personas en la clase. Use
la forma correcta del verbo* **estar** *y el adverbio o adjetivo.*

Modelo   cerrado: el libro, las ventanas
         El libro está cerrado.
         Las ventanas están cerradas.

1. abierto: los cuadernos, la ventana
2. cerrado: la puerta, los libros
3. enfermo: un alumno, unas alumnas
4. cansado: la profesora, los estudiantes
5. contento: yo, Eva
6. triste: Fernando, Inés y Rosa
7. enojado: un estudiante, dos personas
8. aburrido: Ricardo y Paco, Rosa
9. bien: Eva y yo, Juan Hidalgo
10. mal: un alumno, unas alumnas

EJERCICIO 11   Preguntas personales

Conteste en español en oraciones completas.

1. En este (this) momento, ¿está usted bien o mal?
2. ¿Está usted cansado(a)? ¿triste? ¿enfermo(a)? ¿enojado(a)? ¿contento(a)?

¡Qué buen día para estar con los amigos en la playa! Málaga, España.

3. Y ustedes, ¿están bien? ¿Están contentos(as)? ¿Están un poco (*a little bit*) cansados(as)?
4. Ustedes no están aburridos(as), ¿verdad (*right*)?
5. ¿Está usted contento(a) con las clases aquí en la universidad?
6. ¿Está usted contento(a) con la vida (*life*) social aquí en la universidad?
7. En este momento, ¿dónde está su (*your*) familia? **Mi** (*my*) . . . Y sus abuelos, ¿están aquí? ¿Están en la playa? ¿en las montañas? ¿en el campo?

IV. Ser versus estar

A. Usos de ser

Observe the varying uses of **ser**:

1. Ella **es abuela**.*   *She is a grandmother.*
   Él **es profesor**.*   *He is a professor.*
   Yo **soy católico**.*   *I am (a) Catholic.*
   Soy mexicano.*   *I am (a) Mexican.*
   Soy de Monterrey.   *I am from Monterrey.*

Ser denotes *identity* indicating *who* or *what the subject is* and *where the subject is from.*

*NOTE: After **ser**, the indefinite article is omitted before unmodified nouns of vocation, religion, and nationality.

2. ¿Cómo **es su padre**?   *What is your father like?*
    Es alto y **moreno**.   *He is tall and dark-haired.*
    Mi madre **es inteligente** y muy   *My mother is intelligent and very*
      simpática.   *nice.*

Ser indicates *what the subject is like* by denoting characteristics or qualities native, natural, or normal to the person or thing described.

3. **¿Qué hora es?**   *What time is it?*
    Son las ocho.   *It is eight o'clock.*
    ¿Qué día es hoy?   *What day is it today?*
    Es el ocho de octubre.   *It's the eighth of October.*
    Hoy es lunes.   *Today is Monday.*

Ser is used with expressions of time (hours, days, dates, and the like).

4. El coche **es de** Juan.   *The car is John's.*
    Es mi motocicleta.   *It's my motorcycle.*
    La bicicleta **es para él**.   *The bicycle is for him.*

Ser is used to show possession (see Chapter 5) and destination (for whom or for what something is destined).

B. Usos de estar

Observe the varying uses of **estar**.

1. **¿Cómo están ustedes?**   *How are you?*
    Estoy enfermo.   *I am sick.*
    Pepe **está cansado**.   *Pepe is tired.*
    Mónica **está triste**.   *Monica is sad.*
    Las ventanas **están abiertas**. *The windows are open.*
    La puerta **está cerrada**.   *The door is closed.*

Estar tells *in what state* or *condition* the subject is *at a given time*, indicating a state or condition that is not native or natural to the person or thing described.

2. **La casa está en el campo**.   *The house is in the country.*
    Estamos en la ciudad.   *We are in the city.*

Estar denotes location by telling *where the subject is*.

C. <u>Ser</u> o <u>estar</u>

Observe the use of **ser** and **estar** with the same adjective.

Diego **es pálido**.	*Diego is pale. (has a pale complexion)*
Teresa vio un fantasma y **está pálida**.	*Teresa saw a ghost, and she looks pale.*
El profesor **es monótono** y **aburrido**.	*The professor is monotonous and boring.*
Los alumnos **están aburridos**.	*The students are bored.*
Carmen **es muy bonita**.	*Carmen is very pretty.*
Pepita **está** muy **bonita** hoy.	*Pepita looks good today.*
La fruta **es** muy **buena**.	*The fruit is very good. (quality)*
La fruta **está buena** hoy.	*The fruit looks good today. (condition)*

The use of **ser** or **estar** with a given adjective can change or slightly alter that adjective's meaning or emphasis. With **ser** the adjective denotes a characteristic or trait; with **estar** it denotes a condition.

EJERCICIO 12   Identidad, características, condiciones y localización

Conteste en español en oraciones completas para dar (in order to give) *información sobre* (about) *tres personas muy importantes—usted, su profesor(a) y el presidente.*

1. ¿Quién es usted?   (*Who are you?*)
2. ¿Cómo es usted?   (*What are you like?*)
3. ¿Cómo está usted?   (*How are you?*)
4. ¿Dónde está usted?   (*Where are you?*)
5. ¿Cómo es su (*your*) casa/apartamento? **Mi** . . .
6. ¿Dónde está su casa/apartamento?
7. ¿Quién es el (la) profesor(a) de español?
8. ¿Cómo es el (la) profesor(a)?
9. ¿Cómo está el (la) profesor(a)?
10. ¿Dónde está el (la) profesor(a)?
11. ¿Quién es el presidente de los Estados Unidos?
12. ¿Cómo es el presidente?
13. ¿Cómo está el presidente (probablemente)?
14. ¿Dónde está el presidente (probablemente)?

EJERCICIO 13   Una profesora estupenda

*Describa a la profesora (cómo es o está, dónde está). Use **ser** o **estar** según las indicaciones.*

Modelo   fantástica
      Es fantástica.

1. interesante	5. contenta	9. inteligente
2. buena	6. mexicana	10. bien
3. aquí	7. en la clase	11. extraordinaria
4. excelente	8. de México	12. estupenda

EJERCICIO 14   Información personal

Indique en forma afirmativa o negativa si (if) las referencias se aplican a las personas mencionadas.

> Modelo   usted: ¿muy fuerte?
> **Sí, soy (No, no soy) muy fuerte.**
> ¿cansado(a)?
> **Sí, estoy (No, no estoy) cansado(a).**

1. usted: ¿simpático(a)?, ¿inteligente?, ¿bien?, ¿contento(a)?, ¿en la clase?
2. su (*your*) padre: ¿aquí?, ¿americano?, ¿católico?, ¿ingeniero?, ¿enfermo?
3. su madre: ¿religiosa?, ¿española?, ¿en la playa?, ¿profesora?, ¿triste?
4. su hermano(a): ¿feo(a)?, ¿divertido(a)?, ¿en la escuela?, ¿aburrido(a) con la escuela?, ¿muy jóven?
5. su tío: ¿rico?, ¿generoso?, ¿en la Florida?, ¿de la Florida?, ¿mal?

EJERCICIO 15   Una conversación

Usted y su amigo(a) conversan de sus familias. Háganse preguntas y contéstense. (Ask each other questions, and answer each other.)

1. ¿Dónde está tu familia?
2. ¿Cómo está la familia?
3. ¿Cómo es tu padre?
4. ¿Cómo es tu madre?
5. ¿Tienes hermanos(as)? ¿Cómo se llaman?
6. ¿Cómo es tu hermano(a)?
7. ¿Dónde están tus abuelos?
8. ¿Cómo son?

ACTIVIDAD   Una breve presentación

Describa para (for) la clase una persona que es muy importante en su vida (life), indicando:

> ¿Cómo se llama?
> ¿Quién es? (profesión, nacionalidad, etc.)
> ¿Cómo es?
> ¿Cómo está? (probablemente)
> ¿Dónde está en este momento?

V. El verbo irregular ir en el presente
The irregular verb ir (to go) in the present tense

Study the forms of the irregular verb **ir** in the present tense and the sample sentences.

ir *to go*

yo **voy**	*I go, do go, am going*	**Voy** a (*to*) la clase.
tú **vas**	*you go, do go, are going*	¿**Vas** a la clase?
usted **va**	*you go, do go, are going*	¿**Va** usted al museo?
él **va**	*he goes, does go, is going*	Él **va** a la playa.
ella **va**	*she goes, does go, is going*	Ella **va** a las montañas.
nosotros **vamos**	*we go, do go, are going*	**Vamos** a Miami.
vosotros **vais**	*you go, do go, are going*	¿**Vais** a San Antonio?
ustedes **van**	*you go, do go, are going*	¿**Van** ustedes a San Juan?
ellos **van**	*they go, do go, are going*	Ellos **van** a visitar San Francisco.
ellas **van**	*they go, do go, are going*	Ellas **van** a estar en Santa Bárbara.

NOTE 1:   **Ir a** + infinitive means *to be going to . . .* , indicating an action yet to occur.

Voy a visitar Monterrey.   *I am going to visit Monterrey.*
Vamos a estar allí siete días.   *We are going to be there seven days.*

NOTE 2:   **Vamos a** + infinitive, used affirmatively, can also mean *let's*.

¡Vamos a conversar!   *Let's converse.*
¡Vamos a practicar!   *Let's practice.*

EJERCICIO 16   ¿Quién va? (*Who is going?*)

Conteste en español según el modelo.

Modelo   ¿Quién va a la ciudad? (Yo)
Yo voy a la ciudad.

1.   ¿Quién va a la playa? (Rosa, Rubén y yo, mis hermanas, tú, ustedes)
2.   ¿Quién va a la fiesta? (mis amigos, vosotros, Alfonso e Inés, yo, nosotros)

EJERCICIO 17   Con frecuencia

Conteste en español en oraciones completas para indicar adónde van con frecuencia.

Con frecuencia . . .

1.   ¿Va usted a conciertos?
2.   ¿Va usted a partidos (*games*) de fútbol?

3. ¿Va usted a restaurantes?
4. ¿Van ustedes al centro de la ciudad?
5. ¿Van ustedes a la playa?
6. ¿Van ustedes a las montañas?
7. ¿Van ustedes a muchas fiestas?

EJERCICIO 18   ¡Vamos a viajar¡ (*Let's travel.*)

Indique que las personas van al país mencionado para visitar la capital.

> Modelo   Yo: (Puerto Rico) (San Juan)
> **Voy a Puerto Rico.**
> **Voy a estar en San Juan.**

1. Yo: (España) (Madrid); (La Argentina) (Buenos Aires)
2. Nosotros: (Venezuela) (Caracas); (Colombia) (Bogotá)
3. Javier: (Chile) (Santiago); (El Ecuador) (Quito)
4. Isabel y Julia: (Cuba) (La Habana); (Costa Rica) (San José)

VI. Las contracciones
Contractions

There are only two contractions in Spanish:

> **a + el = al; de + el = del**

Observe the combinations.

> Voy **al** campo.   *I am going to the country.*
> *but:*
> Voy **a la** ciudad.   `I am going to the city.*
> Voy **a los** conciertos.   *I am going to the concerts.*

The word **a** (preposition meaning *to*) combined with the masculine singular article **el** becomes **al**.

> Soy **del** campo.   *I am from the country.*
> *but:*
> Soy **de la** ciudad.   *I am from the city.*
> Tengo fotos **de la** casa.   *I have photos of the house.*

The preposition **de** (meaning *from, about,* or *of*) combined with the masculine article **el** becomes **del**.

EJERCICIO 19   Una gran (*great*) excursión

Repita las preguntas sustituyendo los nombres entre paréntesis para indicar otras posibilidades en la gran excursión.

Modelo   ¿Vas a *la catedral?* (el restaurante)
¿Vas al restaurante?

1. ¿Vas a *la ciudad?* (el concierto, la conferencia, el teatro, el drama, el museo, el hotel)
2. ¿Hay un mapa aquí *del centro?* (el metro, la ciudad, el museo, la catedral)
3. ¿Tienes las direcciones *a la conferencia?* (el metro, el teatro, la catedral, el hotel)
4. ¿Tienes fotos *del drama?* (la ciudad, la catedral, el concierto, el museo, los estudiantes, las personas en el grupo)

ACTIVIDAD   Un retrato (*portrait*) personal

Escriba, y posiblemente presente en forma oral, un retrato personal en que usted presenta:

1. información personal (características físicas, personalidad, condiciones);
2. información sobre (*about*) una persona con quien se asocia mucho (características, condiciones, localización);
3. adónde ustedes dos van con mucha frecuencia.

PANORAMA CULTURAL ■

La familia hispana

La familia hispana es generalmente *más grande* que la familia norteamericana. ¿*Por qué? Porque* en la familia hispana es costumbre tener más hijos y *también* es costumbre que los abuelos y *algunas veces otros* parientes *vivan* en la *misma* casa con los padres y los hijos.

larger
why/because/also
sometimes/others/live/same

En la tradición hispana el padre es el *jefe* de la familia y tiene la responsabilidad de *sustentar* a la familia. La mujer, jefa de la casa, *se encarga* de los hijos, de *su* educación *ética* y religiosa, y de la unión y *concordancia entre* los varios miembros familiares. Ella es el *corazón* de la familia. Muchas familias hispanas tienen una *criada* o sirvienta que vive con la familia y *cuida de* los *quehaceres* domésticos.

head
support/is in charge
their/ethical/harmony
between heart
maid/takes care of
chores

Hoy día se notan varios *cambios* en la familia hispana, particularmente en familias de la clase *media.* Dos de los cambios más notables son: (1) la decisión de muchas mujeres *por tener* más educación y la oportunidad de entrar en el mundo profesional, y (2) más *libertad para* los jóvenes, y en particular para las chicas. En generaciones *pasadas* una chica *nunca podía salir* con un chico *sin* la presencia de un pariente.

nowadays/changes
middle
in favor of having
freedom for
past/never could go out
without

A *pesar de* los cambios, la familia hispana *se mantiene* muy unida. Todos están en la casa a la hora de *comer* y todos se reúnen con frecuencia para ce-

in spite of/maintains itself
eating

Toda la familia se reúne para celebrar ocasiones importantes. Cali, Colombia.

lebrar ocasiones importantes—*cumpleaños*, aniversarios, fiestas familiares como la quinceañera[1] y *días festivos* religiosos.

birthdays
holidays

Los *apellidos*

surnames, last names

¿*Cómo se llama?*

La familia Gutiérrez   La familia Ortega

José Gutiérrez (novio)   Carmen Ortega (novia)

José Gutiérrez (esposo)   Carmen Ortega de Gutiérrez (esposa)

hijo

Juan Gutiérrez Ortega

En los países hispanos la esposa conserva su *primer* apellido y también *toma* el primer apellido del esposo. Carmen Ortega es de la familia Gutiérrez. El hijo *puede* tener el apellido de su padre y *el de* su madre. de esta manera el hijo se identifica con las familias de los dos padres, *pero* el primer apellido del padre es el que continúa *por* generaciones.

first
takes
can/that of
but
through

[1]Cuando una señorita cumple (*turns*) quince años (*years*), hay una fiesta y celebración muy grande llamada quinceañera.

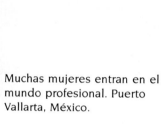

Muchas mujeres entran en el mundo profesional. Puerto Vallarta, México.

¿CUÁNTO RECUERDA USTED?

Complete las oraciones en la columna A con las conclusiones en la columna B.

	A	B
1.	Los abuelos y otros parientes . . .	a. . . . los niños y la unión entre los familiares.
2.	El hombre tiene la responsabilidad . . .	b. . . . cuida de los quehaceres domésticos.
3.	La madre se encarga de . . .	c. . . . entrar en el mundo profesional.
4.	La madre es . . .	d. . . . a la hora de comer.
5.	La criada o sirvienta . . .	e. . . . para celebrar ocasiones importantes.
6.	Se notan cambios . . .	f. . . . viven en la misma casa.
7.	Muchas mujeres deciden . . .	g. . . . de su padre y de su madre.
8.	Todos están en la casa . . .	h. . . . de sustentar a la familia.
9.	Se reúnen con frecuencia . . .	i. . . . en las familias de la clase media.
10.	El hijo puede tener el apellido . . .	j. . . . el corazón de la familia.

INTEGRACIÓN VISUAL: CAPÍTULO 2 ■

EJERCICIO 2.1   Ser + características

El señor Andrade

Ejemplo   El señor Andrade _____.
El Señor Andrade es profesor.
(pregunta personal) ¿Es su
padre o su madre profesor o
profesora?

Victor   Horacio

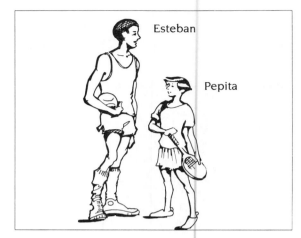

Esteban

Pepita

Rosa   Luisa

Mónica   El ogro

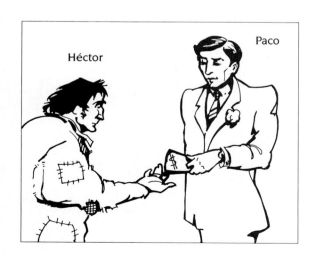

Héctor   Paco

El abuelo

Juanito

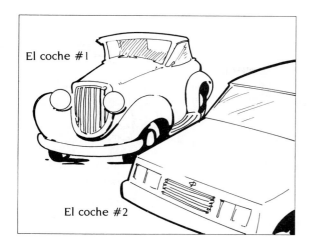

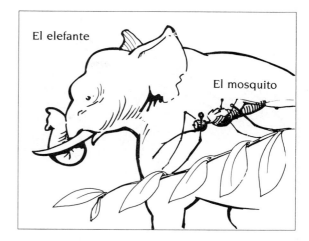

EJERCICIO 2.2   Estar + localización y condición

Ejemplo   ¿Dónde estamos?
Estamos en la escuela.

Alfonso

Alfonso

Alfonso

Alfonso

Julia

REPASO DE VOCABULARIO ACTIVO ■

Adjetivos

abierto(a)	contento(a)	fuerte	pequeño(a)
aburrido(a)	débil	gordo(a)	pobre
alto(a)	delgado(a)	grande	rico(a)
amable	difícil	guapo(a)	rubio(a)
antipático(a)	divertido(a)	hermoso(a)	serio(a)
bajo(a)	enfermo(a)	inteligente	simpático(a)
bonito(a)	enojado(a)	joven	tonto(a)
bueno(a)	fácil	malo(a)	triste
cansado(a)	feo(a)	moreno(a)	viejo(a)
cerrado(a)	flaco(a)	nuevo(a)	

Adverbios

allí   **mal**   **bien**
aquí   **muy**

Conjunciones

but

y   **o**   **pero**

Preposiciones

to   *of*

a   **de**

Pronombres personales

yo	**él**	**vosotros(as)**	**ellas**
tú	**ella**	**ustedes**	
usted	**nosotros(as)**	**ellos**	

Sustantivos

la **abogada**	la **enfermera**	la **médica**	el **padre**
el **abogado**	el **enfermero**	el **médico**	los **padres**
la **abuela**	la **escuela**	las **montañas**	el **pariente**
el **abuelo**	la **esposa**	la **muchacha**	el **perro**
la **amiga**	el **esposo**	el **muchacho**	la **persona**
el **amigo**	la **familia**	la **mujer**	la **playa**
el **auto**	la **hermana**	la **mujer de negocios**	la **prima**
el **bebé**	el **hermano**	la **nena**	el **primo**
el **campo**	la **hija**	el **nene**	la **sobrina**
el **carro**	el **hijo**	la **nieta**	el **sobrino**
la **casa**	el **hombre**	el **nieto**	la **tía**
la **ciudad**	el **hombre de negocios**	la **niña**	el **tío**
el **coche**	la **ingeniera**	el **niño**	la **universidad**
la **chica**	el **ingeniero**	la **novia**	
el **chico**	la **madre**	el **novio**	

Verbos

estar   **ser**   **ir**

hay

AUTOEXAMEN Y REPASO #2 ■

I. Vocabulario: la familia

Indique la persona que corresponde a la definición. (Indicate the person that corresponds to the definition.)

Modelo   El padre de mi padre
     abuelo

1. La madre de mi madre
2. El hijo de mi hermano
3. La hija de mi tía
4. El hermano de mi padre
5. La hija de mi hija
6. El amigo íntimo de una señorita
7. Un niño muy pequeño

II. El verbo ser

Indique que la descripción no es correcta. Siga (follow) *el modelo.*

Modelo   yo/viejo(a)
No soy viejo(a). Soy joven.

1. yo/tonto(a)
2. tú/feo
3. nosotros/débiles
4. ellas/altas
5. Carlos/rubio
6. vosotros/pobres
7. usted/gorda
8. las clases/difíciles

III. El verbo estar

Indique que la información no es correcta. Siga el modelo.

Modelo   yo/bien
No estoy bien. Estoy mal.

1. yo/triste
2. tú/enfermo
3. nosotros/mal
4. mis hermanos/en la ciudad
5. el coche/aquí
6. las puertas del coche/abiertas

IV. Ser versus estar

Describa a la familia, etc., usando la forma correcta de **ser** *o* **estar** *según las indicaciones* (according to the cues).

1. grande/su casa
2. viejo/su carro
3. jóvenes/los padres
4. japonés/el padre
5. abogada/la madre
6. muy simpática/la hija
7. en la Florida/la familia
8. de la Florida/los tíos
9. en la playa/los niños
10. muy contenta/la familia

V. El verbo **ir**

Indique adónde van las personas.

> Modelo   la playa/yo
> **Voy a la playa.**

1. la escuela/Roberto y Pablo
2. la universidad/nosotros
3. la clase/tú
4. un restaurante/el profesor Martínez
5. la cafetería/yo
6. la residencia de estudiantes/vosotros

VI. Repaso del Capítulo 2

A. *Conteste en oraciones completas.*

questions

1. ¿Cómo es usted? —— Soy inteligente
2. ¿Cómo es su madre?   Es muy amable
3. ¿Cómo es el presidente?
4. ¿Cómo son sus amigos? — Son divertidos, amables, y jóvenes
5. ¿Cómo está usted?
6. ¿Están usted y sus amigos en la universidad? Sí, Estamos allí.
7. ¿Va usted a la clase los sábados? No, no voy a la clase los Sabados.
8. ¿Van ustedes al centro de la ciudad con frecuencia? Sí vamos al centro con frecuencia.
9. El profesor (la profesora), ¿va a estar   a estar en la
    en la clase el domingo? No, no va en clase el domingo.

B. *Traduzca al español.*

1. She is rich, intelligent, and beautiful. es
2. She is the daughter of the professor. es
3. The door is open, and the students are in the class. estar
4. Are you tired? (you = **ustedes**) estan ,
5. No, I'm not tired. I'm bored.   estoy
6. Are you going to the country on Sunday? (you = **tú**) vas al campo
7. My parents are going to be there. (my = **mis**) van a estar

■CAPÍTULO■

3

Goals for communication
- Buying foods at the market
- Ordering meals in a restaurant
- Talking about daily activities
- Asking for specific information
- Expressing likes and dislikes

Cultural exploration
- Foods of the Hispanic world
- Eating times
- Specialty food stores

VOCABULARIO EN EL MERCADO ■

Vamos al **mercado** público.	*market*
¿Qué **carnes** tienen hoy?	*meats (f.)*
el **bistec**	*steak*
la **chuleta de cerdo**	*pork chop*
el **jamón**	*ham*
el **pollo**	*chicken*
la **salchicha**, el **chorizo**	*sausage*
el **tocino**	*bacon*
Hay **mariscos** ¿verdad?	*seafood, shellfish*
el **camarón**	*shrimp*
la **langosta**	*lobster*
el **pescado**	*fish*

En los mercados públicos venden una variedad de frutas y legumbres de la región. Pisca, Perú.

Aquí están las **legumbres** o los **vegetales**.	*vegetables*
el **ajo**	*garlic*
el **arroz**	*rice*
la **cebolla**	*onion*
los **frijoles**	*beans*
los **guisantes**	*peas*
las **judías** (España), las **habichuelas**	*green beans*
la **lechuga**	*lettuce*
el **maíz**	*corn*
la **patata**, la **papa**	*potato*
el **tomate**	*tomato*
la **zanahoria**	*carrot*

Hay muchas **frutas** buenas.	*fruits*
la **cereza**	*cherry*
la **fresa**	*strawberry*
el **limón**	*lemon*
la **manzana**	*apple*
el **melocotón** (España), el **durazno**	*peach*
la **naranja**	*orange*

la **pera**	pear
la **piña**	pineapple
el **plátano** (España), la **banana**	banana
la **sandía**	watermelon
la **uva**	grape

**México fue el primero
en dar al viejo mundo los siguientes productos**

tomate	vainilla	chile
maíz	aguacate	chicle
papaya	cacahuete	chocolate
piña	calabazas	frijol
tabaco		

EJERCICIO 1   Vamos al mercado

Conteste en español según el dibujo. (Answer in Spanish according to the drawing.)

1. ¿Qué frutas venden en el mercado? (*What fruits do they sell at the market?*) **Venden** . . .
2. ¿Qué legumbres venden las señoras?
3. ¿Qué carnes vende el hombre?
4. ¿Qué mariscos vende?

EJERCICIO 2   Mi comida (*food*) favorita

Conteste según el modelo.

>   Modelo   ¿Cuál (*which*) es su carne favorita?
>   **Mi carne favorita es el jamón.**

1. ¿Cuál es su fruta favorita?
2. ¿Cuál es su marisco favorito?
3. ¿Cuál es su legumbre favorita?
4. ¿Cuál es su carne favorita?
5. ¿Cuál es su restaurante favorito?

EJERCICIO 3   Más comida

Conteste en español en oraciones completas.

1. En la cafetería, ¿sirven (*do they serve*) mucho pollo? **Sí, (No, no) sirven** . . .
   ¿muchas chuletas de cerdo? ¿mucho jamón? ¿mucho bistec? ¿camarones? ¿langosta? ¿pescado?
2. Por la mañana, ¿qué carnes sirven?
3. ¿Qué legumbres o vegetales sirven con frecuencia?
4. Vamos a preparar una sopa (*soup*) extraordinaria. ¿Qué ingredientes necesitamos (*do we need*)? **Necesitamos** . . .

"Buenos días, doña Rosa, hoy necesito dos kilos de pollo . . ." Barcelona, España

CONVERSACIÓN ▪

Doña¹ Rosa está en el mercado público y **habla** *con doña María, vendedora de* **frutas**.

DOÑA ROSA	Buenos días, doña María. Hoy **necesito frutas**.
DOÑA MARÍA	Pues, tenemos **naranjas**, **piñas** y **bananas**.
DOÑA ROSA	A ver . . . Deme un kilo² de **bananas** y una **piña**, por favor.
DOÑA MARÍA	Muy bien. Aquí están . . . y **mañana llegan fresas** del campo.
DOÑA ROSA	¡Magnífico! Bueno, doña María, ¿**cuánto** es?
DOÑA MARÍA	Cien pesos³ en total, señora.
DOÑA ROSA	Muchas gracias. Hasta mañana.

NOTE 1:   Title of respect given to a married woman, used before the first name only. **Don** is the masculine equivalent.

NOTE 2:   1.00 kilo (kilogram) = 2.20 pounds.

NOTE 3:   Monetary unit used in Mexico, Colombia, Chile, Uruguay, Cuba, and the Dominican Republic.

Doña Rosa is at the public market and is talking with Doña María, a fruit vendor.

PAPA LEON KILO DE $85 A $59	SALCHICHA VIENA ZWAN KILO DE $985 A $759	QUESO ZIZ GRUYERE 8 REBANADAS (180 GRS.) DE $320 A $246

DOÑA ROSA	*Good morning, doña María. Today I need fruit.*
DOÑA MARÍA	*Well, we have oranges, pineapples, and bananas.*
DOÑA ROSA	*Let's see. . . . Give me a kilo of bananas and a pineapple, please.*
DOÑA MARÍA	*Very well, here they are . . . and tomorrow strawberries are arriving from the country.*
DOÑA ROSA	*Wonderful! Well, doña María, how much is it?*
DOÑA MARÍA	*One hundred pesos total.*
DOÑA ROSA	*Thank you very much. See you tomorrow.*

ACTIVIDAD   Mini-drama: En el mercado

Usted y un(a) amigo(a) de la clase de español, preparen un diálogo oral entre (between) un (a) vendedor(a) y la persona que necesita comprar (to buy) legumbres umbres, carnes, etc., en el mercado público. Usen las construcciones de la Conversación.

USTED	**Buenos días, doña (don) . . . hoy necesito. . . .**
VENDEDOR(A)	**Pues, tenemos . . . etc.**

En los supermercados grandes y modernos venden todo tipo de productos. Caracas, Venezuela.

ESTRUCTURA ▪

I. El presente de los verbos regulares -ar
The present tense of regular -ar verbs

All verbs in Spanish fall into three groups:

1. Verbs with infinitives ending in **-ar**, for example, **estudiar** (*to study*)
2. Verbs with infinitives ending in **-er**, for example, **vender** (*to sell*)
3. Verbs with infinitives ending in **-ir**, for example, **escribir** (*to write*)

A. Ejemplos de los verbos -ar

comprar	*to buy*	**necesitar**	*to need*
desear	*to want, desire*	**preparar**	*to prepare*
estudiar	*to study*	**tomar**	*to take, drink, eat*
hablar	*to speak, talk*	**trabajar**	*to work*
llegar	*to arrive*		

B. La conjugación de los verbos -ar en el presente

Study the present-tense conjugation of the regular verb **hablar** and the corresponding English translations. (A regular verb is one that follows a set pattern of conjugation.)

Infinitive: **hablar**

-**ar** *endings*		*conjugation*	
(yo)	**-o**	Habl**o** italiano.	*I speak Italian.*
(tú)	**-as**	¿Habl**as** portugués?	*Do you speak Portuguese?*
(usted)	**-a**	¿Habl**a** usted alemán?	*Do you speak German?*
(él)	**-a**	Él no habl**a** ruso.	*He doesn't speak Russian.*
(ella)	**-a**	Ella no habl**a** chino.	*She doesn't speak Chinese.*
(nosotros)	**-amos**	Habl**amos** mucho en la clase.	*We speak a lot in class.*
(vosotros)	**-áis**	¿Habl**áis** bien el español?	*Do you speak Spanish well?*
(ustedes)	**-an**	¿Habl**an** ustedes un poco?	*Do you speak a little bit?*
(ellos)	**-an**	Ellos habl**an** con el médico.	*They are speaking with the doctor.*
(ellas)	**-an**	¿Habl**an** ellas con un acento?	*Do they speak with an accent?*

**ESPECIALES EN VIGENCIA DESDE
EL JUEVES 7 AL DOMINGO 10 DE NOVIEMBRE, 1985.**

Present-tense conjugations of regular **-ar** verbs drop the **-ar** from the infinitive and to the remaining stem add the endings indicated.

The present tense in Spanish corresponds to three English forms:

Raúl **habla español**.
$\begin{cases} \textit{Raúl speaks Spanish.} \\ \textit{Raúl is speaking Spanish.} \\ \textit{Raúl does speak Spanish.} \end{cases}$

NOTE: When two consecutive verbs follow a subject, only the first is conjugated.

Necesito estudiar.   *I need to study.*
Desean tomar una siesta.   *They want to take a nap.*

EJERCICIO 4   ¿Dónde trabaja? ¿Y qué lengua habla?

Indique dónde trabajan las personas y qué lengua hablan.

Modelo   él/Hong Kong
Trabaja en Hong Kong y habla chino.

1.	yo:	Madrid	5.	nosotros:	Moscú
2.	tú:	París	6.	vosotros:	Roma
3.	él:	Berlín	7.	ustedes:	Lisboa
4.	usted:	Tokio	8.	ellas:	Londres

EJERCICIO 5   El (la) profesor(a) necesita información.

Conteste según el modelo.

Modelo   ¿Quién (*who*) estudia el vocabulario? (yo)
Yo estudio el vocabulario.

1.   ¿Quién estudia los verbos? (nosotros, tú, yo)
2.   ¿Quién habla en español? (yo, ustedes, Elena y yo)

3. ¿Quién prepara las tareas? (Mónica, tú, Eva y Paco)
4. ¿Quién llega a tiempo (*on time*)? (los estudiantes, el (la) profesor(a), nosotros

EJERCICIO 6   Preguntas personales

El (la) profesor(a) necesita más información. Conteste en español en oraciones completas.

1. ¿Estudia usted mucho?
2. ¿Necesita usted estudiar más (*more*)?
3. ¿Desea usted estudiar más?
4. ¿Prepara usted bien las lecciones?
5. ¿Llega usted a la clase a tiempo?
6. ¿A qué hora llega usted?
7. Y durante (*during*) la clase . . .
    ¿habla usted español?
    ¿habla usted inglés?
    ¿toma usted una siesta?
    ¿toma usted Coca-Cola?

VOCABULARIO

mucho	*much, a lot*
poco	*little (quantity)*
hoy	*today*
mañana	*tomorrow*
ahora	*now*
temprano	*early*
tarde	*late*
más tarde	*later*
a tiempo	*on time*
esta mañana/tarde	*this morning/afternoon*
esta noche	*tonight*
todo el día	*all day*
toda la mañana/tarde/noche	*all morning/afternoon/night*
todos los días	*every day*
todas las mañanas/tardes/noches	*every morning/afternoon/night*
por la mañana/tarde/noche	*in the morning/afternoon/evening, at night*

EJERCICIO 7   Tú y yo

Exercises in the text entitled **Tú y yo** are to be done orally, in pairs. You and a classmate take turns asking each other questions using the **tú** form of the verb and the information indicated. Listen to, and if necessary, correct each other's responses.

Háganse preguntas y contéstense. (Ask each other questions, and answer each other.)

> Modelo trabajar/todo el día
> (pregunta) **¿Trabajas todo el día?**
> (respuesta) **(Sí,) (No, no) trabajo todo el día.**

1. comprar/muchas Coca-Colas
2. comprar/mucha fruta
3. trabajar/por la mañana
4. trabajar/por la tarde o por la noche
5. estudiar/mucho o poco
6. estudiar/todos los días
7. necesitar/estudiar esta noche
8. necesitar/estudiar toda la noche
9. llegar/a la clase temprano
10. llegar/a la clase tarde
11. desear/hablar con el (la) profesor(a) más tarde
12. desear/tomar una siesta esta tarde
13. estar/cansado(a) ahora

BISTEC NORMAL DE RES
KILO
DE $1,090 A
$835

II. El presente de los verbos regulares -er, -ir
The present tense of regular -er, -ir verbs

A. Ejemplos de los verbos -er, -ir:

aprender	*to learn*	**vender**	*to sell*	**escribir**	*to write*
beber	*to drink*	**abrir**	*to open*	**vivir**	*to live*
comer	*to eat*				

B. La conjugación de los verbos -er, -ir en el presente

Study the present-tense conjugations of the verbs **comer** and **vivir** and the corresponding English translations.

Infinitive: **comer**

-er endings   *conjugation*

-er endings	conjugation	
-o	Com**o** mucha fruta.	*I eat a lot of fruit.*
-es	¿Com**es** en la cafetería?	*Do you eat in the cafeteria?*
-e	¿Com**e** usted ajo?	*Do you eat garlic?*
	Él com**e** muchas cebollas.	*He eats a lot of onions.*
	Ella com**e** muchos frijoles.	*She eats a lot of beans.*
-emos	Com**emos** tarde.	*We eat late.*
-éis	¿Com**éis** a las nueve?	*Do you eat at nine?*
-en	¿Com**en** ustedes carne?	*Do you eat meat?*
	Ellos no com**en** aquí hoy.	*They are not eating here today.*
	¿Com**en** ellas bien?	*Do they eat well?*

Infinitive: **vivir**

-ir *endings*   *conjugation*

-o	Viv**o** en la ciudad ahora.	*I am living in the city now.*
-es	¿Viv**es** en el campo?	*Do you live in the country?*
-e	¿Viv**e** usted en la residencia de estudiantes?	*Are you living in the dormitory?*
	¿No viv**e** él en la Florida?	*Doesn't he live in Florida?*
	Ella viv**e** en Miami.	*She lives in Miami.*
-imos	Viv**imos** aquí.	*We live here.*
-ís	¿Viv**ís** allí?	*Do you live there?*
-en	¿No viv**en** ustedes en Caracas?	*Don't you live in Caracas?*
	Ellos viv**en** en Bogotá.	*They are living in Bogotá.*
	Ellas no viv**en** en Lima.	*They don't live in Lima.*

Present-tense conjugations of regular **-er** and **-ir** verbs drop the **-er** and **-ir** from the infinitive and to the remaining stem add the endings indicated. The **-er** and **-ir** verbs have the same endings except in the **nosotros** (we) and **vosotros** (you, familiar plural) forms.

> NOTE: The present tense in Spanish may also be used to refer to the very immediate future.

Comen aquí esta noche.   *They are eating (will eat) here tonight.*

No estudio ahora. Estudio más tarde.   *I won't study now. I will study later.*

EJERCICIO 8   Estamos en México.

Indique las actividades de las personas según el modelo.

> Modelo   Vendemos computadoras. (Miguel)
> **Vende computadoras.**

1. Vivimos en la capital. (yo, Fernando, tú, nosotros)
2. Aprendo el español. (vosotros, nosotros, ustedes, yo)
3. Marta escribe a la familia. (yo, nosotros, vosotros, ella)
4. Comen tortillas. (nosotros, tú, yo, los niños)
5. Bebo tequila. (ustedes, tú, Paco, yo)

EJERCICIO 9   Muy enfermo(a)

Indique lo que ustedes, los estudiantes, NO hacen cuando están enfermos(as).

> Modelo   yo . . . preparar la lección.
> **No preparo la lección.**

1. yo . . . escribir los ejercicios
    estudiar
    abrir el libro de español
    aprender el vocabulario
    trabajar
    ir a la cafetería   no boy
    comer bien
2. nosotros . . . (repita)
3. Unos alumnos . . . (repita)

```
┌─────────────────────┐
│    ZANAHORIA        │
│       KILO          │
│   DE $149.50 A      │
│      $90            │
└─────────────────────┘
```

EJERCICIO 10   Preguntas para usted y para sus amigos

Conteste en español en oraciones completas.

1. ¿Aprende usted MUCHO español en esta (*this*) clase?
2. ¿Aprenden ustedes MUCHO en todas las clases?
3. ¿Escribe usted a la familia con frecuencia?
4. ¿Escriben ustedes a los abuelos con frecuencia?
5. ¿Come usted en la cafetería todos los días?
6. ¿Comen ustedes en restaurantes todos los días?
7. ¿Vive usted en la residencia de estudiantes?
8. ¿Viven ustedes en un apartamento?
9. ¿Necesita usted una bicicleta?
10. ¿Necesitan ustedes un coche?
11. ¿Desea usted comprar un coche? ¿vender un coche?
12. ¿Desean ustedes estar aquí? ¿ir a Acapulco? ¿ir a Alaska?

EJERCICIO 11   ¿Cuánto vocabulario recuerda usted?
(*How much vocabulary do you remember?*)

Complete las oraciones con dos o más palabras o expresiones para indicar una variedad de posibilidades.

Modelo   Voy a estudiar . . .
          Voy a estudiar toda la noche.
                        todo el día.
                        mañana.
                        el vocabulario.
                        etc.

1. Voy a aprender . . .
2. Voy a escribir . . .   to arrive
3. Voy a llegar . . .
4. Voy a trabajar . . .
5. Necesito preparar . . .
6. Necesito abrir . . .
7. Necesito vender . . .
8. Deseo comprar . . .
9. Deseo comer . . .

VOCABULARIO   LA COMIDA

la **comida**	food, main meal	la **merienda**	afternoon snack
el **desayuno**	breakfast	la **cena**	supper, dinner
el **almuerzo**	lunch		

¿Qué vamos a comer?

el **cereal**	cereal	la **aceituna**	olive
el **huevo**	egg	la **sopa**	soup
el **pan**	bread	el **bocadillo**	sandwich
el **pan tostado**	toast	(España),	
el **queso**	cheese	el **sandwich**	
la **ensalada**	salad	la **hamburguesa**	hamburger

¿Qué **bebidas** vamos a tomar?   drinks, beverages

el **agua**[1]	water (f.)	la **gaseosa**	soft drink
el **agua mineral**	mineral water	el **jugo**	juice
(con gas, sin gas)	(carbonated,	la **leche**	milk
	uncarbonated)	el **té**	tea
el **café**	coffee	el **vino**	wine
la **cerveza**	beer		

¿Qué hay de **postre**?   dessert

la **galleta**	cookie	el **pastel**	pie, pastry
el **helado**	ice cream	la **torta**	cake

¿Qué necesitamos?

el **azúcar**	sugar	la **pimienta**	pepper
la **crema**	cream	la **sal**	salt
el **hielo**	ice	el **aceite**	oil
la **mantequilla**	butter	el **vinagre**	vinegar
la **mermelada**	jam		

Las especialidades de la casa son muy buenas. Venezuela.

¿Cómo vamos a preparar la comida?

a la parrilla	*grilled*	**revuelto**	*scrambled*
asado	*roasted*	**caliente**	*hot (temperature of things)*
frito	*fried*	**frío**	*cold*

NOTE 1: **Agua** is feminine even though it has the article **el**, for example, **el agua fría**. The plural form is **las aguas**.

NOTE 2: Spanish uses the preposition **de** (*of*) to join two nouns for the purpose of description.

helado de vainilla	*vanilla ice cream*
torta de chocolate	*chocolate cake*
jugo de naranja	*orange juice*

EJERCICIO 12 ¡Vamos a comer!

¿Asocia usted las siguientes comidas con el desayuno, el almuerzo o la cena?

Modelo huevos fritos
el desayuno

1. pan tostado con mantequilla y mermelada
2. sopa y ensalada
3. pastel de manzana con helado de vainilla
4. un coctel de camarones
5. huevos revueltos con tocino

¿Que hay de comer? Madrid, España.

El bistec más famoso del mundo, a la parrilla. Argentina.

6. jugo de naranja
7. un bocadillo de jamón y queso
8. arroz con pollo, pan y vino
9. café caliente con crema y azúcar
10. una hamburguesa con papas fritas

EJERCICIO 13   Tú y yo

Háganse preguntas y contéstense.

Modelo   tomar/crema en el café
         (pregunta) **¿Tomas crema en el café?**
         (respuesta) **(Sí,)(No, no) tomo crema en el café.**

1. tomar/azúcar en el té
           hielo en el vino
           aceite y vinagre en la ensalada
           cebollas en la hamburguesa
2. necesitar/mucha sal en la comida
           mucha pimienta en la comida

mucha mermelada en el pan
mucha mantequilla en las patatas
3. beber/mucha cerveza
    mucha leche
    mucho café
    jugo de tomate
    vino
4. comer/mucho ajo
    muchas aceitunas
    mucha pizza
    mucho helado
    muchos postres
5. desear/los huevos fritos o revueltos
    una sopa caliente o una sopa fría
    la carne a la parrilla o asada
    una gaseosa o una cerveza
    el helado de fresa o el helado de chocolate
    el pastel de manzana o el pastel de limón

ACTIVIDAD   Mini-dramas: En el restaurante

En grupos de dos o tres estudiantes, preparen diálogos orales entre uno o dos clientes y el camarero (waiter) o la camarera en un restaurante.

   Tópicos: (a) el desayuno
               (b) el almuerzo (o) la comida
               (c) la cena

Posibles preguntas (del camarero o de la camarera):

1. ¿Qué desea usted para el desayuno? ¿para el almuerzo? ¿para la cena?
2. ¿Qué desea usted para beber? ¿y de postre?
3. ¿Qué desea usted en la hamburguesa? ¿en el bocadillo? ¿en la ensalada?
4. ¿Qué más desea usted?
5. ¿Desea usted la cuenta (*bill*)?

¡RECUERDEN LAS EXPRESIONES DE CORTESÍA!

III. Palabras interrogativas
Interrogatives

¿qué?[1]	*what?*	**¿Qué** día es hoy?
		¿Qué es una merienda?
¿cómo?	*how?*	**¿Cómo** está su padre?
¿cuándo?	*when?*	**¿Cuándo** llega?
¿por qué?	*why?*	**¿Por qué** llega por la noche?
¿quién? ¿quiénes?	*who?*	**¿Quiénes** van a la estación?
¿cuál? ¿cuáles?[1]	*which one?*	**¿Cuál** de los postres desea?
	which ones?	**¿Cuáles** va a comprar?

¿cuánto? ¿cuánta?	*how much?*	**¿Cuánto** es?
¿cuántos? ¿cuántas?	*how many?*	**¿Cuántas** galletas desea?
¿dónde?	*where?*	**¿Dónde** viven?
¿adónde?	*(to) where?*	**¿Adónde** van?
¿de dónde?	*from where?*	**¿De dónde** son?

NOTE 1: **Qué** is used to obtain a definition or explanation; **cuál(es)** is used to ask for a choice and is not generally used in front of a noun.

NOTE 2: Without written accents, some of the words listed above are conjunctions and relative pronouns introducing dependent clauses. The most common are:

que　*that, which, who*

　¿Qué museo vas a visitar?　*What museum are you going to visit?*

　Voy a visitar el museo **que** está en la plaza.
　I am going to visit the museum that is on the plaza.

lo que　*what, that which*

¿Qué vas a comprar en el centro?	*What are you going to buy downtown?*
Voy a comprar **lo que** necesito.	*I am going to buy what I need.*

cuando　*when*

¿Cuándo vas a estudiar?	*When are you going to study?*
Voy a estudiar **cuando** llego a la residencia de estudiantes.	*I am going to study when I arrive at the dormitory.*

porque　*because (written as one word)*

¿Por qué estudias?	*Why do you study?*
Estudio **porque** necesito aprender.	*I study because I need to learn.*

EJERCICIO 14　Interrogación

Conteste en español en oraciones completas.

1.　¿Quién es el presidente (la presidenta) de la universidad?
2.　¿Qué estudia usted aquí en la universidad? ¿matemáticas? ¿ciencia política? ¿inglés? ¿historia? ¿arte? ¿psicología?
3.　¿Por qué estudia usted? **Estudio para** (*in order to*) . . .
4.　¿Cuándo estudia usted?
5.　¿Cuántas alumnas hay en la clase? ¿Y cuántos alumnos?
6.　¿Dónde vive usted ahora?
7.　¿De dónde es usted?
8.　¿Adónde va usted cuando termina la clase? ¿a la cafetería? ¿a la clase de historia? ¿a la residencia de estudiantes?

EJERCICIO 15   Muchas preguntas para Diego

Diego, visitante de España, habla con ustedes. Usando las palabras interrogativas, y a base de las declaraciones de Diego, ¿cuántas preguntas puede (can) usted formular?

Modelo   (declaración de Diego) Estudio mucho.
    ¿Dónde estudia usted?
    ¿Cuándo estudia usted? etc.

1. Trabajo mucho.
2. Tengo una familia muy grande.
3. Mis abuelos son de Rusia.
4. Voy a la playa frecuentemente.
5. Tomo vino con el almuerzo y con la cena.
6. Deseo comprar un coche americano.
7. Voy a estar en Nueva York por una semana. El lunes voy al museo de arte.
8. Mi amigo llega mañana.

ACTIVIDAD   La entrevista (*The interview*)

Usando las palabras interrogativas, usted necesita solicitar información de una persona en la clase en una entrevista oral.

Posible información:

nombre (*name*)	(¿Cómo . . . ?)
origen	(¿De dónde . . . ?)
residencia	(¿Dónde . . . ?)
la familia	(¿Cómo . . . ? ¿Cuántos(as) . . . ?)
comida favorita	(¿Cuál . . . ?)
bebida favorita	(¿Cuál . . . ?)
estudios	(¿Qué . . . ?)

Prepárese (prepare yourself) para presentar la información a la clase.

IV. Gustar
To be pleasing (to like)

Gustar, *to be pleasing*, is used to translate the English *to like*. Thus, *I like the house*, becomes in Spanish, *The house is pleasing to me*. Observe the patterns of **gustar** to express *I like, you like,* and so on.

Me* gusta comer.	*I like to eat.*
¿**Te gusta** el pescado?	*Do you (fam. sing.) like fish?*
No **le gustan** las cebollas.	*He/she doesn't like onions.*

***Me**, **te**, **le**, **nos**, **os**, and **les** are indirect-object pronouns meaning *to me, to you,* etc. They will be studied in detail in Chapter 9.

Señor, ¿**le gusta** la comida?	*Sir, do you like the meal?*
No **nos gusta** el café.	*We don't like coffee.*
¿**Os gustan** los camarones?	*Do you (fam. pl.) like shrimp?*
Les gusta beber vino.	*They/you like to drink wine.*

Reference to person + **gustar** + thing(s) liked

me
te
le[1]   **gusta** + singular noun or infinitive
nos   **gustan** + plural noun
os
les[1]

Gustar is used in the third person singular and plural. The singular form is used when one thing is liked. The plural form is used when several things are liked.

NOTE 1: Because **le** and **les** have multiple meanings, a clarification may be necessary.

(A usted) le gusta comer.
(A él)
(A ella)
(A José)

(A ustedes) no **les gusta** estudiar.
(A ellos)
(A ellas)
(A mis hermanos)

EJERCICIO 16   ¿Qué hay para la cena?

*Usted pregunta, ¿**Qué hay para la cena?** y su (your) mamá indica una comida. ¿A usted le gusta o no la comida indicada?*

Modelo   bistec
¡Ah! me gusta el bistec. (o)
¡Ay! no me gusta el bistec.

¿Qué hay para la cena?

1. langosta
2. chuletas de cerdo
3. guisantes
4. pescado

5. camarones
6. frijoles
7. coliflor

8. hamburguesas
9. "perros calientes"
10. sopa de ajo

EJERCICIO 17   Los gustos (*tastes*)

Indique los gustos diferentes de las personas.

> Modelo   A su (*your*) hermano(a) ¿le gusta beber cerveza?
> **Sí, (No, no) le gusta beber cerveza.**

1. A su hermano(a) ¿le gusta trabajar?
   ¿comer pizza?
   ¿cocinar?
   ¿estar en casa?
   ¿ir a la playa?
2. A ustedes ¿les gustan las fiestas?
   ¿la comida en la cafetería?
   ¿la clase de español?
   ¿las clases difíciles?
   ¿los profesores fáciles?
3. A los niños, generalmente, ¿les gusta el helado?
   ¿los guisantes?
   ¿las galletas OREO?
   ¿el pescado?

Menú de la semana

Publicamos el menú que será servido en las escuelas públicas de instrucción primaria del condado de Dade, durante la semana escolar que comienza el lunes 2 de diciembre y termina el viernes 6:

LUNES 2
Platos Principales
Macarrones con queso al horno . Hamburguesa de pollo. Huevos duros. Requesón. Emparedado de ensalada de huevo.

Frutas y Vegetales
Elemental: Popsicle de Jugo de frutas. Secundaria: Jugo. Melocotones con guarnición de cereza. Habichuelas al estilo sureño. Buñuelitos de papa. Pan de maíz. Galleticas de avena. Leche.

EJERCICIO 18   Tú y yo

Háganse preguntas y contéstense.

> Modelo   la universidad
> (pregunta) **¿Te gusta la universidad?**
> (respuesta) **Sí (No, no) me gusta.**

1. estudiar
2. hablar español
3. ir a museos de arte
4. tomar exámenes
5. la comida italiana
6. la comida china
7. la comida mexicana
8. las papas fritas de McDonald's
9. las hamburguesas de McDonald's
10. los "perros calientes"
11. la pizza
12. el ajo
13. las cebollas
14. las aceitunas
15. la cerveza
16. el vino
17. la leche
18. las chicas en la clase de español
19. los chicos en la clase de español
20. el (la) profesor(a) de español

ACTIVIDAD   Una cena especial

Usted va a invitar a su amigo(a) a una cena especial. Usted y su amigo(a) hablan de:

1. el día de la cena, la hora, dónde, etc.;
2. las comidas (legumbres, carnes, bebidas, postres, etc.) que le gustan más a su amigo(a);
3. lo que usted va a preparar.

PANORAMA CULTURAL ▨

La comida hispana

La comida hispana es *rica*, interesante y muy variada. Representa los muchos países situados en tres continentes y *también* las influencias de varias culturas: la india, la negra, la europea. Vemos la variedad de comida comparando algunos de los *platos* hispanos más típicos*:

delicious
also

dishes

el **gazpacho**—España: sopa fría *hecha* de tomates, *pepino*, cebollas, *pimiento verde*, ajo, aceite de oliva, vinagre.

made/cucumber
green pepper

la **tortilla**—España: huevos *batidos* fritos con patatas, cebollas, etc. Comida caliente o fría.

beaten

la **paella**—España: plato de arroz *sazonado* con *azafrán*, con carnes (pollo, chorizo, etc.) y/o una gran variedad de mariscos, y con legumbres (guisantes, cebolla, etc.).

seasoned/saffron

el **flan**—España: un postre hecho de huevos, leche, azúcar y vainilla, con un *almíbar* de caramelo.

syrup

los **churros**—España: *masa* de *harina*, cilíndrica, frita. Frecuentemente se sirven con café con leche o con chocolate caliente.

dough/flour

el **arroz con pollo**—Puerto Rico, Cuba: plato hecho de arroz, pollo, legumbres (tomates, guisantes, *garbanzos*, cebolla).

chick-peas

la **empanada**—España, la Argentina, Chile, Cuba, etc.: masa de harina *rellena* generalmente con carne, cebollas, huevos, aceitunas, etc. Frita u *horneada*.

stuffed
baked

la **tortilla**—México, la América Central: de origen indígena, torta *plana* hecha de maíz. Acompaña el desayuno, el almuerzo y la cena. La base de platos famosos mexicanos como enchiladas y tacos.

flat

frijoles—México, Guatemala, Honduras, Cuba, Puerto Rico: producto del Nuevo Mundo. En México se comen *aun* en el desayuno con huevos, tortillas y chiles. En Cuba el frijol negro es típico, servido con arroz.

even

el **asado**—Argentina: carne asada. Frecuentemente a la parrilla, *se adoba* con varias horas de anticipación con sal, pimienta, ajo, aceite y vinagre.

marinated

*These dishes, though commonly associated with a particular country or countries, are often enjoyed throughout the Spanish-speaking world.

¡Mmmmmmm! Churros y chocolate. España.

La tortilla acompaña el desayuno, el almuerzo y la cena. Guadalajara, Mexico.

Las horas de comer varían en el mundo hispano. Generalmente el desayuno se sirve temprano por la mañana, a las seis o siete, y se come poco—pan, mermelada y café o café con leche. El almuerzo, la comida principal, se sirve entre la una y las tres de la tarde y la cena entre las ocho y las diez de la noche. Las horas de la comida *dan* oportunidad para *largas* conversaciones de *sobremesa*.

give/long
after-dinner

Las *tiendas* de especialidades

stores

En el mundo hispano, *además de* los mercados públicos y los supermercados, *se ven* frecuentemente tiendas pequeñas donde se vende un artículo o producto especial. Por ejemplo, una tienda donde venden leche o productos de la leche se llama una lechería, o donde venden pan, una panadería. ¿Cómo se llaman las tiendas en que venden pasteles? ¿carnes? ¿tortillas? Son pastelería, carnicería, tortillería.

besides
are seen

¡Qué rica (*delicious*) está la
paella! España.

¿CUÁNTO RECUERDA USTED?

Complete las oraciones en la columna A con las conclusiones en la columna B.

A	B
1. El gazpacho es . . .	a. . . . es de orígen indígena.
2. La tortilla hecha de maíz . . .	b. . . . masa rellena con carne, cebollas, etc.
3. La paella es . . .	c. . . . un plato típico español de arroz, mariscos, carnes, etc.
4. El asado es . . .	d. . . . con chocolate caliente.
5. Los churros se sirven . . .	e. . . . en la pastelería.
6. El flan es . . .	f. . . . típico de la Argentina.
7. La empanada es . . .	g. . . . una sopa fría.
8. Las horas de la comida dan oportunidad . . .	h. . . . un postre hecho de huevos, leche, azúcar y vainilla.
9. El almuerzo es . . .	i. . . . la comida principal.
10. Se venden pasteles . . .	j. . . . para largas conversaciones de sobremesa.

INTEGRACIÓN VISUAL: CAPÍTULO 3 ▪

EJERCICIO 3.1 Vocabulario, El mercado

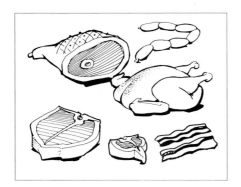

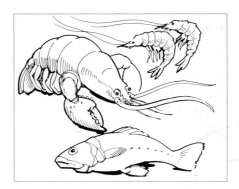

EJERCICIO 3.2 Vocabulario, La comida

EJERCICIO 3.3   Palabras interrogativas

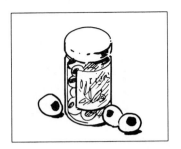

Ejemplo   ¿Qué son?
Son aceitunas.

EJERCICIO 3.4 Gustar

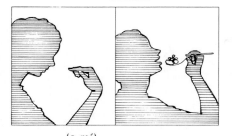

(a mí)

Ejemplo (a mí)
Me gusta comer.

(a ti)

(a usted)

(a Esteban)

(a Pepita)

(a nosotros)

(a ustedes)

(a ellos)

(a ellas)

REPASO DE VOCABULARIO ACTIVO ■

Adjetivos y expresiones adjetivales

asado   **frito**
caliente   **revuelto**
frío   **a la parrilla**

Adverbios y expresiones adverbiales

ahora   **tarde**   **por la mañana/tarde/noche**
hoy   **temprano**   **toda la mañana/tarde/noche**
mañana   **a tiempo**   **todas las mañanas/tardes/noches**
mucho   **esta mañana/tarde/noche**   **todo el día**
poco   **más tarde**   **todos los días**

Palabras interrogativas

¿adónde?   **¿cuánto(a)?** how much   **¿por qué?** why
to where
¿cómo?   **¿cuántos(as)?** how many   **¿qué?** what
¿cuál(es)?   **¿de dónde?** of who   **¿quién(es)?** who
¿cuándo?   **¿dónde?** where

Conjunciones y pronombres relativos

cuando   **porque** because
lo que   **que**

Sustantivos

el aceite oil   la **fruta**   el **pan**
la **aceituna**   la **galleta** cookie   el **pan tostado**
el **agua**   la **gaseosa** soft drink la **papa** potatoe

el **ajo**
el **almuerzo**
el **arroz**
el **azúcar**
la **banana**
la **bebida**
el **bistec**
el **bocadillo**
el **café**
el **camarón**
la **carne**
la **cebolla**
la **cena**
el **cereal**
la **cereza**
la **cerveza**
el **chorizo**
la **chuleta de cerdo**
la **comida**
la **crema**
el **desayuno**
el **durazno**
la **ensalada**
la **fresa** _strawberry_
los **frijoles**

los **guisantes**
las **habichuelas**
la **hamburguesa**
el **helado**
el **hielo**
el **huevo**
el **jamón**
la **judía** _beans_
el **jugo** _juice_
la **langosta** _lobster_
la **leche**
la **lechuga**
la **legumbre** _veg_
el **limón**
el **maíz**
la **mantequilla** _butter_
la **manzana**
el **marisco** _seafood_
el **melocotón**
el **mercado**
la **merienda** _noon snack_
la **mermelada**
la **naranja**

el **pastel**
la **patata**
la **pera** _pear_
el **pescado** _fish_
la **pimienta**
la **piña**
el **plátano** _banana_
el **pollo**
el **postre**
el **queso** _cheese_
la **sal**
la **salchicha** _s_
la **sandía** _watermelon_
la **sopa**
el **té**
el **tocino** _bacon_
el **tomate**
la **torta** _cake_
la **uva** _grapes_
el **vegetal**
el **vinagre**
el **vino** _vine_
la **zanahoria** _carrot_

Verbos

abrir
aprender
beber
comer
comprar
desear

escribir
estudiar
gustar
hablar
llegar
necesitar

preparar
tomar
trabajar
vender
vivir _live_

AUTOEXAMEN Y REPASO #3 ■

I. Vocabulario: el mercado, la comida

¿Qué palabras asocia usted con las siguientes referencias?

Modelo   la sal
          la pimienta

1. el aceite
2. el café
3. el cereal
4. los mariscos
5. frutas cítricas
6. una fruta muy, muy grande

7. carne salada (*salty*)
8. ingredientes típicos de una ensalada
9. ingredientes típicos de un bocadillo
10. bebidas alcohólicas
11. un postre muy famoso americano
12. un postre muy, muy, muy frío

II. Los Verbos -ar, -er, -ir

Sustituya el verbo para indicar opciones diferentes.

1. Compra frutas todos los días. (necesitar, vender, desear)
2. Desean comida mexicana. (preparar, comprar, vender)
3. ¿Trabajas aquí? (estudiar, comer, vivir)
4. Estudio todos los ejercicios. (aprender, escribir, preparar)
5. Hablamos mucho en la clase. (estudiar, aprender, escribir)

III. Palabras interrogativas

Haga una pregunta pidiendo (asking for) *la información según el modelo.*

> Modelo   El señor Fulano no es el profesor.
> **¿Quién es?**

1. Felipe no bebe vino.
2. Ana no vive en Madrid.
3. Roberto no es de Buenos Aires.
4. Alberto no trabaja por la mañana.
5. Elena no va al mercado.
6. Eduardo no necesita tres carros.
7. ¡No se llama Lucinda!
8. La clase de matemáticas no es mi clase favorita. Qual es

IV. El verbo gustar

Indique los gustos de las personas diferentes.

> Modelo   Me gusta el helado. (ella)
> **Le gusta el helado.**

1. Me gusta la sandía. (ellos, tú, nosotros)
2. Les gusta comer. (yo, Alberto, nosotros)
3. No nos gustan las habichuelas. (ellas, yo, usted)
4. ¿Le gustan los camarones? (ustedes, vosotros, tú)

V. Repaso del Capítulo 3

A. *Conteste en oraciones completas.*

1. ¿Qué come usted en el desayuno (*for breakfast*)?
2. ¿Qué come usted en la cena?
3. ¿Cuál es su bebida favorita?

4. ¿Cuál es su postre favorito?
5. ¿Cuál es su fruta favorita?
6. ¿De dónde es usted? *Wherr are you from?*
7. ¿Dónde vive usted? *Where do you live?* *Vivo en Clinton.*
8. ¿Cuándo estudia usted? *Vivo en C*
9. ¿Llega usted a clase a tiempo todos los días?
10. ¿Aprenden ustedes el español? ¿el ruso?
11. ¿Escriben ustedes todos los ejercicios?
12. ¿Le gustan a usted los estudiantes de la clase de español?

B. *Traduzca al español.*

1. Do you need the cream and the sugar? (you = **tú**)
2. They need the salt and the pepper.
3. We are buying fruits and vegetables at the market today.
4. Where are you going now? (you = **tú**)
5. Why does he study all night?
6. How many books are they selling?
7. Who is preparing the dinner?
8. Do you want to eat here tonight? (you = **tú**)
9. Do they like Mexican food?
10. We like wine.

midterm stuff

Necesitas la crema y el azúcar?

Compramos frutas y legumbres en el mercado.

Adonde vas, ahora?

Cuántos libros venden?

Les gusta l comida mexicana?

VI. Repaso: ir + a + infinitivo; ser vs. estar

A. *Indique lo que las personas van a hacer (to do) esta noche. Haga oraciones con las palabras indicadas.*

1. yo/estudiar
2. mi hermano/trabajar
3. Teresa y Linda/preparar la comida
4. nosotros/comprar una pizza
5. tú/leer toda la novela

B. *Usted está en un restaurante. Indique la característica, la condición, etc. usando la forma correcta de **ser** o **estar**.*

1. ¡Ah! ¡El café/caliente!
2. Camarero, la sopa/fría.
3. La torta/de chocolate ¿verdad?
4. Camarero, ¿dónde/el helado?
5. No me gusta este restaurante. El servicio/horrible.

CAPÍTULO 4

Goals for communication
- Talking about the body and ailments
- Expanding our expression of daily activities
- Stating preferences, wants, and capabilities
- Counting

Cultural exploration
- Hispanic life—personal perspectives

VOCABULARIO EL CUERPO Y LAS ACTIVIDADES

La **cabeza** incluye: *head*

el **pelo**[1]	*hair*	la **boca**	*mouth*
las **orejas**	*ears*	los **labios**	*lips*
la **cara**	*face*	los **dientes**	*teeth*
los **ojos**	*eyes*	la **lengua**	*tongue*
la **nariz**	*nose*		

Otras partes del **cuerpo** son: *body*

el **cuello**	*neck*	la **espalda**	*back*
los **hombros**	*shoulders*	el **pecho**	*chest, breast*
los **brazos**	*arms*	el **estómago**	*stomach*
las **manos**	*hands*	las **piernas**	*legs*
los **dedos**	*fingers*	los **pies**	*feet*

97

¿Está usted enfermo(a)? **¿Tiene usted . . . ?**

dolor (*m*.) de garganta	*sore throat*	un **resfriado**	*cold*
dolor de estómago	*stomach ache*	**tos**	*cough* (f.)
		fiebre	*fever* (f.)
dolor de cabeza	*headache*		

Las actividades y otros verbos útiles:

abrazar	*to hug*	**esquiar**	*to ski*
amar	*to love*	**fumar**	*to smoke*
bailar	*to dance*	**llamar**	*to call*
besar	*to kiss*	**leer**	*to read*
buscar	*to look for*	**limpiar**	*to clean*
caminar	*to walk*	**manejar**	*to drive*
cantar	*to sing*	**mirar**	*to look* (at)
cocinar	*to cook*	**nadar**	*to swim*
correr	*to run*	**pintar**	*to paint*
deber	*ought to, should, to owe*	**tocar**	*to touch, to play (instruments)*
descansar	*to rest*	**usar**	*to use*
escuchar	*to listen (to)*		

Los **deportes:**	*sports*
el **equipo**	*team*
jugar al básquetbol	*to play basketball*
jugar al béisbol	*to play baseball*
jugar al fútbol	*to play soccer*
jugar al fútbol americano	*to play football*
jugar al tenis	*to play tennis*

Otras palabras útiles:

la **mentira**	*lie*	la **verdad**	*truth*

NOTE 1: Colors of hair include: **pelo canoso,** *gray or white hair;* **pelo castaño,** *brown hair;* **pelo rojo (pelirrojo),** *red hair (red-haired, -headed);* **pelo rubio,** *blonde hair*

EJERCICIO 1 Las actividades y las partes del cuerpo humano

Es el sábado por la tarde y los estudiantes están en el parque.
A. *Identifique las actividades de los estudiantes según el dibujo.*

Modelo   Manuel y Eva:
         Hablan.

1. Manuel y Eva:
2. Rubén (con la guitarra):
3. Julia (con el libro y la radio):
4. Javier:
5. Pepita: **Juega** (*She is playing*). . .

¡Vamos a bailar! Un baile folklórico de Panamá.

B. Identifique las partes del cuerpo

1. de Manuel

2. de Eva

EJERCICIO 2   El cuerpo y las actividades

¿Qué partes del cuerpo usa usted en las actividades indicadas?

> Modelo   tocar el piano
> **Para** (*in order to*) **tocar el piano uso las manos y los dedos.**

1. nadar	5. abrazar	9. escuchar
2. correr	6. besar	10. manejar
3. mirar	7. leer	11. comer
4. pintar	8. bailar	12. esquiar

EJERCICIO 3   Usted y sus actividades

Conteste en oraciones completas.

1. ¿Le gusta a usted cocinar?
   ¿mirar la televisión?
   ¿escuchar la radio?
   ¿correr? ¿nadár? ¿esquiar?
   ¿pintar? ¿bailar? ¿cantar?
   ¿tocar la guitarra? ¿el piano? ¿el violín? ¿la trompeta?
   ¿jugar al fútbol? ¿al tenis? ¿al básquetbol? ¿al béisbol?

Shood

2. ¿Debe usted estudiar más (*more*)?
   ¿usar el laboratorio más?
   ¿leer más?
   ¿descansar más?
3. ¿Deben ustedes fumar?
   ¿tomar mucha cerveza?
   ¿mirar la televisión toda la noche?
   ¿limpiar el cuarto (*room*) todas las semanas?
4. Generalmente, ¿cuándo mira usted la televisión? ¿Cuáles son sus (*your*) programas favoritos? **Mis . . .**
5. Generalmente, ¿quién cocina en su familia? ¿Quién limpia la casa?
6. ¿Canta usted bien o mal?
   ¿Baila usted bien o mal?
   ¿Pinta usted bien o mal?
   ¿Cocina usted bien o mal?
   ¿Nada usted bien o mal?

CONVERSACIONES ▪

Es sábado. Eva y Manuel, estudiantes universitarios, **hacen** *sus planes para el día.*

MANUEL	Eva, ¿qué vamos a **hacer** hoy?
EVA	No **sé,** Manuel. **Debo limpiar** el cuarto y estudiar un poquito pero . . .
MANUEL	¡Qué aburrido! ¿Porqué no **llamamos** a Javier para ver si **quiere jugar al tenis** o **nadar** en la piscina con nosotros?
EVA	Bueno, me gusta la idea, y posiblemente esta tarde **podemos** comprar unos refrescos y **mirar** el partido de fútbol en la televisión.
MANUEL	**Oye,** ¿**sabes** que esta noche hay un concierto en el centro?
EVA	¡Magnífico! **Podemos caminar** allí pero . . . ¡Ah! ¡Javier **tiene** un coche! Él **puede manejar.** Vamos a llamarle.

It is Saturday. Eva and Manuel, university students, are making their plans for the day.

MANUEL	*Eva, what are we going to do today?*
EVA	*I don't know, Manuel. I ought to clean the room and study a bit, but. . . .*
MANUEL	*How boring! Why don't we call Javier to see if he wants to play tennis or go swimming in the pool with us?*
EVA	*Good. I like the idea, and perhaps this afternoon we can buy some refreshments and watch the football game on T.V.*
MANUEL	*Listen, did you know that tonight there is a concert downtown?*
EVA	*Great! We can walk there but. . . . Oh! Javier has a car! He can drive. Let's call him.*

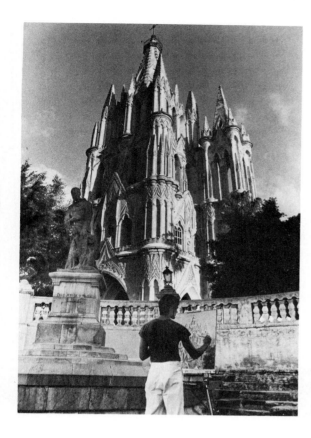

San Miguel de Allende, México, ciudad de artistas. ¿Te gusta pintar?

¿CUÁNTAS ACTIVIDADES RECUERDA USTED?

Use las palabras siguientes para indicar lo que los estudiantes probablemente **van a hacer** *o* **no van a hacer** *según la conversación.*

Modelo   Manuel/a Javier
Manuel va a llamar a Javier.

1. Eva/el cuarto
2. Eva y Manuel/al tenis
3. Javier/en la piscina
4. Todos/unos refrescos

5. Todos/el partido de fútbol
6. Todos/al concierto
7. Javier/su coche
8. Todos/estudiar

Pepita visita la oficina del doctor Lema.

DR. LEMA   Buenas tardes, Pepita. ¿Qué problema **tienes**?
PEPITA   **Tengo tos** y un **dolor de garganta** horrible.
DR. LEMA   A ver si **tienes fiebre** . . .
PEPITA   Creo que sí, doctor, y también estoy muy cansada porque no **puedo dormir**.

DR. LEMA   Parece que tienes un **resfriado** muy serio. Lo que necesitas es **descansar** mucho, tomar mucho líquido y tomar aspirina tres veces al día.

PEPITA   Está bien, doctor. Muchas gracias por su atención. **Llamo** por teléfono si **tengo** más problemas.

Pepita visits the office of doctor Lema.

DR. LEMA   *Good afternoon, Pepita. What problem do you have?*

PEPITA   *I have a cough and a horrible sore throat.*

DR. LEMA   *Let's see if you have a fever . . .*

PEPITA   *I think so, doctor, and I am also very tired because I can't sleep.*

DR. LEMA   *It seems that you have a very bad cold. What you need is to rest a lot, drink a lot of liquid, and take aspirin three times a day.*

PEPITA   *Okay, doctor. Thank you for your attention. I will call on the phone if I have more problems.*

PREGUNTAS

Conteste en oraciones completas.

1.   ¿Qué problemas tiene Pepita?
2.   ¿Cuál es la diagnosis del médico?
3.   ¿Qué necesita Pepita?
4.   ¿Qué va a hacer Pepita si tiene más problemas?
5.   ¿Tiene usted dolor de garganta? ¿Tiene tos? ¿Tiene fiebre? ¿Tiene resfriado?
6.   ¿Qué necesita usted?

ESTRUCTURA ▪

I. La a personal
The personal a

Observe the element in the Spanish sentences that is not found in the English translation.

¿Por qué no llamamos **a** Javier?	*Why don't we call Javier?*
Pepita busca **al** médico y después va a buscar un taxi.	*Pepita is looking for the doctor and afterwards is going to look for a taxi.*

The Spanish personal **a** precedes a direct object that is a noun referring to a person or persons. The personal **a** has no English equivalent or translation.

> Subject + verb + personal a + direct object (person)

NOTE: The personal **a**, like the preposition **a**, contracts with the masculine singular article **el** to form **al**.

EJERCICIO 4   ¿Qué busca usted? (o) ¿A quién busca usted?

Un accidente ha ocurrido y usted habla con muchas personas, buscando información. Complete las oraciones con (with) *o sin* (without) *la **a** personal según las referencias.*

> Modelo   Busco . . . mi hermano.
> **Busco a mi hermano.**

Busco . . . el Dr. Lema

el médico	el policía
las enfermeras	una ambulancia
una solución	el hospital
la oficina del abogado	un taxi
la abogada	los padres de mi amigo

EJERCICIO 5   Preguntas muy personales

*Conteste en oraciones completas, usando la **a** personal.*

1.   ¿A quién (whom) besa usted?
2.   ¿A quién abraza usted?
3.   ¿A quién llama usted por teléfono con mucha frecuencia?
4.   ¿A quién ama usted?
5.   ¿A quién escucha usted?
      ¿A quién NO escucha usted?
6.   ¿A quién mira usted con mucho interés o con mucha curiosidad?

II. Verbos con y̲o̲ irregular en el presente
Verbs with irregular y̲o̲ form in the present tense

Observe the irregular **yo** forms of the following verbs:

hacer	to do, make	**Hago** la tarea todos los días.
poner	to put, place	**Pongo** los libros en la mesa.
salir (de)[1]	to leave, go out (of)	**Salgo** de la clase a tiempo.
ver	to see	**Veo** a mis amigos.
traer	to bring	**Traigo** los cuadernos a la clase.
dar	to give	**Doy** la información al profesor.
traducir	to translate	**Traduzco** las oraciones al inglés.
oír	to hear	**Oigo** el autobús.

hacer:	**hago,** haces, hace, hacemos, hacéis, hacen
poner:	**pongo,** pones, pone, ponemos, ponéis, ponen
salir:	**salgo,** sales, sale, salimos, salís, salen
ver:	**veo,** ves, ve, vemos, veis, ven
traer:	**traigo,** traes, trae, traemos, traéis, traen
dar:	**doy,** das, da, damos, dais, dan
traducir:	**traduzco,** traduces, traduce, traducimos, traducís, traducen
oír:[2]	**oigo,** oyes, oye, oímos, oís, oyen

El fútbol (soccer) es un deporte muy popular en el mundo hispano. Argentina.

NOTE 1: **Salir** is followed by the preposition **de** when the subject is leaving or going out of a place.

Salen **de** la cafetería.   *They are leaving the cafeteria.*

NOTE 2: **Oír** has a spelling change of *i* to *y* in the second person singular and in the third person singular and plural forms.

EJERCICIO 6   Felipe y yo

Felipe es un alumno muy malo. Indique que usted NO hace las cosas (things) *que él hace.*

Modelo   Felipe trae bebidas a la clase.
Yo no traigo bebidas a la clase.

1. Felipe trae comida a la clase.
2. Felipe hace la tarea en la clase.
3. Felipe traduce las lecciones al inglés.
4. Felipe da respuestas incorrectas.

5. Felipe sale de la clase temprano.
6. Felipe pone los pies en el escritorio.

CONSEJO (*advice*)
**El hecho de que tengamos dos orejas y una sola boca es un consejo de
la Naturaleza para que hablemos la mitad y escuchemos el doble.**

refrán: **Quien no oye consejo no llega a viejo.**

EJERCICIO 7 Por todas partes

Todas las personas en la familia **ven** *y* **oyen** *a Lolita constantemente, porque . . . ¡ella está por todas partes* (everywhere)*!*

Modelo ver y oír . . . mis abuelos
        Ven y oyen a Lolita por todas partes.

Ver y oír . . .

1. yo
2. mi mamá
3. nosotros

4. yo
5. mis hermanos
6. tú

Saber y conocer

Spanish has two verbs meaning *to know*. Observe the differences in the way
they are used, and study their conjugations.

conocer *to know*

Conozco bien al profesor. *I know the professor well.*
Conocemos la ciudad de *We know (are acquainted with) Mexico
México. City.*
Deseo **conocer** a *I want to know (meet) Carmen.*
Carmen.

saber *to know*

Sé el número de teléfono. *I know the telephone number.*
Saben donde vivo. *They know where I live.*
Sabe jugar al tenis. *He knows how to play tennis.*

conocer: **conozco,** conoces, conoce, conocemos, conocéis, conocen
saber: **sé,** sabes, sabe, sabemos, sabéis, saben

Conocer means *to know* in the sense of *to be acquainted with* or *to be familiar
with* PEOPLE or PLACES. It also means *to meet*. **Saber** means *to know* FACTS
or INFORMATION and *to know how to do something,* to possess SKILLS.

EJERCICIO 8   Buscamos . . .

A. *Buscamos a personas de mucho talento.*

1. ¿Sabe usted bailar bien?
2. ¿Sabe usted tocar el piano?
   ¿la guitarra?
3. ¿Sabe usted cantar bien?
4. ¿Sabe usted pintar bien?
5. ¿Sabe usted nadar bien?
6. ¿Sabe usted jugar al fútbol?
   ¿al tenis?

B. *Buscamos mucha información.*

1. ¿Sabe usted donde vive el presidente de la universidad?
2. ¿Sabe usted donde vive el profesor (la profesora) de español?
3. ¿Sabe usted el número de teléfono del profesor (de la profesora)?
4. ¿Sabe usted qué día es hoy?
5. ¿Sabe usted qué hora es?

C. *Ahora buscamos a personas con mucha experiencia o curiosidad.*

1. ¿Conoce usted la ciudad de México? ¿Madrid? ¿París? ¿Los Ángeles? ¿Chicago? ¿Nueva York?
2. ¿Conoce usted el arte de Picasso? ¿el arte de Veláquez? ¿la música de Segovia? ¿la música de los Beatles?
3. ¿Desea usted conocer al presidente de los Estados Unidos? ¿al presidente de México? ¿al líder de la Unión Soviética?
4. ¿Desea usted conocer personalmente a Bill Cosby? ¿a James Bond? ¿a la princesa Diana?

EJERCICIO 9   Sí on no, saber o conocer

*Indique si (if) usted **sabe** o **no sabe, conoce** o **no conoce** según las referencias.*

> Modelo   hablar francés
> **Sí, (No, no) sé hablar francés.**
> Los Ángeles
> **Sí, (No, no) conozco Los Ángeles.**

1. hablar español
2. todas las respuestas
3. todo el vocabulario
4. a la profesora (al profesor) de español
5. a todos los estudiantes en la clase
6. jugar al fútbol americano
7. tocar el violín
8. el arte de Diego Rivera
9. San Francisco
10. los museos de arte en San Francisco

EJERCICIO 10   Tú y yo

Háganse preguntas y contéstense.

> Modelo   qué/instrumentos musicales/saber tocar
> (pregunta) **¿Qué instrumentos musicales sabes tocar?**
> (posible respuesta) **Sé tocar el violín.**

1. cuándo/hacer/la tarea
2. leer o traducir/el *Panorama cultural*
3. qué/traer/a la clase de español
4. dónde/poner/los papeles/cuando/entrar/en la clase
5. a quién/conocer/muy bien/en la clase de español
6. oír/al profesor (a la profesora)/en este (*this*) momento
7. a quién/ver/frecuentemente/en la cafetería
8. con quién/salir/los sábados por la noche
9. qué/deportes/saber jugar
10. qué no saber hacer/muy bien

III. Verbos con cambios en la raíz en el presente
Stem-changing verbs in the present tense

Observe where the stem changes occur in the following verbs:

dormir (ue)   *to sleep*   Él **duerme** aquí.
                                                  Nosotros **dormimos** allí.
querer (ie)   *to want, wish, love*   ¿**Quieres** salir ahora?
                                                  ¿**Queréis** ir al restaurante?
pedir (i)   *to ask for*   **Pido** crema para el café.
                                                  Pedimos vino.

> Stem-changing verbs in the present tense change *o* → *ue*, *e* → *ie*, and
> *e* → *i* in all persons except **nosotros** and **vosotros**.

dormir: **due**rmo, **due**rmes, **due**rme, dormimos, dormís, **due**rmen
querer: qu**ie**ro, qu**ie**res, qu**ie**re, queremos, queréis, qu**ie**ren
pedir: p**i**do, p**i**des, p**i**de, pedimos, pedís, p**i**den

jugar (ue)[1]   *to play (sports)*
poder (ue)   *to be able, can*
volver (ue)   *to return*
entender (ie)   *to understand*
cerrar (ie)   *to close*
preferir (ie)   *to prefer*
repetir (i)   *to repeat*

NOTE 1:   The verb **jugar** (*to play*) is unique because *u* changes to *ue*.

Juego al fútbol y mi hermana **juega** al básquetbol.
Jugamos bien.

refrán: **Querer es poder.**

A los jóvenes les gusta
la música "rock."
Concierto en el Parque
de Chapultepec,
México, D.F.

EJERCICIO 11 ¿Quién quiere salir?

Indique quién o quiénes optan por las posibilidades mencionadas.

Modelo ¿Quién quiere salir? (los estudiantes)
Los estudiantes quieren salir.

1. ¿Quién quiere ir a la fiesta?
   (yo, Francisco, tú, nosotros, los alumnos)
2. ¿Quién puede manejar?
   (vosotros, la profesora, tú, yo, nosotros)
3. ¿Quién prefiere ir a un restaurante?
   (yo, Juan y Julio, tú, nosotros, Pancho)
4. ¿Quién quiere salir ahora?
   (los alumnos, yo, la profesora, nosotros)

EJERCICIO 12 Un día sin clases

Indique si (if) usted hace o no hace las siguientes cosas en un día sin clases.

Modelo jugar al fútbol
Sí, (No, no) juego al fútbol.

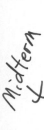

1. dormir mucho
2. cerrar los libros
3. salir de la residencia de estudiantes (de la casa)
4. jugar al tenis
5. ir a la ciudad
6. pedir una pizza
7. mirar la televisión
8. escuchar la radio
9. estudiar
10. descansar
11. volver a casa

EJERCICIO 13   Paco no . . .

*Forme oraciones con vocabulario apropiado para indicar que **nosotros** hacemos ciertas actividades pero **Paco** no.*

Modelo   (entender) . . .
> **Entendemos español.**
> **Paco no entiende español.**

1. En la clase (repetir) . . .
2. En la clase (poder) . . .
3. Por la noche (cerrar) . . .
4. Por la noche (dormir) . . .
5. Los viernes por la noche (querer) . . .
6. Todos los sábados (jugar) . . .
7. En un restaurante (pedir) . . .

EJERCICIO 14   Tú y yo

Háganse preguntas y contéstense.

Modelo   qué postre/preferir
> (pregunta) **¿Qué postre prefieres?**
> (posible respuesta) **Prefiero el helado.**

1. cuántas horas/dormir (generalmente)
2. dormir/en la clase de español
3. qué deportes/jugar
4. qué deportes/no jugar
5. qué/poder hacer bien
6. qué/no poder hacer bien
7. qué coche/preferir manejar
8. preferir/coches americanos o coches japoneses
9. con (*with*) quién/querer salir
10. cuándo/querer salir
11. adónde/querer ir
12. preferir/comer en la cafetería o en un restaurante
13. qué comidas/preferir
14. qué bebidas/pedir (generalmente)
15. qué postre/pedir (generalmente)

IV. Verbos con cambios en la raíz y con yo irregular en el presente

Stem-changing verbs with irregular yo form in the present tense

Observe the irregular **yo** form and the stem changes of the following verbs.

venir (ie)	*to come*	**Vengo** ahora.
		¿Vienen mañana?
decir (i)	*to say, tell*	**Digo** la verdad.
		Dicen que no vienen.
tener (ie)	*to have*	**Tengo** un problema.
		¿Tiene dolor de cabeza?

venir: **vengo,** vienes, viene, venimos, venís, vienen
decir: **digo,** dices, dice, decimos, decís, dicen
tener: **tengo,** tienes, tiene, tenemos, tenéis, tienen

> refranes: **Quien tiene dinero tiene compañeros.**
> **Quien mucho tiene más quiere.**
> **Decir y hacer son dos cosas y la segunda es la dificultosa.**

EJERCICIO 15   Vamos al parque.

Conteste según el modelo.

>Modelo   ¿Quién tiene un coche? (yo)
>**Yo tengo un coche.**

1. ¿Quién tiene los refrescos? (los alumnos, Marta, yo, nosotros)
2. ¿Quién viene al parque? (nosotros, yo, tú, vosotros)
3. ¿Quién dice que es un día fantástico? (la profesora, yo, nosotros, todos los alumnos)

EJERCICIO 16   Preguntas personales

Conteste en oraciones completas.

1. ¿Dice usted la verdad a los padres?
2. ¿Dicen ustedes mentiras a los profesores?
3. Cuando usted habla del profesor (de la profesora), ¿qué dice usted?
4. ¿Viene usted a la clase a tiempo todos los días? ¿y ustedes?
5. ¿Vienen ustedes a la clase de español todos los días?
6. ¿Quién no viene a la clase a tiempo?
7. ¿Tiene usted dolor de cabeza hoy? ¿de estómago? ¿de garganta?
8. ¿Tiene usted pies grandes? ¿un estómago grande? ¿una boca grande? ¿mucho pelo en el pecho? (Muy personal, ¿verdad?)

ACTIVIDADES

A. *El señor (o la señora) "C"*

1. Un(a) alumno(a) pasa a la pizarra y dibuja (*draws*) una caricatura basada en la letra "C".
2. Ahora la clase habla del señor (o de la señora) "C", usando mucha imaginación.
   ¿De dónde es?
   ¿Quién es?
   ¿Cómo es?
   ¿Qué tiene? ¿Qué no tiene?
   ¿Dónde está ahora?
   ¿Qué hace frecuentemente? ¿Qué no hace?

B. *Mini-drama: En la oficina del médico*

Usted y un(a) amigo(a) de la clase de español preparan un diálogo oral entre (*between*) un(a) médico(a) y un(a) paciente. Use sólo (*only*) palabras y estructuras que usted sabe.

VOCABULARIO SUPLEMENTARIO

la **diarrea**	*diarrhea*
embarazada, encinta	*pregnant*
examinar	*to examine*
la **fractura del brazo,** etc.	*broken arm*, etc.
la **gripe**	*flu*
los **problemas digestivos**	*digestive problems*
los **problemas psicológicos**	*psychological problems*
los **síntomas**	*symptoms*

V. Números
(30–100)

treinta	30	**sesenta**	60
treinta y uno	31	**setenta**	70
treinta y dos	32	**ochenta**	80
cuarenta	40	**noventa**	90
cincuenta	50	**cien**	100

NOTE: **Uno**, even when part of a higher number, becomes **un** or **una** to agree with a masculine or feminine noun.

veinti**ún** libros	*21 books*
setenta y **una** mujeres	*71 women*

EJERCICIO 17   Los números hasta cien

1. Vamos a contar
   a. de cinco a cien—5, 10, 15, . . .
   b. de diez a cien—10, 20, . . .
2. Matemáticas

70	20	30	60	90	89	100	50
+10	+14	+23	+15	−28	−10	−7	−15

EJERCICIO 18   ¿Cuánto cuesta?

(**dólares** = *dollars*)

1. Una noche en un hotel elegante—dos personas
2. Una cena para dos en un restaurante elegante
3. Los libros de texto para dos clases

4. Una lámpara para su escritorio
5. Una radio pequeña
6. Un diccionario bueno
7. Una bicicleta para niños
8. Una visita a la oficina del médico
9. Una visita al dentista

ACTIVIDAD   Un conflicto de personalidades

Usted y su compañero(a) de cuarto (*roommate*) tienen muchos problemas.
Usted tiene dos opciones.

A. *Escriba a su mamá o papá una carta (letter)* (**Querida mamá,** etc.) *en que
usted explica por qué existen los problemas.*

B. *Converse con un(a) compañero(a) de clase explicándole la situación.*

Hable posiblemente de lo que su compañero(a) de cuarto hace o no hace; lo
que él/ella prefiere o quiere hacer tarde por la noche; lo que usted no puede
hacer a causa de (*because of*) él/ella, etc.

PANORAMA CULTURAL ■

La vida hispana

Elena, estudiante de la Universidad de Salamanca, habla con estudiantes americanos
sobre la vida hispana.

Me llamo Elena. Soy de Salamanca. Quiero explicarles *algo* de nuestra   *about/life*
vida aquí en España. Primero *pienso* que la filosofía de vida aquí es un poco   *something*
diferente. Los españoles no piensan sólo en el trabajo. Aquí, el trabajo es   *think*
importante en que forma una parte necesaria de la vida, pero también forman una parte muy importante la *amistad*, los amigos, la familia, la diver-   *friendship*
sión—el *calor* humano.   *warmth*

Voy a explicar lo que quiero decir usando mi familia como ejemplo. Un
día de trabajo típico para mi papá:
Suena el *despertador* a las 7:00 de la mañana. Mi papá desayuna en casa   *rings/alarm*
escuchando las noticias por el receptor de radio. A las 8:00 comienza su día
de labor que continúa hasta las 14 o 14:30 horas. Normalmente vuelve a
casa para almorzar con la familia pero *a veces* toma el almuerzo fuera de   *at times*
casa con personas que colaboran o trabajan con él. A las 16 horas vuelve a
su trabajo y trabaja hasta las 19 horas en que *regresa* a casa. En casa fre-   *returns*
cuentemente pasa una hora leyendo *revistas* o libros profesionales y cena-   *magazines*
mos más o menos a las 21 horas. Pasamos mucho tiempo de sobremesa
conversando sobre las actividades del día. *Después* miramos un programa de   *after*
televisión, leemos un *diario* o *tal vez* una novela favorita. A veces *paseamos* por   *newspaper/perhaps/stroll*
la plaza para conversar con amigos, etc. Normalmente todos *nos acostamos* a   *go to bed*
las 23:30 horas o un poco más temprano.

Un amigo del mundo hispano.

Mi hermano Pepe y yo somos estudiantes universitarios. Vivimos en casa con la familia pero *seguimos* la misma rutina de mi padre. *N*os *levantamos* a las 8:30 o 9:00 y estudiamos por la mañana. A veces hacemos *cosas* de la casa *ayudando* a mamá. Tomamos el almuerzo con la familia y a las 16 horas entramos en las clases, saliendo a las 20 horas. Volvemos a casa para cenar y después de conversar con la familia, estudiamos un poco. A veces salimos a la *calle* para estar con unos amigos y a la medianoche a la *cama*.

follow/get up

things

helping

street/bed

Los fines de semana tenemos una rutina diferente. Como la ciudad de Salamanca es pequeña se conoce a todo el mundo. *Por eso* nos gusta pasar mucho tiempo con los amigos en alguna terraza de algún café tomando un refresco y *charlando*. Muchas veces vemos una *película* porque a todos los españoles nos gusta ir al cine. A mi hermano le gusta ir de fiesta con su novia. Ellos, con sus amigos, se sientan en las terrazas cuando hace buen tiempo y en invierno entran en los bares o en las discotecas.

therefore

chatting/film

Los domingos normalmente vamos a *misa* a las 12 horas. Por la tarde nos gusta mucho el excursionismo, las *salidas* en familia o en grupo al campo, a *orillas* de los ríos, playas, etc. También nos gusta ver videos y televisión pero preferimos estar *juntos* como familia conversando y charlando.

mass

departures

shores

together

En cuanto a otros *pasatiempos* y actividades, a mi hermano le gusta ir a las *corridas de toros*, pero a mi personalmente me gustan más los deportes como el esquí, la *natación* y el fútbol, que es muy popular aquí en España.

as for/pastimes

bullfights

swimming

Bueno, como ustedes pueden ver tenemos una vida buena aquí, con mucho énfasis en la familia, en la conversación, y en general una vida, me imagino, *menos apresurada* que la vida en los Estados Unidos.

less hurried

HORA POR HORA

Indique las actividades diarias del padre de la familia y las de Elena y Pepe en la agenda de compromisos (appointment book).

miércoles
25 de noviembre

7:00	_____	_____
8:00	_____	_____
9:00	_____	_____
10:00	_____	_____
11:00	_____	_____
12:00	_____	_____
13:00	_____	_____
14:00	_____	_____
15:00	_____	_____
16:00	_____	_____
17:00	_____	_____
18:00	_____	_____
19:00	_____	_____
20:00	_____	_____
21:00	_____	_____
22:00	_____	_____
23:00	_____	_____
24:00	_____	_____

¿CUÁNTO RECUERDA USTED?

Comprensión aural: ¿cierto o falso?
Responda cierto (true) o falso (false) a las declaraciones.

_____ 1. La filosofía de vida es un poco diferente en España.
_____ 2. Los españoles sólo piensan en el trabajo.
_____ 3. Una parte muy importante de la vida es el calor humano.
_____ 4. La ciudad de Salamanca es grande.
_____ 5. Les gusta a los españoles pasar tiempo conversando con los amigos y con la familia.
_____ 6. Los domingos por la tarde les gusta salir en familia o en grupo al campo.
_____ 7. Prefieren ver videos y televisión más que conversar.
_____ 8. El fútbol no es muy popular en España.
_____ 9. En general, la vida en España es menos apresurada que la vida en los Estados Unidos.

INTEGRACIÓN VISUAL: CAPÍTULO 4

EJERCICIO 4.1   Vocabulario, El Cuerpo

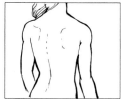

Ejemplo   ¿Qué parte del cuerpo es?
Es la espalda.

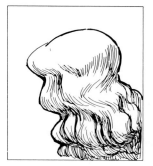  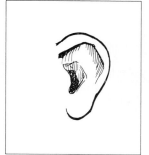 

  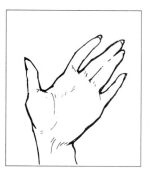 

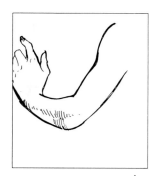   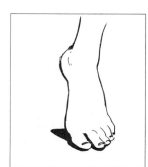

EJERCICIO 4.2 La a personal

Manuel   Eva

Ejemplo   ¿A quién mira Manuel?
Mira a Eva.
(preguanta personal) ¿A quién mira usted?

_____

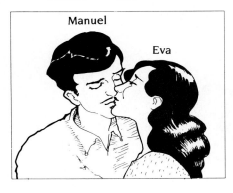

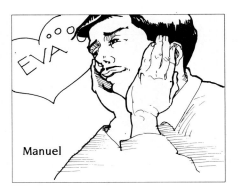

EJERCICIO 4.3 Verbos con <u>yo</u> irregular en el presente

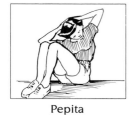

Pepita

Ejemplo

Hace los ejercicios.
¿Y usted?
Hago los ejercicios también (*also*).

EJERCICIO 4.4 Verbos con cambios en la raíz + infinitivos

Ejemplo ¿Qué puede hacer Luisa?
Puede nadar.
(pregunta personal) ¿Puede usted nadar?

Inés

Paco e Inés

Alfonso

REPASO DE VOCABULARIO ACTIVO ▨

Sustantivos

el **básquetbol**	el **deporte**	el **fútbol**	el **pecho**
el **béisbol**	el **diente**	el **hombro**	el **pelo**
la **boca**	el **dolor de cabeza**	el **labio**	el **pie**
el **brazo**	el **dolor de estómago**	la **lengua**	la **pierna**
la **cabeza**	el **dolor de garganta**	la **mano**	el **resfriado**
la **cara**	el **equipo**	la **mentira**	el **tenis**
el **cuello**	la **espalda**	la **nariz**	la **tos**
el **cuerpo**	el **estómago**	el **ojo**	la **verdad**
el **dedo**	la **fiebre**	la **oreja**	

Verbos

abrazar	**deber**	**llamar**	**repetir** (i)
amar	**decir** (i)	**manejar**	**saber**
bailar	**descansar**	**mirar**	**salir**
besar	**dormir** (ue)	**nadar**	**tener** (ie)
buscar	**entender** (ie)	**oír**	**tocar**
caminar	**escuchar**	**pedir** (i)	**traducir**
cantar	**esquiar**	**pintar**	**traer**
cerrar (ie)	**fumar**	**poder** (ue)	**usar**
cocinar	**hacer**	**poner**	**venir** (ie)
conocer	**jugar** (ue)	**preferir** (ie)	**ver**
correr	**leer**	**querer** (ie)	**volver** (ue)
dar	**limpiar**		

Números

treinta	**cincuenta**	**setenta**	**noventa**
cuarenta	**sesenta**	**ochenta**	**cien**

AUTOEXAMEN Y REPASO #4 ▥

I. Vocabulario: el cuerpo y las actividades

¿Qué verbos o actividades asocia usted con las siguientes partes del cuerpo?

Modelo   las manos
          tocar el piano
          etc.

1. los pies y las piernas
2. los brazos
3. los labios
4. los ojos
5. las orejas
6. el estómago
7. los brazos y las piernas
8. las manos

II. La a personal

*¿Con o sin **a**?*

1. Veo . . . (mi amigo, la casa, los muchachos)
2. Conozco . . . (la señorita, el señor Lorca, la ciudad de Nueva York)

III. Verbos con yo irregular en el presente

Indique quién o quiénes participan en las actividades académicas.

Modelo   dar exámenes difíciles/el profesor
          Da exámenes difíciles.

1. oír las instrucciones/yo, tú
2. traer los papeles/yo, ella
3. no hacer errores/yo, nosotros
4. poner las preguntas en la pizarra/yo, vosotros
5. ver los ejemplos/yo, ustedes
6. traducir las oraciones/yo, usted
7. saber las respuestas/yo, ellas
8. salir a la una/yo, nosotros
9. conocer al director de la escuela/yo, tú

IV. Los verbos con cambios en la raíz

Hágale preguntas a Carlos según el modelo.

Modelo   entender la lección
          Carlos, ¿entiendes la lección?

1. dormir en la clase
2. repetir las respuestas en el laboratorio
3. entender bien el español
4. querer estudiar esta noche
5. preferir descansar
6. jugar al béisbol
7. poder nadar bien
8. volver a la universidad en septiembre

V. Verbos con cambios en la raíz y con yo irregular

¡Francisco es perfecto! El profesor quiere saber quién o quiénes hacen lo que hace Francisco.

1. Francisco dice la verdad. ¿Quién más dice la verdad?
   (yo, nosotros, ellos)
2. Francisco tiene una solución. ¿Quién más tiene una solución?
   (yo, nosotros, ustedes)
3. Francisco viene a todas las clases. ¿Quién más viene a todas las clases?
   (Carmen, yo, tú)

VI. Números (30–100)

Matemáticas.

1. 20 + 13 =   2. 30 + 14 =   3. 40 + 15 =   4. 50 + 16 =
5. 60 + 17 =   6. 70 + 18 =   7. 80 + 19 =   8. 90 + 10 =

VII. Repaso del Capítulo 4

A. *Conteste en oraciones completas.*

1. ¿Cuáles son las partes de la cara?
2. ¿Qué partes del cuerpo usa usted para nadar?
3. ¿A qué hora sale usted de la residencia de estudiantes?
4. ¿Qué trae usted a la clase?
5. ¿Viene usted a clase a tiempo todos los días?
6. ¿Prefieren ustedes los profesores fáciles o los profesores difíciles?
7. En la clase de español, ¿a quién conoce usted bien?

B. *Traduzca al español.*

1. I know that he is here.
2. Does he know how to swim?
3. Can she play the piano?
4. What do you want to do now?
   (you = **tú**)
5. We ought to go to class.
6. He is looking at María and looking for an answer.

VIII. Repaso: Interrogativos; gustar

A. *Preguntas. Usando las palabras interrogativas, formule preguntas solicitando más información.*

1. Los estudiantes no vuelven mañana.
2. Varios equipos no vienen el sábado.
3. Ernesto no puede manejar al partido.
4. Los estudiantes no están aquí.
5. No quieren ir a la fiesta.

B. *Traduzca.*

1. My brother likes to dance. **A mi hermano . . .**
2. My sisters like to sing.
3. We don't like to clean the house, but we like to cook.
4. I like sports.
5. Eva, do you like hamburgers?

■CAPÍTULO■

5

Goals for communication
- Purchasing and discussing clothes
- Expressing physical feelings and needs
- Talking about the weather and seasons
- Describing an action in progress
- Indicating possession

Cultural exploration
- Hispanics in the United States

VOCABULARIO LA ROPA ■

¿Qué **ropa** vas a **llevar**?   clothing; to wear, take, carry

la **ropa interior**	underwear	los **blujeans,**	
la **blusa**	blouse	los **vaqueros**	jeans
la **falda**	skirt	la **camisa**	shirt
el **vestido**	dress	la **camiseta**	T-shirt, undershirt
las **medias**	stockings	la **corbata**	tie
los **calcetines**	socks	la **chaqueta**	jacket
los **zapatos**	shoes	el **traje**	suit
los **pantalones**	pants	el **traje de baño**	bathing suit

¿Y para el frío y la lluvia (rain)?

el **abrigo**	coat	el **suéter**	sweater
las **botas**	boots	el **impermeable**	raincoat
los **guantes**	gloves	el **paraguas**	umbrella
el **sombrero**	hat		

Otras **cosas** que necesitamos llevar: *things*

la **bolsa**	*purse, bag*	las **gafas de sol**	*sunglasses*
la **cartera**	*wallet*	las **joyas**	*jewelry*
las **gafas**, los **lentes**	*glasses*	el **reloj**	*watch, clock*

Otras palabras y expresiones útiles:

el **regalo**	*gift*	**corto**	*short*
la **talla**	*size*	**largo**	*long*
costar (ue)	*to cost*	**limpio**	*clean*
ir de compras	*to go shopping*	**sucio**	*dirty*
barato	*cheap*	**otro**	*other, another*
caro	*expensive*		

los colores:

amarillo	*yellow*	**negro**	*black*
anaranjado	*orange*	**pardo**	*brown*
azul	*blue*	**rojo**	*red*
blanco	*white*	**rosado**	*pink*
gris	*gray*	**verde**	*green*
morado	*purple*		

VOCABULARIO SUPLEMENTARIO

el **anillo**	*ring*	los **calzoncillos**	*undershorts*
el **arete**	*earring*	la **camisa de**	
el **collar**	*necklace*	**dormir**	*nightgown*
la **pulsera**	*bracelet*	los **pijamas**	*pajamas*
la **bata**	*robe*	el **sostén**	*bra*
las **bragas**	*underpants*		

YA ES PRIMAVERA

El Corte Inglés

Este año, hay mil posibilidades de combinar la moda: Faldas, blusas, bermudas, chaquetas... Todo puede coordinarse en estilo y color. Con pocas prendas se puede cambiar mucho, porque en Primavera hay momentos alegres, sofisticados, serenos o deportivos... y una sóla moda:
La de El Corte Inglés.

El Corte Inglés es un almacén en España.

EJERCICIO 1   En la tienda (*store*) de ropa

Conteste en oraciones completas según el dibujo.

1.   ¿Qué lleva la mujer que entra en la tienda?
2.   ¿Qué ropa lleva el hombre-maniquí (*mannequin*) elegante?
3.   ¿Qué ropa lleva el otro hombre-maniquí?
4.   ¿Qué otros artículos ve usted allí?
5.   ¿Qué lleva la mujer-maniquí de pelo negro?
6.   ¿Qué lleva la otra mujer-maniquí?
7.   ¿Qué otro artículo ve usted allí?
8.   ¿Cómo se llama la tienda? ¿Venden ropa cara o barata allí?

EJERCICIO 2   Preguntas personales

Conteste en oraciones completas.

1.   ¿Qué ropa lleva usted hoy?
2.   ¿Qué ropa lleva usted cuando va a un restaurante elegante?
3.   ¿Qué ropa necesita usted llevar a Alaska? ¿y a Puerto Rico?
4.   ¿De qué color es su camisa? ¿blusa? ¿vestido? ¿suéter?
5.   ¿Prefiere usted faldas largas o faldas cortas?
6.   ¿Lleva usted calcetines limpios o sucios hoy?
7.   ¿Quién lleva joyas hoy? ¿Qué joyas?
8.   ¿Le gusta a usted ir de compras?
9.   ¿Va usted de compras frecuentemente?
10. ¿Adónde prefiere usted ir de compras?

En muchos pueblos andinos llevan la ropa tradicional de la región. Pisac, Perú.

EJERCICIO 3   Una cuestión de gusto (A *matter of taste*)

¿Qué va bien con (goes well with) *estos* (these) *artículos de ropa?*

1. una chaqueta azul
2. un suéter rosado
3. una corbata amarilla
4. pantalones grises
5. una blusa morada

EJERCICIO 4   ¿Es caro o barato?

Indique si en su opinión los artículos son caros o son baratos.

> Modelo   La camisa cuesta 55 dólares
> **¡Es cara!**

1. El impermeable cuesta 60 dólares.
2. La bolsa cuesta 98 dólares.
3. El traje cuesta 75 dólares.
4. La cartera cuesta 89 dólares.
5. Los zapatos cuestan 15 dólares.
6. Los blujeans cuestan 100 dólares.
7. La corbata cuesta 5 dólares.

CONVERSACIÓN ■

*Felipe **va de compras** a una tienda muy elegante. Busca un **regalo** para el cumpleaños de **su** madre.*

DEPENDIENTA	¿En qué puedo servirle, señor?
FELIPE	**Estoy buscando** un regalo especial para **mi** madre.
DEPENDIENTA	Muy bien. Tenemos toda clase de artículos para damas: **vestidos**, **faldas**, **blusas**, **joyas**. . . .
FELIPE	Quiero ver unas blusas, por favor, de manga **corta**, en la **talla** treinta y seis.
DEPENDIENTA	Esta blusa **azul** es muy elegante.
FELIPE	¿Cuánto **cuesta**?
DEPENDIENTA	Dos mil pesetas,[1] señor.
FELIPE	Muy bien, señora. **Llevo** la blusa, y aquí tiene **mi** tarjeta de crédito.

NOTE 1: $1.00 (U.S.A.) = approximately 110 Spanish pesetas (1988).

¡Vamos de compras!
Zapatería, Madrid, España.

¡Cuánto me gusta este vestido! Tienda, San José, Costa Rica.

Philip goes shopping at a very elegant store. He is looking for a birthday gift for his mother.

CLERK	*How can I help you, sir?*
PHILIP	*I'm looking for a special gift for my mother.*
CLERK	*Fine. We have all kinds of articles for women: dresses, skirts, blouses, jewelry. . . .*
PHILIP	*I would like to see some blouses, please, short-sleeved, in size thirty-six.*
CLERK	*This blue blouse is very elegant.*
PHILIP	*How much does it cost?*
CLERK	*Two thousand pesetas, sir.*
PHILIP	*That'll be fine, Ma'am. I'll take the blouse, and here is my credit card.*

PREGUNTAS

Conteste en oraciones completas.

1. ¿Qué busca Felipe?
2. ¿Qué artículos tiene la tienda?
3. ¿Qué quiere ver Felipe? ¿En qué talla?
4. ¿Qué color prefiere?
5. ¿Cuánto cuesta?

True
False
False
False
True

ACTIVIDAD   Mini-drama: Vamos de compras.

Usted y un(a) amigo(a) de la clase de español, preparen una conversación entre usted y el dependiente (la dependienta) de una tienda. Use sólo palabras y estructuras que usted sabe.

¡Desea comprar aretes, una pulsera o un collar? Joyería, México, D. F.

ESTRUCTURA ▪

I. Expresiones con tener
Expressions with tener

Study the following expressions with **tener** and their English equivalents.

tener (mucha) **hambre**	*to be (very) hungry*	**¡Tengo** mucha **hambre!**
tener (mucha) **sed**	*to be (very) thirsty*	**¿Tienes** sed?
tener (mucho) **frío**	*to be (very) cold (persons)*	El niño **tiene frío.**
tener (mucho) **calor**	*to be (very) hot (persons)*	La niña **tiene calor.**
tener (mucho) **sueño**	*to be (very) sleepy*	**Tenemos** mucho **sueño.**
tener (mucho) **miedo**	*To be (very) afraid*	**¿Tienes miedo** de las serpientes?
tener **razón**	*to be right*	Mi madre **tiene razón.**
no tener **razón**	*to be wrong*	Mi hermano **no tiene razón.**
tener (número) **años**	*to be (number) years old*	**Tiene** trece **años.**

tener que + infinitive	*to have to*	**Tengo que** estudiar esta noche.
tener ganas de + infinitive	*to feel like*	**Tengo ganas de** salir.

EJERCICIO 5   ¿Qué tiene Carlos?

*Indique la expresión con **tener** que corresponde a cada (each) situación.*

1. Carlos quiere comer un bistec con cebollas, patatas, pan y ensalada.
2. Carlos quiere beber una cerveza, una limonada y una Coca-Cola con hielo.
3. ¡Carlos necesita dormir!
4. ¡Ay! ¡Carlos ve una serpiente, un tigre y un león y no puede escapar!
5. ¡Carlos necesita dos suéteres, un abrigo, un sombrero y guantes!
6. Carlos necesita abrir la ventana porque la temperatura está a cien grados Fahrenheit o a treinta y siete grados centígrados.
7. Carlos dice la verdad. ¡Tiene la información correcta!
8. Hay un error. ¡Carlos no tiene la información correcta!

EJERCICIO 6   Obligaciones

Indique por qué las personas no pueden ir al concierto.

> Modelo   yo/estudiar
> **Tengo que estudiar.**

1. Elena/trabajar
2. Nosotros/limpiar la casa
3. Tú/hacer la tarea
4. Mis hermanas/ir de compras
5. Yo/leer una novela para mi clase
6. Fernando/escribir una composición

EJERCICIO 7   Preferencias

*Es el sábado por la mañana. ¿**Tiene** usted **ganas** o **no tiene ganas de** hacer las cosas indicadas?*

> Modelo   estudiar
> **Sí (No, no) tengo ganas de estudiar.**

1. dormir
2. trabajar
3. ir de compras
4. limpiar el cuarto (*room*)
5. leer una novela romántica
6. jugar al tenis
7. escuchar la radio
8. mirar la televisión
9. tomar un desayuno muy grande
10. caminar por el parque

EJERCICIO 8 Tú y yo . . . y mi profesor(a)

A. *Háganse preguntas (usando la forma **tú** del verbo) y contéstense.*

1. tener/frío/ahora
2. tener/calor
3. tener/mucho sueño
4. tener/hambre
5. qué/querer comer/cuando/tener/mucha hambre
6. tener/sed
7. qué/querer beber/cuando/tener/mucha sed
8. tener/miedo/de las serpientes
   . . . de los elefantes
   . . . de los tigres
   . . . de los profesores
9. tener/razón/con mucha frecuencia
10. cuántos/años/tener
11. qué/tener que/hacer/hoy
12. qué/tener ganas de/hacer/hoy
13. tener ganas de/salir de la clase/temprano

B. *Ahora contesten las preguntas personales de su profesor(a).*

1. En su familia, ¿quién tiene razón con mucha frecuencia? ¿Y quién *no* tiene razón?
2. Hablando de su familia, ¿cuántos años tiene su madre? ¿y su padre? ¿y su abuela? ¿y usted?
3. ¿Sabe usted cuántos años tiene el (la) profesor(a) de español? ¿Tiene usted una opinión?
4. ¿Tiene usted ganas de estudiar español hoy? ¿Por qué sí o no?
5. ¿Qué tiene que hacer su madre hoy? ¿y su padre?

EJERCICIO 9 Hoy . . . preferencias y obligaciones

*Indique sus preferencias y obligaciones usando la forma **yo** del verbo y un infinitivo apropiado. (No repita los infinitivos.)*

Modelo   necesitar
Hoy necesito descansar.
Hoy . . .

1. preferir (ie)
2. deber
3. querer (ie)
4. tener que
5. tener ganas de
6. poder (ue)
7. ir a

II. El tiempo, los meses y las estaciones
The weather, months, and seasons

A. El tiempo

Observe the verb that is used in Spanish to express most weather conditions.

¿Qué tiempo hace?	*What's the weather like?*
Hace buen tiempo.	*It's good weather.*
Hace mal tiempo.	*It's bad weather.*
Hace (mucho) **frío.**	*It's (very) cold.*
Hace (mucho) **calor.**	*It's (very) hot.*
Hace fresco.	*It's cool.*
Hace sol.	*It's sunny.*
Hace viento.	*It's windy.*
Llueve.	*It's raining.*
la **lluvia**	*rain*
llover (ue)	*to rain*
Nieva.	*It's snowing.*
la **nieve**	*snow*
nevar (ie)	*to snow*

Refranes: **Después de la lluvia sale el sol.**
Al mal tiempo . . . buena cara.

B. Los meses

enero	*January*
febrero	*February*
marzo	*March*
abril	*April*
mayo	*May*
junio	*June*
julio	*July*
agosto	*August*
septiembre	*September*
octubre	*October*
noviembre	*November*
diciembre	*December*

NOTE: The names of the months are not capitalized in Spanish.

C. Las estaciones

el **invierno**	*winter*	el **verano**	summer
la **primavera**	*spring*	el **otoño**	autumn

EJERCICIO 10 Los meses, las estaciones y el tiempo

Conteste en oraciones completas.

1. ¿Cuáles son los meses del invierno?
2. ¿Cuáles son los meses de la primavera?
3. ¿Cuáles son los meses del verano?
4. ¿Cuáles son los meses del otoño?
5. ¿Cuál es su estación favorita?
6. ¿Cuál es su mes favorito?
7. ¿Qué tiempo hace hoy?
8. ¿Qué tiempo hace en el verano?
9. ¿Qué tiempo hace en el invierno?
10. ¿Llueve mucho en agosto?
11. ¿Nieva mucho en Alaska?
12. ¿Llueve mucho en Oregón?
13. ¿Nieva mucho en la Florida?
14. ¿En qué mes hace fresco aquí?
15. ¿Dónde hace mucho viento?
16. ¿Qué lleva usted cuando nieva? ¿y cuando llueve? ¿y cuando hace calor?

EJERCICIO 11 ¿Qué tiempo hace?

Use la expresión de tiempo que se aplica a la situación indicada.

Modelo   Voy a caminar en el parque.
Hace buen tiempo. (o) **Hace sol.**

1. Voy a la playa.
2. Llevo impermeable y paraguas.
3. Llevo chaqueta.
4. Llevo gafas de sol.
5. Voy a esquiar.
6. Estoy en una isla tropical muy verde.
7. Estoy en los Andes en el invierno.
8. ¡Estamos en un huracán!

III. El presente del progresivo: estar + el participio presente
The present progressive: estar + the present participle

Observe the present progressive construction (**estar** + present participle) in the following sentences.

Paco e Inés **están mirando** la televisión.

Paco and Ines are watching television. (in the act of)

Elena y yo **estamos comiendo**.

Ellen and I are eating. (in the act of)

Ricardo **está escribiendo** una carta.

Richard is writing a letter. (in the act of)

Function: The present progressive stresses an action as being in progress at a given moment. In contrast, the present tense has a more general time reference.

Estoy trabajando ahora.   *I am working now.*
Trabajo todos los días.   *I work (am working) every day.*

Formation:
The present progressive is formed as follows:

> a conjugated form of **estar** + present participle

Regular present participles are formed as follows:

$$\text{infinitive minus} \begin{Bmatrix} \textbf{-ar} \\ \textbf{-er} \\ \textbf{-ir} \end{Bmatrix} + \begin{Bmatrix} \textbf{-ando} \\ \textbf{-iendo} \\ \textbf{-iendo} \end{Bmatrix}$$

look mirar	mir**ando**
eat comer	com**iendo**
escribir	escrib**iendo**

Irregular present participles include:

see decir (i)	**diciendo**	*read* leer	**leyendo**
ask pedir (i)	**pidiendo**	*hear* oír	**oyendo**
repetir (i)	**repitiendo**	*bring* traer	**trayendo**
dormir (u)	**durmiendo**		

Observe that **estar** changes to reflect person and tense, but the present participle does not change in form.

Estoy leyendo.   **Estamos leyendo.**
¿Estás leyendo?   **¿Estáis leyendo?**
Está leyendo.   **Están leyendo.**

NOTE: The verbs **ir** and **venir** are not used in the progressive.

EJERCICIO 12   Un lunes por la noche

Indique lo que los estudiantes están haciendo.

Modelo   yo: usar la computadora
Estoy usando la computadora.

1. Yo: aprender el vocabulario, repetir las palabras, escribir los ejercicios
2. Linda: mirar la televisión, escuchar la radio, descansar
3. Paco y Pepe: estudiar, leer, dormir
4. Eva y Manuel: hablar del examen, preparar una presentación, comer una pizza

EJERCICIO 13   Todos los días y ahora

Indique que las personas están participando en la actividad **ahora.**

>   Modelo   Mi hermano nada todos los días.
>   **Está nadando ahora.**

1. Mi amigo juega al básquetbol todos los días.
2. Yo corro todos los días.
3. Mi madre camina por el parque todos los días.
4. Inés baila todos los días.
5. Nosotros trabajamos todos los días.
6. Esteban hace ejercicios todos los días.
7. Mónica toca el piano todos los días.
8. El bebé toma una siesta todos los días.

EJERCICIO 14   En este momento

Indique lo que su amigo(a) *está haciendo según los objetos que tiene.*

>   Modelo   Tiene un cigarrillo.
>   **Está fumando.**

Tiene . . .

1. una Coca-Cola
2. muchos ingredientes:
   huevos, leche, azúcar
3. un coche nuevo
4. una guitarra
5. una radio
6. un pastel
7. libros y cuadernos
8. un bolígrafo
9. una novela

EJERCICIO 15   ¿Qué están haciendo (probablemente)?

Indique varias posibles actividades que están ocurriendo en las situaciones indicadas.

>   Modelo   en la clase de español
>   **Los estudiantes están hablando en español.**
>   etc.

1. un sábado en la casa de una familia americana
2. un novio y una novia en el parque
3. en la residencia de estudiantes: el lunes por la noche
4. en la residencia de estudiantes: el viernes por la noche
5. en la playa
6. en un restaurante

IV. Los posesivos
The possessives

There are three ways to show possession in Spanish.

A. Posesión con <u>de</u>

Observe the word order and the use of **de** in the following examples.

Es **el sombrero de** Juan.	*It is John's hat.*
Son **las gafas del** profesor.	*They are the professor's glasses.*
¿**De quién** es el impermeable?	*Whose raincoat is it?*

Spanish uses **de** (*of*) to indicate possession; there is no *'s* in Spanish. Similarly, the equivalent of *whose* is **¿de quién?**

EJERCICIO 16   ¿De quién es?

Estudiante #1 hace una pregunta y estudiante #2 contesta la pregunta según el modelo.

Modelo   el suéter/Ana
   #1 ¿De quién es el suéter?
   #2 Es el suéter de Ana.

1. la bolsa/María
2. el abrigo/la muchacha
3. el sombrero/el señor López
4. las joyas/la señora López
5. los zapatos/el profesor
6. el paraguas/Roberto

B. Los adjetivos de posesión antes del nombre
Possessive adjectives used before the noun

Possession can also be shown by use of possessive adjectives. Observe the varying forms of the possessive adjectives and their usage.

mi, mis	*my*	**Mi** sombrero y **mis** gafas no están aquí.
tu, tus	*your*	¿Dónde está **tu** abrigo? ¿y **tus** botas?
su, sus	*your, his, her, its*	**Su** chaqueta y **sus** pantalones son nuevos.
nuestro(a), nuestros(as)	*our*	**Nuestra** abuela y **nuestros** padres llegan mañana.
vuestro(a), vuestros(as)	*your*	¿Van a venir **vuestro** tío y **vuestras** primas?
su, sus	*your, their*	**Su** hermano y **sus** sobrinos viven en California.

In Spanish the possessive adjectives used before the noun agree in number with the *thing possessed*, not with the possessor. **Nuestro** and **vuestro** have feminine forms (both singular and plural) and agree in gender as well.

NOTE: If the owner referred to by **su** or **sus** is not clear by context, clarify in the following manner:

Es **su** libro. = Es el libro **de él. (de ella, de usted, de ellos, de ellas, de ustedes)**

Son **sus** libros. = Son los libros **de él. (de ella,** etc.)

EJERCICIO 17 La ropa está limpia.

La ropa sale de la lavadora automática (washer) *y de la secadora* (dryer). *Indique que las personas tienen su propia* (own) *ropa.*

Modelo   yo: calcetines
Tengo mis calcetines.

1. yo: camisa, camisetas, pijamas
2. nosotros: pantalones, ropa interior, chaquetas
3. tú: blujeans, camisa de dormir, suéteres *tenemos nuestra blujeans.*
4. Elena: vestido, blusas, faldas
5. Diego y Paco: trajes de baño, calcetines, ropa
6. vosotros: ropa interior, camisas, sombreros

EJERCICIO 18 Una excursión

Al (upon) *volver de una excursión hay muchas cosas en el autobús. Conteste las preguntas de la directora* (del director) *según los modelos.*

Modelo   El suéter, ¿es de usted?
Sí (No, no) es mi suéter.

1. La chaqueta, ¿es de usted?
2. Las gafas, ¿son de usted?
3. Las botas, ¿son de Pepe?
4. El sombrero, ¿es de Pepe?
5. La radio, ¿es de ustedes?
6. Los cuadernos, ¿son de ustedes?

Modelo   Señorita, ¿dónde está su cámara?
Mi cámara está aquí.

7. Señorita, ¿dónde está su bolsa?
8. Señorita, ¿dónde están sus libros?
9. Señor, ¿dónde están sus cuadernos?
10. Señor, ¿dónde está su cartera?
11. Señorita, ¿dónde está mi paraguas?
12. Señor, ¿dónde están mis gafas de sol?

C. Los adjetivos de posesión después del nombre
Possessive adjectives used after the noun

Observe the longer forms of the possessive adjectives, their placement in relation to the noun, and their usage.

mío(a), míos(as)	*my, (of) mine*	Una amiga **mía** vive aquí.
tuyo(a), tuyos(as)	*your, (of) yours*	Muchas amigas **tuyas** están aquí.
suyo(a), suyos(as)	*your, (of) yours; his, (of) his; her, (of) hers; its*	Unos parientes **suyos** llegan mañana.
nuestro(a), nuestros(as)	*our, (of) ours*	Una prima **nuestra** vive aquí.
vuestro(a), vuestros(as)	*your, (of) yours*	¿Son ellas amigas **vuestras**?
suyo(a), suyos(as)	*your, (of) yours; their, (of) theirs*	El perro **suyo** es increíble.

The longer forms of the possessive adjectives are used after the noun. They
are used for emphasis and to express the equivalent of the English *of mine, of
yours*, etc.

Possessive adjectives used after the noun agree in number and gender
with the *thing possessed*, not with the possessor.

NOTE 1:   If what the owner means by **suyo(-a, -os, -as)** is not clear by
context, clarify in the following manner:

Es una amiga **suya**. = Es una amiga **de él**. (**de ella, de usted, de ellos, de ellas, de ustedes**)
Son unas amigas **suyas**. = Son unas amigas **de él**. (**de ella**, etc.)

NOTE 2:   The addition of the definite article to the after-the-noun form of the possessive adjective creates the possessive pronoun. After **ser** the article is omitted except for emphasis.

Mario tiene **mi** cámara.	Tiene **la mía**.	*He has mine.*
Van a vender **sus** libros.	Van a vender **los suyos**.	*They are going to sell theirs.*
Son **nuestras** cosas.	Son **nuestras**. (o) Son **las nuestras**.	*They are ours.*

EJERCICIO 19 ¿Quiénes llegan mañana?

A. *Indique quién llega mañana según el modelo.*

Modelo   Unos tíos míos llegan mañana. (Una tía . . .)
Una tía mía llega mañana.

1.   Un pariente tuyo llega mañana. (Una sobrina . . .) (Unos primos . . .)
2.   Unos amigos nuestros llegan mañana. (Unas amigas . . .) (Un tío . . .)
3.   Una amiga mía llega mañana. (Unos parientes . . .) (Un amigo . . .)
4.   Unas primas suyas llegan mañana. (Un primo . . .) (Una hermana . . .)

B. *Todos los visitantes van a salir, pero hay artículos de ropa, etc. abandonados por todas partes. Tu madre quiere saber de quién son pero hay diferencias de opinión.*

Modelo   Mamá dice: ¿De quién es la camisa? Pues, yo digo . . .
Pues, yo digo que es mía.

1.   ¿De quién son los calcetines?
Pues, yo digo . que son mios   Tú dices . . .
Mi hermano dice . . .   Mis primos dicen . . .
2.   ¿De quién es el paraguas?
Mi hermana dice . . .   Tú dices . . .
Yo digo . . .   Mis tíos dicen . . .
3.   ¿De quién son las camisetas?
Mi padre dice . . .   Nosotros decimos . . .
Mis hermanos dicen . . .   Ustedes dicen . . .

EJERCICIO 20 Tú y yo

Háganse preguntas y contéstense según el modelo.

Modelo   el libro
#1: **Yo tengo mi libro. ¿Tienes el tuyo?**
#2: **Sí (No, no) tengo el mío.**

1.	la tarea	5.	la chaqueta
2.	el examen	6.	el paraguas
3.	los cuadernos	7.	el impermeable
4.	el suéter	8.	las botas

ACTIVIDAD La tempestad (*The storm*)

Usted y dos compañeros(as) suyos(as) (de la clase de español, ¡claro!) están acampando en una sección muy remota de las montañas. De pronto (suddenly) viene una tempestad (lluvia, nieve y vientos fuertes) que destruye la carpa (tent) y muchos artículos de ropa. Hablen de:

1. las condiciones en que ustedes están;
2. las sensaciones que tienen (frío, miedo, etc.);
3. lo que tienen que hacer;
4. la condición y la localización de los artículos de ropa, etc.

PANORAMA CULTURAL ▪

Los hispanos en los Estados Unidos

There is much evidence of hispanic culture today in the US.

①Hay *gran* evidencia de la cultura hispana *hoy día* en los Estados Unidos. Se oye la lengua española en todas partes del país, se comen los *alimentos* y condimentos en restaurantes y en fiestas; se oye el ritmo latino del tango y de la samba en la música; se ve la influencia española en la arquitectura; se observa a representantes hispanos en los deportes como el béisbol, el boxeo y el fútbol y en programas de televisión, radio y en el *cine.*

great/nowadays

foods

movies

La lengua y cultura hispanas son evidentes en muchos aspectos de la vida norteamericana. Queens, Nueva York.

Se calcula la población hispana en más o menos 20 millones de personas. Esta población se divide en dos grupos—uno que se compone de hispanos *cuyos ascendientes* españoles exploraron y colonizaron una gran parte de *este* país en los *siglos* 16, 17 y 18, y otro que se compone de inmigrantes, muchos de *los cuales han llegado* en las *últimas* décadas.

whose ancestors
this/centuries
whom have arrived/last

La mayor parte de la población hispana—unos 8.7 millones—es de México. Estas personas residen principalmente en el oeste y el *suroeste* (de Tejas, a Colorado, a California). *Otro* grupo *bastante* grande son los puertorriqueños que, *por* ser de Puerto Rico, un estado *libre* asociado a los Estados Unidos, llegan como *ciudadanos*. Es interesante observar que más puertorriqueños viven en Nueva York que en San Juan, la capital de Puerto Rico.

southwest
another/quite
because of/independent
citizens

Otro grupo de gran importancia son los cubanos, aproximadamente un millón, que residen principalmente en el sur de la Florida. Unos 500.000 viven en Miami, una sección de *la cual* se llama la "pequeña Habana".

which

En años más recientes, por razones políticas o económicas, muchos inmigrantes hispanos van llegando de los países de la América Central, la mayor parte de Nicaragua, Guatemala y El Salvador. *También* llegan otros de la República Dominicana en las Antillas, de Colombia, El Ecuador, la Argentina y de España.

also

Gran parte de los hispanos vienen a los Estados Unidos porque oyen en la radio y ven en la televisión y en las *películas* la ilusión de una vida *mejor*. Noventa *por ciento* de ellos deciden ir a las ciudades grandes porque *creen* que allí hay más oportunidad de *empleo*. También en las ciudades *encuentran* el *compañerismo* de otros hispanos que *ya* viven allí, y buscan conservar la lengua, las costumbres y la cultura hispana en general. *Desgraciada-*

films
better/percent
believe/employment
find/companionship/already
unfortunately

Las aspiraciones de los jóvenes hispanos se manifiestan en forma artística. San Francisco, California.

Los obreros agrícolas se organizaron en los años 60 bajo la dirección de César Chávez para proclamar la solidaridad de los campesinos mexicanos. Los Estados Unidos de América.

Henry Cisneros, alcalde (*mayor*) de San Antonio, Tejas, es buen ejemplo de la creciente influencia política de los hispanos en los Estados Unidos.

Edward James Olmos, famoso actor hispano-norteamericano de televisión y de cine.

El tráfico y consumo de drogas es un problema social que requiere de tu participación

mente el gran influjo a las ciudades produce en *algunos* casos condiciones terribles—secciones o *barrios* congestionados y *superpoblados*, problemas de educación, crimen, malnutrición y desempleo—problemas de los cuales *quisieron* escapar.

some
neighborhoods/overpopulated

wanted

A *causa de* la llegada *cada* año de más inmigrantes y la *edad* joven de la población hispana, se pronostica que *para* el año 2000 unos 30–35 millones de personas de origen hispano residirán en los Estados Unidos y que formarán el 11–12 por ciento de la población total de este país. *Por eso* cada año se notan más la influencia de la cultura hispana y su importancia e influencia política y económica en la vida *diaria* de los Estados Unidos.

because of/each/age

by

therefore

daily

EJERCICIO DE MAPA

A base de la información en el Panorama Cultural, y a base de su experiencia personal, indique en el mapa los estados en que usted sabe que hay gran evidencia de la cultura hispana (lengua, población, etc.).

¿CUÁNTO RECUERDA USTED?

*Comprensión aural: ¿cierto o falso? Responda **cierto** o **falso** a las declaraciones.*

_____ 1. Se observa a representantes hispanos en la televisión o en el cine.

_____ 2. Se calcula la población hispana en más o menos dos millones de personas.

_____ 3. Los españoles exploraron gran parte de los Estados Unidos en los siglos 16, 17 y 18.

_____ 4. La mayor parte de la población hispana es de México.

_____ 5. La mayor parte de la población hispana reside en el oeste y en el suroeste de los Estados Unidos.

_____ 6. Los puertorriqueños llegan a los Estados Unidos como ciudadanos.

_____ 7. Los cubanos viven principalmente en Nueva York.

_____ 8. Muchos inmigrantes llegan hoy día de la América Central.

_____ 9. La mayor parte de los inmigrantes deciden ir a las ciudades grandes.

_____ 10. Se pronostica que para el año 2000 unos cincuenta millones de personas de origen hispano residirán en los Estados Unidos.

INTEGRACIÓN VISUAL: CAPÍTULO 5 ■

EJERCICIO 5.1 Vocabulario, La ropa

Javier

Inés

Mónica

Tomás

Antonio

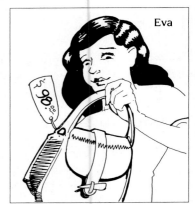
Eva

Elena

Linda

Catalina

EJERCICIO 5.2   Expresiones con <u>tener</u>

Rosa

Ejemplo   ¿Qué tiene Rosa? **Tiene miedo.** (pregunta personal) ¿Tiene usted miedo de los ratoncitos (*mice*)?

Paco

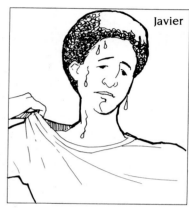
Javier

Esteban

Javier y Pepita

Luisa y Rosa

Julia

la abuela

el padre

EJERCICIO 5.3 Tener que … tener ganas de …

Alfonso

Ejemplo   ¿Qué tiene que hacer Alfonso?
Tiene que cocinar (o) preparar la comida.
(pregunta personal) ¿Tiene usted que cocinar todas la noches?

Ricardo

Alfonso

el señor Gómez

Inés

Pepita

Rosa

Paco e Inés

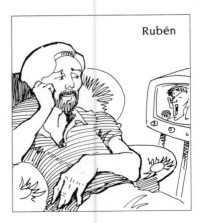

Rubén

EJERCICIO 5.4   El tiempo, los meses, las estaciones

Ejemplo   ¿Qué tiempo hace?
Hace sol.
¿En qué estación hace
mucho sol?
Hace mucho sol en el verano.

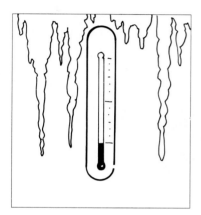

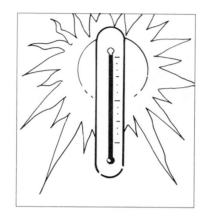

EJERCICIO 5.5   El presente del progresivo

Rubén

Ejemplo   ¿Qué está haciendo Rubén?
Está tocando la guitarra.

Julia

Esteban

Manuel y Eva

Paco

Mónica

Pepita y Javier

Rosa

Inés e Isabel

EJERCICIO 5.6   Los posesivos

Ejemplo   (yo)
Tengo mi sombrero.

Ejemplo   ¿De quién es el sombrero?
El sombrero es mío.

 (yo)

 (yo)

 (yo)

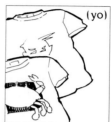 (yo)

 (tú)

 (tú)

 (tú)

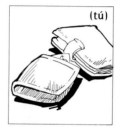 (tú)

 (nosotros)

 (nosotros)

 (nosotros)

 (nosotros)

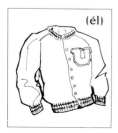 (él)

 (ellos)

 (ella)

 (ellas)

REPASO DE VOCABULARIO ACTIVO ▪

Adjetivos

anaranjado	limpio	blanco	pardo
barato	otro	gris	rojo
caro	sucio	morado	rosado
corto	amarillo	negro	verde
largo	azul		

Adjetivos de posesión (antes del nombre)

mi (-s)	nuestro (-a, -os, -as)
tu (-s)	vuestro (-a, -os, -as)
su (-s)	su (-s)

Adjetivos de posesión (después del nombre)

mío (-a, -os, -as)	nuestro (-a, -os, -as)
tuyo (-a, -os, -as)	vuestro (-a, -os, -as)
suyo (-a, -os, -as)	suyo (-a, -os, -as)

Sustantivos

el abrigo	la chaqueta	los lentes	el sombrero
los blujeans	la corbata	las medias	el suéter
la blusa	la cosa *thing*	los pantalones	la talla
la bolsa	la falda	el paraguas	el traje
las botas	las gafas	el regalo	el traje de baño
los calcetines	las gafas de sol	el reloj	los vaqueros
la camisa	los guantes	la ropa	el vestido
la camiseta	el impermeable	la ropa interior	los zapatos
la cartera	las joyas		

Verbos

costar (ue)	llevar	llover (ue)	nevar (ie)

Expresión idiomática

ir de compras

Expresiones con tener

tener (mucho) calor	tener razón	tener . . . años
tener (mucho) frío	no tener razón	tener ganas de
tener (mucha) hambre	tener (mucha) sed	tener que
tener (mucho) miedo	tener (mucho) sueño	

Meses

enero	**abril**	**julio**	**octubre**
febrero	**mayo**	**agosto**	**noviembre**
marzo	**junio**	**septiembre**	**diciembre**

Estaciones

el **invierno**   la **primavera**   el **verano**   el **otoño**

Tiempo

✳ **¿Qué tiempo hace?** **Hace fresco.**   **Hace** (mucho) **frío.** **Llueve.**
Hace buen tiempo. **Hace sol.**   **Hace** (mucho) **calor.** **Nieva.**
Hace mal tiempo. **Hace viento.**

AUTOEXAMEN Y REPASO #5 ▪

I.   Vocabulario: la ropa

¿Qué artículos de ropa típicamente cubren (cover) *las partes del cuerpo indicadas?*

Modelo   la cabeza
          el sombrero

1. las manos
2. los pies
3. los brazos, hombros, espalda y pecho
4. las piernas
5. más o menos todo el cuerpo

II.   Expresiones con <u>tener</u>

*Indique la expresión con **tener** que corresponde a cada* (each) *situación.*

1. Voy a comer.
2. Voy a beber.
3. Van a dormir.
4. Carlos ve una serpiente grande.
5. ¡Vamos a abrir la ventana!
6. ¡Queremos sopa caliente y café caliente!
7. El profesor dice que yo tengo la respuesta correcta.
8. El profesor dice que tú no tienes la respuesta correcta.

III.   El tiempo, los meses y las estaciones

Indique los meses y el tiempo que corresponden a la estación.

Modelo   la primavera
          meses: **marzo, abril, mayo**
          tiempo: **hace fresco, hace sol, llueve**

1. el verano
2. el otoño
3. el invierno

IV. El presente del progresivo

Para indicar lo que están haciendo las personas en este momento, cambie las oraciones al presente del progresivo.

Modelo   Él fuma.
           Él está fumando.

1. El niño duerme la siesta.
2. Leo la novela.
3. Escriben a sus padres.
4. Comemos bocadillos de jamón y queso.
5. Miras la televisión.
6. Escuchan la radio.

V. La posesión con de

Indique quiénes son las personas.

Modelo   el hijo (la señora López)
           Es el hijo de la señora López.

1. la niña (el señor Martínez)
2. el esposo (Elena)
3. la novia (Felipe)
4. la prima (Carlota)

VI. Los posesivos

Conteste las preguntas indicando de quién son los artículos. Confirme su declaración.

Modelo   ¿De quién es el sombrero? ¿Es tuyo?
           Sí, es mi sombrero.
           ¿Seguro? (*Are you sure?*)
           Sí, es mío.

1. ¿De quién son las gafas? ¿Son tuyas?
2. ¿De quién es el reloj? ¿Es de Teresa?
3. ¿De quién es la chaqueta? ¿Es de Juan?
4. ¿De quiénes son los suéteres? ¿Son de ustedes?
5. ¿De quiénes son las botas? ¿Son de tus amigos?

VII. Repaso del Capítulo 5

A. *Conteste en oraciones completas.*

1. ¿Qué ropa llevan las mujeres a un restaurante elegante? ¿y los hombres?
2. ¿Qué ropa va a llevar usted a Alaska? ¿y a la Florida?
3. ¿De qué color son las manzanas? ¿y las bananas? ¿y los guisantes? ¿y las cebollas?
           Son rojas

④ ¿Qué tiempo hace hoy? *Hace buen tiempo OR Llueve.*
⑤ ¿Qué tiene que hacer usted mañana? *Tengo que ir a la clase. trabajar.*
⑥ ¿Qué está haciendo usted en este momento? *Estoy estudiando.*
7. ¿De quién es el coche que está enfrente de su casa? *escribiendo.*
⑧ ¿Dónde están sus libros de español? *Están aquí. escuchando.*

B. *Traduzca al español.*

1. What is she doing? (*in the act of*)
2. I am very hungry.
3. I feel like eating a hamburger and French fries.
4. It's very cold today!
5. I am going to wear my long coat, my gloves, and my brother's boots.
6. Our parents are going shopping tomorrow.
7. Their friends and a friend of ours are arriving tonight.

VIII. Repaso: ser y estar + adjetivos; verbos con cambios en la raíz (presente, presente del progresivo)

A. *Indique la condición o la característica de los artículos. Use **ser** o **estar**, y la forma correcta del adjetivo.*

1. sucio: los calcetines, la blusa, las panti-medias
2. limpio: el suéter, la chaqueta, los blujeans
3. caro: la ropa buena, las joyas, los abrigos de Inglaterra (*England*)
4. barato: los zapatos de mi hermano, la corbata del profesor, las sandalias de Marta
5. rojo, blanco y azul: la falda, las camisas, los sombreros

B. *Haga dos declaraciones indicando (1) lo que las personas **hacen** en general, y (2) lo que **están haciendo** en este momento.*

1. Felipe/decir la verdad
2. mis hermanas/dormir la siesta
3. ¿tú?/jugar al fútbol
4. yo/pedir limonada con la pizza
5. mi madre/cerrar las ventanas

■CAPÍTULO■

6

Goals for communication
- Talking about places and things in the city
- Narrating actions and events in the past
- Referring to indefinite and negative persons, things, and times
- Counting and indicating dates

Cultural exploration
- Spain: geographical and historical perspectives

VOCABULARIO LA CIUDAD ▨

La **plaza** está en el **centro** de la ciudad.   *square; center, downtown*

De la plaza vemos muchos **edificios:**   *buildings*

un **almacén**	*department store*		
un **banco**	*bank, bench*	un **rascacielos**	*skyscraper*
una **biblioteca**	*library*	un **restaurante**	*restaurant*
una **catedral**	*cathedral*	un **café**	*cafe*
una **iglesia**	*church*	un **bar**	*bar*
un **museo**	*museum*	un **teatro**	*theater*

En una **calle** hay varias **tiendas:**   *street; stores*

una **joyería**	*jewelry shop*	una **peluquería**	*hairdresser*
una **librería**	*bookstore*		

155

En la **avenida** vemos: *avenue*
  mucha **gente,**   *people*
  la entrada al **metro,**   *metro, subway*
  la **parada de autobús,**   *bus stop*
  un **autobús,**   *bus*
  un **taxi,**   *taxi*
  una **bicicleta,**   *bicycle*
  una **motocicleta,**   *motorcycle*
  y en la distancia un **parque.**   *park*

Otras palabras útiles:

el **cine**	*movies*	el **pueblo**	*town, village; people*
la **película**	*film*	el **lugar**	*place*
el **dinero**	*money*		

Verbos útiles:

andar	*to go, walk;*	**pasar**	*to happen, to pass,*
	to work, run		*spend* (time)
	(machinery)	**pensar*** (ie)	*to think*
entrar (en)	*to enter, go into*	**recordar** (ue)	*to remember*
esperar	*to wait for,*	**visitar**	*to visit*
	to hope		

*NOTE: **pensar** + infinitive means *to intend.*

Pienso estudiar esta noche.   *I intend to study tonight.*

  Pensar en means *to think about.*

Pienso en mi familia.   *I think about my family.*

  Pensar de means *to think of (have an opinion).*

¿Qué **piensas del** presidente?   *What do you think of the president?*

EJERCICIO 1   En el centro de la ciudad

Conteste en oraciones completas según el dibujo.

1.   ¿Cómo se llama el restaurante/café?
2.   ¿Qué están haciendo las personas que están sentadas (*seated*) a la mesa?
3.   ¿Cómo se llama el almacén?
4.   ¿Cuántas personas entran en el almacén?
5.   ¿Qué espera la señora vieja que está sentada en el banco?
6.   ¿Qué busca el hombre que está en la avenida?
7.   ¿Cómo se llama el teatro?
8.   Si (*if*) queremos ir al cine esta noche, ¿qué película podemos ver?
9.   ¿Cómo se llama el banco?
10.   ¿Qué otros edificios ve usted en la distancia?

EJERCICIO 2   Preguntas generales

Conteste en oraciones completas.

1.   ¿Piensa usted ir a Europa? ¿a África? ¿a la América del Sur?
2.   ¿Qué lugares piensa usted visitar?
3.   ¿En qué ciudades hay rascacielos famosos? ¿museos famosos? ¿muchos almacenes?
4.   Cuando usted está en una ciudad grande, ¿prefiere usted andar en el metro, en autobús o en taxi?
5.   ¿Tiene usted una bicicleta? ¿una motocicleta? ¿Anda(n) bien?
6.   ¿En qué ciudad/pueblo vive su familia? ¿Tiene su ciudad/pueblo almacenes grandes? ¿museos de arte? ¿un parque? ¿muchas iglesias?
7.   ¿Qué ve usted generalmente en las calles o en las avenidas de una ciudad grande?
8.   ¿Va usted al cine frecuentemente?
9.   ¿Qué películas le gustan a usted? ¿las películas románticas? ¿las de ciencia ficción? ¿las cómicas?
10.   Hablando de ciudades, ¿recuerda usted en qué ciudad de los Estados Unidos viven muchos cubanos? ¿puertorriqueños?

EJERCICIO 3 ¿Adónde vamos?

¿A qué lugares vamos para (in order to) . . . ?

1. comprar libros
2. comprar joyas
3. comer
4. leer, estudiar y pensar
5. ver las obras (*works*) de artistas famosos
6. adorar a Dios (*God*)
7. depositar dinero
8. cortarnos (*to cut*) el pelo
9. ver una película
10. ver un drama
11. comprar ropa
12. descansar en el centro de la ciudad
13. tomar cerveza y vino

CONVERSACIÓN ▪

Ana está sentada en un **café** *en la Avenida José Antonio en Madrid.* **Espera** *a Roberto.*

ANA   Hola, Roberto. Por fin **llegaste. ¿Qué pasó?**

ROBERTO   Lo siento pero cuando **entré** en la calle de Alcalá vi que un **autobús** había chocado con un **taxi. Nadie** se **lesionó** pero ¡qué lío de **gente**! Los policías no me **permitieron** pasar.

ANA   Pues, no importa. **Ya pedí algunas** tapas. Mientras tomamos **algo,** puedes contarme de tus vacaciones en Barcelona.

Vamos a tomar un cafecito y conversar. Café/restaurante, Buenos Aires, Argentina.

ROBERTO	Maravilloso. **Pasé** una semana fantástica allí. **Visité** varios **lugares** de interés: la famosa **catedral,** el puerto, el Paseo de Colón,[1] y . . .
ANA	¿Viste **algunas** de las obras de Picasso en el **Museo** de Arte Moderno?
ROBERTO	Claro. ¡Qué impresionantes! **Pasé** toda una tarde allí.
ANA	Roberto, ¿recordaste traerme **algún** recuerdo de Barcelona?
ROBERTO	Sí, como no. **Encontré algo** muy especial para ti.

NOTE 1:   Paseo de Colón—a major avenue fronting the port, where a statue of Christopher Columbus is a focal point.

Ana is seated at the cafe on the avenue José Antonio in Madrid. She is waiting for Robert.

ANA	*Hi, Robert. You finally arrived. What happened?*
ROBERT	*I am sorry, but when I entered Alcalá Street, I saw that a bus had collided with a taxi. No one was hurt, but what a conglomeration of people! The policemen didn't let me pass.*
ANA	*Well, it doesn't matter. I already ordered some appetizers. While we are eating and drinking something, you can tell me about your vacation in Barcelona.*
ROBERT	*Great. I spent a fantastic week there. I visited various places of interest: the famous cathedral, the port, the Paseo de Colón. . . .*
ANA	*Did you see some of Picasso's works in the Museum of Modern Art?*
ROBERT	*Of course. How impressive! I spent one whole afternoon there.*
ANA	*Robert, did you remember to bring me a souvenir from Barcelona?*
ROBERT	*Yes, of course. I found something very special for you.*

¿CUÁNTO RECUERDA USTED?

Complete.

1. Ana está . . .
2. El café está . . .
3. Roberto llega . . .
4. En el accidente un autobús había chocado con . . .
5. Ana y Roberto pueden hablar mientras . . .
6. Roberto visitó varios lugares de interés en Barcelona. Son . . .
7. En el Museo de Arte Moderno podemos ver . . .
8. Roberto tiene para Ana . . .

ACTIVIDAD

A un(a) compañero(a) en la clase de español, describa su pueblo/ciudad y los edificios/lugares de interés que tiene.

ESTRUCTURA ▨

I. El pretérito de verbos regulares
The preterit (past) tense of regular verbs

A. Los verbos -ar

Study the preterit-tense conjugation of the verb **cantar** and the corresponding English translations.

-ar *endings*   **cantar** *to sing*

-é	Cant**é** anoche.	*I sang last night.*
-aste	¿Cant**aste**?	*Did you sing?*
-ó	Cant**ó** bien.	*He sang well.*
-amos	Cant**amos** mal.	*We sang badly.*
-asteis	¿Cant**asteis** ayer?	*Did you sing yesterday?*
-aron	Cant**aron** en la ópera.	*They sang in the opera.*

To form the preterit tense of regular **-ar** verbs, drop the **-ar** from the infinitive and to the remaining stem add the endings indicated.

The preterit tense in Spanish corresponds to two English forms:

Raúl **cantó** anoche.   *Raúl sang last night.*
Raúl did sing last night.

B. Los verbos -er, -ir   *Simple past tense*

Study the preterit-tense conjugations of the verbs **aprender** and **escribir**.

-er, -ir *endings*   **aprender** *to learn,* **escribir** *to write*

-í	Aprend**í** los verbos y escrib**í** la tarea.
-iste	¿Aprend**iste** los verbos y escrib**iste** la tarea?
-ió	Aprend**ió** los verbos y escrib**ió** la tarea.
-imos	Aprend**imos** los verbos y escrib**imos** la tarea.
-isteis	¿Aprend**isteis** los verbos y escrib**isteis** la tarea?
-ieron	Aprend**ieron** los verbos y escrib**ieron** la tarea.

To form the preterit tense of regular **-er** and **-ir** verbs, drop the **-er** or **-ir** from the infinitive and to the remaining stem add the endings indicated.

NOTE 1:   The preterit forms of **ver** do not have the written accent.

Vi la película dos veces.   ¿**Vio** usted el accidente?

NOTE 2:   Spelling changes occur in the **yo** form of the preterit of verbs ending in **-gar, -car,** and **-zar** in order to maintain the same sound as in the infinitive.

jugar: yo ju**gué**   abrazar: yo abra**cé**   buscar: yo bus**qué**
tocar: yo to**qué**   llegar: yo lle**gué**

NOTE 3:   In the third person singular and plural endings in verbs like **leer** and **oír,** the *i* is changed to *y* when the *i* is preceded by a vowel.

leer: él le**y**ó, ellos le**y**eron   oír: él o**y**ó, ellos o**y**eron

VOCABULARIO   Asociado con el tiempo (*tense*) pretérito o con el pasado

anoche	*last night*	el **viernes** (etc.)	
ayer	*yesterday*	**pasado**	*last Friday, etc.*
la **semana pasada**	*last week*	el **año pasado**	*last year*
el **fin de semana**		**ya**	*already*
pasado	*last weekend*		

refrán: **De rico a pobre pasé,
y sin amigos me quedé.**

EJERCICIO 4   ¿En qué actividades participaron?

Indique las actividades en que participaron las personas.

Modelo   Anoche yo . . . bailar
Anoche bailé.

1. Anoche yo . . .
    hablar por teléfono
    estudiar mi vocabulario
    mirar la televisión
    comer mucho
    salir temprano
2. Ayer mi madre . . .
    trabajar en la tienda
    visitar a mi tío
    preparar la comida
    leer una novela
    escribir a mi abuela
3. La semana pasada nosotros . . .
    ver tres películas
    caminar por el parque
    nadar en el océano
    jugar al tenis
    descansar

4. El año pasado mis hermanos . . .
    pintar la casa
    vender la casa
    comprar un coche
    pasar un mes en Barcelona
    vivir en un apartamento
5. El viernes pasado, ¿tú . . . ?
    tomar el examen
    ver a tu novio(a)
    salir con tus amigos
    manejar al centro
    volver a tu casa
6. El fin de semana pasado, ¿vosotros . . . ?
    escuchar la radio
    escribir a la familia
    llamar a casa
    limpiar el cuarto
    beber mucho

¡Qué impresionante es
este almacén! México, D. F.

EJERCICIO 5   ¿Cuándo?¡Ayer!

*Conteste las preguntas para indicar que usted participó en muchas actividades
ayer.*

> Modelo   ¿Cuándo trabajó usted?
> **Trabajé ayer.**

1.   ¿Cuándo salió usted de la ciudad?
2.   ¿Cuándo llegó usted?
3.   ¿Cuándo manejó usted al centro?
4.   ¿Cuándo comió usted en el restaurante?
5.   ¿Cuándo visitó usted el museo?

> Modelo   ¿Cuándo llegaron usted y su hermano(a) a la casa?
> **Llegamos ayer.**

6.   ¿Cuándo limpiaron la casa?
7.   ¿Cuándo prepararon la comida?
8.   ¿Cuándo comieron la torta?
9.   ¿Cuándo bebieron la leche?
10.   ¿Cuándo llamaron a los abuelos?
11.   ¿Cuándo salieron?

EJERCICIO 6 La semana pasada

¿Participó usted o no participó en las siguientes actividades?

> Modelo   La semana pasada . . .
> entrar en una iglesia o sinagoga
> **Si, (No, no) entré en una iglesia o sinagoga.**

La semana pasada . . .

1. visitar a los abuelos
2. escuchar la radio
3. abrazar a su madre
4. ver una película
5. escribir a su familia
6. caminar al centro

7. usar una computadora
8. bailar el tango
9. comer una pizza
10. limpiar el cuarto
11. leer un libro interesante
       leí

EJERCICIO 7 Un día de excursión en la ciudad

El profesor (la profesora) llega al centro muy tarde el día de una excursión.
Aprende que los estudiantes ya participaron en las actividades planeadas.

> Modelo   Juan, ¿Vas a entrar en la catedral?
> **No, señor (señora, señorita), ya entré en la catedral.**
> ¿y Diego?
> **Diego ya entró también (*also*).**

1. ¿Vas a visitar el museo? ¿y Carmen?
2. ¿Vas a tomar una bebida? ¿y Linda y Lupe?
3. ¿Vas a comprar libros en la librería? ¿y Paco?
4. ¿Vas a ver la película? ¿y Manuel y Eva?
5. ¿Vas a comer en la plaza? ¿y Alfonso?
6. ¿Vas a llamar un taxi? ¿y los otros?
    ¡Ay! ¡Dios mío! ¡Qué tarde llegué!

EJERCICIO 8 Tú y yo

Háganse preguntas y contéstense según el modelo.

> Modelo   qué/estudiar/anoche
> (pregunta) **¿Qué estudiaste anoche?**
> (posible respuesta) **Estudié el español anoche.**

1. qué/comer/anoche
2. qué/beber/anoche
3. qué deporte/jugar/el año pasado
4. qué/comprar/la semana pasada
5. a quién/besar o abrazar/la semana pasada
6. a quién/llamar/la semana pasada
7. a qué hora/salir de la residencia de estudiantes/anoche
8. a qué hora/volver a la residencia de estudiantes/anoche
9. a qué hora/llegar a la clase/hoy
10. cuándo/aprender el vocabulario
11. cuándo/estudiar los verbos
12. cuándo/escribir el examen

ACTIVIDAD Actores y actrices

1. Diez estudiantes seleccionan diez actividades de la lista y, enfrente de la clase, presentan en forma dramática su actividad.
2. Los otros estudiantes indican lo que sus compañeros **están haciendo**.

   Modelo **Diego está jugando al tenis.**

3. Los actores dejan de (*stop*) presentar su actividad y los otros indican la actividad que cada individuo **presentó**.

   Modelo **Diego jugó al tenis.**

4. El actor (la actriz) confirma la respuesta.

   Modelo **Sí, jugué al tenis.**

abrazar	cocinar	fumar	nadar
abrir/cerrar	comer	jugar	pintar
bailar	correr	leer	tocar
beber	entrar/salir	limpiar	trabajar
cantar	escribir	manejar	

II. El pretérito: verbos con cambios en la raíz
Preterit tense: stem-changing verbs

Observe the following verbs that have a stem change in the preterit tense.

dormir (ue, u)	*to sleep*	Yo **dormí** en la casa.
		Él **durmió** en el hotel.
preferir (ie, i)	*to prefer*	Nosotros **preferimos** el bistec.
		Ellos **prefirieron** la langosta.
pedir (i, i)	*to ask for*	¿**Pediste** el vino rojo?
		¿**Pidieron** ustedes el vino blanco?

Verbs ending in **-ir** that are stem-changing in the present tense (*o*→*ue*, *e*→*ie*, *e*→*i*) also change in the preterit. The change (*o*→*u* and *e*→*i*) occurs in the third person singular and plural.

dormir: dormí, dormiste, durmió, dormimos, dormisteis, durmieron [también **morir** (ue, u), *to die*]

preferir: preferí, preferiste, prefirió, preferimos, preferisteis, prefirieron

pedir: pedí, pediste, pidió, pedimos, pedisteis, pidieron [también **repetir** (i, i)]

NOTE: Verbs that change *o*→*u*, *e*→*i* in the preterit make the same change in the *-ing* form.

Estoy **repitiendo** los ejercicios.
Muchos animales están **muriendo**.

Los jóvenes andan por Las Ramblas, avenida principal en Barcelona, España.

EJERCICIO 9   ¡Un accidente horrible!

En la avenida principal que está en el centro de la ciudad hubo (there was) un accidente horrible. ¿Qué pasó?

> Modelo   Pedí información (tú)
> **Pediste información.**

1. Pedimos información. (ellos, yo, tú, mi hermana, el policía)
2. Mi madre repitió las instrucciones del policía. (yo, mis hermanas, tú, vosotros, mi hermano)
3. Preferí no hablar a las víctimas. (nosotros, mi padre, mi madre, los niños, el médico)
4. ¡Gracias a Dios! las personas no murieron. (los padres, el bebé, las hermanas, la abuela)

EJERCICIO 10   Usted y yo

Háganse preguntas (formales) y contéstense según el modelo.

> Modelo   pedir/bistec en el restaurante
> (pregunta) **¿Pidió usted bistec en el restaurante?**
> (posible respuesta) **No, no pedí bistec.**

1. cuántas horas/dormir/anoche
2. dormir/bien o mal
3. comer/en un restaurante recientemente (Sí . . .)

no pedí la langosta

4. pedir/langosta   *no pedí la langosta*
5. qué comidas/pedir
6. qué comida/preferir

7. qué bebida/pedir
8. preferir/la comida o las bebidas
9. preferir/la comida o la conversación

EJERCICIO 11   Preguntas a todos los estudiantes

Contesten según el modelo.

Modelo   ¿Qué pidieron ustedes en la pastelería?
         Pedimos pasteles de limón.

nosotros form
Pedimos

1. ¿Qué pidieron ustedes en el banco?
2. ¿Qué pidieron ustedes en la librería?
3. ¿Qué pidieron ustedes en el almacén?
4. ¿Qué pidieron ustedes en la panadería?
5. ¿Estudiaron ustedes mucho anoche?
6. ¿Repitieron el vocabulario?
7. ¿Repitieron los verbos?
8. ¿Repitieron la conversación?
9. ¿Durmieron ustedes doce horas anoche?
10. ¿Durmieron ustedes muy poco? *Dormimos*

III. Palabras afirmativas y negativas
Affirmative and negative words

Compare the affirmative and negative expressions in the sample sentences.

alguien	*someone, somebody*	**Alguien** entró en la catedral.
alguno (-a, -os, -as)	*some, some one*	**Algunos** niños salieron.
algo	*something*	Vi **algo** interesante.
siempre	*always*	**Siempre** recuerdo el incidente.
a veces	*sometimes, at times*	**A veces** pienso en el incidente.
también	*also*	**También** hablo del incidente.
o . . . o	*either . . . or*	**O** mi tío **o** mi tía van a visitar el lugar.
nadie	*no one, nobody*	**Nadie** entró en la catedral.
ninguno (-a)	*not one, none, not any*	**Ningún** niño vio el incidente.
nada	*nothing, not anything*	No vi **nada** en la catedral.
nunca	*never, not ever*	**Nunca** oí la música.
tampoco	*neither, not either*	**Tampoco** oí la voz.
ni . . . ni	*neither . . . nor*	**Ni** mi tío **ni** mi tía volvieron.

```
┌─────── FERIA DEL LIBRO EN ───────┐
│            LIBRERIA AVILA         │
│      15%-25% y 50% descuento      │
│       262-0744 8558 S.W. 8th Street, Miami │
└──────────────────────────────────┘
```

NOTE 1: In a negative sentence in Spanish, the verb is either preceded by **no** and followed by the longer negative or preceded by the longer negative alone.

no + verb + negative

Carlos **no** sale **nunca.**
No está abierta **ninguna** ventana.

negative + verb

Carlos **nunca** sale.
Ninguna ventana está abierta.

NOTE 2: **Alguien** and **nadie,** when they are objects of the verb, are preceded by the personal **a.**

Veo **a** alguien en la casa.
No veo **a** nadie allí.

NOTE 3: **Alguno** and **ninguno** become **algún** and **ningún** before a masculine singular noun. **Ninguno** has no plural form.

Vamos a México **algún** día.
No veo **ningún** disco.

> refrán: **Sobre gustos no hay nada escrito.**
> **¡Más vale tarde que nunca!**

EJERCICIO 12   Dos amigos

A. En la casa encantada (*haunted*)

Usted y su amigo(a) están caminando por una casa encantada. Su amigo(a) tiene muchas preguntas, probablemente porque tiene miedo. Conteste en la forma negativa.

Modelo   ¿Ves algo allí?
         No, no veo nada allí.

1. ¿Ves algo extraño (*strange*)?
2. ¿Ves a alguien allí?
3. ¿Oyes algo?
4. ¿Oyes a alguien?
5. ¿Buscas algo?
6. ¿Buscas a alguien?
7. ¿Necesitas algo aquí?
   Pues, entonces (*well, then*)
   ¡vámonos ahora!

B. En un día de excursión, a la hora de comer

Su amigo(a) no tiene mucha comida en su bolsa y tiene hambre y sed, pero usted no tiene ninguna de las cosas que pide.

> Modelo   ¿Tienes algunas bebidas?
> **No, no tengo ninguna (bedida).**

1. ¿Tienes algunos bocadillos?
2. ¿Tienes algunas manzanas?
3. ¿Tienes algunos duraznos?
4. ¿Tienes algunas galletas?
5. ¿Tienes algunos pasteles?
6. ¿Tienes algunos chocolates?
7. ¿Tienes alguna comida?

EJERCICIO 13   Pobre Paco

El (la) pesimista y el (la) optimista están hablando del pobre Paco.

> Modelo   El/la pesimista dice: Paco no tiene ningún pariente.
> El/la optimista dice: **Sí, ¡tiene algunos parientes!**

El/la pesimista dice:

1. Paco no tiene ningún amigo.
2. Paco no tiene ninguna amiga.
3. Paco no conoce a nadie aquí.
4. Paco no dice nada en la clase.
5. Paco nunca va a las fiestas.
6. Paco no tiene ni motocicleta ni bicicleta.
7. Paco no tiene nada.
8. Paco no ama a nadie.

EJERCICIO 14   Acciones idénticas

Su padre o madre dice que su hermano(a) hizo (did) o no hizo las cosas indicadas. Indique que usted hizo o no hizo la misma (same) acción.

> Modelo   (madre o padre:)   Tu hermano(a) llamó a casa.
> **Pues, llamé a casa también.**
> (madre o padre:)   Tu hermano no vendió sus libros.
> **Pues, no vendí mis libros tampoco.**

1. Tu hermano(a) caminó al almacén.
2. Tu hermano(a) compró muchas cosas.
3. Tu hermano(a) pasó la tarde en la biblioteca.
4. Estudió mucho.
5. No salió con sus amigos.
6. No volvió a casa tarde.

EJERCICIO 15 ¿Siempre, a veces o nunca?

*Indique si (if) usted participa en las actividades siguientes **siempre, a veces** o **nunca**.*

Modelo   decir la verdad
Siempre (etc.) **digo la verdad.**

1. decir mentiras
2. dormir con la ventana abierta
3. cantar en la ducha (*shower*)
4. mirar la televisión por la mañana
5. caminar a la clase
6. andar en bicicleta a la clase
7. entender al profesor
8. venir a clase a tiempo
9. escuchar a su madre
10. escuchar a su hermano(a)
11. beber mucha cerveza en las fiestas
12. fumar
13. comer postres
14. pensar en su novio(a)
15. dar dinero a los pobres

EJERCICIO 16 Preguntas personales

Conteste en oraciones completas.

1. ¿Compró usted algo ayer? (¿Qué?)
2. ¿Estudió usted con alguien anoche? (¿Con quién?)
3. ¿Vio usted algo divertido en la televisión anoche? (¿Qué?)
4. ¿Salió usted con alguien anoche? (¿Con quién?)
5. ¿Habló usted por teléfono con algunos amigos? (¿Con quiénes?)
6. ¿Comió usted en algún restaurante? (¿Cuál?)
7. ¿Tomó usted o vino o cerveza con la comida?
8. ¿Hay alguien en su cuarto en este momento? ¿en su carro?
9. ¿Tiene usted algo en la mano en este momento? ¿en el estómago? ¿en la cabeza?

¡Vamos al cine! ¿Cuál de las películas prefieres?

ACTIVIDAD   La historia triste de los señores Nadie

Escriba un cuento en que usted narra las actividades del señor y de la señora Nadie. Use las palabras indicadas.

1. El señor y la señora Nadie/nunca
2. a veces
3. ningún amigo
4. nadie
5. tampoco
6. ni él ni ella
7. algunas personas
8. siempre
   ¡Qué triste!

IV. Los números (100 y más)
Numbers (100 and up)

cien	100	**ochocientos(as)**	800
ciento un(o), una	101	**novecientos(as)**	900
doscientos(as)	200	**mil**	1000
trescientos(as)	300	**dos mil**	2000
cuatrocientos(as)	400	**cien mil**	100.000
quinientos(as)	500	**doscientos mil**	200.000
seiscientos(as)	600	**un millón (de)**	1.000.000
setecientos(as)	700	**dos millones (de)**	2.000.000

NOTE 1:   In large numbers in Spanish, the decimal point frequently replaces the comma used in the United States. In amounts of money, the comma is frequently used in place of the decimal point.

NOTE 2:   In Spanish, numbers above 1000 are never read by hundreds.

1971 = mil novecientos setenta y uno.

NOTE 3:   When a number is a multiple of 100 and/or ends in *one*, it agrees in gender with the noun it modifies.

cuatrocient<u>as</u> <u>una</u> mujeres   401 *women*
ciento <u>un</u> hombres   101 *men*
ciento <u>una</u> mujeres   101 *women*

NOTE 4:   In Spanish there is no **y** between hundreds and a smaller number, even though we often say *and* in English.

205 = doscientos cinco
520 = quinientos veinte

EJERCICIO 17   Los números de cien

A. *Usted recibió $1.000 de un tío rico (en billetes de $50). Cuente el dinero:*
50, 100, . . .

B. *¿Sabe usted el año?*

1.   ¿Puede usted identificar . . . ?
     ¿el año de su nacimiento (*birth*)?
     ¿el año del nacimiento de su madre o padre? (¿Cuántos años tiene?)
     ¿el año del nacimiento de su abuelo o abuela? (¿Cuántos años tiene?)
     ¿el año del nacimiento de su profesor(a) de español?
2.   ¿Cuál es el año correcto de . . . ?
     ¿la Primera Guerra Mundial? 1914 o 1920
     ¿la Segunda Guerra Mundial? 1949 o 1939
     ¿cuando Cristóbal Colón llegó al Nuevo Mundo? 1607 o 1492
     ¿cuando terminó la Guerra Civil de los Estados Unidos? 1865 o 1812
     ¿la Declaración de Independencia? 1793 o 1776

EJERCICIO 18   ¿Cuánto cuestan dos?

El señor Olasis es muy, muy rico. Frecuentemente compra regalos extraordinarios para sus dos nietos favoritos. ¿Cuánto dinero necesita para comprar dos de las cosas indicadas?

1.   Un abrigo cuesta $150. **Dos cuestan . . .**
2.   Una televisión cuesta $250.
3.   Un estéreo cuesta $425.
4.   Un tractor cuesta $700.
5.   Un coche nuevo cuesta $12.000.
6.   Una casa nueva cuesta $125.000.
7.   Una mansión cuesta $500.000.

V. ¿Cuál es la fecha?
What is the date?

Observe the word order for expressing dates in Spanish.

> **Es el cuatro de julio.**
> **Es el diez y ocho de septiembre.**
> **Es el primero de abril de mil novecientos noventa.**

The word order for dates in Spanish is:

> article + number + **de** + month (+ **de** + year)

NOTE: The ordinal number **primero,** not the cardinal **uno,** is used for *first*.

¡Qué pintoresca es esta plaza, típica de muchas en el mundo hispano! Segovia, España.

VOCABULARIO

la **fecha**	*date*
el **año**	*year*
el **cumpleaños**	*birthday*
la **Navidad**	*Christmas*
Feliz Navidad	*Merry Christmas*
el **Año Nuevo**	*New Year*
Próspero Año Nuevo	*a prosperous new year*
las **Pascuas**	*Easter, Christmas*
Felices Pascuas	*Happy Easter, Merry Christmas*

EJERCICIO 19   ¿Cuál es la fecha?

A. *Hable con cinco o seis compañeros(as) de la clase de español para saber la fecha de sus cumpleaños.*

    Modelo   ¿Cuándo es tu cumpleaños?
              Mi cumpleaños es el ocho de octubre.

B. *Conteste en oraciones completas para indicar la fecha.*

1. ¿Cuál es la fecha de hoy? (día, mes, año)
2. ¿Cuál es la fecha del Día de la Independencia de los Estados Unidos? (día, mes, año)
3. ¿Cuál es la fecha de la Navidad?
4. ¿Cuál es la fecha del Año Nuevo?
5. ¿Cuál es la fecha del cumpleaños de la profesora (del profesor)?

ACTIVIDAD Un día con mi padre

Usted visitó la oficina de su padre que está en el centro de la ciudad. Use las palabras indicadas para narrar las experiencias del día.

1. yo/salir de/9:30 . . .
2. tomar/metro a . . .
3. llegar . . .
4. entrar en . . .
5. ver/nadie . . .
6. llamar/nadie/contestar . . .
7. pensar en . . .
8. oír/algo . . .
9. abrir . . .
10. ver/padre . . .

11. mi padre y yo/salir a . . .
12. tomar/almuerzo . . .
13. yo/pedir . . .
14. él/pedir . . .
15. hablar de . . .
16. visitar . . .
17. 4:00/él/volver . . .
18. yo/volver . . .

¡Qué día más agradable!

PANORAMA CULTURAL

España

Capital: Madrid
Lengua oficial: Castellano (español)
Gobierno: Monarquía constitucional
Area: 504.750 kilómetros cuadrados (194.885 millas cuadradas)
Población: 40 millones (estimada)
Moneda: Peseta
Productos principales: Aceitunas, naranjas, *trigo*, vino, automóviles, cemento, químicas, ropa, barcos, *hierro*.

wheat
iron

Clima: Variado como su naturaleza—zonas de máxima precipitación en el norte, zonas de máxima aridez en el centro y en el sur; en las periferias (cantábrica y mediterránea) climas muy favorables.

PREGUNTAS

1. Mirando el mapa, indique cuáles son los límites geográficos de España.
   a. Al norte España está limitada geográficamente por _____.
   b. Al este España está limitada por _____.
   c. Al oeste España está limitada por _____.
   d. Al sur España está limitada por _____.
2. ¿Cuáles son los cinco ríos de más importancia?
3. ¿Dónde está situada la capital?
4. ¿Cuáles son tres ciudades de importancia que están situadas en el sur?
5. ¿Cuáles son dos ciudades de importancia que dan al Mar Mediterráneo?
6. ¿Cómo se llaman las islas que están en el Mar Mediterráneo?
7. ¿Qué países tienen fronteras (*borders*) con España?

8. ¿Cómo se llaman las montañas que están entre España y Francia?
9. ¿Cómo se llama el estrecho que separa España de Marruecos?
10. Mirando la variedad geográfica de España, ¿cómo describe usted el clima?

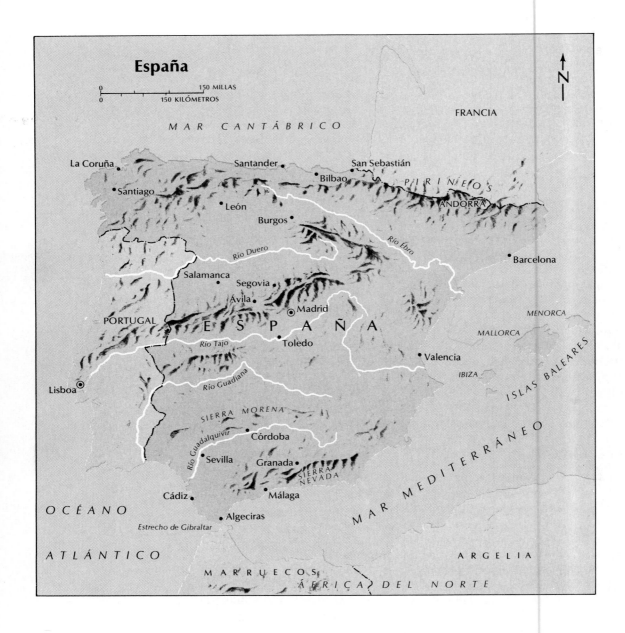

España histórica

La historia de España es larga y variada. Si analizamos esta historia, es fácil *señalar* varios períodos históricos que han contribuído profundamente a la formación de lo que hoy día llamamos España.

if
point out

Los romanos—Los romanos dominaron la península *ibérica desde* el año 218 A.C. hasta 409 D.C. *Dejaron* su marca clara en la forma de un buen sistema de gobierno, el *derecho* romano, una lengua común (el latín), *vías de comunicación* (caminos y *puentes*) y otros monumentos (teatros, coliseos, acueductos, etc.) que son testimonios de su gran civilización.

Iberian from
B.C./A.D./left
law/means
bridges

Los moros—Los moros *empezaron* su conquista de la península en el año 711 D.C. y entre ese año y 1492 establecieron la civilización más brillante de todo el occidente. Siendo famosos como filósofos, poetas, médicos, agricultores, ingenieros y arquitectos, los moros contribuyeron mucho a los *conocimientos* científicos y artísticos del día. También construyeron *mezquitas*, palacios, bibliotecas y escuelas impresionantes. Hoy día podemos ver buena evidencia de su genio en lugares como la famosa Mezquita de Córdoba y la hermosa Alhambra de Granada.

began

knowledge
mosques

Los Reyes Católicos, Fernando e Isabel—*Después de* unos 700 años de conflicto con los moros y *entre sí*, los cristianos, unidos *por fin bajo* Isabel de Castilla y Fernando de Aragón, *derrotaron* a los moros que se *habían retirado* a la ciudad de Granada. Cuando los moros abandonaron la ciudad en 1492,

after
among themselves/finally
under
defeated/had withdrawn

La Alhambra, el maravilloso palacio construído por los moros, tiene en su patio central la hermosa fuente (*fountain*) de los leones. Granada, España

La influencia romana se nota en este impresionante acueducto. Segovia, España.

España *quedó* unificada en lengua, religión y dirección política. En ese *mismo* año Cristóbal Colón descubrió y empezó la exploración del Nuevo Mundo en nombre de los *Reyes Católicos* y en nombre de España, una nueva nación que empezaba a realizar su destino y su misión.

was/same

Catholic monarchs

El imperio español—Dos reyes, Carlos I y Felipe II reinaron durante el período más glorioso de España (1492 hasta los *mediados* del *siglo* diecisiete). Carlos I, rey de España y nieto de Fernando e Isabel, pronto *llegó a ser* emperador de Alemania con el nombre de Carlos V. Con su nuevo título *heredó* un imperio que incluía una gran parte de Europa y los territorios conquistados en el Nuevo Mundo. Cuando Felipe II, su hijo, heredó el *trono* en 1556, su imperio ya comprendía entre sus posesiones España, Portugal, territorios en el norte de África, los Países *Bajos*,[1] gran parte del Nuevo Mundo y varias islas en el Océano Pacífico. España, bajo Carlos y Felipe, se vio obligada a defender sus vastos territorios *contra* los ingleses, los franceses y otros, y su religión contra los protestantes y los *musulmanes*. Los españoles *vencieron* a los turcos en la famosa Batalla de Lepanto en 1571, pero *perdieron* su "Armada Invencible" contra los ingleses en 1588, una *derrota* que señaló el principio de su decadencia política y militar.

middle/century
became
inherited

throne

low

against
Muslims
conquered/lost
defeat

La guerra civil y Franco—España *había* pasado por años de caos político, cuando en 1936 el General Francisco Franco volvió de África a la península ibérica para iniciar una *guerra* contra el gobierno republicano. Con la *ayuda* de los alemanes y los italianos sus fuerzas salieron victoriosas después de 3 años de conflicto trágico en que hermano *luchaba* contra hermano, padre contra hijo. Como dictador, Franco controló el destino de España desde 1939 hasta su *muerte* en 1975. Durante este período de dictadura los espa-

had

war/help

fought

death

[1]Today this area includes the Netherlands, Belgium, and Luxembourg.

Molinos de viento y un castillo. Consuegra.

El Alcázar, Segovia.

Los campos de Andalucía producen uvas y vino extraordinarios.

¡Qué bello es el pueblo de Ojén! Andalucía.

ESPAÑA

Sección impresionante de la Mezquita (*mosque*). Córdoba.

¡Qué fascinante es caminar por las calles pintorescas temprano por la mañana.

Una vista de la ciudad de Segovia del Alcázar.

La ciudad de Córdoba es famosa por sus patios.

Dos jóvenes se dan flores para celebrar las Pascuas (*Easter*).

Vista panorámica de Barcelona con la estatua de Colón.

ñoles perdieron ciertas libertades pero *a la vez* pasaron por un período *at the same time* necesario de estabilidad política.

El proceso democratizador—Con la muerte de Franco se estableció una monarquía constitucional bajo el rey Juan Carlos I de Borbón. Durante estos *últimos* años el país ha pasado por un proceso democratizador: nuevas insti- tuciones democráticas, elecciones *libres*, varias reformas económicas y políti- cas, y más libertades individuales. A *pesar de* ciertos momentos de crisis y dificultades la *confianza* del pueblo español en su gobierno y en su país va *creciendo*, y el futuro de España *parece* más optimista, *sobretodo* con su reciente entrada en el Mercado Común de Europa.

last
free
in spite of
confidence
growing/seems/especially

¿CUÁNTO RECUERDA USTED?

A. *¿Asocia usted las siguientes referencias con los romanos o con los moros?*

1. bibliotecas y escuelas
2. 711–1492
3. sistema de gobierno
4. conocimientos científicos y artísticos
5. 218 A.C.–409 D.C.
6. derecho
7. la Mezquita de Córdoba
8. caminos, puentes y acueductos
9. la Alhambra de Granada
10. teatros y coliseos

B. *¿Qué asocia usted con las siguientes referencias?*

1. Fernando e Isabel
2. 1492
3. Carlos I
4. Felipe II
5. el imperio español bajo Felipe II
6. 1588
7. 1936–1939
8. el General Francisco Franco
9. Juan Carlos I de Borbón

INTEGRACIÓN VISUAL: CAPÍTULO 6 ▪

EJERCICIO 6.1 Vocabulario, La ciudad

EJERCICIO 6.2 El pretérito de verbos regulares

Javier

Ejemplo la casa
Javier pintó la casa.

Javier

Jaime

Javier y Jaime

EJERCICIO 6.3   El pretérito: verbos con cambios en la raíz

Ejemplo   la planta/morir
La planta murió.

Juanito

Juanito

Juanito y Elena

Juanito y Elena

los tíos

Juanito

EJERCICIO 6.4   Palabras afirmativas y negativas

  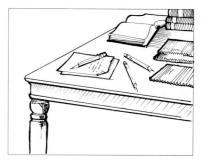

REPASO DE VOCABULARIO ACTIVO ▪

Sustantivos

el **almacén**	el **centro**	la **librería**	la **película**
el **año**	el **cine**	el **lugar**	la **peluquería**
el **autobús**	el **cumpleaños**	el **metro**	la **plaza**
la **avenida**	el **dinero**	la **motocicleta**	el **pueblo**
el **banco**	el **edificio**	el **museo**	el **rascacielos**
la **biblioteca**	la **fecha**	la **Navidad**	el **restaurante**
la **bicicleta**	la **gente**	la **parada de autobús**	el **taxi**
la **calle**	la **iglesia**	el **parque**	el **teatro**
la **catedral**	la **joyería**	las **Pascuas**	la **tienda**

Verbos

andar	**morir** (ue)	**recordar** (ue)
entrar (en)	**pasar**	**visitar**
esperar	**pensar** (ie)	

Expresiones de tiempo

anoche	el **fin de semana pasado**	el **viernes** (etc.) **pasado**
ayer	la **semana pasada**	**ya**
el **año pasado**		

Palabras afirmativas y negativas

algo	**nada**	**nunca**	**siempre**
alguien	**nadie**	**ni . . . ni**	**también**
alguno (-a, -os, -as)	**ninguno** (-a)	**o . . . o**	**tampoco**
a veces			

Números (de cien)

cien	**cuatrocientos**	**setecientos**	**mil**
doscientos	**quinientos**	**ochocientos**	**un millón (de)**
trescientos	**seiscientos**	**novecientos**	

AUTOEXAMEN Y REPASO #6 ▪

I. Vocabulario: la ciudad

¿Qué palabra(s) del vocabulario asocia usted con las siguientes referencias?

1. libros
2. catedral
3. transportación
4. esperar
5. visitar
6. ir de compras
7. cine

II. El pretérito de verbos regulares

Diga usted lo que las personas hicieron ayer.

Modelo   llegar tarde/Eduardo
Eduardo llegó tarde.

1. trabajar/yo
2. salir temprano/yo
3. comprar un abrigo/tú
4. comer en el restaurante/tú
5. llevar un vestido nuevo/ella
6. leer el menú/ella
7. bailar/nosotros
8. beber vino/nosotros
9. escuchar la música/vosotros
10. abrir los regalos/vosotros
11. manejar/ellos
12. volver a casa/ellos

III. El pretérito de verbos con cambios en la raíz

Hágales preguntas a Ana, y a Carlos y Felipe, según el modelo.

Modelo   repetir el número
Ana, ¿repitió usted el número?
Carlos y Felipe, ¿repitieron ustedes el número?

1. pedir el arroz con pollo
2. preferir el helado de fresas
3. dormir bien

IV. Palabras afirmativas y negativas

Conteste en oraciones negativas.

1. ¿Hay algo en el autobús?
2. ¿Hay alguien en el taxi?
3. ¿Hay algunas personas en la catedral?
4. ¿Va usted o al museo o al parque?
5. ¿Siempre va usted a la librería Galdós?
6. ¿Va usted a la biblioteca también?

V. Los números (de cien)

Usted va de compras en un almacén muy, muy caro en la ciudad de Nueva York. ¿Cuánto dinero necesita usted para comprar las cosas indicadas?

1. Las botas cuestan $150 y el abrigo $400.
2. El traje cuesta $440 y las camisas $200.
3. El vestido cuesta $275 y los zapatos $100.
4. El sofá cuesta $1500 y la lámpara $230.
5. La silla cuesta $280 y la mesa $700.

VI. Repaso del Capítulo 6

A. *Conteste.*

1. ¿Estudió usted mucho anoche? *Sí, estudié.*
2. ¿Comió usted una pizza? *No, no comí una pizza.*
3. ¿Qué pidió usted en el restaurante? *Pidí carne (meat).*
4. ¿Usted y sus amigos bebieron todas las Coca-Colas?
5. ¿Visitaron ustedes la biblioteca?
6. ¿Cuántas horas durmieron ustedes anoche? *Dormimos seis horas.*
7. ¿Cuál es la fecha de hoy? (día, mes, año) *Es el nueve de noviembre de mil novecientos noventa y dos.*

B. *Traduzca.*

1. They did not see the film.
2. Did you call last night? (you = **tú**)
3. Did someone ask for a taxi?
4. He bought something interesting in the department store.
5. The date of her birthday is October 8, 1943.

VII. Repaso: verbos con cambios en la raíz (tiempo presente); presente, progresivo, pretérito

A. *Diga que Carlos generalmente hace (o no hace) las cosas indicadas.*

Modelo   Carlos cerró la tienda a las dos.
   Generalmente cierra la tienda a las dos.

1. Volvió a casa temprano.
2. No entendió los problemas.
3. Pidió más información.
4. No recordó las instrucciones.
5. Prefirió esperar.
6. No pensó en llamar.
7. No durmió bien.

B. *Complete para indicar que la acción **ocurre, está ocurriendo** u **ocurrió** en el tiempo indicado.*

· Modelo   cantar bien/yo: En general, . . .
   En general, canto bien.

1. bailar bien/yo: En general, . . . ; Ahora . . . ; Anoche. . . .
2. aprender el vocabulario/nosotros: En la clase de español . . . ; Ahora . . . ; Ayer. . . .
3. escribir a la familia/él: Normalmente, . . . ; Ahora . . . ; La semana pasada. . . .
4. esperar el autobús/ellos: En general . . . ; Ahora . . . ; Ayer, por una hora. . . .

▪C A P Í T U L O▪

7

Goals for communication
- ▪ Talking about places and things identified with nature
- ▪ Narrating actions and events in the past
- ▪ Locating in space and time
- ▪ Stating purpose, destination, and cause

Cultural exploration
- ▪ Spain: a cultural perspective

VOCABULARIO EL CAMPO Y LA NATURALEZA

| En el **campo** hay una **hacienda.** | *country, field; ranch, farm* |
| Vemos muchos **animales:** | *animals* |

el **caballo**	*horse*	la **gallina**	*chicken*
el **burro**	*donkey*	la **oveja**	*sheep*
la **vaca**	*cow*	el **gato**	*cat*
el **cerdo**	*pig*		

Y también **insectos:**	*insects*		
las **arañas**	*spiders*	y una **culebra/**	*snake*
las **moscas**	*flies*	una **serpiente**	
los **mosquitos**	*mosquitoes*		

En el **río** vi un **pez** grande	*river; fish*
y muchos **peces** pequeños.	*fish* (pl.)
¿Desea usted **pescar**?	*to fish*

En el campo vemos:

la **tierra**	land, earth	el **bosque**	woods, forest
la **hierba**	grass	y una **choza**	hut
las **flores**	flowers	en la distancia.	
los **árboles**	trees		

¿Y en el **cielo**?	sky	las **nubes**	clouds
la **luna**	moon	y muchos **pájaros**	birds
las **estrellas**	stars		
el **sol**	sun		

¿Desea usted **viajar**?		to travel	
Vamos a **hacer un viaje**		to take a trip	
al **desierto**	desert	a la **isla**	island
a la **selva**	jungle	al **mar**	sea
al **valle**	valley	o al **océano**.	ocean

Allí vamos a jugar en la **arena**	sand
y ver los **barcos**.	boats

refranes: **El árbol se conoce por sus frutos.**
Los pájaros de la misma pluma vuelan juntos.
En boca cerrada no entran moscas.

EJERCICIO 1   En el campo

Conteste en oraciones completas según el dibujo.

1. ¿Cuántas gallinas ve usted?
2. ¿Qué está haciendo una de las gallinas?
3. ¿Qué animal está comiendo el maíz?
4. ¿Qué animal está corriendo?
5. ¿Qué animal posiblemente tiene miedo del perro?
6. ¿Qué tipo de plantas ve usted cerca (*near*) del gato?
7. En la hacienda hay una casa pequeña. ¿Cómo se llama esta (*this*) clase de casa?
8. ¿Qué animal está cerca del árbol?
9. ¿Qué animal está cerca del río?
10. ¿Qué está comiendo la vaca?
11. ¿Qué ve usted en la distancia?

EJERCICIO 2   Preguntas generales

Conteste en oraciones completas.

1. ¿Prefiere usted pasar las vacaciones en el campo o en la ciudad? ¿en las montañas o en la playa?

¡Qué cuadro impresionante forma la combinación de montañas, río, valle y pueblo! Ollantaytambó Perú.

2. ¿Prefiere usted nadar en el océano, en un lago o en un río?
3. ¿Le gusta a usted pescar? ¿Dónde?
4. ¿Le gustan a usted los animales? ¿Cuáles?
5. ¿Prefiere usted los perros o los gatos? ¿Tiene usted un perro (gato)? ¿Cómo se llama?
6. ¿Viajó usted a algún lugar interesante el verano pasado? ¿Adónde? ¿Le gustó? ¿Por qué?
7. ¿Le gusta a usted viajar?
8. ¿Va usted a hacer un viaje este verano? ¿Adónde?
9. ¿Desea usted visitar la selva y el río Amazonas? ¿Por qué?
10. ¿Qué es el Sahara? ¿Puerto Rico? ¿el Mediterráneo? ¿el Misisipi?
11. ¿De qué color es la hierba? ¿el cielo? ¿el sol?
    ¿De qué color son las nubes? ¿y sus flores favoritas?

EJERCICIO 3   Identificación

Dé (give) *la palabra que corresponde a la definición.*

Modelo   Toma leche.
         el gato

1. Produce leche
2. Muchos árboles
3. Es amigo del hombre
4. Canta muy bonito
5. Produce huevos
6. Su carne se llama jamón
7. Tierra entre (*between*) montañas
8. Producen lluvia
9. Lo que usamos en lagos, ríos, etc.
10. Los suéteres vienen de este animal
11. Muchas personas tienen miedo de este reptil
12. Está en el cielo por la noche; es grande
13. Son de muchos colores bonitos
14. Hay muchas en el cielo de noche
15. Nadan en los ríos, lagos, etc.
16. Una casa muy pequeña en el campo

CONVERSACIÓN ■

*Ricardo y Jaime, amigos **de** hace años, un día se encontraron por casualidad en la calle. **Fueron a** un café **para** hablar.*

RICARDO Jaime, ¿recuerdas que como muchachos **fuimos** un verano **a** la **hacienda de** tus abuelos?

JAIME Sí, ¡cómo no! **Estuvimos** allí **por** un mes. ¡Qué cosas más ridículas **hicimos**!

RICARDO Sí. ¿Recuerdas que **vinieron** a visitarnos unos primos tuyos **de** la ciudad? ¡Qué miedo **tuvieron** cuando **vieron los animales**! No **quisieron** hacer nada.

JAIME Y no **pudimos** resistir la tentación **de** molestarlos un poco. Una noche **pusimos** unos insectos **en** su cama. ¡Qué malos **fuimos**!

RICARDO **En** otra ocasión, **al andar por** el **bosque,** les **dijimos** que había un **animal** grotesco **cerca de** allí. ¡Qué rápido corrieron **a** la casa!

JAIME Cuando **supieron** que era una mentira, se **pusieron** furiosos **con nosotros. Salieron para** la ciudad y nunca **volvieron.** ¡Qué lástima!

RICARDO Sí. Ahora siento lo que **hicimos.** Pero **en** ese momento, ¡qué gusto nos **dio**!

Ricardo and Jaime, friends from years ago, met by chance one day in the street. They went to a cafe to talk.

RICARDO *Jaime, do you remember that as boys we went one summer to your grandparents' farm?*

JAIME *Yes, of course. We were there for a month. What ridiculous things we did!*

RICARDO   *Yes. Do you remember that some cousins of yours from the city came to visit us? How frightened they were when they saw the animals! They refused to do anything.*

JAIME   *And we couldn't resist the temptation to annoy them a little. One night we put insects in their bed. How bad we were!*

RICARDO   *On another occasion, when walking through the woods, we told them that there was a grotesque animal near there. How quickly they ran to the house!*

JAIME   *When they found out that it was a lie, they became furious with us. They left for the city and never returned. What a shame!*

RICARDO   *Yes. I regret now what we did. But at that moment, what joy it gave us!*

PREGUNTAS

Conteste en oraciones completas.

1. ¿Dónde se encontraron Ricardo y Jaime?
2. ¿Para qué fueron a un café?
3. ¿Cuánto tiempo pasaron en la hacienda de los abuelos?
4. ¿Quiénes llegaron de la ciudad?
5. ¿De qué tuvieron miedo los primos?
6. ¿Qué pusieron Jaime y Ricardo en la cama de los primos?
7. Un día, ¿por dónde caminaron los muchachos?
8. ¿Había o no había un animal grotesco en el bosque?
9. ¿Para dónde salieron los primos? ¿Volvieron a la hacienda?

ESTRUCTURA ▦

I. El pretérito: los verbos irregulares <u>ser</u>, <u>ir</u> y <u>dar</u>

Observe the irregular preterit forms of the verbs **ser, ir,** and **dar.**

Alguien entró. ¿Quién **fue**? **Fue** Mario.

Someone entered. Who was it? It was Mario.

¿**Fueron** al café para hablar? Sí, **fuimos** ayer.

Did you go to the cafe to talk? Yes, we went yesterday.

¿**Diste** la presentación a la clase? Sí, la **di** el lunes.

Did you give the presentation to the class? Yes, I gave it on Monday.

ser *to be*   **ir** *to go*   **dar** *to give*

fui	fuimos	fui	fuimos	di	dimos
fuiste	fuisteis	fuiste	fuisteis	diste	disteis
fue	fueron	fue	fueron	dio	dieron

NOTE: **Ser** and **ir** have the same forms in the preterit; the context generally clarifies the meaning.

EJERCICIO 4   Un grupo de músicos famosos

Usted y varios amigos suyos son músicos famosos. Indique quiénes fueron los líderes del grupo en años pasados y qué hicieron como grupo e individualmente.

> Modelo   Fui a Londres. (nosotros)
> **Fuimos a Londres.**

1. Por un mes Inés fue el líder del grupo. (Ana, yo, Pedro, tú)
2. Fuimos a muchas ciudades diferentes. (yo, tú, mis amigos, el grupo)
3. Una semana Inés dio cuatro conciertos. (yo, el grupo, Paco y Juan, Pepe y yo)
4. Fuimos a los conciertos en un autobús especial. (mis amigos, yo, Linda, todos)

EJERCICIO 5   Preguntas personales

Conteste en oraciones completas.

1. ¿Adónde fue usted anoche? ¿y ustedes?
2. Esta mañana, ¿fueron ustedes a la librería? ¿a la biblioteca? ¿a la cafetería?
3. ¿Adónde fue usted el verano pasado? ¿Su familia fue también? ¿y sus abuelos?
4. El año pasado ¿dio usted dinero a una causa noble o buena? ¿Cuánto dinero? (muy personal, ¿verdad?) Y sus padres, ¿dieron dinero a la universidad?
5. Ahora, pensando en su familia, ¿de dónde es usted? ¿De dónde es su madre? ¿y su padre? ¿De dónde son o fueron sus abuelos? ¿Y de dónde fueron sus bisabuelos (*great grandparents*)?

II. El pretérito: otros verbos irregulares

A. Verbs with <u>u</u> or <u>i</u> in the preterit stem

Observe the irregular stem and the irregular endings of **estar** (*to be*) in the preterit tense.

(yo) **Estuve** allí por un mes.	(nosotros) **Estuvimos** en el desierto.
(tú) ¿**Estuviste** en la hacienda?	(vosotros) ¿**Estuvisteis** en el lago?
(ella) **Estuvo** en la selva.	(ustedes) ¿**Estuvieron** en el mar?

Other verbs that have an irregular stem and the endings **-e, -iste, -o, -imos, -isteis, -ieron** in the preterit include:

Infinitive   Preterit stem
Other verbs with *u* in the stem

andar	**anduv-**	**Anduve** por el bosque.
poder	**pud-**	No **pudiste** resistir la tentación.
poner	**pus-**	**Puso** unos insectos en su cama.
saber	**sup-**	**Supimos** el resultado.
tener	**tuv-**	**Tuvieron** que volver a la ciudad.

Verbs with *i* in the stem

hacer	**hic-**	¡Qué cosas ridículas **hizo**[1]!
querer	**quis-**	No **quisimos** hacer nada.
venir	**vin-**	**Vinieron** a visitarnos de la ciudad.

NOTE 1:   The third person singular form of **hacer** is **hizo.**

NOTE 2:   Some verbs may have additional meanings in the preterit.

Supe la respuesta.	I *found out* the answer.
Quise hablar con ella.	I *tried* to speak with her.
No **quiso** contestar.	She *refused* to answer.

B. Verbs with **j** in the preterit stem

Observe the irregular stem and the irregular endings of **traer** (*to bring*) in the preterit tense.

(yo) **Traje** mis cosas.	(nosotros) **Trajimos** las nuestras.
(tú) ¿**Trajiste** las tuyas?	(vosotros) ¿**Trajisteis** las vuestras?
(él) **Trajo** las suyas.	(ellos) **Trajeron** las suyas.

Other verbs that have a *j* in the stem and the endings **-e, -iste, -o, -imos, -isteis, -eron** in the preterit include:

Infinitive	Preterit stem	
decir	**dij-**	**Dijimos** la verdad.
traducir	**traduj-**	No **tradujeron** las oraciones.

EJERCICIO 6   Un viaje a la selva

Indique lo que su tío y las personas de la familia hicieron en preparación para (for) *el viaje y durante* (during) *el viaje a la selva.*

> Modelo   Mi tío vino a la casa. (mis hermanos)
> **Mis hermanos vinieron a la casa.**

1.   Mi tío hizo las preparaciones. (mis hermanos, nosotros, yo, tú)
2.   Mi tío puso las cosas en el JEEP. (mis hermanos, nosotros, yo, tú)
3.   Mi tío trajo la comida. (mis hermanos, nosotros, yo, vosotros)
4.   Mi tío anduvo por la selva. (mis hermanos, nosotros, yo, tú)
5.   Mi tío estuvo allí ocho días. (mis hermanos, nosotros, yo, mi hermana)
6.   Mi tío tuvo una experiencia fantástica. (mis hermanos, nosotros, yo, la familia)

EJERCICIO 7   Preguntas personales

Conteste en oraciones completas.

1.   ¿Dónde estuvo usted anoche? ¿y sus amigos(as)?
2.   ¿Anduvo usted por (*through*) el centro de la ciudad? ¿y sus amigos(as)?
3.   ¿Tuvo usted que estudiar anoche? ¿y ustedes?

4. ¿Quiso usted estudiar? ¿y ustedes?
5. ¿Pudo usted concentrar? ¿y su compañero(a) de cuarto?
6. ¿Hizo usted la tarea? ¿y ustedes?
7. ¿Tradujo usted el *Panorama Cultural*? ¿y ellos?
8. ¿Supo usted todas las respuestas? ¿y sus compañeros(as) de clase?
9. Señorita, ¿dijo usted algo importante?
   ¿y usted, señor? ¿y ustedes? ¿y ellos?

EJERCICIO 8   Tú y yo

Háganse preguntas y contéstense según el modelo.

> Modelo   qué/decir
> (pregunta) **¿Qué dijiste?**
> (posible respuesta) **Dije "buenas tardes".**

1. qué cosas/traer/a la clase hoy
2. dónde/poner/las cosas
3. estar/en la biblioteca/anoche
4. poder aprender/todos los verbos
5. qué/querer hacer/anoche
6. qué/tener que hacer/anoche
7. adónde/ir/el fin de semana pasada
8. andar/en el parque
9. ir/de compras
10. qué otras cosas/hacer

EJERCICIO 9   Varias posibilidades

Respondiendo a las preguntas, indique varias posibilidades para explicar lo que hicieron o dónde estuvieron las personas mencionadas.

> Modelo   Ana vino del mercado. ¿Dónde puso las cosas?
> (posibles respuestas) **Puso las cosas en la mesa.**
> **Puso las cosas en el escritorio.**
> **Puso las cosas en el carro.**

1. Ana vino a la clase. ¿Qué trajo?
2. Tina no pudo venir a la clase. ¿Qué tuvo que hacer?
3. Pedro tuvo un examen. ¿Qué no pudo hacer?
4. La profesora (el profesor) estuvo enfrente de la clase. ¿Qué dijo?
5. Lola no vino a clase ayer. ¿Dónde estuvo?
6. Lola no quiso estudiar. ¿Qué hizo?

ACTIVIDADES

A. Situaciones

Con un(a) compañero(a) o en grupos, describan oralmente (en el pretérito) las posibles actividades de las personas en las situaciones indicadas.

1. Tú pasaste las vacaciones de la primavera en la Florida (California, etc.) el año pasado. ¿Adónde fuiste y qué hiciste?
2. Tú y un(a) amigo(a) pasaron el fin de semana en la ciudad de Nueva York (Los Ángeles, Chicago, etc.). ¿Qué vieron y qué hicieron ustedes?
3. (Fulano—*So-and-so*) llegó a la clase el lunes por la mañana muy cansado. ¿Qué hizo y qué *no* hizo durante el fin de semana?
4. (Fulano y Fulana) hicieron un viaje a España el verano pasado. ¿Qué vieron y qué hicieron?

B. Presentaciones orales

Prepare una breve (brief) *presentación hablando de su aventura* (real o imaginaria):

1. en el campo (en la selva, en el desierto, en una isla), o
2. en una ciudad.

Incluya: *a.* cuándo estuvo allí (mes, estación, días, etc.)
          b. lugares que visitó y lo que hizo allí
          c. dónde durmió
          d. lo que comió, y dónde comió

El conflicto perpetuo entre mar y tierra. Concepción, Chile.

III. Preposiciones
Prepositions

A. Algunas preposiciones comunes

a	*to, at*	¿Quién viene **a** la casa? ¿Quién está **a** la puerta?
en	*in, on, at*	Mi libro no está **en** la clase.
		No está **en** la mesa.
		Está **en** casa (*at home*).
al + infinitive	*upon*	**Al** llegar a casa, vi a mi amigo.
de	*from, of, about*	Es **de** Francia.
		Habló **de** su familia.
con	*with*	Llegó **con** su hermano.
sin	*without*	Llegó **sin** sus padres.
durante	*during*	Estuvo aquí **durante** las vacaciones.
entre	*between, among*	Puso el coche **entre** los dos árboles.
en vez de	*instead of*	Habló con sus amigos **en vez de** trabajar.
antes de	*before*	Salió **antes de** comer.
después de	*after*	Salió **después de** comer.
cerca de	*near*	Su gato está **cerca del** coche.
lejos de	*far from*	Su gato está **lejos del** coche.
dentro de	*inside*	Su gato está. . . .
fuera de	*outside*	
debajo de	*beneath, under*	
encima de	*on top of, above*	
detrás de	*behind*	
delante de	*in front of*	
enfrente de	*in front of, opposite*	
al lado de	*beside*	

EJERCICIO 10   Mi gato Rodolfo

Para indicar los gustos (tastes) *de su gato Rodolfo, cambie las oraciones usando la preposición de significado contrario.*

> Modelo   Rodolfo viene a la casa.
> **Rodolfo viene de la casa.**

1. Rodolfo prefiere su comida *con* leche.
2. Rodolfo duerme *debajo de* la mesa.
3. Rodolfo está *detrás del* sofá.
4. Rodolfo sale *después del* desayuno.
5. Rodolfo corre *dentro de* la casa.
6. Rodolfo está *cerca del* perro.

EJERCICIO 11   Preguntas generales

Conteste en oraciones completas.

1. Generalmente, ¿qué hace usted *al* llegar a una fiesta? ¿*al* volver a la residencia de estudiantes? ¿*al* salir de la clase de español?
2. Generalmente, ¿qué hace *durante* las vacaciones?
3. Generalmente, cuando hace mucho frío, ¿qué lleva usted *debajo del* abrigo? ¿*encima de* la cabeza? ¿*en* los pies?
4. Ahora, pensando en sus padres, ¿viven ellos *cerca de* o *lejos de* la universidad? ¿Dónde viven?
5. ¿Tiene su familia un perro o un gato? ¿Duerme *dentro de* o *fuera de* la casa?
6. En este momento, ¿*entre* qué personas está usted sentado(a)? ¿y *al lado de* qué persona? ¿y *detrás de* qué persona? ¿y *enfrente de* qué persona?

B. Preposiciones con infinitivos

Observe the verb form that follows prepositions in Spanish.

Después de **estudiar,** vamos al cine.	*After studying, we are going to the movies.*
Antes de **salir,** necesitamos llamar a Mario.	*Before leaving, we need to call Mario.*

In Spanish, a verb following a preposition is in the infinitive form. In contrast, English uses the *-ing* form.

EJERCICIO 12   Expresión personal

Complete las ideas indicando actividades, que para usted, son apropiadas.

1. Siempre pienso antes de. . . .
2. No debemos manejar después de. . .
3. Miramos la televisión en vez de. . . .
4. No puedo aprender el español sin. . . .
5. Fui al centro en vez de. . . .
6. Hice la tarea antes de. . . .
7. Comí la torta después de. . . .
8. No puedo estar contento sin. . . .

ON FINAL

IV. Las preposiciones por y para

Por and **para** both mean *for*, but they convey different ideas and can be translated in different ways.

A. Uses of por

1. Looking back to the cause ⟵――――

   for = because of, for the sake of
   on account of
   on behalf of

   Trabajan **por** sus siete hijos.
   Es inocente **por** ser joven.
   Mi padre no pudo venir. Vine **por** él.

2. Duration of time
   for = during

   Estuvimos en México **por** tres años.

3. Movement in and around a given place
   along, down, by, through

   Caminamos **por** la avenida.
   Viajamos **por** las montañas.

4. In exchange for
   for

   Compré una camisa **por** quince dólares.
   Gracias **por** el regalo.

5. *To get* with a verb of motion
   for, to get, in search of

   Fui al banco **por** dinero.
   Volví al hotel **por** mi suéter.

> refrán: **Más sabe el diablo por viejo que por diablo.**

EJERCICIO 13 Mi abuela

*Conteste las preguntas usando **por** para describir la situación.*

1. Cuando su abuela estuvo muy enferma,
   ¿qué hizo usted por ella?
   ¿llamar al médico? **Sí (No, no) llamé al médico por ella.**
   ¿limpiar la casa?
   ¿comprar la comida?
   ¿preparar la comida?
   ¿ir de compras?
2. ¿Por cuánto tiempo estuvo enferma su abuela?
   ¿un mes? **Sí, (No, no) estuvo enferma por un mes.**
   ¿un día?
   ¿una semana?
   ¿dos meses?
   ¿un año?

3. El médico dijo que ella necesitaba caminar. *walk*
   ¿Por dónde anduvieron ustedes?
   ¿la calle? **Sí (No, no) anduvimos por la calle.**
   ¿el parque?
   ¿la avenida?
   ¿el río?
   ¿el bosque?

EJERCICIO 14   Fuimos de compras.

A. *Indique por qué ustedes fueron a los lugares indicados. ¿Qué buscaron allí?*

    Modelo   la tienda
             Fuimos a la tienda por chocolates.

1. el mercado
2. la librería
3. la joyería

4. la panadería
5. la pastelería
6. el almacén

B. *Imagínese que usted fue a un almacén. Haga una lista de seis cosas que usted compró. Indique cuánto costó cada artículo.*

    Modelo   **un suéter**
             Compré un suéter por treinta dólares.

1. Compré un(a) . . . por. . . .
2. . . .
3. . . .

4. . . .
5. . . .
6. . . .

B. Uses of para

1. Purpose, pointing to the goal, objective ⟶

   for = in order to
       (+ infinitive)

   Estudio **para** aprender.
   Fui a la playa **para** descansar.

2. Future limit in time (time goal) ⟶

   for = by

   Tenemos que escribir la composición
       para el lunes.

3. Destination (physical, geographical goal) ⟶

   for = headed for, toward,
       destined for

   Salió **para** Madrid ayer.
   El sofá nuevo es **para** el apartamento.

4. Recipient ⟶

   for = destined for
   in the employment of

   Los chocolates son **para** su hermana.
   Trabaja **para** una compañía de
       chocolates. (The company is a
       recipient of his/her labor.)

EJERCICIO 15   ¿Para qué? ¿Para cuándo? ¿Para dónde?

1. ¿Para qué estudia usted?
    ¿ser ingeniero(a)? **Sí, (No, no) estudio para ser ingeniero(a).**
    ¿ser profesor(a)?
    ¿ser médico(a)?
    ¿ser policía?
    ¿ser abogado(a)?
    ¿ser mujer (hombre) de negocios?
2. Ustedes tienen muchas tareas diferentes. ¿Para cuándo necesitan terminar (*finish*) las tareas siguientes?
    aprender el vocabulario   **Necesitamos aprender el vocabulario para mañana.**
    aprender las preposiciones
    leer el Panorama Cultural
    terminar el capítulo
3. Cuando usted y sus amigos van al centro, ¿para qué van a los lugares indicados?
    al museo   **Vamos al museo para ver el arte.**
    al restaurante
    al cine
    al parque
    a la biblioteca
    al bar
4. Durante las próximas vacaciones todos los estudiantes salen para lugares diferentes.
    ¿Para dónde sale usted?
    ¿las montañas? **Sí, (No, no) salgo para las montañas.**
    ¿la playa?
    ¿una isla?
    ¿su casa?
    ¿la luna?
    ¿otro planeta?

EJERCICIO 16   Regalos ¿para quién?

Haga una lista de cinco regalos que usted compró el año pasado e indique para quién(es) fueron los regalos.

    Modelo   una corbata
          Compré una corbata para mi padre.

1. Compré un(a). . .para. . . .
2. . . .
3. . . .
4. . . .
5. . . .

El misterio y la belleza
del bosque tropical.
Venezuela.

EJERCICIO 17   ¡A Buenos Aires!

*Complete las oraciones usando **por** o **para** para describir su viaje a Buenos Aires.*

>   Modelo   Fuimos a la agencia/hacer las reservaciones
>   **Fuimos a la agencia para hacer las reservaciones.**

1. Hicimos las reservaciones/el ocho de octubre
2. Salimos/Buenos Aires
3. Estuvimos allí/una semana
4. Caminamos/la Avenida San Martín
5. Fuimos a la Plaza de Mayo/ver la catedral
6. Fuimos al almacén/comprar regalos
7. Compramos una bolsa/mi tía
8. Compramos zapatos/120 australes
9. Volví al hotel/mi cámara
10. Hicimos planes/visitar los Andes

EJERCICIO 18   Las vacaciones de primavera

*Dentro de unas semanas usted y sus amigos van a salir de la universidad para las vacaciones de primavera. Imagínense que se van a una playa. Conteste las preguntas usando **por** o **para** en`sus respuestas.*

1. ¿Para dónde salen?
2. ¿Para cuándo necesitan hacer las reservaciones?
3. ¿Para qué van?
4. ¿Por qué decidieron ir a ese lugar?
5. ¿Por cuánto tiempo van a estar allí?
6. Mientras (*while*) allí, ¿por dónde van a caminar/andar?
7. ¿Para quién van a comprar regalos? ¿Por cuánto dinero (más o menos)?
8. ¿Para cuándo necesitan volver a la universidad?

ACTIVIDAD Un viaje a Madrid

*Imagínense que el verano pasado usted(es) fueron a Madrid. Describan su viaje usando **por** o **para** en sus oraciones.*

Modelo   Salimos **para** Madrid el cuatro de julio.

V. Pronombres complementos de preposiciones
Pronouns that are objects of prepositions

¿El regalo es para **mí**?   ¿Dónde está? ¿enfrente de **él**?
Sí, es para **ti**.   No, perdón, está enfrente de **ella**.

Object-of-preposition pronouns

mí	*me*	**nosotros(as)**	*us*
ti	*you* (familiar)	**vosotros(as)**	*you* (familiar)
usted	*you* (formal)	**ustedes**	*you* (formal)
él	*him*	**ellos**	*them*
ella	*her*	**ellas**	*them*

Except for **mí** and **ti,** object-of-preposition pronouns are the same as subject pronouns.

NOTE 1: The preposition **con** + **mí** or **ti** becomes **conmigo** (*with me*) or **contigo** (*with you*), respectively.
¿Quieres venir **conmigo**?
¡Sí! Voy **contigo**.

NOTE 2: Subject, not prepositional, pronouns are used after the preposition **entre.**
No hay diferencia entre **ella** y **yo**.

EJERCICIO 19 Preguntas personales

Conteste en oraciones completas.

1. Tu novio(a), ¿va al cine contigo? ¿Estudia contigo? ¿Come en la cafetería contigo? ¿Pasa todo el día contigo?

2. ¿Quieres ir al cine conmigo? ¿con él? ¿con ella? ¿con nosotros?
3. ¿Vas a comprar un regalo para mí? ¿para él? ¿para ellos?
4. Tengo una torta de chocolate deliciosa aquí. ¿Para quién es? ¿para ti? ¿para ustedes?
5. Y ahora una pregunta muy interesante . . . ¿hablas de mí fuera de la clase? ¿Qué dices?

ACTIVIDAD   ¿Es usted artista?

En la pizarra o en papel, dibuje (draw) *un rectángulo grande. Dibuje una línea en medio del rectángulo que representa el horizonte. Ahora siga* (follow) *las instrucciones.*

1. Son las seis de la tarde. Dibuje el sol en el horizonte.
2. Hay muchos pájaros en el cielo. Dibuje tres o cuatro pájaros.
3. Podemos ver muchas nubes. Dibuje dos o tres nubes en el cielo.
4. En el centro está la casa de sus abuelos. Dibuje una casa con puerta y ventanas.
5. Enfrente de la casa hay flores y hierba. Dibuje la hierba y muchas flores bonitas.
6. Ahora dibuje un árbol grande al lado de la casa.
7. Sus abuelos tienen muchos animales. Dibuje: un perro al lado del árbol; un cerdo enfrente del árbol; un gato encima de la casa; y una vaca o una gallina entre el árbol y la casa.
8. En la distancia vemos un lago o un río. Dibuje un lago pequeño o un río muy lejos de la casa.
9. Ahora escriba el nombre del artista (su nombre) dentro del dibujo, y el precio (price) debajo del dibujo.

En el centro de Madrid vemos la famosa estatua de Don Quijote de la Mancha y Sancho Panza, dos personajes literarios creados por Cervantes. Madrid, España.

PANORAMA CULTURAL ▪

El carácter español

Al visitar España en persona vemos *pronto* que el país es un museo monu-
mental y único que presenta un *conjunto* variadísimo de estilos artísticos.
Las numerosas corrientes artísticas de *tiempos* pasados y presentes y de influencias *extranjeras* se han combinado para producir en el español un genio
creativo y *singular*, un carácter especial.

    Este carácter, *a la vez* austero y frívolo, religioso e irrespetuoso, práctico
e idealista, independiente e increíblemente patriótico, se revela por medio
del arte, *sea* en forma escrita, aural o visual.

Literatura—Al examinar tres personajes literarios de fama universal, El Cid,
don Quijote y don Juan Tenorio, podemos ver los contrastes y las contradicciones que existen en el carácter español.

El Cid es el héroe de uno de los grandes poemas épicos de la literatura
europea, ''El Cantar de Mío Cid'', escrito en el siglo XII. Pero El Cid, como
hombre de su época, *era* más que un campeón en batallas *contra* los moros;

quickly
totality
times
foreign
unique
at the same time

be it

was/against

El Cid Campeador era el más famoso de los héroes
épicos españoles. Burgos, España.

Los niños visitan el Museo del Prado para admirar
los cuadros de Velázquez. Madrid, España.

era religioso, inteligente y prudente; era vasallo *fiel* a su *rey* pero independiente por sus altos valores morales; era un buen padre y esposo. En resumen era un símbolo de las aspiraciones de una nación nueva porque era el
héroe nacional con quien la gente española podía y *todavía* puede identifi-
carse.

faithful/king

still

Don Quijote es el protagonista central de la primera novela moderna,
"El ingenioso hidalgo don Quijote de la Mancha". Esta novela es una sátira
de los libros de *caballería*, pero representa también una visión total y *compleja*
de la vida española. Don Quijote y su compañero Sancho Panza son antité-
ticos: donde uno es valiente, el otro es *cobarde*; donde uno es idealista, el
otro es práctico. Los dos se complementan para formar una imagen de España y del español del siglo XVII *tanto como* del español de hoy.

chivalry/complex

cowardly

as much as

Don Juan Tenorio, personaje de ficción en dos dramas, uno del siglo
XVII y el otro del siglo XIX, es un hombre irrespetuoso, cínico, satírico, irres-
ponsable, egoísta, gran *amante* de las mujeres, héroe rebelde y finalmente
símbolo del machismo latino. Pero es una personalidad que, por su espíritu
de independencia, *libertad* y deseo de *romper* con los convencionalismos sociales *cautiva* la imaginación de los españoles y de todo el mundo.

lover

freedom/break
captures

El arte—Un examen de las *obras maestras* de famosos pintores españoles revela que los contrastes y las contradicciones del carácter español también
son evidentes en el arte. En los *cuadros* de El Greco, Diego Velázquez, Barto-

masterpieces

paintings

La Vista de Toledo. El Greco.

¿Qué observa usted en este cuadro de Pablo
Picasso?

En su opinión, ¿qué representan los relojes en este cuadro de Salvador Dalí?

En sus "Caprichos" Goya criticaba los abusos y las supersticiones de la sociedad.

Andrés Segovia, guitarrista
español de fama mundial.

lomé Murillo y Francisco Goya,[1] todos maestros de siglos pasados, *igual que*   *just as*
en la singularidad de los cuadros de Pablo Picasso, Juan Miró y Salvador
Dalí del siglo XX, se puede observar *temas*, estilos e imágenes que reflejan, o   *themes*
chocan con, la realidad personal o social del pintor y del espectador. (Véanse   *clash*
ejemplos en las fotografías que *siguen*.)   *follow*

La música—La variedad, la energía y la pasión de la música española también nos ayudan a entender el carácter espanõl. Primero debemos escuchar
las *canciones* de tradición folklórica, *sobretodo* el ''cante flamenco'', que, de ori-   *songs/above all*
gen *andaluz*, es sin *duda* el más conocido de los cantares populares. Es una   *Andalusian/doubt*
combinación de cantos y bailes que en *sonido* y movimiento presentan los   *sound*
temas de amor, pasión y muerte. Despés es necesario oír los contrastes
que se encuentran en la música de compositores nacionales como Manuel
de Falla, Isaac Albéniz, Pablo Casals (famoso violoncelista) y en la música
de Andrés Segovia, que *casi* solo ha elevado la guitarra de un *nivel* folklórico   *almost/level*
a un nivel de elegancia clásica mundial.

España moderna—Al entrar en la nueva época de la monarquía constitucional, una época de nuevas libertades, de más independencia individual y
de más optimismo nacional, *es de esperar* que la expresión artística *florezca*   *it is to be expected/*
más que nunca. En la pintura, la escultura y en el cine,[2] los españoles están   *flourish*
formando una ''nueva *ola*'' de artistas. Frecuentemente toman su inspiración   *wave*
de temas y maestros del pasado, pero también van *añadiendo* su *propia* visión   *adding/own*
única de la realidad española.

NOTE 1:   El Greco (1541–1614), Velázquez (1599–1660), Murillo (1617–1682), Goya (1746–1828).

NOTE 2:   Algunos ejemplos incluyen Luis Buñuel, Pilar Miró, José Luis Garcí (directores de cine); Chema Cobo, y Zush (pintores); Susanna Solano (escultora).

¿CUÁNTO RECUERDA USTED?

A. *¿Con quién asocia usted las siguientes características, descripciones o referencias? ¿Con El Cid, don Quijote o don Juan?*

1. héroe de un gran poema épico
2. rebelde
3. idealista
4. campeón contra los moros
5. Sancho Panza
6. buen padre y esposo
7. cínico
8. religioso
9. primera novela moderna
10. símbolo de las aspiraciones de una nación nueva
11. libros de caballería
12. símbolo del machismo latino

B. *¿Con qué asocia usted las siguientes referencias? ¿Con la música o el arte?*

1. flamenco
2. El Greco
3. Manuel de Falla
4. Velázquez
5. Picasso
6. Pablo Casals
7. Goya
8. Andrés Segovia
9. Dalí

INTEGRACIÓN VISUAL: CAPÍTULO 7 ▪

EJERCICIO 7.1   Vocabulario, El campo y la naturaleza

EJERCICIO 7.2   El pretérito: los verbos irregulares

Ejemplo   andar

Paco anduvo por la calle.

EJERCICIO 7.3 Preposiciones

Manuel   Pepita   Javier

     Eva   Alfonso   Isabel

EJERCICIO 7.4 Preposiciones

EJERCICIO 7.5   Por vs. para

Ejemplo   ¿Por dónde anda Paco?
Anda por la calle.

REPASO DE VOCABULARIO ACTIVO ■

Sustantivos

el **animal**	el **cielo**	el **insecto**	el **pájaro**
la **araña**	la **culebra**	la **isla**	el **pez**
el **árbol**	la **choza**	el **lago**	el **río**
la **arena**	el **desierto**	la **luna**	la **selva**
el **barco**	la **estrella**	el **mar**	la **serpiente**
el **bosque**	la **flor**	la **mosca**	el **sol**
el **burro**	la **gallina**	el **mosquito**	el **tiempo**
el **caballo**	el **gato**	la **nube**	la **vaca**
el **campo**	la **hacienda**	el **océano**	el **valle**
el **cerdo**	la **hierba**	la **oveja**	

Verbos

pescar **viajar**

Expresiones idiomáticas

hacer un viaje

Preposiciones

a	**con**	**después de**	**entre**
al	**de**	**detrás de**	**en vez de**
al lado de	**debajo de**	**en**	**fuera de**
antes de	**delante de**	**encima de**	**lejos de**
cerca de	**dentro de**	**enfrente de**	**sin**

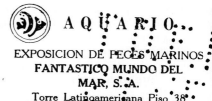

Pronombres complementos de preposiciones

mí	**nosotros(as)**
ti	**vosotros(as)**
usted	**ustedes**
él	**ellos**
ella	**ellas**

AUTOEXAMEN Y REPASO #7 ■

I. Vocabulario: el campo y la naturaleza

¿Qué palabras del vocabulario asocia usted con las palabras siguientes?

Modelo el pescado
el pez
el sol
la luna, el cielo, etc.

1. el jamón	7. la hierba
2. el pollo	8. la isla
3. el bistec	9. la selva
4. los árboles	10. las nubes
5. la arena	11. pescar
6. el barco	

II. El pretérito: los verbos irregulares

Conteste las preguntas para indicar las actividades, etc. de las personas.

Modelo ¿Quién tradujo la lectura? (Yo)
Yo traduje la lectura.

1. ¿Quién vino a clase temprano? (yo, usted) *vine, vino*
2. ¿Quién no supo la respuesta? (yo, ellos) *supe, supieron*
3. ¿Quién no pudo hacer el ejercicio? (ella, nosotros) *pude, pudimos*
4. ¿Quién tuvo que salir? (vosotros, tú) *tú tuviste*
5. ¿Quién anduvo en motocicleta? (yo, mi hermana) *anduvé anduvé*
6. ¿Quién fue al museo? (nosotros, mis primos) *fuemos, fueron*
7. ¿Quién dio la presentación? (yo, mis padres) *di, dieron*
8. ¿Quién no estuvo allí? (Carmen, mis amigos) *estuvé, estuvieron*
9. ¿Quién quiso volver a casa? (nosotros, tú)

III. Preposiciones

A. *Para indicar las preferencias, cambie las oraciones usando la preposición de significado contrario.*

Modelo No quiero el bistec *con* cebollas.
Quiero el bistec sin cebollas.

1. No quiero vivir *lejos de* las montañas.
2. No quiero estar *dentro de* la casa.
3. No quiero poner los libros *debajo del* escritorio.
4. No quiero poner la planta *delante del* sofá.
5. No quiero hablar *antes de* comer.

ON FINAL OPPOSITE

B. *Complete con una actividad apropiada.*

1. Fui al cine en vez de *estudiar* .
2. Hablé con mis padres antes de *comer* .
3. Salí de la casa después de *dormir* .
4. No puedo vivir sin *agua* .

C. *Por* vs. *Para*. *Complete las oraciones para indicar lo que usted hizo.*

1. Trabajé/el banco *para*
2. Trabajé/ir a México *para*
3. Salí/México el 6 de marzo *para*
4. Estuve allí/un mes *por*
5. Anduve/todo el país *por*
6. Compré un libro de arte/mi madre *para*
7. Compré el libro/diez mil pesos *por*

IV. Repaso del Capítulo 7

A. *Conteste.*

1. ¿Hizo usted un viaje el año pasado? ¿Adónde fue? ¿Le gustó? *Hice un viaje a Canada a la playa.*
2. Viajando por todo el mundo, ¿qué contrastes ve usted en la geografía? **Veo montañas,** . . .
3. Mirando el cielo, ¿qué cosas ve usted? *Veo los nubes y las (stars) estralla.*
4. ¿Qué hizo usted anoche? *Yo fui al cine.*
5. Al entrar en la clase, ¿qué dijo usted al profesor (a la profesora)? *No dije nada. (I said nothing)*
6. Y al llegar, ¿dónde puso usted su abrigo? *Puse mi abrigo en la silla.*
7. ¿Qué va a hacer usted esta noche después de comer?
8. ¿Quiere usted ir al cine conmigo?
9. ¿Para qué estudia usted?
10. ¿Por cuántos años va usted a estar en la universidad?

B. *Traduzca.*

1. When we went to Chile, we traveled through the desert.
2. We were able to see the Andes and the Pacific Ocean.
3. We were there for two months.
4. Instead of going to restaurants, we bought fruits and "empanadas" from the vendors.
5. One day we walked downtown to buy gifts.
6. I have something interesting for you.

V. Repaso: verbos con <u>yo</u> irregular en el presente; posesión

A. *Cambie las oraciones para indicar que la acción ocurre en el presente.*

1. Fui a la biblioteca. *Voy*
2. Tuve que estudiar. *Tengo que es!*
3. Vine a la clase. *Vengo*
4. Traje churros. *Triago*
5. Puse los churros en el escritorio. *Pongo*
6. Di los churros a los estudiantes. *Doy*
7. Salí de la clase. *Salgo*
8. Dije "adiós" a mis amigos. *Digo*
9. Fui a la clase de gimnasia. *Voy*
10. Hice muchos ejercicios. *Hago*

GOOD

B. *Exprese la posesión en una manera diferente.*

Modelo   Es mi perro.
   El perro es mío.
   Es (el) mío.

ON EXAM

1. Es nuestra hacienda.
2. Los gatos son de ella. *Son suyos   Los gatos son suyos.*
3. ¿Son tus caballos? *Los caballos son tuyos.*
4. La vaca es de ellos. *La vaca es suya.*
5. Son mis animales. *Los animales son míos.*

■CAPÍTULO■

8

Goals for communication
- Describing the house and home, and its contents
- Narrating and describing past states, events, and conditions
- Expressing a time reference for ongoing or completed actions
- Pointing out things and persons

Cultural exploration
- Mexico: geographical and historical perspectives

VOCABULARIO EL HOGAR ■

Una **casa** no es un **hogar** sin la familia.	*house; home*		
¿Qué **cuartos** tienes en tu casa?	*rooms*		
dos **alcobas**/		una **cocina**	*kitchen*
recámaras	*bedrooms*	un **comedor**	*dining room*
un baño	*bathroom, bath*	una **sala**	*living room*

La casa tiene dos **pisos.**	*floors, stories*		
una **escalera**	*stairs*	un **garaje**	*garage*
una **chimenea**	*chimney, fireplace*	y un **jardín**	*garden, yard*
un **sótano**	*basement*		

Los **muebles** y otras cosas:	*furniture*		
el **sofá**	*sofa*	la **cama**	*bed*
el **sillón**	*easy chair*	el **estante**	*bookshelf, shelf*

la **cómoda**	chest of drawers	el **cuadro**	picture, painting;
el **ropero**	closet	en la **pared**	wall
la **lámpara**	lamp	el **televisor**	television set
la **luz**	light	el **tocadiscos**	record player
las **cortinas**	curtains	el **disco**	record
la **alfombra**	carpet, rug;	la **radiograbadora**	radio/tape recorder
en el **suelo**	floor	el **cassette**	cassette

En el baño hay una **bañera**,	bathtub		
una **ducha**	shower	un **espejo**	mirror
un **retrete** (España);		**jabón** (m.)	soap
un **inodoro**	toilet	y **toallas.**	towels
un **lavabo**	sink (bathroom)		

¿Y en la cocina?

la **estufa**	stove	la **copa**	glass, goblet
el **fregadero**	sink	el **tenedor**	fork
el **refrigerador**	refrigerator	el **cuchillo**	knife
el **plato**	plate, dish	la **cuchara**	spoon
la **taza**	cup	la **servilleta**	napkin
el **vaso**	glass		

Verbos útiles:

alquilar	to rent	**subir; subir a**	to go up, climb;
apagar	to turn off		to get on
encender (ie),		**lavar**	to wash
poner	to turn on	**había**[1]	there was; there
bajar; bajar de	to go down; to get off		were

Otras palabras útiles:

el **vecino**	neighbor	**muchas veces**	often (on many
una vez	once (on one occasion)		occasions)

NOTE 1: **Había**, like **hay**, denotes existence, but in the past. It is always used in the singular form.

Había muchas casas atractivas allí.
There were many attractive houses there.

EJERCICIO 1 La casa

Conteste en oraciones completas según el dibujo.

1. ¿Qué hay en la sala?
2. ¿Qué hay en el comedor?
3. En la cocina, ¿dónde lavamos los platos?
4. ¿Qué aparato (*appliance*) usamos para cocinar la comida?

La familia pasa mucho tiempo conversando y mirando la television en la sala. Madrid, España.

5. ¿Qué otro aparato ve usted en la cocina?
6. ¿Qué cosas ve usted en el estante que está en la cocina?
7. Según el reloj, ¿qué hora es?
8. ¿Qué hay en el baño?
9. ¿Qué muebles tiene la alcoba?
10. ¿Qué hay en la ventana?
11. En el otro cuarto, ¿qué cosas hay en el estante?
12. ¿Qué más hay en el cuarto?
13. ¿Dónde está la escalera?
14. ¿Cuántos pisos tiene la casa?

EJERCICIO 2 Preguntas personales

Conteste en oraciones completas.

1. ¿Cuántas alcobas hay en su casa? ¿Cuántos baños? ¿Cuántos pisos?
2. ¿Tiene su casa un jardín? ¿un garaje? ¿un sótano? ¿una chimenea?
3. En su hogar, ¿cuál es su cuarto favorito? ¿Por qué?
4. En su familia, ¿generalmente quién cocina? ¿Quién lava los platos? ¿Quién lava la ropa? ¿Quién limpia la casa?
5. ¿Le gustan a usted sus vecinos? ¿Por qué sí o por qué no?

EJERCICIO 3 Identificación

A. *Dé la palabra que corresponde a la definición.*

1. El cuarto donde preparamos la comida
2. El cuarto donde comemos

3. El cuarto donde dormimos
4. El cuarto donde tomamos una ducha
5. El cuarto donde recibimos a nuestros amigos
6. Lo que usamos para lavar el cuerpo
7. Lo que miramos para ver nuestra cara
8. Lo que usamos para subir y bajar de un piso a otro
9. Lo que apagamos de día y encendemos de noche
10. Lo que hacemos cuando no queremos comprar la casa
11. Donde ponemos los trajes, vestidos, camisas, etc.
12. Donde ponemos los coches y muchas otras cosas que no deben estar en la casa

B. *Dé una definición que corresponde a la palabra.*

1. el tenedor
2. la cuchara
3. la taza
4. el vaso
5. la servilleta
6. la cómoda
7. el estante
8. el lavabo
9. el fregadero
10. la estufa
11. el jardín
12. el sótano
13. la cama

EJERCICIO 4   Asociación

¿Qué cosas o actividades asocia usted con las siguientes palabras?

   Modelo   el plato   **comer, la comida, la cena**, etc.

1. la cama
2. la luz
3. encender
4. bajar
5. el jabón
6. el cassette
7. el disco
8. la ventana
9. la escalera
10. el televisor
11. el sillón
12. el tenedor
13. cocinar
14. la música

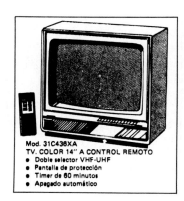

Mod. 31C436XA
TV. COLOR 14" A CONTROL REMOTO
• Doble selector VHF-UHF
• Pantalla de protección
• Timer de 60 minutos
• Apagado automático

CONVERSACIÓN ▪

Hace seis meses que Gonzalo *busca* un apartamento para *alquilar*. Está hablando por teléfono con la agente de bienes raíces.

LA AGENTE	Ya sé que usted busca un apartamento nuevo con dos **alcobas**, pero, ¿qué aspectos no le gustaron del que **vimos hace dos meses?**
GONZALO	**ése era** demasiado caro y no **estaba** cerca del metro.
LA AGENTE	¿Y el que **vimos hace dos semanas?**
GONZALO	Pues, en **ése** la cocina **era** demasiado pequeña, no **tenía refrigerador** y no **había** balcón.
LA AGENTE	Ah, espere, acabo de recibir noticia de uno que tiene dos **pisos**, una **sala** grande, **comedor**, **baño** con **ducha** y **bañera**, y ¡está cerca de la ruta de autobús!
GONZALO	Bueno. Mañana tengo un día libre. ¿Es posible verlo por la tarde a las tres?
LA AGENTE	Sí, claro. ¿Por qué no pasa usted por la oficina a las dos y media?
GONZALO	Muy bien. Hasta mañana entonces.

For six months Gonzalo has been looking for an apartment to rent. He is talking on the telephone with the real estate agent.

AGENT	*I already know that you are looking for a new apartment with two bedrooms, but what aspects didn't you like about the one that we saw two months ago?*
GONZALO	*That one was too expensive, and it wasn't near the metro.*
AGENT	*And the one that we saw two weeks ago?*
GONZALO	*Well, in that one, the kitchen was too small, it didn't have a refrigerator, and there was no balcony.*
AGENT	*Oh, wait, I have just received notice of one that has two floors, a large living room, a dining room, a bathroom with shower and tub, and it is near the bus route!*
GONZALO	*Good. Tomorrow I have a free day. Is it possible to see it in the afternoon at three?*
AGENT	*Yes, of course. Why don't you come by the office at two-thirty?*
GONZALO	*Very well. Until tomorrow then.*

PREGUNTAS

Conteste en oraciones completas.

1. ¿Qué busca Gonzalo?
2. ¿Por qué no le gustó el primer apartamento?
3. ¿Por qué no le gustó el segundo apartamento?
4. ¿Cómo es el apartamento que van a ver?
5. ¿Por qué es posible ver el apartamento mañana?
6. ¿A qué hora va a pasar por la oficina?

ACTIVIDADES

1. Usted busca un apartamento o una casa. Su compañero(a) de clase es el (la) agente de bienes raíces. Hablen de lo que usted quiere y de lo que el (la) agente tiene para vender o alquilar.
2. Describa a su compañero(a) de clase la casa o el apartamento en que su familia vive. Primero describa la casa/apartamento en general y después hable de los muebles y otras cosas que usted tiene en su alcoba.

ESTRUCTURA ▪

I. El imperfecto
The imperfect tense

Spanish has two simple past tenses: the preterit and the imperfect. You already know the preterit, used to narrate completed events in the past. The imperfect tense is used to describe the past and to indicate uncompleted or continuous actions. The forms for the imperfect follow.

A. Formación de los verbos regulares en el imperfecto

Los verbos **-ar**
Study the imperfect tense conjugations of the verb **cantar** and the corresponding English translations.

-ar *endings* **cantar** *to sing*

-aba	Cant**aba** todos los días.	*I used to sing every day.*
-abas	¿Cant**abas** en la ducha?	*Were you singing in the shower?*
-aba	Cant**aba** en español.	*She (he) was singing in Spanish.* *You were singing in Spanish.*
-ábamos	Cant**ábamos** bien.	*We sang well.*
-abais	¿Cant**abais** en el teatro?	*Did you used to sing in the theater?*
-aban	Cant**aban** en la ópera.	*They (you) were singing in the opera.*

To form the imperfect tense, regular **-ar** verbs drop the **-ar** from the infinitive and add the endings indicated.

The imperfect tense in Spanish corresponds to three English forms:

Raúl **cantaba** en la ducha.
{
Raúl was singing in the shower.
Raúl used to sing in the shower.
Raúl sang in the shower.
}

Los verbos **-er**, **-ir**

Study the imperfect tense conjugations of the verbs **tener** and **preferir**.

-er, **-ir** *endings*   **tener** *to have;*   **preferir** *to prefer*

-ía	Ten**ía** que estudiar pero prefer**ía** salir.
-ías	Ten**ías** que estudiar pero prefer**ías** salir, ¿verdad?
-ía	Ten**ía** que estudiar pero prefer**ía** salir.
-íamos	Ten**íamos** que estudiar pero prefer**íamos** salir.
-íais	Ten**íais** que estudiar pero prefer**íais** salir, ¿verdad?
-ían	Ten**ían** que estudiar pero prefer**ían** salir.

To form the imperfect tense, regular **-er** and **-ir** verbs drop the **-er** or **-ir** from the infinitive and add the endings indicated.

NOTE: The past progressive is formed by using **estar** in the imperfect tense plus the present participle.

¿Qué **estabas haciendo**?   *What were you doing?*

EJERCICIO 5   Visitando a los abuelos . . . todos los veranos

¿Qué hacían las personas indicadas en la casa de los abuelos?

> Modelo   cantar en la bañera (yo)
> **Cantaba en la bañera.**

1. trabajar en el jardín (nosotros, yo, mis padres)
2. comer pollo frito (nosotros, yo, tú)
3. preparar galletas (mi abuela, nosotros, yo)
4. jugar en el sótano (tú, mis hermanos, yo)
5. dormir en la cama grande y vieja (yo, nosotros, mi hermana)

B. Los verbos irregulares en el imperfecto

There are only three irregular verbs in the imperfect tense.

Cuando **éramos** niños frecuentemente **íbamos** a la casa de una vecina muy especial.	*When we were children, we frequently went to the house of a very special neighbor.*
Veíamos muchas cosas extrañas y exóticas en su casa.	*We used to see many strange and exotic things in her house.*

ser *to be*   **ir** *to go*   **ver** *to see*

era	éramos	iba	íbamos	veía	veíamos
eras	erais	ibas	ibais	veías	veíais
era	eran	iba	iban	veía	veían

EJERCICIO 6 Una familia de profesionales

Indique las profesiones de las personas, adónde iban y qué hacían allí.

Modelo mi madre: enfermera **Era enfermera.**
al hospital **Iba al hospital.**
a los niños **Veía a los niños.**

1. mi hermano y yo: hombres de negocios
   a la capital
   a nuestros clientes
2. tú: médico(a)
   al hospital
   los pacientes
3. mi padre: abogado
   a la oficina
   a sus clientes

4. mis tíos: profesores
   a la universidad
   a los estudiantes
5. yo: agente de bienes raíces
   al centro
   a mis clientes

EJERCICIO 7 Tú y yo cuando estábamos en la escuela secundaria (*high school*) . . .

Háganse preguntas y contéstense según el modelo.

Modelo estudiar mucho
(pregunta) **¿Estudiabas mucho?**
(respuesta) **Sí, (no, no) estudiaba mucho.**

1. tener muchos amigos
2. ir a muchas fiestas
3. ir de compras con frecuencia
4. hablar mucho por teléfono
5. ser tímido(a)
6. ser agresivo(a)
7. mirar mucho la television (¿Qué programas?)
8. tener un(a) novio(a) especial (¿Cómo se llamaba?)
9. jugar algún deporte (¿Cuál?)
10. tocar algún instrumento musical (¿Cuál?)
11. fumar
12. leer muchos libros
13. trabajar (¿Dónde?)
14. escuchar la radio (¿Qué tipo de música?)
15. tener una radiograbadora
16. pensar mucho en el futuro

EJERCICIO 8 Pensando en el pasado

Indique varias posibles actividades que se aplican a las personas en las circunstancias mencionadas.

Model Cuando era un bebé yo . . .
dormía mucho, jugaba con mis pies, tomaba leche,
etc.

1. Cuando yo era un(a) niño(a) pequeño(a) . . .
2. Cuando íbamos a la playa . . .
3. Cuando mis hermanos estaban en el sótano . . .
4. Cuando yo estaba solo(a) en mi casa . . .
5. Cuando mis abuelos venían . . .

II. Pretérito versus imperfecto

Although both the preterit and the imperfect tenses show past time, they convey different meanings. Study the examples, and then relate them to the explanation that follows.

A. El pretérito

1. **Entró en la cocina.**
   Preparó la comida.
   Llamó a sus hermanos.

The preterit denotes a *single, completed past action.*

2. **La semana pasada estuvieron en Arizona.**
   Ayer pasaron por Nuevo México.
   Llegaron aquí a las nueve de la noche.

The preterit denotes an action with a specific *limitation of time,* that is, with a designated beginning and/or ending.

3. **Estuvieron tristes al oír del accidente.**
   Tuvo hambre cuando vio la torta de chocolate.

The preterit denotes a *sudden change of condition.*

B. El imperfecto

1. **Todos los veranos íbamos a la casa de mis abuelos.**
   Siempre pescábamos en el lago.
   Muchas veces dábamos de comer a los animales.

The imperfect denotes a *continuous* or *repeated* past action that was occurring or used to occur over a period of time without a stated beginning or end.

2. **Había luna.**
   Hacía mucho frío cuando llegaron.
   Todo estaba tranquilo.
   Caminábamos en el bosque cuando vimos una casa extraña (*strange*).
   Un hombre estaba durmiendo allí cuando entramos.

The imperfect is used to convey *background description* (often accompanied by an interrupting action in the preterit).

3. **La casa era vieja y pequeña.**
   El hombre tenía pelo largo y blanco.
   Estaba muy triste.
   No sabíamos quién era.
   Queríamos hablar con él.

The imperfect is used to *describe physical characteristics, conditions,* and *mental* and *emotional* attitudes.

4. **Era la una de la tarde.**
   Eran las cuatro y media de la mañana.

The imperfect is used to *tell time* in the past.

EJERCICIO 9   En el pasado

*Indique lo que usted **hacía** todos los días y lo que **hizo** anoche.*

> Modelo   todos los días yo . . .   anoche yo . . .
>   jugar al tenis
>   **Todos los días jugaba al tenis.   Anoche jugué al tenis.**

1. estudiar en la biblioteca
2. ir a la cafetería
3. limpiar mi alcoba
4. mirar la televisión
5. hacer mi tarea
6. lavar la ropa
7. poner la ropa en la cómoda
8. ver a mis amigos
9. apagar las luces
10. subir la escalera

EJERCICIO 10   Una variedad de circunstancias

Usando su imaginación indique lo que usted hacía cuando ocurrieron las siguientes acciones.

> Modelo   ¿Qué hacía usted cuando su amigo llamó?
>   **Lavaba los platos,** etc., **cuando mi amigo llamó.**

1. ¿Qué hacía usted cuando llegó el autobús?
2. ¿Qué hacía usted en la cocina cuando su madre entró?
3. ¿Qué hacía usted en su alcoba cuando su padre entró?
4. ¿Qué hacían ustedes en la clase cuando la profesora (el profesor) llegó?
5. ¿Qué hacían ustedes en la fiesta cuando el policía llegó?
6. ¿Qué hacían ustedes cuando apagaron las luces?

EJERCICIO 11   Mi gato Rodolfo

Describa a su gato Rodolfo y sus actividades usando el pretérito o el imperfecto.

> Modelo   tener pelo gris
>   **Tenía pelo gris.**

1. tener ojos verdes
2. ser gordo y bonito
3. poder entender el español
4. dormir en el sótano

5. muchas veces/subir los árboles
6. una vez/subir la chimenea
7. con frecuencia/estar en la bañera
8. una vez/estar en el retrete
9. todas las mañanas/venir a la cocina
10. una mañana/beber toda la leche
11. un día/comer nuestro pescado
12. muchas veces/tomar la siesta en el sillón
13. una vez/jugar con la lámpara
14. cuando hacía calor/salir de la casa
15. cuando hacía frío/mirar por las ventanas
16. a veces/escuchar el tocadiscos
17. por cinco años/vivir con nosotros
18. una noche/no volver a casa
19. posiblemente/morir
        ¡Qué tristes estuvimos!

Mod. M9711K
RADIOGRABADORA STEREO
CON ECUALIZADOR GRAFICO DE
3 BANDAS
● Cajas desmontables ¡ ● A corriente y a pilas

EJERCICIO 12 Un testigo (*a witness*)

Una noche usted no duerme bien. Oye un ruido (noise) *en la casa de su vecino. ¡Usted es testigo de un robo* (robbery)! *Más tarde usted narra la historia a su amigo. (Use el pretérito o el imperfecto según las indicaciones.)*

1. Son las dos de la mañana.
2. Hace viento.
3. La luna está en el cielo.
4. No hay estrellas.
5. La casa es grande y vieja.
6. Un hombre entra por la ventana.
7. El hombre es alto y flaco.
8. El hombre lleva un sombrero negro.
9. Yo llamo a un policía.
10. El hombre pasa diez minutos en la casa.
11. El hombre sale con una bolsa grande.
12. El hombre ve el auto del policía.
13. El policía dice, "¡ALTO!" (*stop*)
14. Y el hombre corre en la otra dirección.

ACTIVIDAD

Prepare una breve narración original usando el imperfecto y el pretérito. Después repita su narración a un(a) amigo(a) en la clase de español.

Título: Un incidente en la residencia de estudiantes
        (o) La aventura de (*una persona de la clase*)
Incluya: 1. la hora
          2. descripción: de la noche/del día   del escenario
                            del tiempo   de la(s) persona(s) en el
                                                   escenario

3. descripción de las actividades continuadas y/o repetidas de la(s) persona(s)
4. acciones completadas
5. conclusiones—fin de la narración

III. Hacer en expresiones de tiempo
Hacer in expressions of time

A. Observe the construction used in Spanish to indicate an action that *has been going on for a period of time and still is.*

¿Cuánto tiempo[1] **hace que** conocen a sus vecinos?	*How long have you known your neighbors?*
Hace mucho tiempo que conocemos a nuestros vecinos.	*We have known our neighbors for a long time (much time).*
Hace cinco años que alquilo el apartamento.	*I have been renting the apartment for five years.*

Hace + time + **que** + present tense

NOTE 1:   In this context **tiempo** means *time* and does not refer to weather.

NOTE 2:   To indicate an action that *had been going on for some time and still was* up to the moment referred to or implied, Spanish uses: **Hacía** + time + **que** + imperfect tense.

Hacía mucho tiempo que vivía allí.	*I had been living there for a long time.*

EJERCICIO 13   Tú y yo

Háganse preguntas y contéstense según el modelo.

Modelo   estudiar inglés
(pregunta)   **¿Cuánto tiempo hace que estudias inglés?**
(posible respuesta)   **Hace quince años que estudio inglés.**

1. estudiar español
2. estar en la universidad
3. vivir en este (*this*) país
4. salir con (*to go out with*) tu novio(a)
5. conocer al profesor (a la profesora) de español
6. jugar al tenis (golf, básquetbol, fútbol, etc.)
7. tocar el piano (la guitarra, la trompeta, etc.)
8. beber Coca-Cola (cerveza, etc.)

Ahora su profesor(a) posiblemente tiene algunas preguntas para usted. Conteste.

1. ¿Cuánto tiempo hace que usted estudia español? ¿ . . . que juega al golf?
    ¿ . . . que trabaja? etc.

B. Observe the construction used in Spanish to indicate an action that took
place sometime *ago*.

¿Cuánto tiempo hace que llegaste a casa?	*How long ago did you arrive home?*
Llegué hace dos horas.	*I arrived two hours ago.*
Salieron hace cinco minutos.	*They left five minutes ago.*

preterit tense + **hace** + time

NOTE: An alternate word order is:

Hace dos horas que llegó.

EJERCICIO 14 Tú y yo

Háganse preguntas y contéstense según el modelo. ¡En el pretérito!

Modelo comprar un abrigo
(pregunta) **¿Cuánto tiempo hace que compraste un abrigo?**
(posible respuesta) **Compré un abrigo hace tres años.**

¿Desea usted pasar un verano en esta casa con vista al Mar Meditérraneo? Costa Blanca, Alicante, España.

1. escribir a tus padres
2. llamar a casa
3. ir de compras
4. comprar un cassette
5. hacer un viaje
6. nadar en el océano
7. ir a una fiesta
8. comer en un restaurante
9. pedir una pizza
10. limpiar tu cuarto
11. tomar una ducha
12. ir a la biblioteca

Ahora su profesor(a) posiblemente tiene algunas preguntas para usted. Conteste.

1. ¿Cuánto tiempo hace que escribió usted a sus padres? ¿ . . . que llegó usted a clase? etc.

IV. Los demostrativos
Demonstratives

A. Los adjetivos demostrativos

Demonstrative adjectives are used to point out or clarify a specific object or objects. Observe the demonstrative adjectives in the sample sentences.

Esta silla era mía.	*This chair was mine.*
Esa silla era suya.	*That chair was yours.*
Aquella silla era de mi abuela.	*That chair was my grandmother's.*
Este sillón y **estos** cuadros eran suyos.	*This easy chair and these paintings were his.*
Ese plato y **esos** vasos eran suyos.	*That plate and those glasses were his.*

Near speaker	Near person spoken to	Over there
this **este** chico	*that* **ese** chico	*that* **aquel** chico
esta chica	**esa** chica	**aquella** chica
these **estos** chicos	*those* **esos** chicos	*those* **aquellos** chicos
estas chicas	**esas** chicas	**aquellas** chicas

In Spanish there are two words for *that*—one for objects near the person spoken to and one for objects "over there" or far away. Like all adjectives, demonstratives agree with the word they describe in gender and number.

EJERCICIO 15   Comida para el viaje

Estamos en el supermercado y queremos comprar mucha comida para el viaje. ¡Vamos a hacer nuestras selecciones!

Modelo   las galletas
Queremos **estas** galletas, **esas** galletas y **aquellas** galletas.

Flores y plantas adornan los balcones de estas casas en Granada, España.

1. la torta
2. el queso
3. las frutas
4. los pasteles
5. el cereal
6. las bebidas

EJERCICIO 16 ¿Qué ropa llevas?

Imagínese que usted está haciendo la maleta (suitcase) *para su viaje a las montañas. ¿Qué va a llevar?*

> Modelo   camisa
> Debo llevar **esta** camisa.

1. suéter
2. pantalones
3. calcetines
4. camisetas
5. bolsa
6. botas
7. sombrero
8. zapatos
9. chaqueta
10. abrigo

Repita según el modelo.

> Modelo   camisa
> Prefiero llevar **esa** camisa.

1. suéter, etc.

EJERCICIO 17 ¿Qué va a explorar?

Usted llega a su destinación y decide lo que va a explorar.

> Modelo río
> Voy a explorar **ese** río.

1. montaña
2. lago
3. valle
4. ríos

5. bosque
6. montañas
7. lagos
8. valles

Repita según el modelo.

> Modelo río
> También pienso explorar **aquel** río.

1. montaña, etc.

B. Los pronombres demostrativos

Compare the demonstrative pronouns in the sample sentences with the demonstrative adjectives you have already studied.

Quiero ver **esta** lámpara, **ésa** y
  aquélla.
¿Te gustan **estos** platos? No,
  prefiero **ésos.**

I want to see this lamp, that one,
  and that one over there.
Do you like these dishes? No, I
  prefer those.

éste	*this one* (m.)
ésta	*this one* (f.)
éstos	*these* (m.)
éstas	*these* (f.)
ése, aquél	*that one* (m.)
ésa, aquélla	*that one* (f.)
ésos, aquéllos	*those* (m.)
ésas, aquéllas	*those* (f.)

A demonstrative adjective becomes a pronoun with the addition of a written accent over the first e. There is no difference in pronunciation.

EJERCICIO 18 Tú y yo: Cosas para el apartamento

Usted y su amigo(a) están en un almacén grande, buscando cosas para el apartamento. Háganse preguntas y respóndanse según el modelo.

> Modelo el sofá
> (pregunta) ¿Te gusta **este** sofá?
> (respuesta) No, prefiero **ése.**

1.	el sillón	6.	la alfombra
2.	el estante	7.	el espejo
3.	la cómoda	8.	las toallas
4.	la lámpara	9.	los platos
5.	las cortinas	10.	el televisor

C. Los demostrativos neutros   *Neuter demonstratives*

Compare the neuter demonstrative forms (ending in o) with the demonstratives that you previously studied.

¿Qué es **esto**?	*What is this?*
¿Qué es **eso**?	*What is that?*
¡**Eso** es horrible!	*That is horrible!*

esto   *this* (unspecified or unidentifiable)
eso   *that* (unspecified or unidentifiable)

Neuter demonstratives are used only when the identity is unknown or extremely general.

¿Desea usted alquilar un apartamento en el centro de la ciudad? Caracas, Venezuela.

EJERCICIO 19   ¿Qué dicen?

¿Qué expresión corresponde a cada (each) situación?

Expresiones: **¿Qué es esto?**   **¿Qué es eso?**
¡Eso es ridículo!   **¡Eso es horrible!**
¡Eso es maravilloso!

Situaciones:

1. El profesor dice que mañana hay tres exámenes y que los alumnos tienen que escribir quince ejercicios. ¿Qué dicen los alumnos?
2. Usted está en la cafetería y mira su plato de comida que tiene muchas cosas difíciles de identificar. ¿Qué dice usted?
3. Usted y su amigo caminan en el bosque y ven un animal muy extraño (*strange*). ¿Qué dicen ustedes?
4. Usted vio una película anoche. Al fin de la película, todas las personas y todos los animales murieron. ¿Qué dijo usted?
5. El profesor dice que mañana no hay clase, que este semestre no hay examen y que los estudiantes tienen vacaciones de un mes. ¿Qué dicen los estudiantes?
6. Un huracán destruyó completamente el centro de la ciudad. ¿Qué dice usted?

ACTIVIDAD   Memorias

Sus abuelos, a quienes usted visitaba mucho cuando era joven, decidieron vender la casa y alquilar un apartamento en la ciudad. Usted volvió hace una semana a la casa familiar para hacer una visita más.

La ciudad de Puebla, México tiene una vista panorámica del volcán Popocatépetl.

En forma escrita (*written*) . . .

1. describa la casa indicando cuartos, muebles y objetos especiales que usted vio y
2. describa escenas e incidentes del pasado que estos cuartos, objetos, etc. representaban.

PANORAMA CULTURAL* ■

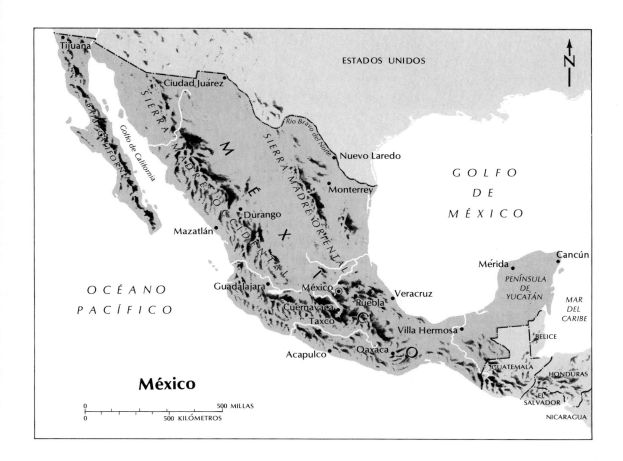

México

Capital: México, Distrito Federal (D.F.)   **Lengua oficial:** Español
Nombre oficial: los Estados Unidos Mexicanos
Area: 1.972.552 kilómetros cuadrados (761.607 millas cuadradas)
Población: 82 millones (estimada)

*Ver fotografías en color de México después de p. 272.

Las impresionantes ruinas de Palenque, ciudad construida por los mayas, están situadas en la selva tropical de Yucatán, México.

Productos: Maíz, frijoles, *algodón*, frutas, *ganado*, tabaco, cereales, le-   *cotton/livestock*
gumbres, pescado, *madera*, cemento, químicas, ropa, *hierro*, *artesanías*, mine-   *wood/iron/crafts*
rales, petróleo
Moneda: Peso

EJERCICIO DE MAPA

1. Mirando el mapa, indique cuáles son los límites geográficos de México.
   a. Al norte México está limitado geográficamente por
      _____ .
   b. Al este está limitado por _____ .
   c. Al oeste está limitado por _____ .
   d. Al sur está limitado por _____ .
2. ¿Dónde está situada la capital?
3. ¿Cuáles son las dos sierras principales?
4. ¿Cómo se llama la península que está al norte de Belice y Guatemala?
5. ¿Cómo se llama la península que se extiende al sur de California?
6. ¿Cuáles son dos ciudades que se encuentran en la frontera con los Estados Unidos?
7. ¿Qué río forma parte de la frontera entre México y los Estados Unidos?

México

México, tres veces más grande que España, es el país *más septentrional* de la   *northernmost*
América Latina. De todos los países de este hemisferio sólo los Estados
Unidos y el Brasil tienen más población que México. Su capital es la ciudad
más grande de este hemisferio y según estudios publicados por las Naciones Unidas la población (18.1 millones) del área metropolitana la hace la
ciudad más grande del *mundo*.   *world*

Las civilizaciones indias—Para entender *mejor* a México, es necesario *repasar* su historia desde el tiempo de los aztecas y los mayas que *poblaban* respectivamente la *meseta* central y la península de Yucatán. Estas civilizaciones indias, y otras anteriores, dan al país una originalidad que no tiene otro país del mundo. El famoso calendario azteca, las pirámides de San Juan Teotihuacán, los templos y monumentos de las *antiguas* ciudades mayas (Palenque, Chichén-Itzá) en el sur, y las *artesanías* indias dan buena evidencia de los avances científicos, arquitectónicos y artísticos de las civilizaciones precolombinas.

better/review
inhabited
plateau

ancient
artifacts

La conquista—En 1519 Hernán Cortés entró en la impresionante capital de los aztecas, Tenochtitlán (donde hoy está situada México, D.F.). Los españoles capturaron al famoso emperador Moctezuma, pero, al ser *derrotados* por los aztecas, tuvieron que escaparse de la ciudad. Volvieron dos años más tarde para destruir la ciudad y poner fin al imperio azteca. Los mayas, *sin embargo*, menos organizados como imperio, resistieron la conquista y la colonización por muchos años.

defeated

however

Los mestizos—Durante el período colonial *se desarrolló* un *tercer* grupo de gente, los mestizos—personas *nacidas* de padres español e indio. Hoy día la mayoría de la población mexicana es mestiza. Los mexicanos contemporáneos tienen mucho *orgullo* en sus orígenes indios y algunos *desprecian* la influencia española interpretada por la conquista. Por ejemplo, no existe en México un monumento dedicado a Hernán Cortés *mientras* el héroe nacional es Cuauhtémoc, el último emperador azteca.

developed/third
born

pride/scorn

while

Independencia—Durante los *siguientes* 300 años, cuando México era colonia de España, los españoles introdujeron en México nuevos métodos para *mejorar* la agricultura y la industria. Pero tambien *sacaron* del país *riquezas* increíbles. En 1810 México declaró su independencia de España, *ganando* su libertad en 1821. Siguió un período de caos y *cambios* políticos y conflicto con los Estados Unidos. Como resultado de estos conflictos México *perdió* posesiones que hoy día *comprenden* los estados de Tejas, Colorado, Kansas, Oklahoma, Wyoming, Nuevo México, Arizona, Nevada, Utah y California.

next

improve/took/riches
winning
changes
lost
include

La revolución—*Bajo* la dictadura de Porfirio Díaz (1876–1911) los mexicanos *perdieron* muchos *derechos* y libertades y los pobres *quedaron* bajo la influencia y control de los ricos (los *hacendados*, los hombres de negocios y los *extranjeros*). En 1910 la gente inició la "revolución" con la *esperanza* de *conseguir* más justicia social y progreso económico. *Sin embargo*, en los últimos años de la revolución los líderes revolucionarios (Francisco "Pancho" Villa, Venustiano Carranza, Emiliano Zapata, etc.) *luchaban entre sí* para *ganar* control del gobierno. Por fin se formó una nueva constitución liberal bajo Carranza, pero el conflicto y el caos continuaban. Algunos mexicanos *creen* que la revolución sigue todavía *por medio de* la continua *búsqueda* de más reformas sociales, políticas y económicas.

under
lost/rights/remained
landowners/foreigners
hope/getting
Nevertheless

fought among themselves
gain

believe/by means of/
search

En la Plaza de las Tres Culturas se encuentran el México indígena, el México español y el México moderno. México, D. F.

México moderno—Aunque México *experimentó* mucho progreso económico durante los años *mediados* de este siglo, todavía la pobreza es su problema dominante. Cada año más personas van a las ciudades en busca de *empleo* o *tratan de cruzar* la *frontera* a los Estados Unidos. El descubrimiento de depósitos grandes de petróleo dieron unos momentos de esperanza, pero la *caída* de *precios* por todo el mundo ha producido una inflación increíble que poco a poco va destruyendo la clase media. ¿El futuro de México? ¿Quién sabe? Depende de la *fuerza* espiritual y física de su gente y su capacidad para continuar, en forma positiva, la "revolución"

experienced
middle
employment
try to/cross/border
fall
prices

strength

¿CUÁNTO RECUERDA USTED?

¿Cómo identifica o con qué asocia usted las referencias históricas?

1. la ciudad más grande de este hemisferio
2. aztecas
3. mayas
4. Hernán Cortés
5. Tenochtitlán
6. Moctezuma
7. personas nacidas de padres indio y español
8. Cuauhtémoc
9. 1810
10. Porfirio Díaz
11. 1910
12. Villa, Carranza y Zapata
13. problemas dominantes de hoy

INTEGRACIÓN VISUAL: CAPÍTULO 8 ▪

EJERCICIO 8.1   Vocabulario, La casa

EJERCICIO 8.2   El imperfecto

EJERCICIO 8.3   Pretérito vs. imperfecto

Ejemplo   ¿Qué hacía Juanito cuando la madre entró?
Juanito hacía la tarea cuando la madre entró.

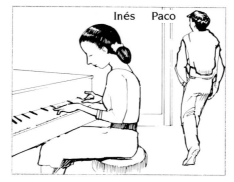

EJERCICIO 8.4 Hacer en expresiones de tiempo

Paco e Inés

Ejemplo media hora
Hace media hora que Paco e Inés bailan.

los novios

la mujer

Eva y Manuel

Pepita

Rubén

Ana

EJERCICIO 8.5   Demostrativos

Ejemplo   ¿Qué necesitas?
Necesito este televisor, ése y aquél.

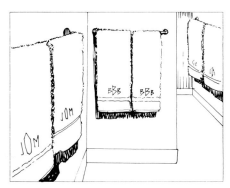

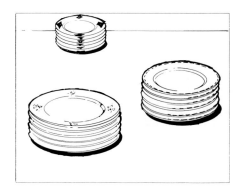

REPASO DE VOCABULARIO ACTIVO ▪

Adjetivos

Adjetivos demostrativos

este	ese	aquel
esta	esa	aquella
estos	esos	aquellos
estas	esas	aquellas

Demostrativos neutros

esto   eso

Sustantivos

la **alcoba**	el **cuchillo**	el **jardín**	la **sala**
la **alfombra**	la **chimenea**	la **lámpara**	la **servilleta**
la **bañera**	el **disco**	el **lavabo**	el **sillón**
el **baño**	la **ducha**	la **luz**	el **sofá**
el **cassette**	la **escalera**	los **muebles**	el **sótano**
la **cama**	el **espejo**	la **pared**	el **suelo**
la **cocina**	el **estante**	el **piso**	la **taza**
el **comedor**	la **estufa**	el **plato**	el **televisor**
la **cómoda**	el **fregadero**	la **radiograbadora**	el **tenedor**
la **copa**	el **garaje**	la **recámara**	la **toalla**
las **cortinas**	el **hogar**	el **refrigerador**	el **tocadiscos**
el **cuadro**	el **inodoro**	el **ropero**	el **vaso**
el **cuarto**	el **jabón**	el **retrete**	el **vecino**
la **cuchara**			

Verbos

alquilar	**encender** (ie)	**había**
apagar	**lavar**	
bajar	**subir**	

Expresiones

muchas veces
una vez

AUTOEXAMEN Y REPASO #8 ▪

I. Vocabulario: el hogar

¿Cuántos muebles y otros objetos puede usted asociar con los cuartos siguientes?

1. la alcoba
2. la sala
3. la cocina
4. el comedor
5. el baño

II. El imperfecto

Diga usted lo que las personas hacían cuando eran niños.

Modelo   tomar jugo de naranja . . . yo
Tomaba jugo de naranja.

1. abrazar a mi abuela . . . yo
2. correr en el parque . . . yo
3. amar a tu perro . . . tú
4. leer muchos libros . . . tú
5. pedir galletas . . . él
6. andar en bicicleta . . . él
7. querer jugar . . . nosotros
8. visitar a nuestros tíos . . . nosotros
9. salir por la tarde . . . vosotros
10. caminar en la avenida . . . vosotros
11. comer mucho helado . . . ustedes
12. hablar todo el día . . . ustedes

III.   ¿Pretérito o imperfecto?

*Exprese, según las indicaciones, lo que usted **hizo** o **hacía** en el pasado.*

> Modelo   (hacer el viaje) El verano pasado . . .
> **El verano pasado hice el viaje.**

1. (ir a la playa) El verano pasado . . .
2. (ir a una sección remota de la playa) Todos los sábados . . .
3. (nadar en un lago) Una vez . . .
4. (nadar en el océano) Muchas veces . . .
5. (correr en la playa) Todos los días . . . .
6. (correr por el pueblo) Ayer . . .
7. (tener una experiencia extraordinaria) Un día . . .
8. (tener experiencias interesantes) Con frecuencia . . .
9. (volver a casa en agosto) Todos los veranos . . .
10. (volver a casa en septiembre) Una vez . . .

IV.   Hacer en expresiones de tiempo

Conteste las preguntas indicando cuánto tiempo hace que (A) usted participa o (B) usted participó en las actividades.

A. Modelo   ¿Cuánto tiempo hace que vives aquí?—un año
   Hace un año que vivo aquí.

1. ¿Cuánto tiempo hace que trabajas aquí?—dos semanas
2. ¿Cuánto tiempo hace que juegas al tenis?—tres meses
3. ¿Cuánto tiempo hace que conoces a tu compañero(a) de cuarto?—un año

B. Modelo   ¿Cuánto tiempo hace que vendiste el coche?—dos días
   Vendí el coche hace dos días.

1. ¿Cuánto tiempo hace que hablaste con tus abuelos?—dos semanas
2. ¿Cuánto tiempo hace que limpiaste tu cuarto?—tres días
3. ¿Cuánto tiempo hace que viste una película?—un mes

V. Los demostrativos

Indique, usando los demostrativos, qué selección(es) usted hizo.

Modelo   Compré las cortinas.
Compré estas cortinas, ésas y aquéllas.

1. Compré el sillón.
2. Compré las toallas.
3. Compré los platos.
4. Compré la lámpara.

VI.   Repaso del Capítulo 8

A. *Conteste.*

1. Usted busca un apartamento para alquilar y habla con el propietario por teléfono. ¿Qué preguntas tiene usted?
2. Usted vio el apartamento ayer. ¿Cómo era? (Use su imaginación.)
3. Cuando la profesora (el profesor) entró en el apartamento a las diez de la noche, ¿qué hacían los estudiantes?
4. ¿Cuánto tiempo hace que usted estudia aquí en la universidad?
5. ¿Cuánto tiempo hace que usted llegó aquí?

B. *Traduzca.*

1. It was midnight.
2. It was very windy.
3. The stars were in the sky.
4. I was sleeping when someone entered the house.
5. I called the policeman at 1:00 A.M.
6. I have been in my room for five hours.
7. He left five minutes ago.
8. This is horrible!
9. This hat and those shoes are his.

VII.   Repaso: palabras afirmativas y negativas; expresiones con <u>tener</u>; expresiones con <u>hacer</u>

A. *Conteste en la forma negativa.*

1. ¿Había alguien en la cocina?
2. ¿Había algo en la estufa?
3. ¿Viste algunos insectos en el comedor?
4. ¿Entraste o en la alcoba o en el baño?
5. ¿Siempre cierras la puerta al salir?
6. ¿También cierras las ventanas?

B. *Usando las expresiones con **tener**, indique el problema o la condición.*

    Modelo   Quería comer.
          Tenía hambre.

1. Quería tomar una Coca-Cola.
2. Necesitaba un suéter.
3. Más tarde, ya no necesitaba el suéter.
4. Al caminar por el bosque, vi una culebra muy, muy larga de muchos colores diferentes.
5. Hacía tres días que no dormía.

C. *Indique el tiempo que hacía (probablemente) en las circunstancias indicadas.*

1. Era enero. Estábamos en Alaska. La luna estaba en el cielo.
2. Era febrero. Había muchas nubes grises. Algo frío y blanco venía del cielo.
3. Era agosto. Estábamos en la playa.
4. Era otoño. Había mucho movimiento en los árboles, y las nubes pasaban rápidamente por el cielo.
5. Era primavera. Para las flores, para la hierba, para los árboles, agua venía del cielo.

La estatua de Chac Mool domina uno de los templos de Chichén-Itzá, Yucatán, México.

CAPÍTULO 9

Goals for communication
- Transacting business at the post office and bank
- Referring to unnamed persons and things
- Describing how something is done

Cultural Exploration
- Mexico: artistic and personal perspectives

VOCABULARIO EL CORREO Y EL BANCO

el **correo**	*mail*
Escribimos una **carta.**	*letter*
Ponemos la carta en el **sobre.**	*envelope*
Escribimos la **dirección.**	*address*
Vamos a la **casa de correos.**	*post office*
Compramos un **sello.**	*stamp*
Ponemos la carta en el **buzón.**	*mailbox*
La carta va **por correo aéreo.**	*by airmail*
Recibimos un **paquete**	*package*
y una **tarjeta postal.**	*postcard*
En el banco vamos a la **ventanilla.**	*cashier's window*
Hablamos con el (la) **cajero(a).**	*teller, cashier*
Ponemos la **firma** en el **cheque.**	*signature; check*
en el **cheque de viajero.**	*traveler's check*

Casa Central de Correos, Plaza de las Cibeles. Madrid, España.

De compras usamos:

un **libro**		**efectivo**	*cash*
de cheques	*checkbook*	**cambio**	*change (exchange)*
una **tarjeta**		**moneda**	*coin (money, currency)*
de crédito	*credit card*		

Mi primo busca **empleo/trabajo**   *job, work*
en el banco.

Máquinas en la oficina: *machines* (f.)

la **calculadora**	*calculator*	la **máquina de escribir**	*typewriter*
la **computadora**	*computer*	el **teléfono**	*telephone*

Verbos útiles:

preguntar	*to ask (questions)*	**ahorrar**	*to save*
contestar	*to answer*	**cambiar**	*to change, exchange*
perder (ie)	*to lose, to miss (trains, etc.)*	**cobrar**	*to cash, to charge*
		devolver (ue)	*to return (something)*
encontrar (ue)	*to find*	**firmar**	*to sign*
empezar (ie)[1]	*to begin*	**invitar**[1]	*to invite*
terminar	*to finish*	**mandar**	*to send, command*
ganar	*to earn, win*	**mostrar** (ue)	*to show*
gastar	*to spend (money)*	**pagar**	*to pay*
depositar	*to deposit*	**prestar**	*to lend*
sacar	*to take out, to take (photos)*	**recibir**	*to receive*

Expresiones idiomáticas:

acabar de + infinitivo	*to have just . . .*
tratar de + infinitivo	*to try to . . .*
echar al correo	*to mail*
escribir a máquina	*to type*
hacer fila	*to make a (stand in) line*

NOTE 1: **Empezar** and **invitar** require the preposition **a** before a following infinitive.

Él **empezó a trabajar.**	*He began to work.*
Me **invitaron a comer.**	*They invited me to eat.*

EJERCICIO I   En el correo y en el banco

Conteste en oraciones completas.

A. *Según el primer dibujo:*

1. ¿Dónde están las personas?
2. El hombre que lleva la cámara, ¿qué necesita comprar?
3. ¿Qué va a mandar la abuela?
4. El abuelo tiene un sobre grande. ¿Qué escribió en el sobre?
5. ¿Qué está haciendo la mujer joven?
6. ¿Qué está haciendo el niño?
7. ¿Cuál es la fecha?

B. *Según el segundo dibujo:*

1. ¿Dónde están las personas?
2. ¿Cómo se llama el banco?
3. Probablemente, ¿qué va a hacer el hombre con su dinero?
4. ¿Qué está haciendo la mujer?
5. ¿Qué máquinas tiene la cajera?
6. ¿Qué máquinas hay en el escritorio de la otra mujer?
7. ¿Qué está haciendo ella? ¿Qué más hace en su trabajo?
8. ¿Qué encontró el niño?

EJERCICIO 2   Preguntas personales

Conteste en oraciones completas.

1. ¿Qué tiene usted que hacer hoy?
2. ¿Qué tuvo usted que hacer anoche?
3. ¿Qué tiene usted ganas de hacer ahora?
4. ¿Qué tuvo usted ganas de hacer anoche?
5. ¿Qué acaba usted de hacer?
6. ¿Qué está usted tratando de hacer?
7. ¿Trabajó usted el verano pasado? ¿Cuánto ganó usted por hora? ¿Qué hizo usted con su dinero?

8. Aquí en la universidad, ¿en qué gasta usted su dinero?
9. ¿Escribe usted a sus padres frecuentemente? ¿Llama usted por teléfono?
10. ¿Recibe usted paquetes de sus padres?
11. ¿Qué cosas le gusta a usted recibir por correo?
12. ¿Cuándo empieza usted a estudiar por la noche?
13. ¿Sabe usted escribir a máquina? ¿usar una computadora? ¿Cuál?

EJERCICIO 3   La historia de una carta

Narre "la historia de una carta" cambiando los infinitivos al pretérito.

Modelo   yo: buscar papel
         Busqué papel.

1. yo: escribir la carta
         poner la carta en el sobre
         escribir la dirección en el sobre
         ir a la casa de correos
         ir a la ventanilla
         comprar sellos
         poner sellos en el sobre
         ir al buzón
         echar la carta al correo

2. mi amigo(a):   recibir la carta
                  abrir el sobre
                  sacar la carta
                     del sobre
                  leer la carta
                  contestar la carta
                  estar contento(a)

¿Necesita usted cambiar
dinero? Sevilla, España.

Las personas hacen fila en la casa de correos.
Madrid, España.

EJERCICIO 4   Asociación

¿Qué verbos o nombres asocia usted con las palabras siguientes?

Modelo   el cajero
la ventanilla, cobrar cheques, etc.

1. el cheque
2. el dinero
3. las matemáticas
4. la máquina de escribir
5. el buzón
6. el sobre
7. el paquete
8. la carta

9. cobrar
10. pagar
11. mandar
12. hacer fila
13. ganar
14. perder
15. dar

CONVERSACIONES ▦

En la **casa de correos**

EMPLEADO	Buenos días, señorita. ¿En qué puedo **servirle**?
LINDA	Quiero **mandar** esta **carta** a mis amigos en los Estados Unidos.
EMPLEADO	¿Cómo quiere **mandarla**? ¿**Por correo aéreo** o certificada?
LINDA	**Correo aéreo,** por favor.
EMPLEADO	**Le** cuesta cuatrocientos veinte pesos en **sellos.**
LINDA	Gracias, señor. ¿Dónde debo **echarla**?
EMPLEADO	Allí, a la derecha, en el **buzón.**

At the post office

CLERK	*Good morning, Miss. How can I help you?*
LINDA	*I want to send this letter to my friends in the United States.*
CLERK	*How do you want to send it? Air mail or certified?*
LINDA	*Air mail, please.*
CLERK	*That will cost you four hundred twenty pesos in stamps.*
LINDA	*Thank you, sir. Where should I deposit (mail) it?*
CLERK	*There, to the right, in the mailbox.*

En el banco

CAJERA	Buenos días, señor. ¿En qué puedo **servirle**?
CLIENTE	Quiero **cobrar** este **cheque de viajero,** por favor.
CAJERA	Muy bien, ¿Puede **mostrarme** su identificación?
CLIENTE	Aquí **la** tiene. ¿A cuánto está el **cambio** hoy?
CAJERA	**Se** lo digo en un momento. A ver . . . ciento cuarenta al dólar americano.
CLIENTE	¿Puede **darme** el dinero en billetes de cincuenta y cien?
CAJERA	Sí, señor. ¿**Me** hace el favor de **firmar** el **cheque**?
CLIENTE	Ah, sí. . . . Aquí está. . . . Muchas gracias por su ayuda.

In the bank

TELLER	*Good morning, sir. How can I help you?*
CUSTOMER	*I want to cash this traveler's check, please.*
TELLER	*Very well. Can you show me your identification?*
CUSTOMER	*Here it is. What is the exchange rate today?*
TELLER	*I will tell you in a moment. Let's see . . . one hundred forty to the American dollar.*
CUSTOMER	*Can you give me the money in bills of fifty and one hundred?*
TELLER	*Yes, sir. Will you do me the favor of signing this check?*
CUSTOMER	*Oh, yes. . . . Here it is. . . . Many thanks for your help.*

ACTIVIDAD Conversaciones

1. Algunos estudiantes de la clase sirven como dependiente/dependienta en una casa de correos y otros sirven como cajero/cajera en un banco.
2. Los otros estudiantes van al banco y van a la casa de correos para hacer tareas (*tasks*) específicas.
3. Escogiendo (*selecting*) de la lista de posibilidades, conversen con las personas apropiadas.

En la casa de correos

1. comprar sellos
2. mandar una carta a _____
3. mandar un paquete a _____
4. mandar una tarjeta postal a _____
5. buscar/pedir cartas
6. buscar un paquete de _____
7. buscar empleo

En el banco

1. cambiar dinero
2. cobrar un cheque muy grande
3. depositar mucho dinero
4. comprar cheques de viajero
5. sacar mucho dinero
6. pedir una tarjeta de crédito
7. buscar empleo

USE SU CREDITO DURANTE ESTE
HISTORICO EVENTO DE AHORROS!...
AÑADASELO A SU CUENTA
PRESENTE...
ABRA UNA NUEVA CUENTA
O USE SU VISA O MASTERCARD

¡RECUERDEN LAS EXPRESIONES DE CORTESÍA!

ESTRUCTURA ▪

I. Pronombres de complemento directo
Direct-object pronouns

Observe the direct-object pronouns and their position in relation to the verb.

¿Cómo mandaste **la carta**? **La** mandé por correo aéreo.
How did you send the letter? I sent it by air mail.

¿Cuándo vas a mandar **el paquete**? Voy a mandar**lo** mañana.
When are you going to send the package? I am going to send it tomorrow.

¿Dónde están **los sellos**? Estoy buscándo**los** ahora.
Where are the stamps? I am looking for them now.

The direct object receives the action directly through the verb. The following forms are used when the direct object is a pronoun.

me	me	¿Por qué no **me** esperaste?
te	you	**Te** esperé media hora.
lo	you (m.), him, it (m.)	Aquí viene el autobús. ¿**Lo** ves?
la	you (f.), her, it (f.)	¿Tienes mi cartera? Sí, **la** tengo

nos	us	**Nos** llamaron anoche.
os	you	¿No **os** llamaron?
los	you (m.), them (m.)	¿Cuándo vas a llamar**los**?
las	you (f.), them (f.)	¿Tienes las direcciones? Sí, estoy buscán-do**las** ahora.

In Spanish, the direct-object pronoun is placed directly *before* a conjugated verb, and generally *after* and *attached to* an infinitive or present participle.

> NOTE: An accent mark is added to the present participle to preserve the original stress pattern.

Estamos **terminándolo.**

EJERCICIO 5   Las invitaciones

Manolo va a tener una fiesta. Él invita a todas las personas que quieren ir a la fiesta. Indique usted a quién él invita según el modelo.

> Modelo   Paco quiere ir.
>   Manolo **lo** invita.

1. *Yo* quiero ir. **Manolo . . .**
2. *Nosotros* queremos ir.
3. *Tú* quieres ir.
4. *Cecilia* quiere ir.
5. *Vosotros* queréis ir.
6. *Carlota y Lupe* quieren ir.
7. *Juanita y Mario* quieren ir.
8. *Eduardo* quiere ir.

EJERCICIO 6   Conociendo a muchas personas

Conteste las preguntas para indicar a quién usted conoce o a quién usted quiere conocer.

A. ¿Conoce usted . . . ?

> Modelo   ¿Conoce usted a la profesora de inglés?
>   **Sí, (No, no) la conozco.**

1. ¿Conoce usted personalmente al presidente de los Estados Unidos?
2. ¿Conoce usted personalmente al presidente (a la presidenta) de la universidad?
3. ¿Conoce usted bien a la profesora (al profesor) de español?
4. ¿Conoce usted bien a las señoritas de esta clase?
5. ¿Conoce usted bien a los hombres de esta clase?
6. ¿Conoce usted a la familia de la profesora (del profesor)?

B. ¿Quiere usted conocer (*to meet*) a . . . ?

Ahora haga una lista de seis personas famosas (hombres y mujeres) en la política de este país y del mundo.

Modelo   Margaret Thatcher
            ¿Quiere usted conocer a Margaret Thatcher?
            Sí, (No, no) quiero conocerla.

1. . . . ¿Quiere usted conocer a . . . ?
2. . . . ¿y a . . . ?
3. . . .
4. . . .
5. . . .
6. . . .

EJERCICIO 7   Tú y yo

Háganse preguntas y contéstense.
A. *Usted quiere saber si su amigo(a)* **hizo** *o* **no hizo** *las cosas indicadas.*

Modelo   contestar *la carta*
            (pregunta) **¿Contestaste la carta?**
            (respuesta) **Sí, (No, no) la contesté.**

1. comprar *los sellos*
2. mandar *el paquete*
3. recibir *la tarjeta postal*
4. firmar *los cheques de viajero*
5. cobrar *los cheques*
6. depositar *el dinero*
7. gastar *todo el dinero*
8. entender *las direcciones*

B. *Usted quiere saber si su amigo(a)* **va a hacer** *o* **no va a hacer** *las cosas indicadas.*

Modelo   pintar *la casa*
            (pregunta) **¿Vas a pintar la casa?**
            (respuesta) **Sí, (No, no) voy a pintarla.**

1. limpiar *el cuarto*
2. lavar *las camisetas*
3. preparar *la comida*
4. lavar *los platos*
5. hacer *la cama*
6. devolver *los cassettes*

C. *Usted quiere saber si su amigo* **está haciendo** *o* **no está haciendo** *las cosas indicadas.*

Modelo   escribir *los ejercicios*
            (pregunta) **¿Estás escribiendo los ejercicios?**
            (respuesta) **Sí, (No, no) estoy escribiéndolos.**

1. traducir *el Panorama Cultural*
2. leer *la novela DON QUIJOTE*
3. contestar *estas preguntas*
4. escribir *las respuestas*
5. terminar *la tarea*
6. usar *el vocabulario*

EJERCICIO 8 Amor a primera vista (*sight*)

Primero, una demostración del amor a primera vista. Un hombre y una mujer, enfrente de la clase, hacen preguntas con las palabras indicadas y responden según el modelo.

> Modelo   querer conocerme
> (pregunta) **¿Quieres conocerme?**
> (respuesta) **Sí, (No, no) quiero conocerte.**

1. querer invitarme a una fiesta
2. querer llevarme al cine
3. poder llamarme esta noche
4. querer abrazarme
5. querer besarme
6. amarme

Ahora, todos los estudiantes participan, haciéndose preguntas y respondiéndose.

II. Pronombres de complemento indirecto
Indirect-object pronouns

Observe the indirect-object pronouns and their position in relation to the verb.

Jorge **me** dio la carta.	*George gave the letter to me.*
Estoy mostrándo**les** el sello.	*I am showing them the stamp.*
Voy a dar**le** el cheque **a ella** inmediatamente.	*I am going to give her the check immediately.*

The indirect object receives the action indirectly through the verb. It tells *to whom* or *for whom* the action is performed. The following forms are used when the indirect object is a pronoun. (It may be necessary to clarify a third-person indirect-object pronoun with the forms shown in parentheses.)

me	*to (for) me*	¿**Me** dijiste la verdad?
te	*to (for) you*	Sí, **te** dije la verdad.
le	*to (for) you* **(a usted)**	¿Vas a decir**le a ella** lo que pasó?
	him **(a él)**	
	her **(a ella)**	
nos	*to (for) us*	Están comprándo**nos** algo bonito.
os	*to (for) you*	¿No **os** compraron nada?
les	*to (for) you* **(a ustedes)**	Debemos hablar**les a ellos** de esto.
	them **(a ellos)**	
	them **(a ellas)**	

The indirect-object pronoun is placed directly *before* a conjugated verb, and generally *after* and *attached to* an infinitive or present participle.

> NOTE: The indirect-object pronoun is commonly used in conjunction with an indirect-object noun.

Les di un regalo **a mis hermanas.**   **Le** mandé una tarjeta postal **a Eva.**

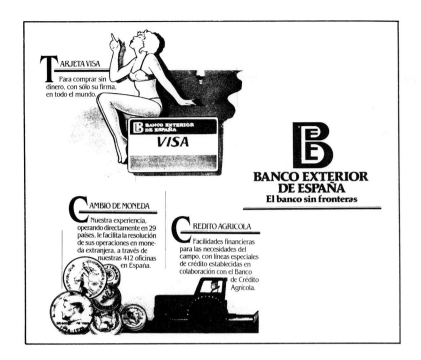

EJERCICIO 9 Un tío muy generoso

Un tío suyo, muy generoso, les dio a todas las personas en la familia lo que necesitaban. Indique usted lo que su tío le dio a cada (each) persona según el modelo.

Modelo   (a mi hermana) un reloj
Mi tío le dio un reloj.

1. (a mí) una máquina de escribir
2. (a mi madre) una calculadora
3. (a mi padre) una radio
4. (a mis hermanas) un tocadiscos
5. (a mis hermanos) una radiograbadora
6. (a ti) una computadora
7. (a nosotros) un coche
8. (a vosotros) un televisor

EJERCICIO 10 La correspondencia

Indique a quién usted escribió.

Modelo   ¿Escribió usted *al abogado?*
          Sí, **le** escribí.

1. ¿Escribió usted *a su madre?*
2. ¿Escribió usted *a sus hermanos?*
3. ¿Escribió usted *a sus amigas?*
4. ¿Escribió usted *al presidente?*

Modelo ¿Acaba usted de mandar la carta *al abogado*?
        Sí, acabo de mandar**le** la carta.

5. ¿Acaba usted de mandar la carta *a su madre*?
6. ¿Acaba usted de mandar la carta *a sus amigas*?
7. ¿Acaba usted de mandar la carta *a sus hermanos*?
8. ¿Acaba usted de mandar la carta *al presidente*?

EJERCICIO 11 Los gustos

Conteste para indicar las preferencias.

1. ¿Le gusta a usted recibir cartas? ¿De quién?
2. ¿Le gusta a su madre recibir cartas? ¿De quién?
3. ¿Le gusta a usted escribir cartas?
4. ¿Le gusta a usted recibir paquetes?
5. ¿Les gusta a ustedes recibir cheques?
6. ¿Le gusta a usted ahorrar dinero? ¿y a sus padres?
7. ¿Le gusta a su padre gastar dinero? ¿Qué le gusta comprar?
   ¿Le gusta a su madre gastar dinero? ¿Qué le gusta comprar?
   ¿Les gusta a los estudiantes gastar dinero? ¿Comprando qué?

EJERCICIO 12 Preguntas

Su profesor(a) tiene muchas preguntas. Contéstelas usando los pronombres de complemento directo o indirecto.

1. Señor (señorita), usted no lleva su chaqueta hoy. ¿La perdió usted? Y usted no lleva su reloj. ¿Lo perdió usted? Y, señor, ¿dónde están sus calcetines? ¿Los perdió usted?
2. ¡Ay! Yo perdí algunas cosas también. No puedo encontrar mis gafas. ¿Las tiene usted? Y mi tarjeta de crédito, ¿la tiene usted? ¡Y mi dinero! ¿Lo tiene usted?
3. ¡Necesito un poco de dinero! ¿Puede usted prestarme un dólar? ¿Puede usted prestarme diez dólares? ¿Puede usted prestarme cien dólares? Y usted, ¿puede prestarme mil dólares? ¡Ustedes son muy generosos!
4. ¿Saben ustedes que mañana es mi cumpleaños? ¿Va usted a traerme un regalo? ¿Va usted a traerme una torta? ¿Va usted a traerme chocolates? ¡Fantástico!

ACTIVIDAD ESCRITA Una carta

Escríbale una carta a un(a) estudiante español(a) que va a vivir con su familia por tres meses. Incluya:

1. su nombre (*name*)
2. su edad (*age*)
3. lo que le gusta y no le gusta hacer

4. descripción de su familia
5. su casa
6. su pueblo/ciudad
7. el tiempo en esta época/estación
8. la ropa que debe traer
9. las cosas que usted quiere mostrarle
10. los lugares que usted quiere visitar con él/ella

VOCABULARIO

Querido(a)	*Dear*	**Abrazos,**	*Hugs*
Estimado(a)	*Dear* (más formal)	**Atentamente,**	*Attentively, Yours*
Con cariño,	*With affection*		*faithfully* (más formal)

III. Dos complementos del verbo
Indirect- and direct-object pronouns with the verb

Observe the indirect- and direct-object pronouns in the sample sentences and their position in relation to each other and to the verb.

¿**Me** trajiste el paquete?
Did you bring me the package?

Sí **te lo** traje.
Yes, I brought it to you.

¿Van a dar**nos** los cheques?
Are they going to give us the checks?

Sí, van a dár**noslos.**
Yes, they are going to give them to us.

When a verb takes both an indirect- and a direct-object pronoun, the *indirect always comes first.* Both object pronouns are placed directly *before* a conjugated verb, and generally *after* and *attached to* an infinitive or present participle.

NOTE: An accent mark is added to an infinitive that has two objects to preserve the original stress pattern.

¿Vas a **mostrármelo**?

Observe the circumstances under which the indirect objects **le** and **les** change to **se.**

¿**Le** diste la carta a Miguel?
Did you give the letter to Miguel?

Sí, **se la** di.
Yes, I gave it to him.

¿**Les** mostraste el sello a tus hermanos?
Did you show your brothers the stamp?

Sí, **se lo** mostré.
Yes, I showed it to them.

When both the indirect and direct object pronouns are in the third person, the *indirect* object pronouns **le** and **les** change to **se.**

$$
\text{le} \atop \text{les} \quad + \quad \begin{cases} \text{lo} \\ \text{la} \\ \text{los} \\ \text{las} \end{cases} = \text{se} \begin{cases} \text{lo} \\ \text{la} \\ \text{los} \\ \text{las} \end{cases}
$$

EJERCICIO 13   El coche nuevo

Anita está muy orgullosa (proud) de su coche nuevo. Quiere mostrárselo a todo el mundo. Indique a quién.

   Modelo   (a Paco)
          Va a mostrárselo.

1. (a mí)   6.   (a vosotros)
2. (a ti)   7.   (a sus primos)
3. (a Pepe)   8.   (a los niños)
4. (a Ana)   9.   (a ti y a mí)
5. (a nosotros)   10.   (a la familia)

EJERCICIO 14   Estudiantes generosos

Los estudiantes de la clase son muy generosos.

a.   Cada estudiante le da a otro estudiante un artículo.
b.   Todos los artículos deben estar encima del escritorio.
c.   Ahora contesten las preguntas del profesor (de la profesora).

   Modelo   (Fulano—*So-and-so*), ¿quién le dio la chaqueta?
          (Fulana—*So-and-so***) me la dio,** etc.

1. . . . ¿quién le dio . . . ?   2. . . .   3. etc.

Ahora, probablemente es una buena idea devolver los artículos. Cada estudiante, al recibir su artículo, debe decir **"Gracias por devolvérmelo(la)"**, *etc.*

EJERCICIO 15   Cosas imaginarias

El profesor (la profesora) tiene muchas cosas imaginarias. Pregúntele al profesor (a la profesora) si quiere . . .

. . . dárselas
. . . mostrárselas
. . . prestárselas
. . . devolvérselas

o **vendérselas** *a usted según el objeto.*

   Modelo   [profesor(a)]   Tengo una torta de chocolate.
          [estudiante]   **¿Quiere usted dármela?,** etc.

Tengo . . .

1. un coche Mercedes
2. un cheque de mil dólares
3. un examen con la nota A+
4. una fantástica novela nueva
5. la bolsa de (*estudiante*)
6. una radiograbadora nueva
7. un libro de texto por dos dólares
8. la chaqueta de (*estudiante*)
9. un vídeo de una película fantástica
10. una copia del examen final

EJERCICIO 16 Tú y yo, amigos(as) fantásticos(as)

Háganse preguntas y contéstense para saber si su amigo(a) **le presta** *o* **no le presta** *las cosas indicadas.*

Modelo   el tocadiscos
(pregunta) **¿Me prestas el tocadiscos?**
(respuesta) **Sí, (No, no) te lo presto.**

1. la calculadora
2. la computadora
3. la máquina de escribir
4. la radiograbadora
5. tu suéter
6. tu abrigo
7. tu chaqueta
8. tu bicicleta
9. tu coche
10. cinco dólares
11. quince dólares
12. cincuenta dólares

¿Es o no es fantástico(a) tu amigo(a)?

EJERCICIO 17   Un(a) estudiante desafortunado(a)

Un(a) estudiante [Fulano(a)] se sienta enfrente de la clase. Imagínense que el (la) estudiante perdió todas sus posesiones en un incendio (fire). Ustedes, siendo generosos, quieren darle algunas cosas.

A. *¿Hay voluntarios? ¿Quién quiere darle algo? Respondan según el modelo.*

   Modelo   [estudiante generoso(a)] **Quiero darle mi libro de español,** etc.

1.   Quiero darle . . .   2.   . . .   3.   etc.

B. *Ahora, ya que Fulano(a) tiene tantas cosas, vamos a saber quiénes se las dieron. Respondan según los modelos.*

   Modelo   ¿Quién le dio el libro de español?
            [estudiante generoso(a)] **Yo se lo di.**

1.   ¿Quién le dio . . . ?   2.   . . .   3.   etc.

EJERCICIO 18   Don (Doña) Perfecto(a)

Usted siempre hace todas las cosas que necesita o debe hacer. Conteste en la forma afirmativa usando los pronombres de complemento directo e indirecto.

   Modelo   ¿Escribió usted *el cheque a su madre?*
            Sí, se lo escribí.

1.   ¿Escribió usted *la carta a su padre?*
2.   ¿Devolvió usted *el libro a su hermana?*
3.   ¿Devolvió usted *los discos a sus amigos?*
4.   ¿Mandó usted *el paquete a su abuelo?*
5.   ¿Mandó usted *las flores a su abuela?*
6.   ¿Mostró usted *la computadora a su amigo?*
7.   ¿Mostró usted *el vídeo a sus amigas?*
8.   ¿Prestó usted *el coche a su hermano?*
9.   ¿Prestó usted *el dinero a la profesora (al profesor)?*

EJERCICIO 19   Regalos por correo

Varias personas recibieron regalos extraordinarios por correo. Haga preguntas para saber quién les mandó los regalos. Use los dos complementos del verbo.

   Modelo   Yo recibí una chaqueta.
            ¿Quién te la mandó?

1.   Yo recibí un suéter.
2.   Luisa recibió un abrigo elegante.
3.   Ana recibió tres discos.
4.   Juan recibió dos camisetas.
5.   Mis hermanos recibieron una radio.
6.   Mi hermana y yo recibimos un cheque grande.
7.   (nombre de estudiante) . . .

IV. Formación de los adverbios
Formation of adverbs

You already know some Spanish adverbs such as **ahora, hoy, mañana, tarde, bien, mal, aquí, allí,** and **muy.** Observe the formation of adverbs that end in **-mente** (the Spanish equivalent of the English *-ly*).

Carlos habla español **perfectamente.**	*Carlos speaks Spanish perfectly.*
Carmen lo aprende **fácilmente.**	*Carmen learns it easily.*

The ending **-mente** is added to the feminine singular form of the adjective, or directly to adjectives that end in **e** or a consonant.

rápido	→ **rápida** →	**rápidamente**	*rapidly*
posible	→	**posiblemente**	*possibly*
personal	→	**personalmente**	*personally*

VOCABULARIO

fácil	*easy*	**posible**	*possible*
frecuente	*frequent*	**probable**	*probable*
general	*general*	**profesional**	*professional*
lento	*slow*	**rápido**	*rapid, fast*
perfecto	*perfect*	**reciente**	*recent*
personal	*personal*		

EJERCICIO 20   Juanito estaba aprendiendo español.

Indique cómo Juanito aprendía español.

> Modelo   La profesora lo conocía profesionalmente. (personal)
> **La profesora lo conocía personalmente.**

1. Ella le hablaba frecuentemente. (rápido)
2. Él le contestaba fácilmente. (lento)
3. Él no podía hablar rápidamente. (perfecto)
4. Aprendió el vocabulario fácilmente. (reciente)
5. Quería aprenderlo perfectamente. (fácil)
6. Generalmente estudiaba mucho. (probable)

Y, ¿cómo habla usted el español?

ACTIVIDAD ESCRITA   Una breve narración: "Un robo en el Banco Nacional"

Indique:

1. lo que hacían las personas en el banco,
2. cuándo y cómo entró el ladrón (*robber*),
3. cómo era el ladrón,
4. lo que hizo el ladrón (**robar,** etc.) y lo que hicieron las personas en el banco.

Use: el tiempo imperfecto, el tiempo pretérito, adverbios y los pronombres de complemento directo e indirecto.

PANORAMA CULTURAL ▪

La voz mexicana—expresión artística y personal

Expresión artística—Las artes siempre *han sido* una parte íntegra de la vida mexicana. Las civilizaciones indias, sobre todo los mayas, ponían mucho énfasis en la decoración artística y religiosa de sus templos y edificios. A los aztecas *les encantaban* la poesía y la música. Cuando llegaron los españoles, trajeron *consigo* sus propias tradiciones y fascinación por las artes—la literatura, la pintura, la arquitectura. La fusión de las dos culturas y razas resultó en una síntesis de dos personalidades y expresiones artísticas diferentes que se reflejan en todo lo que es el México *actual*.

    Se ve en los famosos murales de pintores como José Orozco, Diego Rivera y David Siqueiros,[1] y en las obras literarias de autores como Mariano Azuela, Carlos Fuentes y Octavio Paz,[2] donde se han combinado temas de origen indio, temas de la revolución y temas contemporáneos para *crear* una expresión típicamente mexicana. También se oye en el *sonido* triste y melan-

(margin glosses: have been / loved / with them / present-day / create / sound)

En los murales de Diego Rivera, famoso artista mexicano del siglo 20, se ven temas de la vida indígena y de la historia de México.

cólico de las flautas y de los *tambores* indios, en las trompetas y en los violines de los mariachis,[3] en las canciones folklóricas de la revolución, y en la presentación musical y visual del Ballet Folklórico de México, un *compendio* histórico del alma de México. Pero más que en *cualquier* otro lugar o manera se oye la voz del México histórico, artístico y contemporáneo—sus frustraciones, sus conflictos, su *orgullo* y su *esperanza*—en testimonios personales.

    A *continuación* se encuentran expresiones personales de lo que es ser mexicano en la crisis actual.

Testimonios personales—"Realmente, el *hecho* de *nacer* en México es algo extraordinario. *Debido a* su enorme *riqueza* cultural, expresada en sus artesanías, arquitectura y literatura, y debido a la grandeza de su historia, de *luchas* y héroes, de *esfuerzo* y sacrificio, *fracaso* y victoria, México es un país con un gran potencial de *desarrollo*. A pesar de tener *etapas* muy difíciles y serias, como la actual, es un país con una *esperanza* en el futuro. *Además* México *cuenta con* un pueblo muy especial—*sencillo* y *sabio*, *lleno de* tradiciones, pero *a la vez* dinámico, fuerte, vivaz. Todo esto, *mezclado* con la *belleza* de su territorio, con todo tipo de climas y vegetación, con mil y un lugares que visitar o descubrir hace que no sólo me guste México, *sino* que me *enorgullezca* de ser mexicano."

Víctor (edad: 24 años)

drums

compendium
any

pride/hope
following

fact/being born
due to/richness

struggles
effort/failure
development/periods
hope/besides
relies on/simple/wise/filled with
at the same time/mixed/beauty

but/be proud

Los mariachis, con sus guitarras, violines y trompetas, tocan la música típica y tradicional de México.

"Aquí en la capital donde vivo, hay muchísima gente. Existen muchos problemas de tránsito; los *camiones* van *casi* siempre llenos de gente, y se tiene que esperar mucho en la parada del autobús para poder abordarlo. El empleo *escasea* y los salarios son bajos; el *comerciante* vende muy caro; y las autoridades muchas veces *se corrompen* (esto último es un problema muy fuerte porque el que tiene dinero hace lo que quiere casi *impunemente*). Algo que nos afecta mucho es el *alza* de precios; queremos comprar algo y a la semana *siguiente* cuesta más caro. La contaminación *se ha agravado bastante* en los *últimos tiempos*; casi siempre se ve gris el cielo, y existen muchas enferme-dades *cuyo* origen y curación son desconocidos. *Sin embargo*, el mexicano, acostrumbrado a una vida difícil, *se sobrepone* a los problemas y busca salir *adelante*. *Confiamos en* que un pueblo con tantos años de vida y cultura no puede ser *acabado* y que en el futuro *saldremos* de esta crisis para poder *legar* a nuestros hijos un México con una economía y ecología sana y fuerte.

buses/almost

is scarce/merchant
are corrupt
with impunity
rise
following/has gotten quite bad
recent times
whose/nevertheless
overcomes
forward/trust
destroyed/we will get
out of/leave

Adelina (edad: 23 años)

NOTE 1: José Clemente Orozco (1883–1949), Diego Rivera (1886–1957), David Alfaro Siqueiros (1898–   )

NOTE 2: Mariano Azuela, novelista (1873–1952), Carlos Fuentes, no-velista (1929–   ), Octavio Paz, poeta y ensayista (1914–   )

NOTE 3: Mariachis are musicians who generally play a popular style of music on the violin, guitar, and trumpet.

El famoso Ballet Folklórico se conoce por su representación visual y musical de la tradición e historia de México.

¿CUÁNTO RECUERDA USTED?

¿Con qué o con quién asocia usted las siguientes referencias?

1. Son una parte íntegra de la vida mexicana.
2. Les encantan la poesía y la música.
3. Ponían mucha decoración artística y religiosa en sus templos.
4. Trajeron consigo una fascinación por la literatura, la arquitectura, el arte.
5. Orozco, Rivera, Siqueiros
6. Azuela, Fuentes, Paz
7. Ballet Folklórico de México

PREGUNTAS

Según los dos testimonios personales, ¿cómo contesta usted las siguientes preguntas?

1. En la opinión de Víctor, ¿por qué es México un país con un gran potencial?
2. Según Víctor, ¿cómo es el pueblo de México?
3. ¿Por qué tiene Víctor orgullo en ser mexicano?
4. Según Adelina, ¿cuáles son algunos problemas que existen en la capital?
5. ¿Tiene Adelina confianza en el futuro de México? ¿Qué quiere para las generaciones futuras?

INTEGRACIÓN VISUAL: CAPÍTULO 9 ■

EJERCICIO 9.1   Vocabulario, El correo y el banco

EJERCICIO 9.2 Pronombres de complemento directo

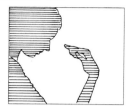

Ejemplo Carlos invitó . . .
Carlos me invitó.

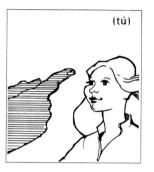
(tú)

(usted)

(Esteban)

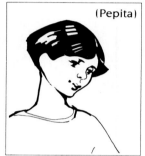
(Pepita)

(nosotros)

(ustedes)

(ellos)

(ellas)

EJERCICIO 9.3   Pronombres de complemento indirecto

(a mí)

Ejemplo   Carlos dio una invitación . . .
Carlos me dio una invitación.

(a ti)

(a usted)

(a Esteban)

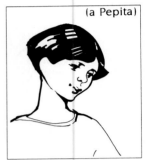
(a Pepita)

(a nosotros)

(a ustedes)

(a ellos)

(a ellas)

EJERCICIO 9.4   Dos complementos del verbo

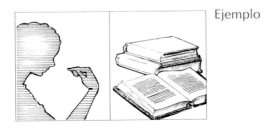

Ejemplo   Carlos prestó . . .
Carlos me los prestó.

(a ti)

(a usted)

(a Esteban)

(a Pepita)
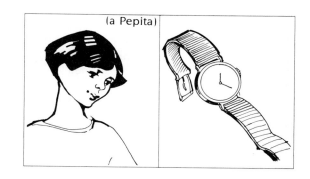

(a nosotros)

(a ustedes)

(a ellos)

(a ellas)

REPASO DE VOCABULARIO ACTIVO ▪

Pronombres de complemento directo

me	lo	nos	los
te	la	os	las

Pronombres de complemento indirecto

me	le	os
te	nos	les

Sustantivos

el **buzón**
el (la) **cajero(a)**
la **calculadora**
el **cambio**
la **carta**
la **casa de correos**
el **cheque**
el **cheque de viajero**
la **computadora**

el **correo**
el **correo aéreo**
la **dirección**
el **efectivo**
el **empleo**
la **firma**
el **libro de cheques**
la **máquina**
la **máquina de escribir**

la **moneda**
el **paquete**
el **sello**
el **sobre**
la **tarjeta de crédito**
la **tarjeta postal**
el **teléfono**
el **trabajo**
la **ventanilla**

Verbos

ahorrar
cambiar
cobrar
contestar
depositar
devolver
empezar (ie)

encontrar (ue)
firmar
ganar
gastar
invitar
mandar
mostrar (ue)

pagar
perder (ie)
preguntar
prestar
recibir
sacar
terminar

Adjetivos

fácil
frecuente
general
lento

perfecto
personal
posible
probable

profesional
rápido
reciente

Expresiones idiomáticas

acabar de + infinitive
tratar de + infinitive
echar al correo

escribir a máquina
hacer fila

Expresiones para cartas

abrazos
atentamente

con cariño
estimado(a)

querido(a)

ista panorámica de la ciudad más grande del mundo.
México D.F.

Esta joven yucateca nos saluda de su casa.

Una día de fiesta. Oaxaca.

os bailes folklóricos de México nos atraen
or su color, movimiento y ritmo.

La estatua del ángel de Chapultepec y el Paseo de

Las ruinas mayas de Tulúm dan al Mar Caribe.
Yucatan.

¡Cúanta variedad de legumbres y frutas existen en los
mercados de México! El mercado de San Juan de Dios
Guadalajara.

¡Tortillas deliciosas! El mercado de Xochimilco, México D.F.

AUTOEXAMEN Y REPASO #9 ■

I. Vocabulario: el correo y el banco

Identifique la palabra según las indicaciones.

1. Lo contrario de *empezar, perder, preguntar, mandar, ahorrar, sacar*
2. Lo que usted escribe en el sobre
3. Donde usted echa la carta para mandarla
4. Algo grande que usted recibe por correo
5. Lo que usted compra al ir a la ventanilla de la casa de correos
6. Usted paga con esto cuando no usa tarjeta de crédito ni cheques.
7. El acto de darle algo a una persona, pero la persona necesita devolverlo
8. El acto de llevar una cosa al lugar donde usted la encontró
9. Lo que usted usa cuando quiere escribir muy rápidamente sin bolígrafo o lápiz

II. Pronombres de complemento directo

A. *El tío Antonio va a Cancún para las vacaciones. Él va a llevar a todas las personas que quieren ir. Indique usted a quién él va a llevar según el modelo.*

> Modelo   *Elena* quiere ir.
>   Antonio va a llevar**la**.

1. *Yo* quiero ir.
2. *Nosotros* queremos ir.
3. *Ustedes* quieren ir.
4. *Mis hermanas* quieren ir.
5. *Mis hermanos* quieren ir.
6. *Pepita* quiere ir.
7. *Tú* quieres ir.
8. *El perro* quiere ir.

B. *Su familia está haciendo los preparativos para el viaje. Conteste las preguntas de su hermano según el modelo.*

> Modelo   ¿Encontraste *el traje de baño?*
>   Sí, **lo** encontré.

1. ¿Encontraste *las gafas de sol?*
2. ¿Compraste *los cheques de viajeros?*
3. ¿Cambiaste *el dinero?*
4. ¿Pagaste *las reservaciones?*
5. ¿Recibiste *la confirmación?*

III. Pronombres de complemento indirecto

Su tía vive en Quito, Ecuador. Indique usted a quiénes ella acaba de escribir muchas cartas.

> Modelo   *José* acaba de recibir una carta.
>   Ella acaba de escribir**le**.

1. *Yo* acabo de recibir una carta.
2. *Ustedes* acaban de recibir una carta.
3. *Mis abuelos* acaban de recibir una carta.
4. *Tú* acabas de recibir una carta.
5. *Nosotros* acabamos de recibir una carta.

IV. Dos complementos del verbo

Un amigo suyo le hace muchas preguntas para saber si ocurrieron las acciones indi-cadas. Conteste usando dos complementos del verbo.

Modelo   ¿Le mostraste *los discos* a Andrés?
           Sí, se los mostré.

1. ¿Le prestaste *la calculadora* a Marcos?
2. ¿Le devolviste *los libros* a Carmen?
3. ¿Le diste *el paquete* a Felipe?
4. ¿Me trajiste *la información?*
5. ¿Me mostraste *los regalos?*
6. ¿Me compraste *los sellos?*
7. ¿Vas a darnos *el dinero?*
8. ¿Vas a prestarnos *la cámara?*
9. ¿Vas a devolvernos *nuestras cosas?*
10. ¿Te di *el cheque?*
11. ¿Te mostré *la foto?*
̃2. ¿Te devolví *el reloj?*

V. Adverbios

Conteste para indicar cómo lo hizo.

Modelo   ¿Cómo lo hizo? (fácil)
           Lo hizo fácilmente.

1. ¿Cómo lo hizo? (rápido)
2. ¿Cómo lo hizo? (profesional)
3. ¿Cuántas veces lo hizo? (frecuente)
4. ¿Cuándo lo hizo? (reciente)

VI. Repaso del Capítulo 9

A. *Conteste.*

1. ¿Qué estás tratando de hacer?
2. ¿Qué acabas de hacer?
3. ¿Quieres prestarme tu bolígrafo?
4. ¿Vas a pedirle a Rosa las respuestas?
5. ¿Le diste la tarea al profesor (a la profesora)?
6. ¿Vas a mostrarle tu cuaderno?

B. *Traduzca.*

1. She does not know me well.
2. I am going to write to her tomorrow.
3. She sent the package to us.

4. Tina, I want to show it to you. (it = **el paquete**)
5. David, can you lend it to them? (it = **el coche**)

VII. Repaso: presente de progresivo; imperfecto; <u>gustar</u>

A. *Indique que Manolo* **está haciendo** *las cosas indicadas* **ahora.**

> Modelo ¿Mandó Manolo *el paquete* ayer?
> **No. Está mandándolo ahora.**

1. ¿Escribió *la carta* ayer?
2. ¿Hizo *la tarea* ayer?
3. ¿Devolvió *los libros* a la biblioteca ayer?
4. ¿Leyó *la novela* ayer?
5. ¿Terminó *el proyecto* ayer?

B. *Indique lo que su abuelo favorito* **hacía.**

> Modelo llamarme por teléfono
> **Me llamaba por teléfono.**

1. mandarme cartas
2. invitarme a su casa
3. prestarme sus libros
4. mostrarme sus fotografías
5. leerme novelas fantásticas
6. decirme cosas extrañas e interesantes
7. quererme mucho

C. ¿Le(s) gustó? ¿Le(s) gustaron?

> Modelo (a mí) el museo
> **Me gustó el museo.**

1. (a Elena) las catedrales
2. (a nosotros) la biblioteca
3. (a mis padres) los almacenes
4. (a ti) el teatro
5. (a mí) los restaurantes

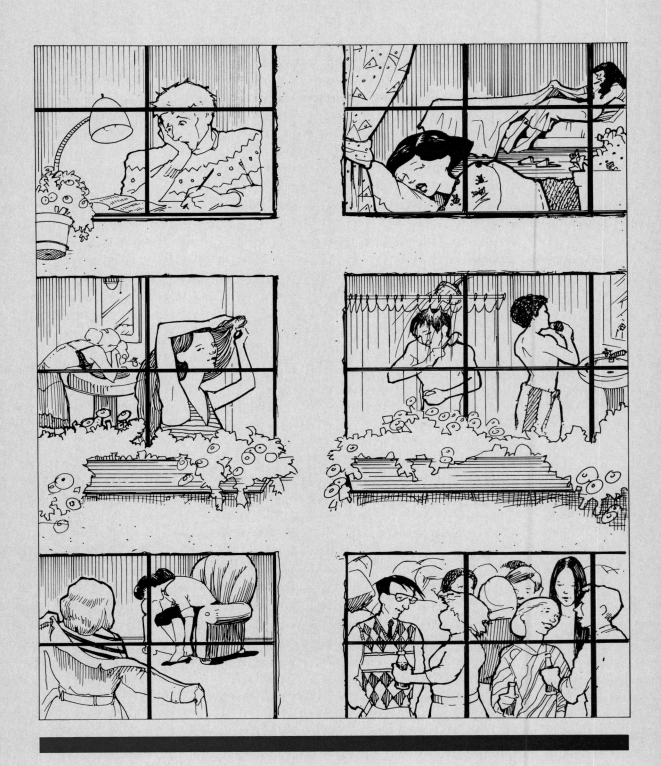

■CAPÍTULO■

10

VOCABULARIO LA RESIDENCIA DE ESTUDIANTES Y LA VIDA DIARIA ■

Muchos estudiantes americanos viven
    en una **residencia de estudiantes**/un   *dormitory*
    dormitorio.
¿Quién es tu **compañero(a) de cuarto**?   *roommate*
Artículos de uso diario:

el **peine**	*comb*	la **pasta de dientes**	*toothpaste*
el **cepillo**	*brush*	la **navaja**	*razor*
el **champú**	*shampoo*	la **crema de afeitar**	*shaving cream*
el **secador de pelo**	*hair dryer*	la **máquina de afeitar**	*electric shaver*
el **cepillo de dientes**	*toothbrush*	el **papel higiénico**	*toilet paper*

Otras palabras útiles:

el **despertador**	*alarm clock*	**sonar** (ue)	*to ring, sound*
el **ruido**	*noise*		

Lo que hacemos—acciones y emociones:

acostarse (ue)	*to go, put to bed*	**sentarse** (ie)	*to sit down*
dormirse (ue, u)	*to go to sleep*	**irse**	*to go away*
despertarse (ie)	*to wake up*	**divertirse** (ie, i)	*to have a good time*
levantarse	*to get up*	**enojarse**	*to get angry*
quitarse (la ropa, etc.)	*to take off*	**preocuparse (por) (de)**	*to worry (about)*
lavarse	*to wash (oneself)*	**quejarse (de)**	*to complain (about)*
bañarse	*to take a bath, bathe*	**sentirse** (bien, mal, etc.)	*to feel*
secarse	*to dry*		
afeitarse	*to shave*	**enamorarse**	*to fall in love*
cortarse	*to cut oneself*	**comprometerse (con)**	*to get engaged (to)*
cepillarse (los dientes, el pelo)	*to brush*	**casarse**	*to get married*
peinarse	*to comb one's hair*	**estar enamorado (a) (de)**	*to be in love (with)*
ponerse (la ropa, etc.)	*to put on*	**estar comprometido(a)**	*to be engaged*
vestirse (i, i)	*to get dressed*		

EJERCICIO 1 La residencia de estudiantes

Conteste en oraciones completas según el dibujo. Son las once de la noche en la residencia.

En el tercer (*third*) piso:

1. El chico que está estudiando, ¿se divierte o se preocupa por los exámenes? **Se . . .**
2. La chica que está cerca de la ventana, ¿se duerme o se acuesta?
3. La otra chica, ¿se levanta o se acuesta (probablemente)?

En el segundo piso:

4. La chica que está enfrente de la ventana, ¿se peina o se cepilla el pelo?
5. La chica que está enfrente del lavabo, ¿se lava o se baña?
6. El chico que está en la ducha, ¿qué hace?
7. El chico que está enfrente del espejo, ¿qué hace?

En el primer (*first*) piso:

8. La chica que está sentada en el sillón no se quita los zapatos. ¿Qué hace?
9. La chica que está cerca de la ventana tiene calor. ¿Qué hace?
10. Los estudiantes que están en la fiesta, ¿se preocupan o se divierten? ¿Qué están haciendo?

EJERCICIO 2   Las cosas que usamos

¿Qué objetos o artículos asocia usted con las siguientes actividades?

1. cepillarse los dientes
2. cepillarse el pelo
3. peinarse
4. afeitarse
5. lavarse el cuerpo
6. lavarse el pelo
7. secarse las manos
8. secarse el pelo
9. despertarse
10. cortarse
11. ponerse
12. sentarse

EJERCICIO 3   Preguntas personales

Conteste en oraciones completas.

1. ¿Vive usted en una residencia de estudiantes?
   ¿Cuánto tiempo hace que usted vive allí?
   ¿Le gusta a usted vivir allí?
   ¿Hay mucho ruido en su residencia por la noche?
2. ¿Tiene usted un compañero(a) de cuarto?
   ¿Le gusta su compañero(a) de cuarto?
   ¿Por qué sí o por qué no?
3. ¿Tiene usted un despertador?
   ¿A qué hora suena?
4. Y ahora, algunas preguntas MUY personales:
   ¿Está usted enamorado(a)? ¿De quién?
   ¿Cuánto tiempo hace que usted conoce a esta persona?
   ¿Estuvo usted enamorado(a) el año pasado?
5. ¿Está usted comprometido(a)?
   ¿Quiere usted estar comprometido(a)?
6. En su opinión, ¿cuál es la edad (age) ideal para casarse?

CONVERSACIÓN ▪

*Ricardo **se ha vestido** y **ha tomado** el desayuno. Ahora, muy impaciente, llama a la puerta del baño y le dice a su hermana:*

RICARDO	Oye, Anita. ¿Todavía no **has terminado**? ¿Cuánto tiempo vas a estar **bañándote**?
ANITA	¡Ya **me he bañado**! Espera un momento, por favor. Estoy **cepillándome los dientes**.
RICARDO	Date prisa. Casi es la hora de salir.
ANITA	¿Quieres **afeitarte**?
RICARDO	¡No! Quiero **peinarme**.
ANITA	¡Caramba, Ricardo! ¡Tú tienes un espejo en tu cuarto donde puedes **mirarte**!
RICARDO	¡Dios mío, Anita! ¡Hace dos horas que estás ahí!

Ricardo has gotten dressed and has had breakfast. Now, very impatiently, he knocks on the bathroom door and says to his sister:

RICHARD   Listen, Anita. Haven't you finished yet? How long are you going to be in there bathing?

ANITA   I have already taken a bath. Wait a minute, please, I'm brushing my teeth.

RICHARD   Hurry up! It's almost time to leave.

ANITA   Do you want to shave?

RICHARD   No! I want to comb my hair.

ANITA   Good grief, Ricardo! You have a mirror in your room where you can look at yourself!

RICHARD   My God,* Anita! You've been in there for two hours!

*Spanish uses such expressions frequently, and they are considered perfectly acceptable.

PREGUNTAS

Conteste en oraciones completas.

1. ¿Dónde está Ricardo?
2. ¿Dónde está Anita?
3. ¿Está Anita bañándose?
4. ¿Está cepillándose el pelo? ¿Qué está cepillándose?
5. ¿Por qué dice Ricardo "date prisa" a su hermana?
6. ¿Quiere Ricardo afeitarse? ¿Qué quiere hacer?
7. ¿Dónde hay otro espejo?
8. Según Ricardo, ¿hace cuánto tiempo que Anita está en el baño?

ESTRUCTURA ▪

I. Pronombres y verbos reflexivos

Reflexive pronouns and verbs

A. Pronombres reflexivos

Observe the following pairs of sentences and the change in meaning created by the addition of the reflexive pronoun.

(Yo) corté la carne.	I cut the meat.
(Yo) **me** corté.	I cut myself.
(Ellos) están lavando la ropa.	They are washing the clothes.
(Ellos) están lavándo**se**.	They are washing themselves.
Debemos vestir a los niños.	We ought to dress the children.
Debemos vestir**nos**.	We ought to get dressed.

Some verbs add the reflexive pronouns (**me**, **te**, **se**, **nos**, **os**, **se**) to show that the doer of the action also receives the action. To indicate this reflexive action in English, *myself, yourself, ourselves,* etc., are commonly used.

Reflexive pronouns, like direct- and indirect-object pronouns, are placed before a conjugated verb, and generally after and attached to an infinitive or present participle.

B. Conjugación de los verbos reflexivos

Reflexive verbs (the combination of reflexive pronoun and verb) are commonly used in Spanish. In the examples below, note that the reflexive pronoun and the subject of the verb represent the same person.

Modelo: **levantarse**   *to get up*

me	**Me levanto** temprano.	*I get up early.*
te	¿**Te levantas** temprano?	*Do you get up early?*
se	¿A qué hora **se levanta** usted?	*At what time do you get up?*
	Ella (Él) **se levanta a las seis.**	*She (He) gets up at six.*
nos	**Nos levantamos** tarde.	*We get up late.*
os	¿**Os levantáis** tarde?	*Do you get up late?*
se	¿**Se levantan** ustedes a las once?	*Do you get up at eleven?*
	Ellos (Ellas) **se levantan** al mediodía.	*They get up at noon.*

NOTE: With reflexive verbs, use the definite article, not the possessive adjective, to refer to a part of one's body or article of clothing.

Quiero lavarme **el** pelo.   *I want to wash my hair.*
Va a ponerse **las** botas.   *He is going to put on his boots.*

EJERCICIO 4   La rutina diaria

Indique quién participa en las actividades siguientes.

Modelo   ¿Quién **se lava** con agua fría? (Yo)
          Yo me lavo con agua fría.

1. ¿Quién **se acuesta** muy tarde? (yo, tú, Felipe, nosotros)
2. ¿Quién **se despierta** muy temprano? (Carmen y Linda, yo, nosotros, vosotros)
3. ¿Quién **se levanta** a las seis? (mi compañero(a) de cuarto, mis padres, tú, yo)
4. ¿Quién **se baña** por la mañana? (tú, Teresa, nosotros, yo)

EJERCICIO 5   Esta mañana

¿Usted hizo o no hizo las cosas indicadas esta mañana?

Modelo   lavarse la cara
          Sí, (No, no) me lavé la cara.

1. despertarse a las cinco
2. levantarse cuando sonó el despertador
3. bañarse
4. lavarse el pelo
5. secarse el pelo con un secador de pelo
6. afeitarse la cara
7. afeitarse las piernas
8. cepillarse los dientes
9. vestirse rápidamente
10. ponerse calcetines limpios

EJERCICIO 6   En el baño

*Su hermano(a) llama a la puerta del baño y pregunta si usted está haciendo las cosas indicadas. Usted dice que no, pero que **va a hacerlas** en un momento.*

Modelo   [su hermano(a)]   ¿Estás lavándote?
          ¡No, pero voy a lavarme en un momento!

1. ¿Estás afeitándote?
2. ¿Estás cepillándote los dientes?
3. ¿Estás bañándote?
4. ¿Estás secándote el pelo?
5. ¿Estás vistiéndote?

EJERCICIO 7   Antes y después

Ustedes tienen la responsabilidad de cuidar (to take care of) *a algunos niños.*

A. *Indique cómo ustedes deben cuidar a los niños.*

Modelo   Antes de lavarnos . . .
          Antes de lavarnos debemos lavar a los niños.

1. Antes de peinarnos . . .
2. Antes de vestirnos . . .
3. Antes de sentarnos . . .
4. Antes de bañarnos . . .
5. Antes de acostarnos . . .

B. *Indique lo que ustedes van a hacerse después de cuidar a los niños.*

Modelo   Después de lavar a los niños . . .
          Después de lavar a los niños, vamos a lavarnos.

1. Después de peinar a los niños . . .
2. Después de vestir a los niños . . .
3. Después de sentar a los niños . . .
4. Después de bañar a los niños . .
5. Después de acostar a los niños .

ACTIVIDAD   Actores y actrices

Ocho estudiantes, enfrente de la clase, presentan en forma dramática ocho actividades (verbos reflexivos) diferentes.

1. Los otros estudiantes de la clase indican lo que cada (each) uno de sus amigos **está haciendo** (presente de progresivo).

Ahora los ocho actores/actrices cesan (stop) las actividades.

2. Los otros estudiantes indican lo que cada uno de sus amigos **hizo** (pretérito).

EJERCICIO 8   Tú y yo

Háganse preguntas y contéstense.

Modelo   a qué hora/dormirse
(pregunta) **¿A qué hora te duermes?**
(posible respuesta) **Me duermo a las once.**

1. a qué hora/acostarse
2. a qué hora/despertarse
3. a qué hora/levantarse
4. cuándo/bañarse
5. cuándo/cepillarse los dientes
6. cuántas veces por semana/afeitarse
7. cómo/sentirse hoy
8. adónde/irse para las vacaciones
9. cómo/divertirse
10. con quién/divertirse
11. dormirse/en las clases a veces (¿Cuáles?)
12. enojarse/frecuentemente (¿Con quién?)
13. preocuparse/mucho (¿De qué?)
14. quejarse/frecuentemente (¿De qué o de quién?)

★

**SE VENDE O
SE ALQUILA**

En Fontainebleau Park
townhouses 3/2 y 2/2,
apartamentos de 2 dor-
mitorios, 2 baños, y 2
dormitorios 1 baño;
sala-comedor. Aire
acondicionado y cale-
facción. Piscina,
canchas de tenis y servi-
cio de seguridad en el
reparto. Teléfono.

856-4752

EJERCICIO 9

Complete las oraciones usando verbos reflexivos.

1. Me gusta . . .
2. Debo . . .
3. Tengo ganas de . . .
4. Esta mañana yo . . .
5. Esta mañana mi compañero(a) de cuarto . . .
6. Cuando éramos niños, antes de la llegada de nuestros abuelos, nosotros siempre . . .
7. El novio y la novia están muy enamorados. Ellos van a . . .

C. El reflexivo para indicar una acción recíproca (*each other*)

Observe the construction used to express a reciprocal action.

Mi novio y yo **nos queremos** mucho.	*My boyfriend and I love each other a lot.*
Marta y Esteban siempre **están besándose** y **abrazándose**.	*Martha and Steven are always kissing (each other) and hugging (each other).*

Nos and **se,** in addition to meaning *ourselves, yourselves,* and *themselves,* also mean *each other.*

EJERCICIO 10   Una historia (*story*) de amor

A. *Usted necesita determinar el orden probable de las actividades siguientes en la ''historia de amor'' de Manuel y Eva. ¿Qué occurrió primero? ¿y segundo? etc.*

encontrarse en el parque	enamorarse	casarse
comprometerse	abrazarse	hablarse
conocerse	mirarse	entenderse
besarse		

B. *Ahora, usando los verbos en el orden determinado, narre la historia indicando lo que* **occurrió.**

>   Modelo   (1) encontrarse en el parque
>   **Manuel y Eva se encontraron en el parque.**

C. *Ahora, usando los mismos verbos, indique lo que usted y su novio(a) hicieron.*

>   Modelo   (1) encontrarse . . .
>   **Nos encontramos en . . .**

II. El se impersonal

Observe the impersonal use of the pronoun **se** in the following sentences.

A. Se as *one* or *they*

No **se debe** fumar.	*One should not smoke.*
Se dice que causa el cáncer.	*They (people) say that it causes cancer.*
¿Cómo **se sale** de este edificio?	*How does one get out of this building?*
Aquí **se habla** español.	*Here one speaks Spanish.*
	(Spanish is spoken.)

When the subject does not refer to a particular person but rather to a *general* or *anonymous reference* (*one, they, people, you*), **se** is used in Spanish with a *third person singular verb.*

B. Se to indicate a passive action

¿Dónde **se vende** pasta de dientes?	*Where is toothpaste sold?*
¿Dónde **se venden** cepillos de dientes?	*Where are toothbrushes sold?*
¿A qué hora **se abren** las tiendas?	*At what time do the stores open?*

When the subject is a *thing* or *things* and emphasis is placed on the passive action itself (subject or subjects are acted upon rather than performing the action), **se** is used with a *third person singular* or *plural* verb.

EJERCICIO 11   Preguntas generales

Un estudiante de Chile hace muchas preguntas para aprender de la vida en la universidad y en la ciudad donde usted vive. Conteste sus preguntas en oraciones completas.

1.   ¿Se come bien en la cafetería?
2.   ¿A qué hora se abre la cafetería?
3.   ¿Se estudia mucho aquí en la universidad?
4.   ¿Se puede estudiar bien en el dormitorio?
      ¿Por qué sí o por qué no?
5.   ¿Dónde se estudia bien?
6.   Generalmente, ¿a qué hora se abre la biblioteca?
7.   ¿Se permite fumar en la biblioteca? ¿y en las clases?
8.   ¿En qué lugares de la ciudad no se debe fumar?
9.   En la ciudad, ¿dónde se compran sellos? ¿y cheques de viajeros?
10. ¿Dónde se vende pan? ¿y leche?
11. ¿Dónde se venden libros? ¿y joyas?
12. Generalmente, ¿a qué hora se cierran los almacenes? ¿y los bancos?

III. El presente perfecto
The present perfect tense

The present perfect tense in Spanish, as in English, indicates an action in the past that has recently been completed. Observe the construction of the present perfect tense in the sample sentences.

He llamado al médico.	*I have called the doctor.*
Los niños se **han levantado** y se **han vestido.**	*The children have gotten up and have gotten dressed.*
Me **ha dicho** que viene pronto.	*He has told me that he is coming soon.*

A. Formación del presente perfecto

> the present tense of **haber** (*to have*) + the past participle

Modelo **terminar**	*to finish*
(yo) **He terminado.**	*I have finished.*
(tú) **¿Has terminado?**	*Have you finished?*
(él, ella, usted) **Ha terminado.**	*He (she) has finished.* *You have finished.*
(nosotros) **Hemos terminado.**	*We have finished.*
(vosotros) **¿Habéis terminado?**	*Have you finished?*
(ellos, ellas, ustedes) **Han terminado.**	*They (you) have finished.*

Modelo **divertirse** — to have a good time
Me **he divertido.** — I have had a good time.
¿Te **has divertido?** — Have you had a good time?
Ella se **ha divertido.** — She has had a good time.

Nos **hemos divertido.** — We have had a good time.
¿Os **habéis divertido?** — Have you had a good time?
Ellos **se han divertido.** — They have had a good time.

NOTE 1: **Haber** means *to have* only as a helping verb before a past participle. **Tener** means *to have* in the sense of possession.

NOTE 2: All object pronouns (direct, indirect, and reflexive) directly precede the helping verb **haber** and follow **no** if the sentence is negative.

Me he sentado cerca de ella.
Le he hablado.
Usted **no me** ha contestado.

B. Formación de los participios pasados *Formation of past participles*

Participios pasados regulares:

> **-ar** verbs: verb stem + **ado** = past participle
> **-er, -ir** verbs: verb stem + **ido** = past participle

Algunos participios pasados irregulares:

abrir	**abierto** (*opened*)	poner	**puesto** (*put, placed*)
decir	**dicho** (*said, told*)	romper	**roto** (*broken*)
escribir	**escrito** (*written*)	ver	**visto** (*seen*)
hacer	**hecho** (*done, made*)	volver	**vuelto** (*returned*)
morir	**muerto** (*died, dead*)	devolver	**devuelto** (*returned*)

EJERCICIO 12 Esta semana

¿Quién ha hecho las actividades indicadas?

Modelo ¿Quién ha estudiado mucho? (nosotros)
(Nosotros) hemos estudiado mucho.

1. ¿Quién ha lavado la ropa? (yo, tú, nosotros, vosotros)
2. ¿Quién ha ido de compras? (Marta, Miguel y Paco, yo, nosotros)
3. ¿Quién ha mirado la televisión? (yo, tú, ustedes, nosotros)

4. ¿Quién ha leído un libro? (nosotros, los estudiantes, la profesora, yo)
5. ¿Quién ha escrito a la familia? (Jaime, tú, nosotros, yo)

EJERCICIO 13 Los inocentes

¿Qué dicen ustedes, los inocentes?

> Modelo oír
> **No hemos oído nada.**

1. decir
2. hacer
3. ver

4. romper
5. abrir
6. devolver

7. comer
8. tomar

EJERCICIO 14 En el baño (otra vez)

*Su hermano(a) llama a la puerta del baño otra vez y pregunta si usted está
haciendo las cosas indicadas. Usted dice que no, que ya las **ha hecho**.*

> Modelo [su hermano(a)] ¿Estás lavándote?
> **No. Ya me he lavado.**

1. ¿Estás afeitándote?
2. ¿Estás cepillándote los dientes?
3. ¿Estás bañándote?

4. ¿Estás peinándote?
5. ¿Estás vistiéndote?
6. ¿Estás secándote el pelo?

EJERCICIO 15 Sus padres quieren saber . . .

*Sus padres quieren saber si usted **ha hecho** o **no ha hecho** las cosas indicadas.
Use los **pronombres** de los complementos directos e indirectos.*

> Modelo ¿usar la computadora?
> **Sí, (No, no) la he usado.**

1. ¿empezar la composición?
2. ¿hacer la tarea?
3. ¿devolver los libros a la biblioteca?
4. ¿poner el dinero en el banco?
5. ¿depositar el cheque?
6. ¿gastar todo el dinero?

7. ¿comprar los libros para la clase?
8. ¿recibir el paquete de tus abuelos?
9. ¿escribir a tu abuelo?
10. ¿escribir a tus hermanas?
11. ¿dar el regalo a tu hermano?
12. ¿mostrar la carta a tu hermano?

EJERCICIO 16 Recientemente

*Para saber lo que sus amigos **han hecho recientemente:***

1. Usando la lista de verbos que se encuentra abajo, todos los estudiantes
   andan por la clase haciéndose preguntas. (Todos deben contestar *en
   oraciones completas.*)
2. Si (*if*) un(a) estudiante responde a una pregunta en el afirmativo (**Sí, he
   . . .**), escriba el nombre de ese(a) estudiante al lado del verbo.

Porque queremos un futuro diferente para todos los peruanos

 Hemos bajado la inflación
Gracias al esfuerzo de productores, comerciantes y amas de casa estamos derrotando a la inflación. Esta es la mejor manera de defender el ingreso de los más pobres.

 Hemos congelado el dólar y el precio de la gasolina Por seis meses más el precio de la gasolina y el dólar seguirán congelados. Por lo tanto, alimentos, transporte y otros servicios seguirán estabilizados.

 Hemos reducido los intereses
Ahora financiar una actividad productiva o una operación comercial cuesta más barato. Porque democratizar el crédito es la mejor manera de reactivar la producción y el consumo.

 Hemos aumentado los salarios
Porque ahora los trabajadores reciben más dinero y su dinero vale más, pudiendo comprar más cosas y alimentos.

 Hemos disminuído el déficit fiscal
Porque gracias a nuevos programas de reactivación estamos aumentando la recaudación, lo que junto a una saludable política de austeridad ha nivelado la balanza entre ingresos y egresos.

3. Continúen haciéndose preguntas hasta encontrar respuestas afirmativas a tantas (*as many*) preguntas como posible. (Incluyan al profesor [a la profesora] en la actividad.)

> Modelo   ir a la biblioteca
> (pregunta) **¿Has ido a la biblioteca recientemente?**
> (respuesta) **Sí (No, no) he ido recientemente.**

¡Atención a los participios pasados irregulares![*]

1. escribir* a tus padres
2. recibir un paquete en el correo
3. volver* a casa
4. limpiar tu cuarto
5. leer una novela (¿Cuál?)
6. ver* una película extraordinaria (¿Cuál?)
7. comer una pizza
8. beber mucha cerveza
9. ir a la iglesia/sinagoga
10. abrazar a un amigo(a)
11. romper* algo
12. viajar a Europa o a México
13. enamorarte (¿De quién?)
14. enojarte (¿Con quién?)
15. preocuparte mucho (¿De qué?)
16. divertirte mucho (¿Dónde?)
17. . . . (¿otras preguntas originales?)

ACTIVIDAD   Escenarios espontáneos

*Usted y un amigo(a) hacen el papel de (play the role of) las personas indicadas. Háganse preguntas y contéstense usando el **presente perfecto**.*

1. el profesor (la profesora) al estudiante (**¿Has hecho la tarea?,** etc.)
2. el (la) estudiante al profesor (a la profesora)

3. la madre al niño (a la niña) pequeño(a)
4. el padre al hijo (a la hija) de 19 años
5. un(a) compañero(a) de cuarto a otro(a)
6. una novia a su novio

IV. El pasado perfecto
The past perfect tense

The past perfect tense indicates an action in the past that *had occurred* prior to other past events.

> Cuando los vecinos llegaron, vieron que el ninõ **había roto** la ventana.
> *When the neighbors arrived, they saw that the child had broken the window.*

Formation:

> the imperfect tense of **haber** + the past participle

Modelo **salir**	*to leave*
(yo) **Había salido** ya.	*I had already left.*
(tú) **¿Habías salido?**	*Had you left?*
(él, ella, usted) **Había salido**.	*He (she, you) had left.*
(nosotros) **Habíamos salido**.	*We had left.*
(vosotros) **¿Habíais salido?**	*Had you left?*
(ellos, ellas, ustedes) **Habían salido**.	*They (you) had left.*

NOTE 1: The past perfect tense is also called the *pluperfect* or in Spanish the **pluscuamperfecto**.

EJERCICIO 17   Antes de la llegada de la tía

*La semana pasada la tía vino de visita. ¿Qué preparativos **había hecho** la familia antes de su llegada?*

> Modelo   nosotros/pintar la alcoba
> **Habíamos pintado la alcoba.**

1. mi padre/cortar la hierba
2. tú/hacer las camas
3. nosotros/limpiar la casa
4. mis hermanas/lavar el carro
5. mi madre/preparar la comida
6. yo/poner las flores en la mesa
7. nosotros/ponernos ropa elegante

V. La voz pasiva
Passive voice

In the active voice the subject is the doer of the action. In the passive voice the subject receives the action of the verb.

El volcán San Pedro y el lago Atitlán. Guatemala.

(active)   **Mi abuelita limpió la casa.**
My grandmother cleaned the house.

(passive)   **La casa fue limpiada (por mi abuelita).**
The house was cleaned (by my grandmother).

(active)   **Carlos escribió las cartas.**
Charles wrote the letters.

(passive)   **Las cartas fueron escritas (por Carlos).**
The letters were written (by Charles).

In Spanish, if the subject is acted upon rather than doing the action, and an agent (doer of the action) is stated or strongly implied, the true passive voice is used.

> True passive: **ser** + *past participle* (+ **por** + *agent*) (agrees with subject)

NOTE: If the *condition* that *results* from the action is stressed rather than the action and agent, Spanish uses **estar** + *the past participle.*

La puerta **está abierta**.   *The door is open.*
Las ventanas **están rotas**.   *The windows are broken.*

Es día de fiesta en
Chichicastenango,
pintoresco pueblo indígena
de Guatemala.

EJERCICIO 18 ¡Mi hermanito lo rompió todo!

*Indique las cosas que **fueron rotas** por su hermanito.*

> Modelo la taza
> **La taza fue rota por mi hermanito.**

1. los platos
2. el vaso
3. las copas
4. el espejo
5. la lámpara
6. el tocadiscos
7. los discos
8. la ventana

EJERCICIO 19 Nuestra abuelita

*La abuelita ha pasado mucho tiempo trabajando. Ustedes vuelvan a casa y encuentran que todo ya **está hecho.** Indique las cosas que **fueron hechas** por ella.*

> Modelo ¡Las camas están hechas!
> **Las camas fueron hechas por ella.**

1. ¡La ropa está lavada!
2. ¡Las cortinas están lavadas!
3. ¡La casa está limpia!
4. ¡Los niños están bañados!

5. ¡Los niños están vestidos!
6. ¡La mesa está puesta (*set*)!
7. ¡La comida está preparada!

ACTIVIDAD

A. *Una conversación*

Usted y su esposo(a) hacen un viaje de negocios a Los Ángeles por tres o cuatro días. Una vecina ha venido a su casa para cuidar a los hijos, Ana, de once años, y Tomás, de nueve años. En Los Ángeles usted llama a casa para saber cómo los hijos (y la vecina) han pasado los dos primeros días. Pregúntele a la vecina si los hijos se han acostado a tiempo, qué han hecho, etc.

B. *Una descripción*

Hace dos años sus padres salieron de vacaciones por unos días. Su hermano(a), de diez y ocho años, invitó a cinco o seis amigos a una fiesta en su casa. Pero, llegaron más de treinta personas que pasaron toda la noche divirtiéndose. Cuando volvieron sus padres y vieron el estado (la condición) de la casa, el patio, el jardín, etc., se pusieron furiosos. Describa en forma escrita lo que había pasado (antes de la llegada de sus padres) y lo que ellos le dijeron a su hermano(a).

El canal de Panamá permite tránsito marítimo entre los océanos Atlántico y Pacfico. Panamá.

PANORAMA CULTURAL* ▪

EJERCICIO DE MAPA

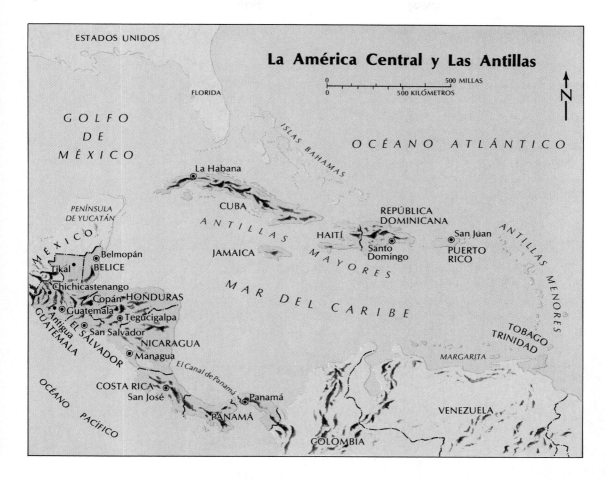

La América Central y Las Antillas

1. ¿Cuáles son los dos países que limitan la América Central en el norte y en el sur?
2. Al pasar del Mar Caribe al Océano Pacífico por el Canal de Panamá, ¿en qué dirección se va? ¿del este al oeste o del norte al sur?
3. ¿Cómo se llama la isla grande que está al sur de Cuba?
4. ¿Cómo se llama la nación que forma la otra mitad (*half*) de la isla en que se encuentra la República Dominicana?
5. ¿Cuál es la isla más grande de las Antillas?
6. ¿Cómo se llaman las islas que están al norte de las Antillas?
7. ¿Cómo se llama el país que está situado al noreste de Guatemala?

*Ver fotografías en color de la América Central y las Antillas después de p. 304.

8. ¿Cuál es la capital de Panamá? ¿de Costa Rica? ¿de Nicaragua? ¿de Honduras? ¿de Guatemala? ¿de El Salvador?
9. ¿Cuál es la capital de Cuba? ¿de la República Dominicana? ¿de Puerto Rico?
10. Mirando el mapa, ¿cómo explica usted la importancia geográfica de Panamá? ¿de la América Central?

La América Central y Las Antillas

La América Central—Los países hispanos que forman el istmo centroamericano, unidos histórica y culturalmente, son seis en total: Guatemala, Honduras, El Salvador, Nicaragua, Costa Rica y Panamá. *Puente* entre la América del Norte y la del Sur, la América Central es una tierra de una *belleza* geográfica que *cautiva* la imaginación.

    Los *paisajes* fantásticos, el clima *templado*, el carácter histórico indo-hispano todos fascinan al visitante. Por todas partes se puede contemplar panoramas que cambian constantemente: las montañas floridas y frescas de Guatemala, los grandes volcanes de El Salvador y Nicaragua, las abruptas montañas *cubiertas* de pinos de Honduras, los grandes lagos interiores de Nicaragua, las playas bonitas de Costa Rica y las densas selvas tropicales de Panamá.

    Aquí en Panamá, debemos *pararnos* un poco para explorar este ''Puente del mundo'', frase que explica perfectamente lo que es el país. Por su estratégica situación geográfica, los españoles usaron esta región durante la Conquista como el centro de donde salieron las expediciones para las costas del Atlántico y del Pacífico de la América del Sur. En el siglo XIX, du-

bridge
beauty
captures
landscapes/temperate

covered

stop

Las ruinas de la antigua ciudad de Tikal se encuentran en la selva de Guatemala.

rante la "fiebre de *oro*" de California, se construyó en Panamá el primer *gold*
ferrocarril transoceánico del continente y en 1914 se inauguró el Canal de *railroad*
Panamá, una maravilla de ingeniería moderna, que permite el tránsito marítimo entre los dos océanos. En tiempos *actuales* Panamá se ha convertido en *present*
el centro bancario y financiero más importante de la región.

Al continuar nuestra exploración de la América Central, nunca podemos
perder la oportunidad de visitar las ruinas impresionantes de la civilización
maya. En Guatemala y Honduras, la grandeza de esta civilización se ve en
las ciudades *antiguas* de Tikal y Copán, ahora conservadas como monumen- *ancient*
tos nacionales. La población india y mestiza de estos países es evidente en
los pueblos remotos de las montañas y en pueblos famosos como Chichicastenango (Guatemala).

El visitante puede ver fácilmente la importancia de la agricultura, industria dominante de todos los países. Se observan plantaciones grandes
de azúcar, cacao, bananas y otras frutas *sabrosas*, y en las faldas de los fér- *tasty*
tiles y majestuosos volcanes se produce café de la *mejor* calidad. *best*

Ésta es la tierra que *deleitó* al mundo con la poesía del nicaragüense *delighted*
Rubén Darío y con la obra literaria del guatemalteco Miguel Angel Asturias
(Premio Nobel de Literatura en 1969).

Pero ésta también es una tierra que ha sufrido mucho—calamidades
naturales como huracanes y *terremotos*, y catástrofes políticas, militares y so- *earthquakes*
ciales provocadas por crueles dictaduras militares. La miseria, la *angustia* y *anguish*
la destrucción causadas por guerras civiles, como las de Nicaragua y El Sal-
vador, interrumpen los *esfuerzos* para *alcanzar* el progreso económico y la esta- *efforts/achieve*
bilidad social. La tragedia es que este conflicto, *sea* entre los "sandinistas" y *be it*

Plaza de la Catedral,
Habana, Cuba.

"contras" de Nicaragua o entre comunistas y ultra-conservadores, o entre otros grupos políticos de *cualquier* país, está destruyendo la productividad económica y humana de esta región. Como siempre, es la gente pobre la que sufre más. ¿Existe la posibilidad de paz? Muchos creen que sí, si se realiza el plan de paz formulado por el presidente de Costa Rica, Oscar Arias Sánchez (Premio Nobel de Paz, 1987).

any

Las Antillas—Los países hispanos de las Antillas son tres: Cuba, La República Dominicana y Puerto Rico. Cuba, la "perla de las Antillas", está situada dentro de la zona tropical a la entrada del Golfo de México. Es la isla *mayor* de las Antillas. Sus profundas y bien formadas *bahías a lo largo de* su costa constituyen excelentes *puertos* y playas. Además de su belleza geográfica, la isla es rica en productos agrícolas y en depósitos minerales. Su población, compuesta por descendientes de españoles y por elementos de la raza negra, ha producido, entre muchas otras cosas, la música rítmica de la "salsa" el bien conocido Ron Bacardí, y azúcar y tabaco de fina calidad. Cuba también ha dado al mundo los genios literarios de José Martí, campeón de la independencia cubana, y Alejo Carpentier, famoso novelista de este siglo. Cuba, en 1959, se convirtió en la primera nación comunista del hemisferio bajo el *liderazgo* de Fidel Castro.

largest
bays along
ports

leadership

La República Dominicana, descubierta por Cristóbal Colón en 1492, es uno de los países más modernos y con más *sabor* de toda América. Santo Domingo, su capital, *cuenta entre* las ciudades coloniales más importantes y bellas del hemisferio. La Universidad de Santo Domingo y su hospital son los más antiguos del Nuevo Mundo. La República Dominicana produce azúcar, cacao, café y frutas para la exportación, pero también es conocida por su música (el "merengue") y jugadores profesionales de béisbol de grandes ligas.

flavor
is ranked among

Puerto Rico, la *tercera* isla hispana de las Antillas, está situado a unas mil millas de la Florida. San Juan, su capital, *cuenta con* "el Viejo San Juan" que, *al igual que* Santo Domingo, es una verdadera joya de arquitectura colonial española. La isla, destino de vacaciones de muchos turistas por su clima agradable, la belleza de sus playas y sus hoteles excelentes, tiene uno de los *niveles de vida* más altos de las Américas. Hace algunos años la economía se basaba en productos agrícolas pero hoy la industria y el turismo contribuyen más a la base económica de la isla.

third
includes
the same as

standards of living

Puerto Rico es un "commonwealth", lo que *quiere decir* que *tanto* puertorriqueños *como* estadounidenses pueden moverse libremente entre los dos países. Hoy día algunos puertorriqueños quieren que Puerto Rico *sea* un estado de los Estados Unidos *mientras* otros buscan la independencia y la nacionalidad puertorriqueña.

means
as well as
be
while

Es de gran importancia que estudiemos y conozcamos mejor todos los países de la América Central y de las Antillas porque su dirección y estabilidad de muchas maneras influyen en las decisiones políticas y económicas de las Américas y de gran parte del mundo.

Una de las atracciones más históricas y populares de Puerto Rico es la fortaleza El Morro, construida por los españoles.

¿CUÁNTO RECUERDA USTED?

¿Con qué países de la América Central o de las Antillas asocia usted las siguientes referencias?

1. el "Puente del mundo"
2. ruinas impresionantes de la civilización maya
3. Miguel Angel Asturias, el Premio Nobel de Literatura
4. guerras civiles
5. la "Perla de las Antillas"
6. uno de los niveles de vida más altos de las Américas
7. una maravilla de ingeniería que permite el tránsito marítimo entre dos océanos
8. un estado "commonwealth"
9. centro bancario y financiero
10. Fidel Castro
11. Oscar Arias Sánchez
12. José Martí y Alejo Carpentier
13. jugadores profesionales de béisbol
14. una isla descubierta por Cristóbal Colón
15. el "Viejo San Juan"
16. Santo Domingo

INTEGRACIÓN VISUAL: CAPÍTULO 10 ■

EJERCICIO 10.1   Vocabulario, La vida diaria

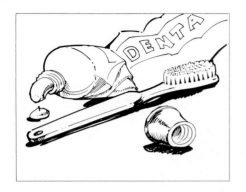

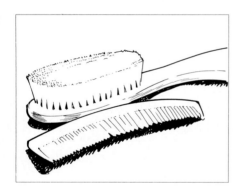

EJERCICIO 10.2   Verbos reflexivos

Juanito

Ejemplo   Son las diez de la noche. ¿Qué hace Juanito?
Se acuesta.
(pregunta personal) ¿A qué hora se
acuesta usted generalmente?

EJERCICIO 10.3   El reflexivo para indicar una acción recíproca—La historia de Manuel y Eva

Manuel   Eva

Ejemplo   ¿Qué hicieron Manuel y Eva?
Se conocieron.

EJERCICIO 10.4   El presente perfecto

Ejemplo   ¿Qué ha hecho Javier?
Ha pintado la casa.

Jaime y Javier

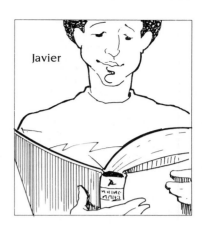

Jaime

Javier

Javier y Jaime

Javier y Jaime

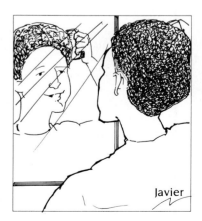

Jaime

Javier

Jaime

Javier

Jaime

Jaime

Javier y Jaime

REPASO DE VOCABULARIO ACTIVO ■

Pronombres reflexivos

me   **te**   **se**   **nos**   **os**   **se**

Sustantivos

el **cepillo**
el **cepillo de dientes**
el **champú**
el **compañero(a) de cuarto**
la **crema de afeitar**

el **despertador**
el **dormitorio**
la **máquina de afeitar**
la **navaja**
el **papel higiénico**

la **pasta de dientes**
el **peine**
la **residencia de estudiantes**
el **ruido**
el **secador de pelo**

Verbos

acostarse (ue)
afeitarse
bañarse
casarse
cepillarse
comprometerse (con)
cortarse
despertarse (ie)
divertirse (ie, i)
dormirse (ue, u)
enamorarse
enojarse
haber

irse
lavarse
levantarse
peinarse
ponerse
preocuparse (por) (de)
quitarse
romper
secarse
sentarse (ie)
sentirse (ie)
sonar (ue)
vestirse (i, i)

Expresiones idiomáticas

estar enamorado(a) (de)   **estar comprometido(a)**

AUTOEXAMEN Y REPASO #10 ■

I Vocabulario: la residencia de estudiantes y la vida diaria

¿Qué verbos asocia usted con las palabras siguientes?

1. el despertador
2. la toalla
3. la silla
4. la ropa
5. los zapatos
6. el pelo
7. los dientes
8. el cuchillo
9. la navaja
10. el jabón
11. la cama
12. el novio y la novia
13. la fiesta
14. los exámenes

II Pronombres y verbos reflexivos

Son las ocho de la mañana en la residencia de estudiantes. Indique las actividades de las varias personas.

Modelo Linda/levantarse
Linda se levanta.

1. mi compañero(a) de cuarto/despertarse
2. yo/levantarse
3. tú/quitarse los pijamas
4. vosotros/vestirse
5. nosotros/preocuparse por el examen
6. Ana y Susana/enojarse
7. yo/irse

Modelo Diego/levantarse
Diego acaba de levantarse.

8. yo/bañarse
9. Felipe/secarse
10. tú/lavarse la cara
11. nosotros/afeitarse
12. ellos/cepillarse los dientes
13. yo/peinarse
14. Pedro/ponerse los calcetines

III El presente perfecto

Indique lo que las personas han hecho en El Ecuador.

Modelo nosotros/llegar al Ecuador
Hemos llegado al Ecuador.

1. yo/caminar por la ciudad de Quito
2. nosotros/visitar la catedral
3. tú/sacar fotos de la plaza
4. Inés/ir al mercado público
5. vosotros/comprar muchas flores
6. mis amigos/escribir muchas tarjetas postales
7. usted/viajar por los Andes
8. yo/subir las montañas
9. tú/ver la selva
10. ustedes/conocer el puerto de Guayaquil
11. yo/hacer muchas cosas interesantes
12. yo/divertirse
13. nosotros/volver a los Estados Unidos

IV El pasado perfecto

Indique lo que había pasado en la clase.

Modelo   Hemos escuchado al profesor.
Habíamos escuchado al profesor.

1. El profesor lo ha dicho.
2. Hemos hecho la tarea.
3. Lupe y Cecilia han escrito los ejercicios.
4. He estudiado el vocabulario.
5. ¿Los has terminado?
6. ¿Ustedes han leído el Panorama Cultural?

V La voz pasiva

Indique por quién las cosas fueron hechas.

Modelo   Mi padre depositó los cheques.
Los cheques fueron depositados por mi padre.

1. El abogado firmó el cheque.
2. Mi tío mandó la dirección.
3. Mi hermano encontró los sellos.
4. Mi hermana recibió los paquetes.
5. La mujer escribió las cartas.

VI Repaso del Capítulo 10

A. *Conteste.*

1. ¿Qué hace usted por la mañana después de levantarse? (verbos reflexivos)
2. ¿Qué hizo su compañero(a) de cuarto al levantarse? (verbos reflexivos)
3. ¿Qué hicieron el novio y la novia? (verbos reflexivos)
4. Usted y su novio(a), ¿se quieren mucho? ¿Se abrazan mucho?
5. En esta universidad, ¿dónde se puede estudiar bien? ¿Y dónde no se puede estudiar bien?
6. En esta universidad, ¿dónde se venden libros? ¿Y dónde se vende comida?
7. ¿Qué ha hecho usted hoy?
8. Usted y sus amigos, ¿se han divertido mucho recientemente?

B. *Traduzca.*

1. I had to go to bed early because I didn't feel well.
2. She got angry and left.
3. We haven't seen her recently.
4. Ana, had they called you?
5. The letter was found by her daughter.

VII Repaso: verbos irregulares en el pretérito; preposiciones; <u>por</u> y <u>para</u>

A. **Muchos viajes.** *Conteste para indicar que usted viajó mucho el año pasado.*

Lago Atitlán. Guatemala.

El mercado de Chichicastenango.
Guatemala.

Mardi Gras. Las Tablas,
Panamá.

Las ruinas mayas de Tikal. Petén. Guatemala.

Temprano por la mañana. Santa Eulalia,
Guatemala.

A AMÉRICA CENTRAL Y LAS ANTILLAS

estre (*country landscape*). Viñales, Cuba.

Las carretas (*ox-carts*) son típicas de las artesanías de Costa Rica. Sarchi, Costa Rica.

El barco "Royal Princess" pasa por el canal de Panamá. Panamá.

En la distancia, la fortaleza El Morro.

Vista panorámica de la capital, Tegucigalpa, Honduras.

Modelo   ¿Has estado en México?
         Sí, estuve en México el año pasado.

1. ¿Has estado en España?
2. ¿Has ido alguna vez a Alaska?
3. ¿Has hecho un viaje a Australia?
4. ¿Has andado por la selva Amazonas?
5. ¿Has tenido muchos problemas con tu coche?

B. *Indique que usted **hizo** las cosas mencionadas **esta mañana.***

Modelo   ¿Has hecho los ejercicios?
         Los hice esta mañana.

1. ¿Has hecho la tarea?
2. ¿Has traído el documento?
3. ¿Has traducido el documento?
4. ¿Has puesto la información en la computadora?
5. ¿Se lo has dicho a tus padres?

C. *Indique dónde están los objetos usando la preposición de significado contrario.*

1. La navaja está debajo de la toalla.
2. El jabón está dentro de la bañera.
3. El papel higiénico está lejos del inodoro.
4. Las toallas están delante de la ducha.

D. *Complete las oraciones indicando las actividades de Tina. Use **por** o **para.***

1. Tina se levantó temprano/ir de compras.
2. Compró un secador de pelo/su hermana.
3. Lo compró/quince dólares.
4. Tenía frío. Volvió a casa/su chaqueta.
5. A su mamá no le gustaba el pelo largo. Tina se cortó el pelo/ella.
6. Anduvo/la ciudad toda la tarde.
7. Cuando volvió a casa estuvo cansada. Se sentó en el sofá/tres horas.
8. Necesita escribir una carta/encontrar empleo.
9. Quiere trabajar/una compañía japonesa.

CAPÍTULO 11

Goals for communication
- Traveling by train and calling by phone
- Talking about what will happen
- Talking about what would happen
- Comparing people, places, and things
- Giving orders and advice to family and friends

Cultural exploration
- South America: geographical and historical perspectives

VOCABULARIO LA ESTACIÓN DE FERROCARRIL Y LAS LLAMADAS TELEFÓNICAS

Llegamos a la **estación de ferrocarril.**	railroad station
Estudiamos el **horario**	schedule
que indica la **salida**	exit, departure
y la **llegada** del **tren.**	arrival; train
¿Hay una **demora**?	delay
Vamos a la **taquilla**	ticket window
para comprar un **billete** (España)/**boleto**	ticket
de **ida y vuelta,**	round-trip
de **primera clase** o	first-class
de **segunda clase.**	second-class
Vamos al **quiosco**	newsstand
para comprar una **revista**	magazine
y un **periódico.**	newspaper

Leemos las **noticias**	*news*
y las **caricaturas.**	*cartoons*

¿Dónde está el **aseo** (España)/**servicio?**	*restroom*
Vamos al **andén.**	*platform, track*
El **maletero** lleva	*porter*
las **maletas**	*suitcases*
o el **equipaje.**	*baggage*
Le damos una **propina.**	*tip*

Buscamos el **teléfono público**	*public telephone*
y la **guía telefónica.**	*phone book*
Hablamos con el (la) **operador(a).**	*operator*
¿Sabes el **código de área?**	*area code*
Podemos **hacer una llamada**	*to make a call*
de **larga distancia,**	*long distance*
común,	*station to station*
de **persona a persona** o	*person to person*
de **cobro revertido.**	*collect*
¡Ay! ¡La **línea** está **ocupada**!	*line; busy*
¿Tenemos el **número equivocado?**	*wrong number*

Otras palabras y expresiones útiles:	
bastante	*enough, quite*
cada	*each, every*
demasiado	*too, too much*
el **país**	*country*
ayudar	*to help*
callarse	*to be quiet*
dejar	*to leave (behind), to let*
marcar	*to dial*
olvidar, olvidarse (de)	*to forget; to forget (about)*
telefonear	*to telephone*
hacer la maleta	*to pack*
ponerse impaciente	*to become impatient*
la **semana que viene**	*next week*
el **año que viene**	*next year*

¿Cuándo llegará el tren?

EJERCICIO I En la estación de ferrocarril

Conteste en oraciones completas según el dibujo.

1. ¿Dónde están todas las personas?
2. ¿Qué quiere comprar el hombre que está enfrente de la taquilla?
3. Probablemente, ¿qué clase de boletos hay?
4. ¿Quién está en los brazos de la madre? ¿y quién se pone impaciente?
5. ¿Qué está haciendo el hombre que está detrás de la madre? ¿A qué hora sale el primer tren?
6. ¿Qué quiere comprar el hombre que está enfrente del quiosco?
7. ¿Quién es el hombre que le ayuda a la señora vieja con su equipaje? ¿Cuántas maletas lleva?
8. ¿Qué está haciendo el hombre que está cerca del teléfono? ¿Y qué va a hacer?
9. ¿Qué lee el hombre que está sentado en el banco?
10. Los jóvenes que están al lado del hombre, ¿se conocen bien? ¿Se aman mucho?
11. ¿Dónde está el tren?
12. ¿Qué están haciendo las personas en el andén?

EJERCICIO 2   Preguntas personales

Conteste en oraciones completas.

1. ¿Cuál es su número de teléfono? ¿y su código de área?
2. ¿Hace usted muchas llamadas de larga distancia? ¿A quién?
3. ¿Hace usted llamadas de cobro revertido frecuentemente? ¿A quién?
4. ¿Ha hecho usted una llamada a otro país? ¿Cuál? ¿Por qué?
5. ¿Se pone usted impaciente
   . . . cuando la línea está ocupada?
   . . . cuando tiene el número equivocado?
   y . . . cuando hay una demora larga en un viaje?
   ¿En qué otras ocasiones se pone usted impaciente?
6. Al comprar un periódico, ¿qué lee usted primero, las noticias, los deportes o las caricaturas? ¿Cuál es su caricatura favorita?
7. ¿Lee usted un periódico todos los días? ¿Cuál?
8. ¿Lee usted revistas frecuentemente? ¿Cuáles?
9. ¿Tiene usted bastante tiempo para leer? ¿estudiar? ¿dormir? ¿divertirse?
10. ¿Estudia usted demasiado? ¿Come usted demasiado? ¿Bebe usted demasiado?
11. ¿Hace el profesor (la profesora) demasiadas preguntas?

EJERCICIO 3   Definiciones

A. *Indique el verbo o la expresión del vocabulario que corresponde a la definición.*

1. el acto de usar el teléfono
2. el acto de indicar el número de teléfono
3. el acto de no hablar o de no hacer ruido
4. el acto de no recordar algo
5. el acto de poner las cosas en la maleta
6. el acto de perder la paciencia

B. *¿Puede usted definir las siguientes palabras?*

1. la llamada de larga distancia
2. la llamada de cobro revertido
3. la operadora
4. el maletero
5. la propina
6. la taquilla
7. el boleto de ida y vuelta
8. el horario

CONVERSACIÓN ▪

*Un pasajero llega de prisa a la **taquilla** de la **estación de ferrocarril**.*

PASAJERO   Buenas tardes. Lo siento pero he llegado un poco tarde. ¿Ha salido el **tren** para Sevilla?

BOLETERO   No, señor. **Saldrá** en cinco minutos.

PASAJERO   ¡Qué suerte! Necesito un **boleto de ida y vuelta,** por favor.

BOLETERO	¿**De primera** o **de segunda clase,** señor?
PASAJERO	**De segunda.** No he tenido tiempo para cambiar mi dinero. ¿Aceptan ustedes cheques de viajero?
BOLETERO	Sí, ¡cómo no! . . . Aquí tiene el **boleto** y su cambio. Y, señor, a la derecha usted puede encontrar un **horario.**
PASAJERO	Muchísimas gracias.
BOLETERO	¡Buen viaje!

A passenger arrives hurriedly at the ticket window of the railroad station.

PASSENGER	*Good afternoon. I'm sorry but I have arrived a bit late. Has the train left for Seville?*
TICKET AGENT	*No, sir. It will leave in five minutes.*
PASSENGER	*What luck! I need a round-trip ticket, please.*
TICKET AGENT	*First or second class, sir?*
PASSENGER	*Second. I haven't had time to change my money. Do you accept traveler's checks?*
TICKET AGENT	*Yes, of course! . . . Here is the ticket and your change. And, sir, to the right you can find a schedule.*
PASSENGER	*Thank you very much.*
TICKET AGENT	*Have a good trip!*

PREGUNTAS

Conteste en oraciones completas.

1. ¿Ha llegado el pasajero demasiado tarde?
2. ¿Cuándo saldrá el tren?
3. ¿Qué tipo de boleto necesita?
4. ¿Cómo paga?
5. ¿Qué se encuentra a la derecha?
6. Al salir el pasajero, ¿qué dice el boletero?

ACTIVIDAD   Conversaciones en la estación de ferrocarril, Sevilla, España

a.   Varios estudiantes hacen el papel de boleteros, vendedores en quioscos y operadores(as) de una compañía telefónica.
b.   Los otros estudiantes, pasajeros en la estación de ferrocarril, conversan con los boleteros, vendedores, etc., para realizar (*fulfill*) las tareas (*tasks*) indicadas.

En las taquillas:

1. comprar un boleto de primera o de segunda clase
2. comprar un boleto de ida y vuelta
3. buscar sus maletas perdidas
4. pedir información (de horarios, equipaje, etc.)
5. hablar de la demora del tren y qué hacer
6. preguntar si (*if*) hay otro tren a X. Usted ha perdido el suyo.

En el quiosco:

7. comprar revistas
8. comprar un periódico
9. quejarse de las revistas pornográficas que venden

Con el (la) operador(a) (teléfono público):

10. hacer una llamada de larga distancia
11. hacer una llamada de cobro revertido
12. hablar con la operadora—la línea que usted está tratando de marcar está ocupada y usted tiene una emergencia.

ESTRUCTURA ▪

I. El futuro
The future tense

A. Formación del futuro

Observe the formation of the future tense of regular **-ar, -er,** and **-ir** verbs.

endings	sample verbs	
-é	Llegar**é** a las ocho.	*I will arrive at eight.*
-ás	¿Cuándo llegar**ás**?	*When will you arrive?*
-á	Ella volver**á** la semana que viene.	*She will return next week.*
-emos	Ir**emos** a la estación.	*We will go to the station.*
-éis	¿Traer**éis** el carro grande?	*Will you bring the large car?*
-án	Estar**án** aquí por un mes.	*They will be here for one month.*

Con AT&T, llamar a México es fácil, rápido y económico

Ahorre la tercera parte (⅓) de la Tarifa Normal en sus llamadas … ¡todos los días de la semana!

Ahora, AT&T le ofrece la tercera parte (⅓) de descuento de la Tarifa Normal en todas sus llamadas marcadas directamente durante el período de Tarifa de Descuento…¡los siete días de la semana! Y es fácil:

Para llamar, siga estos sencillos pasos…

1. Busque en el mapa el código correspondiente a la ciudad que usted desea llamar.*
2. Marque el 011 (Código de Acceso Internacional).
3. Marque el 52 (Código de México).
4. Marque el código de la ciudad.
5. Por último marque el número telefónico local.

The future tense of regular **-ar, -er,** or **-ir** verbs is formed by adding to the *complete infinitive* the endings indicated. The future tells what *will* happen.

Modelo **volver** *to return*

volver**é**	volver**emos**
volver**ás**	volver**éis**
volver**á**	volver**án**

EJERCICIO 4   Resoluciones para el año nuevo

Indique lo que van a hacer las personas el año que viene; use el tiempo futuro.

Modelo   estudiar más (yo)
Estudiaré más.

1.   limpiar el cuarto más frecuentemente (yo, mi compañero(a) de cuarto)
2.   escribir a la familia más frecuentemente (yo, mis hermanos)
3.   ir a la biblioteca más (tú, vosotros)
4.   recibir buenas notas (Anita, yo)
5.   comer menos (*less*) postres (nosotros, mi hermana)
6.   comer más legumbres (yo, tú)
7.   beber menos Coca-Cola (mis amigos, yo)
8.   tratar de tener más paciencia (nosotros, Carlos)
9.   mirar la televisión menos (mi compañero(a) de cuarto, yo)
10.   dormir más (yo, nosotros)
11.   dar menos exámenes (el (la) profesor(a))

EJERCICIO 5   Este verano tú y yo

Háganse preguntas y contéstense según el modelo.

Modelo   estudiar el español
(pregunta) **¿Estudiarás el español?**
(respuesta) **Sí (No, no) estudiaré el español.**

1. ir a la escuela de verano
2. trabajar (¿Dónde?)
3. ganar mucho dinero (¿Cuánto?)
4. ahorrar mucho dinero
5. comprar un coche
6. alquilar un apartamento
7. ir a la playa
8. nadar en el océano
9. jugar al tenis
10. viajar a otro país (¿Adónde?)
11. descansar mucho
12. visitar a tus abuelos (¿Dónde?)
13. vivir con tu familia
14. volver a la universidad

B. Verbos irregulares en el futuro

The following verbs are irregular in the future. Observe that they use:

a.   irregular stems (not the complete infinitive)
b.   regular future endings: **-é, -ás, -á, -emos, -éis, -án.**

Verbs   *future stems*

decir:	**dir-**	Yo le **diré** la verdad.
hacer:	**har-**	¿Cuándo lo **harás**?
poder:	**podr-**	Carlos **podrá** hacerlo mañana.
poner:	**pondr-**	¿Dónde **pondremos** sus cosas?
querer:	**querr-**	¿**Querréis** salir?
saber:	**sabr-**	¿**Sabrán** las direcciones?
salir:	**saldr-**	¿Cuándo **saldrá**?
tener:	**tendr-**	**Tendremos** que hablar con él.
venir:	**vendr-**	**Vendrá** a las cinco.
haber:	**habr-**	¿**Habrá** una reacción favorable?
		Will there be a favorable reaction?

Modelo   **decir**   *to say, tell*

diré	diremos
dirás	diréis
dirá	dir**án**

NOTE: The future perfect tense is formed by using **haber** in the future plus the past participle.

Para el jueves **habré terminado** el proyecto.
By Thursday I will have finished the project.

EJERCICIO 6   Mañana

*Responda a las interrogaciones indicando que usted **hará** las cosas indicadas mañana.*

Modelo   ¿Cuándo vas a venir?
         Vendré mañana.

1. ¿Cuándo vas a hacer las maletas?
2. ¿Cuándo vas a poner las cosas en el sótano?
3. ¿Cuándo vas a salir?
4. ¿Cuándo vas a venir a la universidad?
5. ¿Cuándo vas a tener la información?
6. ¿Cuándo vas a saber cuánto cuesta?
7. ¿Cuándo vas a decirme la verdad?

Repita según el modelo.

Modelo   Y ustedes, ¿cuándo van a venir?
         Vendremos mañana.

EJERCICIO 7   Preguntas personales

Conteste para indicar lo que usted hará.

1.   ¿Qué tendrá usted que hacer esta noche?
2.   ¿Qué querrá usted hacer esta noche?
3.   ¿Qué hará usted este fin de semana?
4.   ¿Qué no podrá hacer este fin de semana?
5.   ¿Qué hará usted la semana que viene? ¿y el verano que viene? ¿y el año que viene?

ACTIVIDAD   La bola de cristal

Imagínense que ustedes pueden, con la ayuda de su bola de cristal, pronosticar el futuro. Trabajando en pares, indique lo que ocurrirá en la vida de su compañero(a) de clase diez años en el futuro.

II. El condicional
The conditional

A. Formación del condicional

Observe the formation of the conditional tense of regular **-ar, -er,** and **-ir** verbs.

endings   *sample verbs*

-ía	Yo viajar**ía** en tren.	*I would travel by train.*
-ías	¿Llevar**ías** a los niños?	*Would you take the children?*
-ía	Juanito comer**ía** durante todo el viaje.	*Juanito would eat during the whole trip.*
-íamos	Nosotros leer**íamos.**	*We would read.*
-íais	¿Descansar**íais**?	*Would you rest?*
-ían	Mis abuelos dormir**ían.**	*My grandparents would sleep.*

The conditional of regular **-ar, -er,** and **-ir** verbs is formed by adding to the complete infinitive the endings indicated. Note that the conditional endings are identical to the imperfect tense endings for **-er** and **-ir** verbs. The conditional tells what *would* happen.

Modelo   **viajar**   *to travel*

viajar**ía**	viajar**íamos**
viajar**ías**	viajar**íais**
viajar**ía**	viajar**ían**

EJERCICIO 8   Un día sin clases

¿Qué harían las personas indicadas?

> Modelo   yo (dormir todo el día)
> **Dormiría todo el día.**

1. yo (dormir tarde, lavar la ropa, limpiar mi cuarto)
2. tú (andar en bicicleta, jugar al tenis, nadar)
3. Marta (llamar a sus padres, escribir a sus abuelos, leer un libro)
4. Nosotros (ir de compras, visitar a nuestros amigos, mirar la televisión)
5. Paco y Pepe (tocar la guitarra, escuchar la radio, descansar)

B. Verbos irregulares en el condicional

The following verbs are irregular in the conditional. Observe that they use:

a. irregular stems
b. regular conditional endings: **-ía, -ías, -ía, -íamos, -íais, -ían.**

verbs   *conditional stems*

decir:	**dir-**	No se lo **diría.**
hacer:	**har-**	¿Lo **harías** tú por él?
poder:	**podr-**	Felipe no **podría** entenderlo.
poner:	**pondr-**	¿Dónde **pondríamos** sus cosas?
querer:	**querr-**	¿**Querríais** hablar con él primero?
saber:	**sabr-**	Los niños **sabrían** lo que pasó.
salir:	**saldr-**	**Saldrían** inmediatamente.
tener:	**tendr-**	**Tendríamos** que dejarlos con la abuela.
venir:	**vendr-**	¿**Vendríais** con nosotros?
haber:	**habr-**	En su opinión, ¿**habría** un problema?
		In your opinion, would there be a problem?

> NOTE: The conditional perfect is formed by using **haber** in the conditional plus the past participle.

Pensaba que **habrían terminado** ya.
I was thinking that they would have finished already.

EJERCICIO 9   Un(a) estudiante ideal . . .

¿Haría o no haría las siguientes cosas?

> Modelo   venir a la clase a tiempo
> **Sí, vendría a la clase a tiempo.**

1. venir a la clase todos los días
2. hacer la tarea

3. salir de la clase temprano
4. saber las respuestas
5. decir mentiras al profesor (a la profesora)
6. tener toda la tarea
7. poder contestar bien
8. querer estudiar
9. poner manzanas en la mesa del profesor (de la profesora)

ACTIVIDAD   Con mucha imaginación . . .

*Trabajando en pares o en grupos pequeños discutan lo que **harían** en los siguientes lugares.*

Modelo   en el almacén
   Compraría ropas.
   Miraría los muebles.
   etc.

1. en la playa
2. en la casa de los abuelos
3. en la ciudad de Nueva York
4. en Puerto Rico
5. en Madrid

6. en Alaska
7. en la estación de ferrocarril
8. en el banco
9. en la casa de correos
10. en la luna

III. Las comparaciones
Comparisons

A. Las comparaciones de igualdad   *Equal comparisons*

Observe the constructions used in Spanish to make equal comparisons.

1. Comparison of general qualities (adjectives and adverbs):

Esta revista es **tan interesante como** ésa.	*This magazine is as interesting as that one.*
Este autor escribe **tan bien como** ése.	*This author writes as well as that one.*

To compare two things or persons with regard to a general quality, use:

tan + adjective (or adverb) + como = *as . . . as*

2. Comparison of quantities (nouns):

Compré **tantos boletos como** tú.	*I bought as many tickets as you did.*
Tenemos **tantas maletas como** Carmen.	*We have as many suitcases as Carmen does.*

To compare equal quantities, use:

> **tanto (-a, -os, -as)** + noun + **como** = *as much (many) . . . as*

NOTE 1:   When the noun reference is omitted, and *two actions* are compared equally, **tanto como** is used.

Él comió **tanto como** tú.   *He ate as much as you.*

NOTE 2:   Also, **tanto** has the additional meaning of *so much* or *so many.*

¡Tiene **tantas** maletas!   *He has so many suitcases!*

Con Mountain Bell sus seres queridos están tan cerca como tomar el teléfono y llamar.

Para que la larga distancia sea más corta.

EJERCICIO 10   Igualdad en la clase de español

Haga comparaciones de igualdad entre estudiantes de la clase de español.

Modelo   (*Nombre de estudiante*) es fantástico(a).
(*Nombre de estudiante*) es fantástico(a) también.
(*Nombre*) es tan fantástico(a) como (*nombre*).

1. _____ es simpático(a). _____ es simpático(a) también. _____ es . . .
2. _____ es generoso(a). _____ es generoso(a) también. _____ es . . .
3. _____ es romántico(a). _____ es romántico(a) también. _____ es . . .
4. _____ es responsable. _____ es responsable también. _____ es . . .
5. _____ es guapo(a). _____ es guapo(a) también. _____ es . . .
6. _____ es extraordinario(a). _____ es extraordinario(a) también. _____ es . . .

Modelo   (*Nombre*) lee muchos libros.
(*Nombre*) lee muchos libros también.
(*Nombre*) lee tantos libros como (*nombre*).

7. _____ lee muchas revistas. _____ lee muchas revistas también. _____ . . .
8. _____ come mucho helado. _____ come mucho helado también. _____ . . .
9. _____ come mucha pizza. _____ come mucha pizza también. _____ . . .
10. _____ tiene muchos amigos. _____ tiene muchos amigos también. _____ . . .
11. _____ tiene muchas amigas. _____ tiene muchas amigas también. _____ . . .

12. _____ gana mucho dinero. _____ gana mucho dinero también. _____ . . .

Modelo   (*Nombre*) y (*nombre*) estudian mucho.
         (*Nombre*) estudia tanto como (*nombre*).

13. _____ y _____ van a la biblioteca mucho. _____ . . .

14. _____ y _____ miran la televisión mucho. _____ . . .

15. _____ y _____ duermen mucho. _____ . . .

16. _____ y _____ trabajan mucho. _____ . . .

EJERCICIO 11   Preguntas de comparación

Conteste para indicar cómo usted se compara con otras personas.

1. ¿Es usted tan inteligente como su profesor(a)?
2. ¿Está usted tan ocupado(a) como su profesor(a)?
3. ¿Está usted tan cansado(a) como su profesor(a)?
4. ¿Tiene usted tanta ropa como su compañero(a) de cuarto?
5. ¿Recibe usted tantas cartas como su compañero(a) de cuarto?
6. ¿Gasta usted tanto dinero como su compañero(a) de cuarto?
7. ¿Estudia usted tanto como su compañero(a) de cuarto?
8. ¿Come usted tanto como Fat Albert?
9. ¿Es usted tan divertido como Eddie Murphy?

B. Las comparaciones de desigualdad y los superlativos   U*nequal comparisons and superlatives*

Observe the constructions used in Spanish to make unequal comparisons.

1.   Regular comparative forms

La clase de español es **más interesante que** la clase de historia.	*Spanish class is more interesting than history class.*
Carlos aprende **más facilmente que** su hermano.	*Carlos learns more easily than his brother.*
Carlos tiene **menos tarea que** su hermano.	*Carlos has less homework than his brother.*

To make an unequal comparison, use:

> **más** (*more*)
>   or   + adjective, adverb, or noun + **que** (*than*)
> **menos** (*less*)

Than is translated by **que** except before a number; in such a case **de** is used.

Él tiene más **de** cincuenta dólares. *He has more than fifty dollars.*

2. Irregular comparative forms

La clase de español es **mejor que** la clase de historia.	*Spanish class is better than history class.*
La clase de matemáticas es **peor que** la clase de historia.	*Math class is worse than history class.*
Mi compañero(a) de cuarto es **menor que** yo.	*My roommate is younger than I am.*
Soy **mayor** que él.	*I am older than he is.*

Spanish has four irregular forms used to express unequal comparisons. These forms *do not* use **más** and **menos.**

ADJECTIVE		ADVERB		COMPARATIVE	
bueno	*good*	**bien**	*well*	**mejor**	*better*
malo	*bad*	**mal**	*badly*	**peor**	*worse*
joven	*young*			**menor**	*younger*
viejo	*old*			**mayor**	*older*

AT&T La mejor decisión.

EJERCICIO 12   Preguntas de comparación

Conteste para indicar las comparaciones.

1. ¿Es su profesor(a) de español más difícil o menos difícil que su profesor(a) de inglés?
2. ¿Es su profesor(a) de español más interesante o menos interesante que su profesor(a) de matemáticas?
3. ¿Es usted más fuerte o menos fuerte que su profesor(a) de español? ¿más guapo(a) o menos guapo(a)?
4. ¿Es usted mayor o menor que su profesor(a) de español?
5. ¿Tiene usted un(a) hermano(a) mayor o menor? ¿Cuál? ¿Cuántos años tiene?
6. En su opinión, ¿es la clase de español mejor o peor que la clase de historia?
7. Personalmente, ¿es este año mejor o peor que el año pasado? ¿Por qué?

EJERCICIO 13   Mi hermano(a) o mi amigo(a) favorito(a)

Haga una comparación igual o desigual entre usted y un(a) hermano(a) suyo(a) o un(a) amigo(a) suyo(a).

> Modelo   serio(a)
> Soy **más serio(a) que** mi hermano(a) o amigo(a).
> Soy **menos serio(a)** que . . .
> Soy **tan serio(a)** como . . .

1. generoso(a)   2. inteligente   3. sentimental

4. responsable   5. alto(a)   6. guapo(a)

Modelo   libros
Tengo **más libros que** mi hermano(a) o amigo(a).
Tengo **menos libros que** . . .
Tengo **tantos libros como** . . .

7. revistas   8. discos   9. ropa
10. camisas   11. zapatos   12. amigos

3. The superlative

Contrast the comparative and superlative forms in the sample sentences.

Pedro es **alto.**   *Pedro is tall.*
Pepe es **más alto.**   *Pepe is taller.*
Paco es **el más alto de** los tres.   *Paco is the tallest of the three.*
   [superlative]

Teresa es **buena** en español.   *Teresa is good in Spanish.*
Tina es **mejor.**   *Tina is better.*
Tonia es **la mejor de** la clase. *Tonia is the best in the class.*
   [superlative]

The superlative is formed by using:

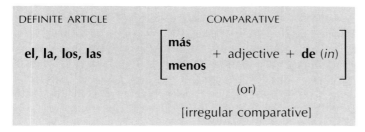

DEFINITE ARTICLE	COMPARATIVE	
el, la, los, las	**más** / **menos** + adjective + **de** (*in*)	
	(or)	
	[irregular comparative]	

EJERCICIO 14   Vamos a comparar . . .

Haga comparaciones entre las tres personas o cosas indicadas; después indique el superlativo según el modelo.

Modelo   restaurantes: McDonald's
                          Howard Johnson's
                          Pierre's en Nueva York
          posibles respuestas:
          COMPARACIONES: **McDonald's es peor (mejor) que Howard**
                          Johnson's, etc.
          SUPERLATIVO: **Pierre's es el mejor de los tres.**

1. hermanos: Paco (10 años)
                          José (12 años)
                          Miguel (14 años)

2. revistas: *People*
                          Time
                          National Geographic
3. periódicos: *National Inquirer*
                          Denver Post
                          New York Times
4. Novelas interesantes: *Tom Sawyer* por Mark Twain
                          Crime and Punishment por Dostoyevski
                          Don Quijote por Cervantes
5. joyerías caras: la joyería en Sears
                          la joyería en Bloomingdales
                          Tiffany's
6. modos de transporte—
   caros/baratos: el taxi
                          el autobús
                          el metro

EJERCICIO 15   En mi opinión

En oraciones completas indique la persona o la cosa que, en su opinión, corresponde a cada categoría.

1. La mejor computadora
2. El mejor coche
3. El peor coche
4. El mejor restaurante de esta ciudad
5. El peor restaurante de esta ciudad
6. El mejor programa de televisión
7. El peor programa de televisión
8. La mejor película (reciente)
9. La peor película (reciente)
10. El actor más popular
11. La actriz más popular
12. El disco más popular
13. El grupo de cantantes más popular
14. El deporte más popular de este país

ACTIVIDAD   . . . y yo

Prepare, en forma escrita o como presentación oral, una comparación entre usted y una persona famosa o entre usted y un(a) estudiante de la clase de español.
Incluya: comparaciones de igualdad
             comparaciones de desigualdad
             superlativos

IV. Los mandatos tú
The tú command forms

To give orders or advice to people you address as **tú,** informal **tú** commands are used. Formal commands will be studied in Chapter 12.

A. El mandato tú afirmativo

Observe the verb forms used to formulate **tú** affirmative commands.

¡Espera, por favor!	*Wait please!*
¡Piensa!	*Think!*
Enciende la luz, por favor.	*Turn on the light, please.*
¡Tráemelo!	*Bring it to me!*
¡Ábrelo!	*Open it!*
¡Cállate!	*Be quiet!*
Siéntate, por favor.	*Sit down, please.*

The regular **tú** command forms are identical to the third person singular (él, ella, usted) form of the present tense indicative.

> NOTE: In all affirmative commands the object pronouns are attached at the end; in this case a written accent mark is added to the command form on the syllable normally stressed.

The irregular **tú** affirmative commands are:

poner	**pon**	**Pon** las cosas en el coche.
salir	**sal**	**Sal** pronto.
tener	**ten**	**Ten** paciencia.
venir	**ven**	**Ven** aquí, por favor.
hacer	**haz**	**Haz**lo ahora.
ser	**sé**	**Sé** bueno.
decir	**di**	**Di**le la verdad.
ir	**ve**	**Ve** a la casa esta noche.

> refrán: **Dime con quien andas y te diré quien eres.**

EJERCICIO 16   ¡Hazlo!

Dígale a su hermano(a) menor que es su obligación o responsabilidad hacer las cosas siguientes.

    Modelo   abrir la puerta
              ¡Abre la puerta!

1. dejar tus cosas aquí
2. contestarme

3. apagar la radio
4. devolverme los discos
5. mostrármelo
6. peinarte
7. vestirte
8. callarte
9. venir aquí
10. hacer tu cama
11. ir a la tienda
12. poner la comida en la mesa
13. tener paciencia
14. decirme la verdad
15. salir, por favor

B. El mandato tú negativo

Observe the verb forms used to formulate tú negative commands.

¡No **fumes**!	*Don't smoke!*
¡No me **hables**!	*Don't speak to me!*
¡No lo **comas**!	*Don't eat it!*
¡No **hagas** eso!	*Don't do that!*
Por favor, no lo **repitas.**	*Please don't repeat it.*
No te **duermas.**	*Don't fall asleep.*

The **tú** negative command forms use:

- the **yo** form of the present indicative
- minus the *o*
- plus **-es** (**-ar** verbs)
  -as (**-er, -ir** verbs)

Modelos

esperar	**espero**	no **esperes**
volver	**vuelvo**	no **vuelvas**
salir	**salgo**	no **salgas**

NOTE: In all negative commands the object pronouns are placed *before* the verb.

Three verbs that are commonly used in commands have an irregular form in the **tú** negative:

dar	no **des**	No me lo **des** ahora.
ir	no **vayas**	Por favor, no **vayas** allí.
ser	no **seas**	No **seas** estúpido.

refranes: **No digas en secreto lo que no quieres oír en público.**
No hagas a otro lo que no quieres que te hagan.

EJERCICIO 17   ¡No lo hagas!

Dígale a su hermano(a) menor que NO haga las siguientes cosas.

Modelo   llevar mis ropas
          No **lleves** mis ropas.

1. mirar la televisión
2. escuchar la radio
3. gastar mi dinero
4. beber mi Coca-Cola
5. dormir en mi cama
6. poner tus pies en el sofá
7. venir a mi cuarto
8. jugar con mi computadora
9. salir esta noche
10. ir a la fiesta
11. ser tonto
12. olvidarte de hacer la tarea
13. preocuparte

EJERCICIO 18   Un(a) hermano(a) mayor horrible

Usted es un(a) hermano(a) mayor horrible. Siempre dice NO cuando su hermano(a) menor le pide algo. Conteste según el modelo.

Modelo   [hermano(a) menor] ¿Me permites (*will you allow me*) usar
                              el sombrero?
          [hermano(a) mayor] **No, no lo uses.**

¿Me permites . . .

1. . . . usar la chaqueta?
2. . . . manejar el coche?
3. . . . llamar a los abuelos?
4. . . . tocar la guitarra?
5. . . . leer esa revista?
6. . . . comer esos chocolates?
7. . . . dar la moneda a mi amigo?
8. . . . mostrar la moneda a mi amigo?
9. . . . devolver el cassette a mi amigo?
10. . . . comprar esta camiseta?

EJERCICIO 19   ¿Sí o no?

Hay un conflicto en su conciencia—¿Hacerlo o no hacerlo? ¿Qué dicen las dos voces (voices) de su conciencia?

Modelo   comerlo
          (#1) **Sí, ¡cómelo!**
          (#2) **No, ¡no lo comas!**

1. beberlo
2. fumarlo
3. comprarlo
4. gastarlo
5. hacerlo
6. decirlo
7. escucharlo
8. repetirlo
9. mirarlo
10. tocarlo
11. abrirlo
12. pagárselo
13. dárselo

EJERCICIO 20   Consejos (*advice*) para su amigo Juan

Dígale a Juan lo que debe hacer y lo que no debe hacer en cada situación.

Seguimos la Carretera Panamericana por el extenso desierto de Atacama. Chile.

Modelo   Juan tiene un problema muy grande.
                (consejos) **Habla con tus padres.**
                No te preocupes.
                etc.

1. Juan tiene una torta de chocolate.
2. Juan tiene un examen muy importante el miércoles.
3. Juan recibió un cheque de $200.
4. Juan va a salir con su novia en quince minutos.
5. Juan mira por la ventana y ve que hace mucho frío y está nevando.
6. Juan perdió sus monedas en el teléfono público.
7. Juan encontró una cartera en la calle.
8. Juan tiene un pariente que está enfermo.
9. A Juan no le gusta el español ni el (la) profesor(a) de español.
10. Juan no tiene suficiente dinero para comprar lo que necesita.

ACTIVIDAD Mandatos para mi compañero(a) de cuarto

*En grupos, formulen para cada situación cinco mandatos **tú** afirmativos y cinco mandatos **tú** negativos dirigidos a un(a) compañero(a) de cuarto.*

1. Un lunes por la noche cuando usted está tratando de estudiar para un examen.
2. Un sábado por la noche, en una fiesta.

3. En la estación de ferrocarril, mientras (*while*) ustedes están esperando el tren.

ACTIVIDAD ESCRITA

Usted y su hermano menor hicieron un viaje en tren para visitar a sus tíos. El tren acababa de salir cuando su hermano aprendió que había dejado su maleta en el tren.

Escriba una carta a sus padres explicándoles cómo usted resolvió la situación: cómo le explicó al empleado lo que había pasado; lo que el empleado dijo que haría; lo que pasó después.

PANORAMA CULTURAL* ▪

EJERCICIO DE MAPA (p. 328)

1. ¿Cuál es el país más grande de la América del Sur? (¿Sabe usted qué lengua se habla allí?)
2. ¿Cuál es el río que se extiende por gran parte del Brasil?
3. Saliendo de Panamá en camino al sur, pasamos por una cordillera (*range*) famosa de montañas. ¿Cuál es? Indique los países por los cuales pasa.
4. ¿Cómo se llama el río que divide la Argentina y el Uruguay?
5. ¿Cuál es el país más largo y estrecho (*narrow*) de la América del Sur?
6. ¿Cómo se llama el lago que se encuentra en la frontera entre el Perú y Bolivia?
7. ¿Qué países tienen fronteras con Paraguay?
8. ¿Qué línea importante pasa directamente por el Ecuador?
9. ¿Cómo se llama el desierto grande que se encuentra en el norte de Chile?
10. ¿Cuál es el país más septentrional (*northerly*) del continente?
11. ¿Cómo se llama el estrecho que se encuentra muy al sur del continente?
12. ¿Cuántas millas o cuántos kilómetros (más o menos) hay entre la frontera del norte de Chile y la Tierra del Fuego en el sur?

La América del Sur

Grandiosidad, inmensidad, extremos, belleza espectacular son palabras que bien definen y describen la geografía de la América del Sur. Al *cruzar* las   *crossing*
montañas nevadas de los Andes, magnífica cordillera, se ve el Aconcagua, el pico más alto de las Américas. En la Argentina encontramos la *pampa* más   *plain*
fértil del mundo, tierra *natal* del *gaucho*. En Chile *se nos presenta* uno de los   *native/cowboy/we are*
desiertos más áridos, el Atacama, y en el Brasil pasamos en barco por el   *confronted with*
Río Amazonas que se extiende por el bosque tropical más grande del mundo.

También hay en el continente una variedad de tipos raciales. En el Brasil (donde se habla portugués) y en las costas tropicales hay un gran nú-

*Ver fotografías en color de la América del Sur después de p. 352.

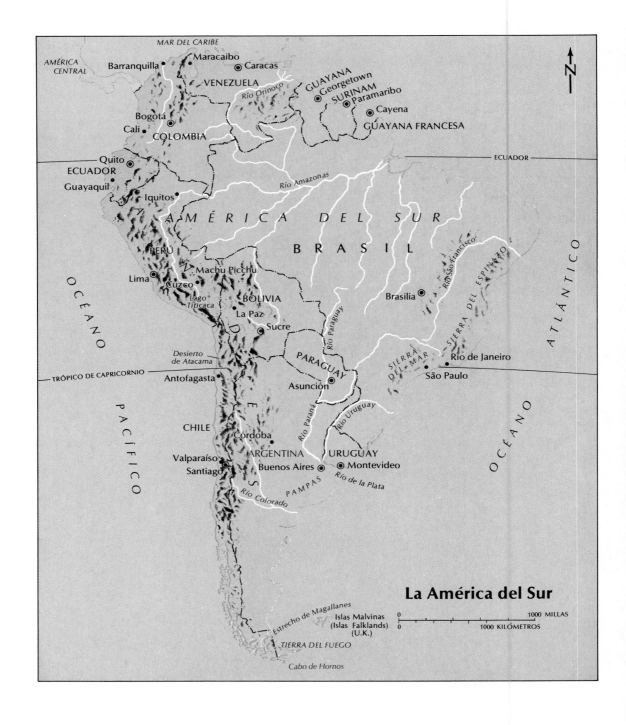

MAR DEL CARIBE

AMÉRICA
CENTRAL

Barranquilla
Maracaibo
Caracas

VENEZUELA
GUAYANA
Georgetown
SURINAM
Paramaribo
Cayena
GUAYANA FRANCESA

Río Orinoco

Bogotá
Cali
COLOMBIA

Quito
ECUADOR
ECUADOR
Guayaquil

Iquitos
Río Amazonas

AMÉRICA   DEL   SUR
BRASIL

PERÚ
Machu Picchu
Lima
Cuzco
Lago
Titicaca
BOLIVIA
La Paz
Sucre
Brasilia

Río São francisco
SIERRA DEL ESPINAZO

OCÉANO

Desierto
de Atacama
PARAGUAY
Río Paraguay
SIERRA
DEL
MAR
Río de Janeiro
São Paulo

TRÓPICO DE CAPRICORNIO
Antofagasta
Asunción

ATLÁNTICO

PACÍFICO
Río Paraná
Río Uruguay

CHILE
Córdoba
ARGENTINA
URUGUAY
Valparaíso
Santiago
Buenos Aires
Montevideo
Río de la Plata
OCÉANO

Río Colorado
PAMPAS

Estrecho de Magallanes
Islas Malvinas
(Islas Falklands)
(U.K.)

TIERRA DEL FUEGO

Cabo de Hornos

La América del Sur

0   1000 MILLAS
0   1000 KILÓMETROS

N

El gaucho y su caballo
son como uno.
Argentina.

mero de negros. En Chile, la Argentina, el Uruguay y el Brasil hay muchos inmigrantes europeos, principalmente de Italia, España, Portugal y Alemania. En países como el Perú, el Ecuador y Bolivia, donde existía el imperio incaico, el indio es el elemento predominante.

El imperio incaico—En las montañas de los Andes, cerca del Cuzco, Perú, se encuentran las ruinas de Machu Picchu, vieja y última capital de los incas, situada a más de ocho mil pies *de altura*. Esta ciudad, como otros sitios históricos, es monumento al *desarrollo* militar, social y cultural de este imperio de unos diez millones de habitantes.

high
development

La conquista—Cuando Francisco Pizarro y sus soldados llegaron a la costa del Perú en busca de riquezas, fama y gloria, los incas ya se encontraban debilitados por una *guerra* civil. Los españoles, con sus armas de *fuego* y caballos (*ambos* desconocidos a los indios) y con gran *atrevimiento* y *engaño*, *vencieron* a los incas en 1532. Después de *exigir* de los indios una fortuna en *oro* y *plata*, mataron al emperador inca Atahualpa y destruyeron gran parte de la civilización incaica. Con su triunfo *sobre* los indios los españoles *ejercieron* control sobre un área del continente (unas tres mil millas) que se extendía desde el Ecuador hasta Chile.

war/fire
both/daring/deception
conquered/demand
gold/silver
over/exercised

La colonización—Después de la desintegración del imperio incaico, los españoles solidificaron su posición en la América del Sur con exploraciones por las dos costas del continente, *creando* pueblos y *fortalezas* en sitios que

creating/fortresses

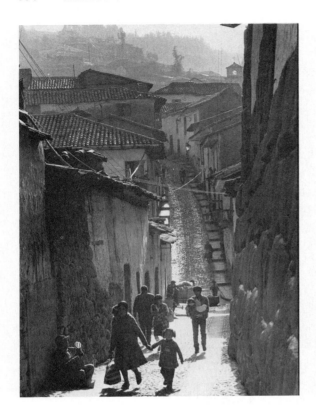

¡Qué fascinante es andar por las calles históricas de Cuzco, antigua capital de los Incas! Cuzco, Perú.

ahora son ciudades famosas y grandes como Buenos Aires, Caracas y Santiago. El continente pasó por tres siglos de colonización, período en el cual la iglesia católica, las universidades, el sistema económico y político y la estructura social se establecieron bajo un estricto régimen español. Para *asegurar* su control sobre un territorio tan vasto y tan lejos de la *patria*, los españoles no quisieron dar privilegios, *derechos* o posiciones de gran importancia o *poder* a los indios o a los mestizos. Como *consecuencia surgieron* tres clases distintas: los españoles y los *criollos* (personas *nacidas* en América de padres españoles), los mestizos, y últimamente los indios. Éstos frecuentemente se vieron obligados a trabajar para los españoles en condiciones y situaciones deplorables.

ensure
homeland
rights
power/result/arose
Creoles/born

La independencia—A fines del siglo diez y ocho las ideas liberales empezaron a llegar a Sudamérica. España, invadida por los soldados franceses bajo Napoleón, *ya no* pudo mantener su control político y militar en el Nuevo Mundo. Los líderes hispanoamericanos como Bolívar (de Venezuela), O'Higgins (de Chile) y San Martín (de la Argentina), inspirados por las revoluciones francesa y norteamericana, reconocieron el momento en que iniciar la *lucha* por su independencia y libertad.

no longer

struggle

Machu Picchu, la
antigua ciudad perdida
de los Incas, está
situada a más de 8.000
pies de altura en los
Andes. Perú.

Después de una lucha *sumamente* larga y difícil, la mayoría de los países
hispanoamericanos habían ganado su independencia *hacia* 1830. Inmediata-
mente cada región empezó a buscar y *desarrollar* su propio sistema de gobierno. Pero a causa de la *falta* de experiencia política, y un *sinfín* de otras
razones, los años después de la independencia fueron marcados por la ines-
tabilidad. En algunos países llegaron al poder *jefes* políticos llamados "caudillos," que en muchos casos *se hicieron* dictadores.

Hoy día—Muchos problemas sociales todavía existen en la América del Sur
y se manifiestan en varias formas—la pobreza, la inflación increíble, la falta
de una buena educación para todos y más. Pero estos problemas y los esfuerzos para resolverlos han dado origen a una literatura extraordinaria. Autores como Gabriela Mistral (Premio Nobel de Literatura, 1945) y Pablo Ne-
ruda de Chile (Premio Nobel de Literatura, 1971), Jorge Luis Borges y Julio
Cortázar de la Argentina, Gabriel García Márquez de Colombia (Premio Nobel de Literatura, 1982), Mario Vargas Llosa del Perú y muchos otros han
ganado fama internacional por la calidad temática y estética de sus *obras*
literarias.

Mirando al futuro, podemos ver que este continente enorme, a causa

extremely
by about
develop
lack/endless number

bosses
became

works

Mujeres y niños vuelven a su pueblo situado en el altiplano de Bolivia, a más de 12.000 pies de altura.

de su población de más de doscientos millones de personas, sus *riquezas* naturales, su gran potencial, y sus problemas *no resueltos*, tendrá una influencia cada vez más profunda en la economía, la política, el pensamiento intelectual y el balance de poder del mundo.

resources

unresolved

¿CUÁNTO RECUERDA USTED?

Asociación. ¿Con qué palabras o frases asocia usted las referencias que siguen?

1. la geografía de la América del Sur
2. Aconcagua
3. pampa
4. Atacama
5. el Río Amazonas
6. inmigrantes europeos
7. Machu Picchu
8. Pizarro
9. Atahualpa
10. 1830
11. tres clases
12. Bolívar, O'Higgins, San Martín
13. independencia
14. caudillos
15. Premio Nobel de Literatura

INTEGRACIÓN VISUAL: CAPÍTULO 11 ■

EJERCICIO 11.1 Vocabulario, La estación de ferrocarril y Las llamadas telefónicas

EJERCICIO 11.2   El futuro

Ejemplo   ¿Qué hará Julia?
Escuchará la música.

Julia

EJERCICIO 11.3 El condicional

Esteban

Ejemplo   ¿Qué haría Esteban?
Dormiría en una hamaca.

EJERCICIO 11.4 Las comparaciones de igualdad

Luisa   Leti

Ejemplo   flaca
**Luisa es tan
flaca como Leti.**

Esteban   Pablo

Víctor

Marcelo

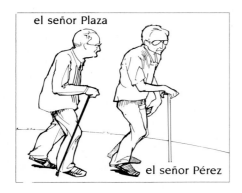

el señor Plaza

el señor Pérez

Oscar

Héctor

Paco   Carlos

Jaime   Lisa

EJERCICIO 11.5   Las comparaciones de desigualdad y los superlativos

Ejemplo   La falda de Tina es corta.
La falda de Nina es más corta.
La falda de Rita es la más
corta de las tres.

Tina   Nina   Rita

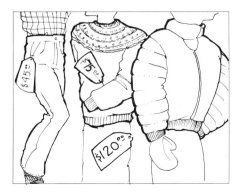

Fifi   Churro   Taco

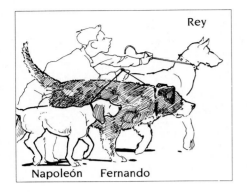

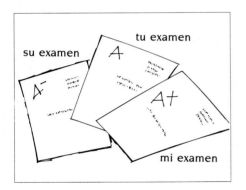

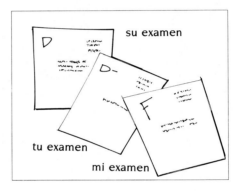

EJERCICIO 11.6 Los mandatos <u>tú</u>

Juanito

Ejemplo   ¿Qué le dice la madre a Juanito?
Acuéstate.

Juanito

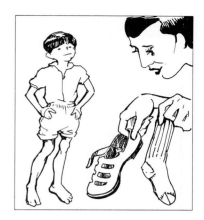

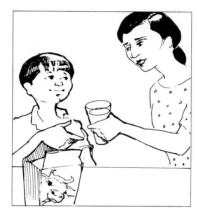

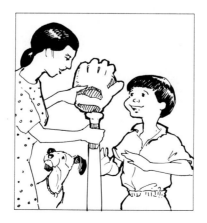

REPASO DE VOCABULARIO ACTIVO ▪

Adjetivos

cada	mejor
equivocado	ocupado
mayor	peor
menor	

Adverbios

bastante	más
demasiado	menos

Sustantivos

el andén	la guía telefónica	el (la) operador(a)
el aseo	el horario	el país
el billete	la llamada	el periódico
el boleto	común	la propina
de ida y vuelta	de cobro revertido	el quiosco
de primera clase	de larga distancia	la revista
de segunda clase	de persona a persona	la salida
la caricatura	la llegada	el servicio
el código de área	la línea	la taquilla
la demora	la maleta	el teléfono público
el equipaje	el maletero	el tren
la estación de ferrocarril	la noticia	

Verbos

callarse	olvidar
dejar	olvidarse (de)
marcar	telefonear

Expresiones idiomáticas

hacer una llamada
hacer la maleta
ponerse impaciente
el año que viene
la semana que viene

Expresiones de comparación

tan . . . como
tanto (-a, -os, -as) . . . como

AUTOEXAMEN Y REPASO #11 ■

I. Vocabulario

¿Qué palabras o expresiones asocia usted con las siguientes referencias?

1. el horario	4. el maletero	7. la llamada
2. la taquilla	5. el quiosco	8. la línea
3. el boleto	6. el periódico	9. el número

II. El futuro

Diga usted lo que las personas van a hacer en el año 2000.

Modelo   Carlos/vivir en Buenos Aires
Carlos vivirá en Buenos Aires.

1. Juanita y Mario/tener muchos hijos
2. yo/alquilar una casa en Acapulco
3. mi esposo(a) y yo/pasar un año en Europa
4. tú/hacer un viaje a Madrid
5. vosotros/volver a la universidad
6. Carlota/ir a Italia
7. Alberto/ser millonario
8. nosotros/poder ir a la luna
9. ustedes/trabajar en Nueva York

III. El condicional

Diga usted lo que las personas harían con un millón de dólares.

Modelo   Carlos/comprar una casa
Carlos compraría una casa.

1. Yo/comprar un Mercedes
2. Alicia/dar el dinero a los pobres
3. Pepe/poner el dinero en el banco
4. Nosotros/viajar a la América del Sur
5. Mónica y Lupe/salir de la universidad
6. Tú/tener muchas vacaciones
7. Ustedes/comer en restaurantes muy caros

IV. Las comparaciones de igualdad

Haga comparaciones de igualdad según los modelos.

Modelo   la clase de inglés/la clase de español (difícil)
La clase de inglés es tan difícil como la clase de español.

1. hombres/mujeres (inteligentes)
2. Roberto/Miguel (alto)
3. Lisa/Rosario (simpática)

Modelo   los Gutiérrez/los Gómez (hijas)
         Los Gutiérrez tienen tantas hijas como los Gómez.

4. los Gutiérrez/los Gómez (dinero)
5. los Gutiérrez/los Gómez (coches)
6. los Gutiérrez/los Gómez (ropa)

V.   Las comparaciones de desigualdad y los superlativos

Haga comparaciones de desigualdad según el modelo.

Modelo   Rodolfo es honesto.
         (Felipe) **Felipe es más honesto que Rodolfo.**
         (Alberto) **Alberto es el más honesto de los tres.**

1. Yo soy fuerte.   3. La carne es buena.
    (mi hermano)   (la ensalada)
    (mi primo)   (el postre)
2. Teresa es bonita.   4. Mis hermanos son malos.
    (Tina)   (mis primos)
    (Nina)   (mis primas)

VI.   Los mandatos <u>tú</u>, afirmativos y negativos

A. *Su madre le dice a usted que debe hacer las siguientes cosas.*

Modelo   volver a casa temprano
         Vuelve a casa temprano.

1. limpiar el cuarto   5. comer las legumbres
2. apagar la radio   6. ser bueno(a)
3. hacer la cama   7. cortarte el pelo
4. poner (*set*) la mesa   8. acostarte temprano

B. *Su madre le dice a usted que NO debe hacer las siguientes cosas.*

Modelo   acostarte tarde
         No te acuestes tarde.

1. beber cerveza   6. ser insolente
2. volver tarde a la casa   7. levantarte tarde
3. ir a la fiesta   8. preocuparte
4. decirme mentiras   9. ponerte impaciente
5. salir con esos muchachos   10. enojarte

VII.   Repaso del Capítulo 11

A. *Conteste.*

1. ¿Qué hará usted este sábado?
2. ¿Qué haría usted en Acapulco?
3. ¿Es usted tan inteligente como su hermano(a)?
4. ¿Tiene usted tantas camisetas como su hermano(a)?

5. ¿Trabaja usted tanto como su hermano(a)?
6. ¿Es usted más guapo(a) o menos guapo(a) que su hermano(a)?
7. ¿Es usted mayor o menor que su hermano(a)?
8. Quién es la persona más generosa de su familia?

B. *Traduzca.*

1. We will leave for the railroad station at 10:00.
2. Who will buy the tickets?
3. He said that we would arrive at midnight.
4. Pepe, would you be able to take my luggage?
5. Carmen has as many suitcases as I do.
6. She is as funny (amusing) as her brother.
7. She is more responsible than he is.
8. She is the best student in our Spanish class.
9. The train has arrived. Come here! Run!
10. Don't leave the magazine on the bench!

VIII. Repaso: pretérito vs. imperfecto; pronombres de complemento directo e indirecto

A. *En la estación de ferrocarril. Indique las experiencias de Gabriel en la estación de ferrocarril. Haga oraciones cambiando los verbos al pretérito o al imperfecto según las indicaciones.*

1. Gabriel/ser un estudiante universitario
2. el sábado pasado él/ir a la estación de ferrocarril
3. muchas personas allí/esperar los trenes
4. muchas personas/leer revistas y periódicos
5. Gabriel/comprar un boleto
6. Gabriel/sentarse en un banco
7. Gabriel/estar allí por dos horas
8. cuando el tren llegó, él/dormir
9. alguien/despertarlo
10. él/correr al andén
11. él/ver el tren
12. haber/muchas personas en el tren
13. Gabriel/subir al tren en el último momento
14. ¡qué suerte (*luck*)/tener!

B. *Conteste las preguntas para indicar lo que usted hará. Cambie los complementos directos e indirectos a pronombres.*

Modelo   ¿Vas a cambiar los cheques?
         Sí, los cambiaré.

1. ¿Vas a escribir a tus abuelos?
2. ¿Vas a hacer las reservaciones?
3. ¿Vas a traer las maletas?
4. ¿Vas a mandar el boleto a tu hermano?
5. ¿Vas a mostrar el horario a tu madre?
6. ¿Vas a dar una propina al maletero?

▪C A P Í T U L O▪

12

VOCABULARIO LA CARRETERA ▪

En la **estación de servicio/gasolina**	service/gas station
el empleado tiene que	
llenar el **tanque** con **gasolina,**	to fill; tank; gasoline
cambiar la **llanta (desinflada),**	(flat) tire
limpiar el **parabrisas,**	windshield
revisar el aceite,	to check
el **aire** en las llantas	air
y la **batería.**	battery
Algunas cosas no **funcionan (funcionar).**	to work [machine]
Es necesario **arreglar/reparar**	to fix, repair
el **limpiaparabrisas,**	windshield wiper
los **frenos** y	brakes
el **motor.**	motor

Andamos por el **camino** y	road
por la **carretera.**	highway
Vamos a **cruzar**	to cross
el **puente** y	bridge
la **frontera.**	border
¡No debe **pararse** allí!	to stop
¡No debe **estacionarse** allí!	to park

Hay mucho **tráfico/tránsito.**	traffic
Un **camión** y un coche tuvieron	truck
un **accidente.**	accident
El **policía** acaba de llegar.	policeman
Quiere ver la **licencia de chófer.**	driver's license
¿Tiene **seguro de automóvil?**	car insurance
¿A cuánta **velocidad** viajaban?	speed
¿A cuántas **millas** por hora?	miles
¿A cuántos **kilómetros?**	kilometers
¿Tendrán que pagar una **multa?**	fine (ticket)

Las direcciones:	
Es necesario **doblar**	to turn
a la derecha	to the right
en la **esquina.**	corner
Y al llegar al **semáforo**	traffic light
doble **a la izquierda.**	to the left
Es necesario **seguir** (i, i)	to continue, follow
recto/derecho	straight, straight ahead
una **cuadra/manzana** más.	block

Expresiones y palabras útiles:	
darse prisa	to hurry up
tener cuidado	to be careful
ahora mismo	right now
otra vez	again
despacio	slowly
pronto	soon, right away
¡Caramba!	Oh, my gosh!
¡Claro!	Of course!
¡Socorro!	Help!
¡Lo siento mucho!	I'm so sorry!
¡Qué barbaridad!	How awful!
¡Qué lástima!	What a shame!
¡Qué lío!	What a mess!

EJERCICIO 1   La carretera

Conteste en oraciones completas según el dibujo.

1.   ¿Dónde está el coche VW?
2.   ¿Cómo se llama la estación de servicio?
3.   ¿Qué ponen en el tanque?
4.   ¿Qué más hace el hombre que llena el tanque?
5.   ¿En qué condición está una de las llantas del coche?
6.   ¿Qué va a hacer el hombre que lleva la llanta?
7.   Probablemente, ¿qué hará el hombre que examina el motor?
8.   ¿Quién es el hombre que está enfrente del semáforo?
9.   Según el policía, ¿qué debe hacer el camión?
10.   El otro coche, ¿debe seguir recto o pararse?
11.   ¿Cómo sabemos que el semáforo no funciona?
12.   ¿Qué acaba de cruzar el camión?
13.   ¿Dónde está el otro coche? ¿Cuál es el número de la carretera?
14.   Al llegar a la esquina, ¿en qué dirección debemos doblar para llegar al centro? ¿Cuántos kilómetros tenemos que viajar?
15.   ¿Qué ve usted en la distancia?

EJERCICIO 2   Preguntas personales y generales

Conteste en oraciones completas.

1.   ¿Ha tenido usted un accidente? ¿Dónde? ¿Cuándo?
2.   ¿Ha recibido usted una multa? ¿Por qué?
3.   ¿Siempre tiene usted cuidado cuando maneja?
4.   Generalmente, ¿manejan los hombres más despacio o más rápidamente que las mujeres?
5.   Cuando su coche tiene una llanta desinflada, ¿puede usted cambiarla?
6.   Cuando el motor de su coche no funciona, ¿puede usted arreglar o repararlo? ¿y los frenos? ¿y el limpiaparabrisas?
7.   ¿Tiene usted que pagar para estacionarse en esta universidad? ¿Cuánto?
8.   Cuando usted lleva su coche a la estación de servicio, ¿qué cosas hace usted generalmente? ¿Y qué cosas hace el empleado de la estación?

EJERCICIO 3   Asociación

¿Qué palabras asocia usted con los siguientes verbos y sustantivos?

Modelo   limpiar
el parabrisas

1.	revisar	5.	cruzar	9.	el semáforo
2.	cambiar	6.	doblar	10.	la esquina
3.	arreglar o reparar	7.	pararse	11.	el tanque
4.	llenar	8.	el parabrisas	12.	el policía

Llene el tanque, por favor. Caracas, Venezuela.

EJERCICIO 4   ¡Caramba!

¿Qué diría usted en las siguientes situaciones? Use las expresiones exclamativas del vocabulario.

> Modelo   Usted ha tenido un accidente en el coche nuevo de su padre.
> **¡Qué barbaridad!**
> etc.

1. Un amigo suyo ha tenido un accidente horrible y está en el hospital.
2. Usted está manejando por el desierto de Arizona y . . . ¡no hay más gasolina en su tanque!
3. Usted está en el centro de la ciudad de Nueva York y ¡su coche tiene una llanta desinflada!
4. El policía le pide a usted su licencia de chófer y ¡usted no la tiene!
5. Llueve mucho y ¡su limpiaparabrisas no funciona!
6. Usted abre la puerta de su coche y ve que todo adentro está muy, muy sucio. Hay papeles, comida vieja, ropa sucia y vieja, etc., etc., por todas partes.
7. Usted aprende que el coche del profesor (de la profesora) fue destruido (*destroyed*) en una catástrofe natural.
8. Su padre le pregunta a usted si quiere un coche nuevo como regalo.

CONVERSACIÓN ■

*El viajero y su familia, después de muchas horas de viaje en coche, llegan a una **estación de servicio.***

VIAJERO	**Parémonos** en esta estación de servicio. Necesitamos **gasolina** y direcciones para llegar al centro.
EMPLEADO	Buenos días, señor. ¿Qué clase de **gasolina** quiere? ¿regular o sin plomo?
VIAJERO	Sin plomo. **Llene** el **tanque,** por favor.
EMPLEADO	¿Qué tal el **aceite**? **¿Quiere que** lo **revise?**
VIAJERO	Sí, y **hágame** el favor de limpiar el **parabrisas. . . .**
EMPLEADO	Bueno, señor, son diez y ocho mil pesos en total.
VIAJERO	Bien. . . . A propósito, ¿puede usted darme las direcciones de cómo llegar al centro?
EMPLEADO	Mire, señor. Al llegar a aquel **semáforo, doble a la izquierda** y **siga derecho** unos dos **kilómetros** hasta encontrarse con la avenida principal.
VIAJERO	Muchísimas gracias.
EMPLEADO	No hay de qué. ¡Que **tengan** un buen viaje!

The traveler and his family, after many hours of car travel, arrive at a service station.

TRAVELER	*Let's stop at this gas station. We need gas and directions to get downtown.*
EMPLOYEE	*Good day, sir. What kind of gasoline do you want? Regular or unleaded?*
TRAVELER	*Unleaded. Fill the tank, please.*
EMPLOYEE	*How's the oil? Do you want me to take a look at it?*
TRAVELER	*Yes, and please clean the windshield. . . .*
EMPLOYEE	*Well, sir, that will be eighteen thousand pesos total.*
TRAVELER	*Fine. . . . By the way, can you give me directions on how to get downtown?*
EMPLOYEE	*Look, sir. When you get to that traffic light, turn to the left and continue straight ahead for more or less two kilometers until you get to the main avenue.*
TRAVELER	*Thanks a lot.*
EMPLOYEE	*You're welcome. Have a good trip!*

PREGUNTAS

Conteste en oraciones completas.

1. ¿Dónde está el viajero?
2. ¿Qué necesita?
3. ¿Qué hace el empleado?
4. ¿Cuánto cuesta?
5. Al llegar al semáforo, ¿en qué dirección se dobla?
6. ¿Está la avenida central lejos de allí? ¿A cuánta distancia?

ESTRUCTURA ■

El subjuntivo
The subjunctive mood

The indicative is an objective mood for stating facts or communicating specific knowledge. All the tenses you have studied to this point are indicative tenses.

The subjunctive, in contrast, is a subjective mood for conveying a speaker's wishes, for expressing a speaker's attitudes, hopes, fears, doubts, uncertainties, and other emotional reactions to events and actions.

In this and subsequent chapters you will be introduced to the forms for the four tenses of the subjunctive (present, present perfect, imperfect, past perfect) plus the uses of the subjunctive forms.

I. El presente de subjuntivo: Formación
The present subjunctive: Formation

Observe the forms of the verbs used to make formal commands and to convey the speaker's wishes, doubts, or emotional reactions regarding the actions of others.

> **Tenga** usted cuidado y **maneje** despacio, por favor.
> *Be careful and drive slowly, please.*
> Su madre quiere que usted **tenga** cuidado y que **maneje** despacio.
> *Her mother wants you to be careful and to drive slowly.*
> Espero que ustedes **tengan** cuidado y que **manejen** despacio.
> *I hope that you all are careful and that you drive slowly.*
> Dudan que **tengamos** cuidado y que **manejemos** despacio.
> *They doubt that we will be careful and that we will drive slowly.*

NOTE: The present subjunctive is usually translated like the present indicative, although it can also have the meaning of *may* or *will*.

The present subjunctive of regular **-ar, -er,** or **-ir** verbs is formed by using the **yo** form of the present indicative minus -o and adding the endings indicated.

-ar endings	Modelo	**estudiar**	**-er, -ir** endings	Modelo	**hacer**
-e	estudi**ø**	estudi**e**	**-a**	hag**ø**	hag**a**
-es		estudi**es**	**-as**		hag**as**
-e		estudi**e**	**-a**		hag**a**
-emos		estudi**emos**	**-amos**		hag**amos**
-éis		estudi**éis**	**-áis**		hag**áis**
-en		estudi**en**	**-an**		hag**an**

Otros modelos

hablar	habl**ø**	habl**e**, habl**es**, habl**e**, habl**emos**, habl**éis**, habl**en**
comer	com**ø**	com**a**, com**as**, com**a**, com**amos**, com**áis**, com**an**
conocer	conozc**ø**	conozc**a** conozc**as**, conozc**a**, conozc**amos**, conozc**áis**, conozc**an**
vivir	viv**ø**	viv**a**, viv**as**, viv**a**, viv**amos**, viv**áis**, viv**an**
salir	salg**ø**	salg**a**, salg**as**, salg**a**, salg**amos**, salg**áis**, salg**an**

NOTE 1: Some verbs have spelling changes in the present subjunctive in order to maintain the same sound as in the infinitive.

-gar $(g \rightarrow gu)$	lle**gue**, lle**gues**, lle**gue**, lle**guemos**, lle**guéis**, lle**guen**
-car $(c \rightarrow qu)$	to**que**, to**ques**, to**que**, etc.
-zar $(z \rightarrow c)$	abra**ce**, abra**ces**, abra**ce**, etc.

NOTE 2: Stem-changing verbs ending in **-ar** and **-er** have stem changes in the present subjunctive in the same persons as the present indicative.

pensar (ie)	p**ie**nse, p**ie**nses, p**ie**nse, pensemos, penséis, p**ie**nsen
volver (ue)	v**ue**lva, v**ue**lvas, v**ue**lva, volvamos, volváis, v**ue**lvan

NOTE 3: Stem-changing verbs ending in **-ir** have an additional change $(o \rightarrow u$ and $e \rightarrow i)$ in the **nosotros** and **vosotros** forms.

dormir (ue, u)	d**ue**rma, d**ue**rmas, d**ue**rma, d**u**rmamos, d**u**rmáis, d**ue**rman
preferir (ie, i)	pref**ie**ra, pref**ie**ras, pref**ie**ra, pref**i**ramos, pref**i**ráis, pref**ie**ran
seguir (i, i)	s**i**ga, s**i**gas, s**i**ga, s**i**gamos, s**i**gáis, s**i**gan

Los verbos irregulares en el presente de subjuntivo

Study the irregular subjunctive forms of these six verbs.

dar	dé, des, dé, demos, deis, den
estar	esté, estés, esté, estemos, estéis, estén
ir	vaya, vayas, vaya, vayamos, vayáis, vayan
saber	sepa, sepas, sepa, sepamos, sepáis, sepan
ser	sea, seas, sea, seamos, seáis, sean
haber	haya, hayas, haya, hayamos, hayáis, hayan

> NOTE: The present subjunctive forms of **haber** are used to form the present perfect subjunctive (which you will study in Chapter 13); **haya** is also the subjunctive form of **hay** (*there is, there are*).

The subjunctive forms presented in this section will be practiced in context in Sections II to V of Chapter 12 and I to III of Chapter 13.

II. Los mandatos usted, ustedes y nosotros (*let's*)
The usted, ustedes, and nosotros (let's) commands

A. Los mandatos usted y ustedes

You have been using and hearing formal command forms of verbs since Chapter 1 (**escriba el ejercicio, contesten en oraciones completas,** etc.). These command forms are identical to the subjunctive forms. Note that the forms for the negative **tú** (informal) commands that you studied in Chapter 11 are also identical to the subjunctive.

Observe the **usted** and **ustedes** (formal) affirmative and negative commands and the change of position of the object pronouns.

Cierre la puerta, por favor.	*Close the door, please.*
Cierren las ventanas también.	*Close the windows, too.*
¡No **salga** usted!	*Don't leave!*
¡No **salgan** ustedes!	*Don't leave!*
Levántese ahora mismo.	*Get up right now.*
No **se siente.**	*Don't sit down.*
Léamelo, por favor.	*Read it to me, please.*
No **se lo lea** a él.	*Don't read it to him.*

The **usted** and **ustedes** affirmative and negative commands are the same as the third person singular and plural present subjunctive forms.

> NOTE: In all affirmative commands the object pronouns are attached at the end; an accent mark is written in the command form on the syllable normally stressed.

In all negative commands the object pronouns are placed *before* the verb.

En la Plaza de la Independencia se observa la arquitectura colonial de Quito. Quito. Ecuador.

Vista panorámica de los Andes y la capital chilena. Santiago, Chile.

El Teatro Colón es impresionante ejemplo de la vida cultural de Buenos Aires. Buenos Aires, Argentina.

LA AMÉRICA DEL SUR

Costa y montañas forman parte del paisaje (*landscape*) hermoso de Venezuela. Puerto de la Guaira, Caracas,

Caracas, como otras capitales sudamericanas, es
ciudad moderna y cosmopolita. Caracas, Venezue

Qué maravilloso es esquiar en los Andes. Portillo,
hile.

El Río Urubamba pasa
por los Andes cerca
de Machu Picchu. Perú.

Escena típica en la pampa argentina.
Argentina.

as incomparables cataratas del
guazú se encuentran en la frontera

EJERCICIO 5 Pues (*well*), ¡hágalo!

La profesora (el profesor) de la clase de español tiene ganas de hacer muchas cosas diferentes. Dígale que haga las cosas indicadas.

Modelo   Tengo ganas de bailar.
          Pues, ¡baile (usted)!

Tengo ganas de . . .

1. comer una paella
2. tomar una copa de vino
3. descansar
4. leer una novela
5. ir a la Florida

6. nadar en el océano
7. dormir en la playa
8. jugar al tenis
9. salir de la clase

EJERCICIO 6 Estudiantes y profesores

A. *Usted es un(a) estudiante en la clase de español. Dé usted mandatos al profesor (a la profesora).*

Modelo   abrir la ventana
          Abra la ventana, por favor.

1. hablar más despacio
2. escribir la respuesta en la pizarra
3. traducir la oración
4. repetir la pregunta otra vez

5. cerrar la puerta
6. escuchar a los estudiantes
7. leer la oración otra vez

B. *Usted es el (la) profesor(a) de la clase de español. Dé usted mandatos a los estudiantes.*

Modelo   estudiar el vocabulario
          Estudien el vocabulario.

1. hacer la tarea
2. venir a clase a tiempo
3. aprender los verbos
4. contestar las preguntas
5. ir a la pizarra ahora mismo

6. sentarse, por favor
7. callarse, por favor
8. darse prisa, por favor
9. volver pronto
10. pensar

EJERCICIO 7 En la estación de servicio

A. *Su coche necesita mucha atención. Hoy, al llegar a la estación de servicio, dígale al empleado que haga las cosas indicadas.*

Modelo   las llantas/cambiar
          Cámbielas, por favor.

1. el aceite/cambiar
2. el tanque/llenar
3. el motor/arreglar
4. los frenos/revisar

5. el parabrisas/limpiar
6. el mapa/traerme
7. la tarjeta de crédito/devolverme

B. *En otra ocasión su coche todavía necesita mucha atención, pero usted tiene mucha prisa (are in a hurry). Dígale al empleado que NO haga las siguientes cosas.*

Modelo   la llanta/cambiar
No la cambie.

1. la batería/cambiar
2. el aceite/revisar
3. el limpiaparabrisas/reparar
4. las ventanas/limpiar

5. el tanque/llenar
6. la llanta desinflada/devolverme
7. las malas noticias/darme

EJERCICIO 8   Las direcciones

Dé usted direcciones a unas personas que buscan la universidad.

Modelo   ir a la calle Juárez
Vayan a la calle Juárez.

1. seguir recto cuatro cuadras
2. pararse en la esquina de Juárez y Morelos
3. doblar a la izquierda
4. cruzar el puente

5. pasar cinco semáforos
6. doblar a la derecha
7. seguir tres cuadras más
8. estacionarse enfrente de la biblioteca

ACTIVIDAD   El laberinto

a. Dos estudiantes salen de la clase.
b. Los otros estudiantes cambian la posición de las sillas y de los escritorios, etc., formando un laberinto.
c. Los dos estudiantes, uno(a) con los ojos cubiertos (covered), entran en la clase. El (la) estudiante con los ojos cubiertos pasa por el laberinto, siguiendo las direcciones del otro (de la otra) estudiante.¿ Tal vez (perhaps) una sorpresa lo (la) espera al final(?)

EJERCICIO 9   Consejos (advice) para Doña Mercedes

Dígale usted a Doña Mercedes lo que debe hacer en cada situación.

Modelo   Doña Mercedes tiene sed.
¡Beba una Coca-Cola!

1. Doña Mercedes tiene mucha hambre.
2. Doña Mercedes tiene mucho frío.
3. Doña Mercedes ha recibido un paquete muy grande en el correo.
4. Doña Mercedes tiene un libro muy interesante que usted quiere leer.
5. Doña Mercedes ha trabajado demasiado y está muy cansada.
6. Doña Mercedes está muy enferma.
7. Doña Mercedes tiene tres coches y necesita dinero.

8. Doña Mercedes está caminando por el parque y hay nieve y hielo en el camino.
9. Doña Mercedes ha preparado unas galletas deliciosas y usted tiene hambre.
10. Doña Mercedes tiene ganas de visitar a sus nietos.

B. Los mandatos <u>nosotros</u>   *The* let's *commands*

In Spanish there are two ways of expressing the command or suggestion *let's*.

El mandato <u>nosotros</u>: subjuntivo

Entremos en la pastelería.	*Let's go into the pastry shop.*
Compremos una torta.	*Let's buy a cake.*
Llevémosla a casa.	*Let's take it home.*
No **la comamos** ahora mismo.	*Let's not eat it right now.*
¡Salgamos!	*Let's leave!*

The first person plural (**nosotros** form) of the present subjunctive can be used to form the *let's* command.

> NOTE 1:   To form the affirmative *let's* command of reflexive verbs, the final **-s** is dropped before adding the reflexive pronoun **nos.**

levantemos → **levantemo** + **nos** → **¡Levantémonos!**
   But the negative is:
¡No nos levantemos!

> NOTE 2:   The verb **ir** or **irse** has an irregular affirmative *let's* command:

¡Vamos! or **¡Vámonos!**   *Let's go!*
   But the negative is the same as the subjunctive:
¡No vayamos! or **¡No nos vayamos!**   *Let's not go!*

El mandato <u>nosotros</u>: *vamos a*

Observe the contrast between these affirmative and negative commands.

¡Vamos a nadar!   *Let's swim!*
¡No nademos!   *Let's not swim!*

The affirmative *let's* command can also be formed by using **vamos a** + infinitive. However, the negative *let's* command returns to the subjunctive form.

EJERCICIO 10   ¡Sí! ¡Hagámoslo!

A. *Indique que ustedes quieren hacer las actividades indicadas.*

   Modelo   ¡Vamos a salir!
         ¡Sí! Salgamos.

Por la noche . . .

1. ¡Vamos a comer!	4. ¡Vamos a cantar!
2. ¡Vamos a beber!	5. ¡Vamos a andar por la ciudad!
3. ¡Vamos a bailar!	6. ¡Vamos a divertirnos!

Por la mañana . . .

7. ¡Vamos a levantarnos!	10. ¡Vamos a vestirnos!
8. ¡Vamos a lavarnos!	11. ¡Vamos a hacer un viaje!
9. ¡Vamos a peinarnos!	

Por la tarde . . .

12. ¡Vamos a la playa!	15. ¡Vamos a tomar el sol!
13. ¡Vamos a nadar!	16. ¡Vamos a escuchar la música!
14. ¡Vamos a jugar al vólibol!	17. ¡Y . . . ahora, vamos a volver a casa

B. *Indique que ustedes NO quieren participar en algunas de las actividades indicadas.*

> Modelo ¡Vamos a salir!
> **No, no salgamos.**

1. ¡Vamos a comer! etc.

C. *Usted y sus amigos tienen un día libre sin clases. Ustedes indican en qué actividades quieren participar.*

> Modelo **Durmamos hasta las diez.**

1. . . . etc.

III. El subjuntivo en mandatos indirectos
The subjunctive in indirect (implied) commands

You have already used the subjunctive form to express a direct command (**¡Venga! ¡Traigan las maletas! Pepito, ¡no corras!**). An indirect or implied command, however, expresses the speaker's wish, desire, preference, recommendation, request, etc., *that someone else do something.* The subjunctive mood is used to express indirect or implied commands.

Quiero que usted **venga** ahora mismo.	*I want you to come[1] right now.*
Recomiendo que traigan las maletas.	*I recommend that you bring the suitcases.*
Pepito, **insisto (en) que** no **corras.**	*Pepito, I insist that you not run.*

Notice that the first clause, expressing the speaker's wish to influence (*I want . . . , I recommend . . . , I insist . . .*), is in the *indicative;* the second clause (*. . . you to come, . . . that you bring the suitcases, . . . that you not run*), is in the *subjunctive.* In Spanish the two clauses are linked by **que.**

Subject #1 influences		Subject #2 influenced
expression of wish to influence	+ **que** +	action influenced
indicative		*subjunctive*

NOTE 1: After the verb that expresses the wish to influence, Spanish uses **que** + subjunctive whereas English, in some instances, uses an object plus infinitive.

Some verbs expressing indirect or implied commands (the wish to influence) include:

decir (i)	*to tell*	Te[1] **digo que** no lo[2] **hagas.**
desear	*to wish, want*	**Deseo que** me lo **muestres.**
insistir (en)	*to insist (on)*	**Insisto que salgas** ahora.
pedir (i, i)	*to request*	Les[1] **pido que** lo **terminen** pronto.
preferir (ie, i)	*to prefer*	**Prefieren que** no **vayamos.**
querer (ie)	*to want*	**Quieren que** les **escribamos.**
recomendar (ie)	*to recommend*	**Recomiendan que llame** frecuentemente.
sugerir (ie, i)	*to suggest*	**Sugerimos que** no **se preocupen.**

NOTE 1: **Pedir** and **decir** are most commonly used with indirect-object pronouns.

NOTE 2: Observe that, in contrast to their position in affirmative direct commands, the direct-object, indirect-object, and reflexive pronouns *precede* the conjugated verb just as they do in the indicative.

If there is no change of subject after the verb that expresses the wish to influence, use the infinitive, not **que** + subjunctive.

ONE SUBJECT	VS.	CHANGE OF SUBJECT
Quiero **ver**lo.		Quiero que tú lo **veas.**
Prefiero **comprar** éste.		Prefiero que Carlos **compre** ése.

EJERCICIO 11   No quiero hacerlo.

A. *Cuando su hermano(a) le pregunta si usted quiere hacer las cosas indicadas, responda que NO. Siga el modelo.*

Modelo   ¿Quieres tocar el piano?
   No, quiero que tú toques el piano.
   (o)
   No, quiero que tú lo toques.

1. ¿Quieres hacer las camas?
2. ¿Quieres limpiar la casa?
3. ¿Quieres preparar la comida?
4. ¿Quieres beber el jugo de tomate?
5. ¿Quieres comer los guisantes?
6. ¿Quieres lavar los platos?
7. ¿Quieres vestir al bebé?
8. ¿Quieres devolver los discos?
9. ¿Quieres apagar las luces?

B. *Su hermano(a) no quiere hacer las cosas tampoco. Sugiera usted que su hermanita Tina las haga.*

Modelo No quiero tocar el piano.
Sugiero que Tina toque el piano.
(o)
Sugiero que Tina lo toque.

1. No quiero hacer las camas.
2. No quiero limpiar la casa.
3. No quiero preparar la comida.
4. No quiero beber el jugo de tomate.
5. No quiero comer los guisantes.
6. No quiero lavar los platos.
7. No quiero vestir al bebé.
8. No quiero devolver los discos a los vecinos.
9. No quiero apagar las luces.

EJERCICIO 12 Recomendaciones del (de la) profesor(a)

A. *Su profesor(a) insiste en que ustedes **hablen** en español. Sustituya el verbo que expresa influencia según el modelo.*

Modelo recomendar
El (la) profesor(a) recomienda que hablemos en español.

1. desear
2. querer
3. sugerir
4. preferir
5. decirnos
6. pedirnos
7. insistir en

B. *¿Qué otras recomendaciones tiene el (la) profesor(a)? Responda según el modelo.*

Modelo estudiar
Recomienda que estudiemos.

1. hacer la tarea
2. escribir los ejercicios
3. ir al laboratorio
4. repetir las palabras
5. venir a clase todos los días
6. llegar a tiempo
7. escuchar bien
8. ser estudiantes buenos
9. no dormirnos en la clase

EJERCICIO 13 Preferencias de sus padres

*Indique usted si sus padres prefieren que usted **haga** o que **no haga** las siguientes cosas.*

Modelo acostarse tarde
Prefieren que no me acueste tarde.

1. acostarse temprano
2. levantarse tarde
3. cortarse el pelo frecuentemente
4. invitar a amigos a la casa
5. traer bebidas alcohólicas a la casa
6. fumar
7. leer revistas pornográficas
8. ver películas que tienen mucha violencia
9. escuchar la música "roc"
10. gastar mucho dinero
11. ahorrar mucho dinero
12. hacer llamadas de cobro revertido
13. recibir buenas notas

EJERCICIO 14   Expresión personal

Indique en qué maneras usted quiere influenciar las acciones de otras personas.
Complete con tantas variaciones como posible.

1. Quiero que mis padres . . .
2. Recomiendo que mi profesor(a) . . .
3. Insisto en que mi compañero(a) de cuarto . . .
4. Prefiero que mi novio(a) . . .
5. Le pido a mi hermano(a) menor que . . .

IV. El subjuntivo con expresiones de emoción
The subjunctive with expressions of emotion

When the speaker expresses emotion/feelings (glad, hopeful, sorry, etc.) *about
the actions or condition of another subject* (whether person or thing), the
subjunctive is used.

Siento que Jaime **esté** tan enfermo.	*I am sorry that Jaime is so sick.*
Espero que la ambulancia **llegue** pronto.	*I hope that the ambulance arrives soon.*

The first clause, expressing the speaker's emotion/feelings, is in the *indicative*;
the second clause is in the *subjunctive*.

expression of emotion	+	**que**	+	actions (condition) of another subject
indicative				*subjunctive*

Some verbs expressing emotion include:

alegrarse (de)	*to be glad (about)*	**Me alegro que estés** aquí.
esperar	*to hope*	**Espero que podamos** ir al cine.
sentir (ie, i)	*to be sorry, regret*	**Siento que haga** tanto frío.

temer	*to fear*	**Temen que llueva.**
tener miedo (de)	*to be afraid*	**Tengo miedo de que haya** un problema.

If there is no change of subject after the expression of emotion, the infinitive is used, not **que** + subjunctive.

ONE SUBJECT   vs.   CHANGE OF SUBJECT

Espero **ir.**   Espero que Pepita **vaya.**

EJERCICIO 15   Temores (*fears*) y esperanzas (*hopes*)

A. *Usted está en el centro de una ciudad grande, en su carro, y **teme** que haya muchos problemas. Indique lo que usted teme según el modelo.*

Modelo   La batería no tiene agua.
          Temo que la batería no tenga agua.

1. Una llanta está desinflada.
2. El carro necesita aceite.
3. El motor no anda bien.
4. El tanque no tiene gasolina.
5. Los frenos no funcionan bien.
6. ¡No hay una estación de servicio aquí!

B. *Ahora exprese lo que usted **espera** según el modelo.*

Modelo   Alguien me ayuda.
          Espero que alguien me ayude.

1. El policía viene.
2. Alguien llega.
3. Alguien se para aquí.
4. Alguien trae gasolina.
5. Alguien llama a casa.
6. Mi madre no se preocupa.
7. Mi padre no se enoja.
8. Mis padres entienden el problema.
9. El mecánico no cobra demasiado.
10. Mis padres me prestan un poco de dinero.

EJERCICIO 16   Su reacción

*Indique su reacción favorable o desfavorable a cada situación. Use **me alegro de que** . . . o **siento que** . . . según los modelos.*

Modelos   No tenemos un examen hoy.
           Me alegro de que no tengamos un examen hoy.
           Carlos está enfermo.
           Siento que Carlos esté enfermo.

1. Hace sol hoy.
2. Lloverá mañana.
3. (Nombre) no está aquí hoy.
4. No hay clase mañana.
5. El examen final será difícil.
6. Mi compañero(a) de cuarto tiene un resfriado.
7. Mi mejor amigo sale de la universidad.
8. Los estudiantes no toman drogas.
9. Mis padres vienen a visitarme.
10. Hay una fiesta muy grande este fin de semana

EJERCICIO 17 Expresión personal

¿Qué posibles acciones de otras personas le causan a usted estas emociones?
Complete con tantas variaciones como posible.

1. Tengo miedo de que . . .
2. Me alegro de que . . .
3. Espero que . . .
4. Siento que . . .

V. El subjuntivo con expresiones de duda, negación e incredulidad
The subjunctive with expressions of doubt, denial, and disbelief

When the speaker expresses doubt, uncertainty, or disbelief *about the actions of someone else,* or denies those actions, the subjunctive is used.

Dudo que puedan hacerlo.	*I doubt that they can do it.*
Niegan que Franco **tenga** la información.	*They deny that Franco has the information.*

The first clause, expressing the speaker's doubt, denial, or disbelief, is in the *indicative*; the second clause is in the *subjunctive*.

expression of doubt/ denial/disbelief	que	actions of someone else
indicative		*subjunctive*

Some expressions of doubt, uncertainty, denial, and disbelief include:

dudar	*to doubt*	**Dudo que** lo **traiga.**
no estar seguro	*not to be sure*	**No estamos seguros que** lo **entiendan.**
negar (ie)	*to deny*	**Niega que sepamos** hacerlo.
no creer	*not to believe*	**No creo que recuerde** el incidente.

NOTE 1: **No dudar, no negar, creer,** and **estar seguro** as expressions of certainty would use the indicative, not the subjunctive.

Creo que **sabe** la respuesta.   *I believe (am sure) that he knows the answer.*

Hagas lo que hagas, siempre hay un modelo especial de Yumas para ti.

Yumas
Tu próxima marca.

Las carreteras extensas y modernas nos llevan por las ciudades de Latinoamérica. Buenos Aires, Argentina.

NOTE 2: Expressions of certainty may become expressions of doubt when used in the interrogative form.

¿Crees que **sepa** la respuesta? *Do you think (not sure) that he knows the answer?*

EJERCICIO 18 Opiniones

Indique si usted **cree** *o* **duda** *las generalizaciones siguientes.*

Modelo Los coches americanos *son* inferiores.
Yo creo que los coches americanos *son* inferiores.
(o)
Yo dudo que los coches americanos *sean* inferiores.

1. Las mujeres son más inteligentes que los hombres.
2. Los profesores son más inteligentes que los alumnos.
3. Los hombres en esta clase son machos.
4. Los estudiantes en esta clase son superiores.
5. Los hombres prefieren a las mujeres inteligentes.
6. Las mujeres prefieren a los hombres ricos.
7. El gobierno (*government*) americano es bueno.
8. La guerra (*war*) es inevitable.
9. La inflación es incontrolable.

EJERCICIO 19 Tú y yo, dudas y negaciones

Usted y un compañero(a) de la clase de español deben hacerse las siguientes declaraciones. Respóndanse usando

Dudo que . . .   **Niego que** . . . o
No estoy seguro que . . .   **No creo que.** . . .

Modelo   (#1) Soy muy, muy rico(a).
         (#2) **No creo que** (etc.) **seas muy, muy rico.**

1. Soy muy, muy inteligente.   5. Soy muy, muy guapo(a).
2. Sé todas las respuestas.   6. Tengo un(a) novio(a) fantástico(a).
3. Gano mil dólares por mes.   7. (otras declaraciones originales . . .)
4. Manejo un Rolls Royce.

EJERCICIO 20   Preguntas personales y conversación

Contesten en oraciones completas y discutan (discuss) *sus opiniones.*

1. ¿Cree usted que el dinero sea indispensable? ¿Por qué?
2. ¿Cree usted que el amor sea indispensable? ¿Por qué?
3. ¿Qué duda usted? Explique por qué.
   ¿ . . . que eliminen las armas nucleares?
   ¿ . . . que eliminen la pobreza (poverty)?
   ¿ . . . que encuentren un remedio al cáncer?
4. ¿Qué espera usted? Explique por qué.
   ¿ . . . que sigamos la exploración de los planetas?
   ¿ . . . que usted y su familia puedan visitar la luna?
   ¿ . . . usemos menos energía nuclear?
   ¿ . . . que podamos controlar la población del mundo?
   ¿ . . . que eliminemos los cigarrillos?

Cada año hay más tránsito y
más contaminación del aire.
México, D.F.

ACTIVIDAD

Usted y su novio(a) son estudiantes en dos escuelas o universidades diferentes que están muy lejos la una de la otra. Quieren verse durante las vacaciones de primavera y hacen sus planes. Usted escribe una carta indicándole a él/ella lo que usted desea o espera que hagan, sus posibles dudas o temores, etc.

PANORAMA CULTURAL ▪

Voces sudamericanas

Cada país hispano de la América del Sur tiene su propia personalidad por su historia, su posición geográfica, su clima, el origen étnico de su gente y su desarrollo económico, social y político.

    A *continuación* podemos leer los "testimonios" personales de dos argen-   *following*
tinos y de un peruano para ver cómo cada uno percibe de un punto de vista distinto a su país natal.

Pregunta: Cuando usted dice "soy argentino", ¿qué *quiere decir*?   *mean*

ANA (30 años, profesora): "Para mí ser argentina no es *solamente* haber nacido   *only*
en esta tierra, sino amarla con sus defectos y sus virtudes. *Más aún*, siento   *even more*

La calle Florida es una de las calles mas famosas de Buenos Aires a causa de sus tiendas finas, hoteles y otros negocios.

un profundo orgullo cuando, al estar en un país extranjero, me preguntan de qué nacionalidad soy, pues aquí están mis *raíces* y todo aquello que quiero."

roots

MARTIN (36 años, ingeniero civil): "En general, los argentinos, especialmente los que están viajando *en el exterior*, sienten gran orgullo cuando pronuncian la frase 'yo soy argentino.' Sin embargo, en muchos casos, esos mismos argentinos se quejan continuamente por todo lo que ocurre en nuestro país, diciendo 'este país *no tiene arreglo*', olvidando que es necesaria una gran cuota de solidaridad y *desinterés* para *superar* nuestros problemas."

abroad

is a hopeless case
unselfishness
overcome
characteristics

Pregunta: ¿Qué aspectos o *rasgos* de la Argentina aprecia usted más?

ANA: "E*n cuanto a* lo que más aprecio en mi país, pues, son dos las cosas por *las que* siento una gran admiración: sus bellezas naturales, algunas de ellas únicas en el mundo, y la intensa vida cultural y artística que se desarrolla en Buenos Aires y que la hacen *estar a la altura de* las grandes capitales del mundo. Pero se debe notar que las grandes distancias que separan Buenos Aires del interior son una *desventaja* para que la gente de esas ciudades pueda *gozar de* todas las manifestaciones culturales y artísticas."

with respect to
which

equal to

disadvantage
enjoy

MARTIN: "Siempre me ha fascinado de la Argentina la diversidad de climas y *paisajes* que tiene su geografía. En particular, siento un especial afecto por nuestra Patagonia en el sur. Me emociona esa idea *abrumadora* de soledad e inmensidad, la idea de un paisaje desolado que se extiende por cientos y

landscapes
overwhelming

Hombre, caballo y ovejas en la inmensidad de Patagonia, Argentina.

cientos de kilómetros desde las enormes extensiones de playas desoladas con aguas frías en el este hasta las altas montañas nevadas en el oeste."

Pregunta: ¿Qué características hacen que la Argentina, el país y su gente, sea diferente de otros países hispanos?

ANA: "Para mí, la Argentina es diferente de los otros países hispanoamericanos porque recibió un contingente de inmigrantes mucho mayor que cualquier otro país de Latinoamérica. Fueron personas audaces que, llegadas de todas partes del mundo, pero especialmente de España e Italia, buscaron en América la *concreción* de un destino. Esta gente contribuyó notablemente al *crecimiento* y al progreso de esta joven nación, haciendo de Buenos Aires una ciudad 'europeizada'." *realization* / *growth*

MARTIN: "Creo que el aspecto cultural es el que nos diferencia de otros países latinoamericanos. En el caso de la Argentina, ha ocurrido que no hubo en su historia, una *mezcla* entre la cultura indígena local y la cultura europea que influenció América *a partir del* siglo XV. Pero, si me permiten, prefiero comentar sobre lo que más me preocupa personalmente, lo que nos identifica y nos *une* a los otros países del continente. Esto es la pobreza, el desempleo, el *analfabetismo, es decir*, los problemas comunes a los países subdesarrollados. En esta última década, estos problemas se han acentuado *debido al* enorme *endeudamiento* externo que *compromete* el desarrollo de estos países. También influyen profundamente en nuestro *nivel* de vida, *empeorando* no sólo el aspecto material sino el aspecto moral y espiritual que están íntimamente relacionados con la *calidad* de vida." *mixture* / *starting with* / *unites* / *illiteracy/that is to say* / *due to/debt/compromises* / *standard* / *deteriorating* / *quality*

Pregunta: Cuando usted dice "soy peruano", ¿qué quiere decir?

Guillermo (62, profesor) nos da su propio testimonio personal de lo que es ser peruano. Su orgullo, su frustración y sus esperanzas se manifiestan en su interpretación de la realidad peruana.

GUILLERMO: "Entre los pueblos y países indo-latinoamericanos y el Perú no hay gran diferencia porque todos tenemos el mismo pasado. Si hay diferencias éstas son de carácter geográfico y de ello resultan formas y costumbres particulares. Por ejemplo en el Perú tenemos tres regiones: costa, sierra y selva. Las formas de vida y de comportamiento son diferentes en cada región: los vestidos, las celebraciones, la música, las danzas, etc., pero si vamos *al fondo* encontramos una base común—la lucha del *poblador* indo-latinoamericano para *sobrevivir*, para defenderse y *aún* para mejorarse. *deeper/inhabitant* / *survive/even*

Se puede decir que el indo-latinoamericano es *humilde*, trabajador, de *conocimiento* elemental, pero la 'civilización' lo hace *preso* fácil, se le explota y se *corrompe* en la ciudad. Allí, en la ciudad *halla* que las diferencias se basan en causas económicas que motivan la existencia de las clases sociales: la clase baja, el indio; la clase media, el mestizaje; la clase rica, los descen- *humble* / *knowledge/prisoner* / *corrupted/finds* dientes de extranjeros. Éstos nos colonizaron y nos trajeron ideas materialistas *encubiertas* por la religión que no profesaban sinceramente sino que les servía para encubrir sus intenciones *avasalladoras* y egoístas.

concealed
enslaving

Hoy en día, me preocupa el *hecho* de que los países desarrollados imponen sus formas de vida y comportamiento, y los países subdesarrollados las adoptan olvidando las costumbres iniciales, *sobre todo* la música y la danza.

fact

especially

En el Perú *a comienzos* de este siglo la gran aspiración era venir a la capital, a Lima. Pero esa aspiración era sólo un *paso* para *alcanzar* una ilusión más alta—la de hacer riqueza para gozar de la vida cosmopolita y viajar a los países desarrollados abandonando la tierra natal.

at the beginning
step/reach

En cuanto a mí, me *quedo* en mi país. Aprecio con todo mi *corazón* el paisaje típico de la región andina, la música y las canciones andinas, la comida típica. Pero lo que más aprecio y lo que más me emociona es ver que uno respete al otro, que los niños tengan lo mejor: educación, casa, *alimento* y *salud*. Mi gran esperanza es que mis hijos puedan trabajar, tener un *título* profesional y que puedan residir en una zona donde haya cultura e *higiene*, en una casa moderna, con jardines y árboles frutales."

stay/heart

food/health
degree
sanitation

Preguntas

Contesten en oraciones completas.

1. Para Ana, ¿qué quiere decir ser argentina?
2. ¿Por qué siente Ana tanto orgullo de su nacionalidad?
3. Según Martín, ¿qué dicen algunos argentinos al quejarse de su país? ¿Qué significa la frase?
4. ¿Cuáles son las dos cosas que Ana aprecia más de la Argentina?
5. ¿Por qué no puede la gente del interior gozar de la cultura que tiene Buenos Aires?
6. ¿Qué parte de la Argentina aprecia más Martín? ¿Por qué?
7. Para Ana, ¿cómo es diferente la Argentina de los otros países hispanoamericanos? ¿Cómo es Buenos Aires?
8. Según Martín, ¿qué tienen en común la Argentina y los otros países del continente?
9. Según Guillermo, ¿qué cosas diferencian a los pobladores indo-latinoamericanos? ¿Cuál es su base común?
10. ¿Cómo describe Guillermo al poblador indo-latinoamericano?
11. Según Guillermo, ¿cómo le afecta al indo-latinoamericano la civilización?
12. ¿Cuál era la aspiración de muchos peruanos a comienzos del siglo? ¿Por qué?
13. ¿Qué le preocupa a Guillermo de lo que está pasando hoy en su país?
14. ¿Por qué se queda Guillermo en el Perú? ¿Cuál es su gran esperanza?

INTEGRACIÓN VISUAL: CAPÍTULO 12 ▪

EJERCICIO 12.1 Vocabulario, La carretera

EJERCICIO 12.2   Los mandatos <u>usted</u> y <u>ustedes</u>

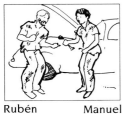

Rubén   Manuel

Ejemplo   Rubén
Cambie su ropa. (o)
Lave su ropa.
Rubén y Manuel
Cambien su ropa. (o)
Laven su ropa.

EJERCICIO 12.3   El subjuntivo en mandatos indirectos

Juanito

Ejemplo   ¿Qué quiere la madre?
**La madre quiere
que Juanito se acueste.**

Juanito

EJERCICIO 12.4   El subjuntivo con expresiones de emoción

Luisa   Pepita

Ejemplo   ¿Qué espera Pepita?
**Espera que Luisa
juegue al tenis con ella.**

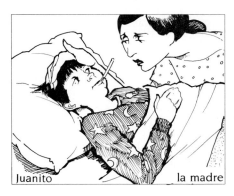

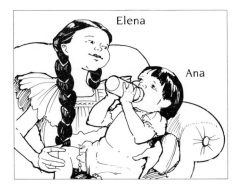

REPASO DE VOCABULARIO ACTIVO ▪

Adverbios

despacio
pronto

Sustantivos

el **accidente**
el **aire**
la **batería**
el **camino**
el **camión**
la **carretera**
la **cuadra**
la **esquina**
la **estación de servicio**
el **freno**
la **frontera**
la **gasolina**
el **kilómetro**
la **licencia de chófer**

el **limpiaparabrisas**
la **llanta (desinflada)**
la **manzana**
la **milla**
el **motor**
la **multa**
el **parabrisas**
el **policía**
el **puente**
el **seguro de automóvil**
el **semáforo**
el **tanque**
el **tráfico**
el **tránsito**
la **velocidad**

Verbos

alegrarse (de)
arreglar
creer
cruzar
doblar
dudar
esperar
estacionarse
funcionar
insistir (en)

llenar
negar (ie)
pararse
recomendar (ie)
reparar
revisar
seguir (i, i)
sentir (ie, i)
sugerir (ie, i)
temer

Expresiones idiomáticas

ahora mismo
darse prisa
no estar seguro

otra vez
tener cuidado

Direcciones

a la derecha
a la izquierda

recto, derecho

Expresiones

¡Caramba!	**¡Qué barbaridad!**
¡Claro!	**¡Qué lástima!**
¡Socorro!	**¡Qué lío!**
¡Lo siento mucho!	

AUTOEXAMEN Y REPASO # 12 ■

I. Vocabulario: La carretera

Conteste.

1. ¿Qué cosas puede revisar el empleado en la estación de servicio? ¿Qué llena? ¿Qué limpia? ¿Qué cambia?
2. ¿Qué dices cuando el motor de tu coche no funciona? ¿Y cuando tu amigo está enfermo?
3. ¿Dónde no debes estacionarte?
4. Un policía te para en la carretera. ¿Qué preguntas te hará (probablemente)?

II. Los mandados usted y ustedes

En una reunión de negocios, indique en la forma de un mandato, lo que sus colegas deben hacer.

Modelo   hacerlo (usted) ahora mismo
      Hágalo ahora mismo.

1. esperar un momento (usted)
2. traérmelo mañana (usted)
3. sentarse aquí (usted)
4. mostrármelo (usted)
5. decirme lo que sabe (usted)
6. volver a las diez (ustedes)
7. no irse enojados (ustedes)
8. escribirme su respuesta (ustedes)

III. Los mandatos nosotros

Contradicciones. ¿Hacerlo o no hacerlo?

Modelo   llamarlo
      Llamémoslo. No, no lo llamemos.

1. hacerlo otra vez
2. salir ahora mismo
3. ir a la discoteca
4. pararse aquí
5. entrar en este restaurante

IV. El subjuntivo—mandatos indirectos, expresiones de emoción, duda y negación

Indique sus reacciones (las de usted) a las posibles actividades de Juanita.

Modelo   querer/pasar las vacaciones en Mazatlán
Quiero que Juanita pase las vacaciones en Mazatlán.

1. alegrarse/ir
2. desear/divertirse mucho
3. preferir/viajar en tren
4. insistir (en)/llevar cheques de viajeros
5. esperar/llegar a tiempo
6. temer/perder las maletas
7. no creer/encontrar el hotel fácilmente
8. dudar/querer volver a casa

V. Repaso del Capítulo 12

A. *Conteste.*

1. ¿Qué quieren los profesores que hagan los estudiantes?
2. ¿Qué espera usted que hagan sus padres?
3. ¿Qué duda usted que haga su compañero(a) de cuarto?

B. *Traduzca.*

1. (usted) Turn to the right at the corner.
2. (usted) Upon arriving at the traffic light, turn to the left.
3. (usted) Continue straight ahead four blocks.
4. (usted) Call us from the gas station.
5. (ustedes) Don't park on the bridge.
6. Let's stop here.
7. Juan, do you suggest that we leave right now?
8. I am glad that the car has enough gas.
9. I am not sure that we can find the house.

VI. Repaso: tiempo futuro; demostrativos

A. *Indique que la acción ocurrirá en el futuro.*

Modelo   Espero que vendan este coche.
Venderán este coche. (o) **Lo venderán.**

1. Espero que compren ese coche.
2. Espero que hagan el viaje.
3. Espero que traigan sus bicicletas.
4. Espero que salgan de la ciudad hoy.
5. Espero que puedan llegar mañana.
6. Espero que tengan cuidado en la carretera.
7. Espero que entiendan nuestras direcciones.

B. *Usted es el dueño* (owner) *de la estación de servicio y habla con el mecánico indicando las cosas que necesitan su atención. Use los demostrativos para indicar cuáles.*

Modelo limpiar/parabrisas
    Limpie **este** parabrisas y **ése.**

1. reparar/motor
2. cambiar/llantas
3. revisar/batería
4. lavar/coches

5. arreglar/camión
6. revisar/motocicleta

■CAPÍTULO■

13

Goals for communication
- Traveling by air
- Expressing reactions, in an impersonal manner, relevant to the actions of another
- Making reference to things or persons that are hypothetical or possibly nonexistent
- Expressing the purpose of an action or the conditions under which it is to take place
- Talking about pending actions
- Expressing reactions relevant to actions or events that have occurred recently

Cultural exploration
- A Trip to the Future through the Past—Seville Expo-92
- Air travel information

VOCABULARIO EL AEROPUERTO ■

Elena va a la **agencia de viajes** para hacer una **reservación.**	*travel agency* *reservation*
Más tarde tendrá que **confirmar** el **vuelo.**	*to confirm* *flight*
Le gusta **volar** (ue). Vuela a todas partes del **mundo.**	*to fly* *world*
Lleva su **cámara** y muchos **rollos de película** porque saca muchas **fotos.**	*camera* *rolls of film* *photos*

¿Para cuándo necesita usted las reservaciones? Agencia de viajes, Madrid, España.

Al llegar al **aeropuerto**	airport
busca la **línea aérea**,	airline
tiene que **facturar** el equipaje,	to check (baggage)
pregunta si el vuelo tiene una **escala**,	stopover (plane)
necesita **conseguir** (i, i)	to get, obtain
su **tarjeta de embarque**,	boarding pass
busca la **puerta**	gate
y en la **sala de espera**	waiting room
tiene que **despedirse de** (i, i) su amigo.	to say good-bye to
En el **avión**	airplane
el **auxiliar de vuelo** o la **azafata**	steward; stewardess
ayuda a los **pasajeros**.	passengers
Elena va a su **asiento**.	seat
Debe **abrocharse** el **cinturón**.	to fasten; seatbelt
Van a **servir** (i, i) la comida.	to serve
El **piloto** anuncia la llegada.	pilot
Al bajar del avión	
va a la **aduana**	customs
donde muestra su **pasaporte**	passport
y otra **documentación**.	documents
Después, va a	
la **sala de reclamación de equipajes**	baggage claim room
para **reclamar** o	to claim
recoger sus maletas.	to pick up
Va a **quedarse** por un mes.	to stay, remain

TARJETA DE EMBARQUE
BOARDING PASS *

INFORMACION AL PASAJERO					
Vuelo	Destin	Hora Límite ↘ Puerta	Acceso a bordo	Su asiento	
IB 956	MAD	19.41 I00		16A	
Flight	Destin	Time Limit ↗ Gate	Entry door	Your seat	
FOR PASSENGER INFORMATION					

Otras expresiones útiles:
por todas partes *everywhere*
todo el mundo *everyone*

EJERCICIO 1 En el aeropuerto

Conteste en oraciones completas según el dibujo.

1. ¿Dónde están las personas?
2. ¿Cómo se llama la línea aérea? ¿En qué país tiene origen esa línea?
3. La mujer que lleva el abrigo, ¿qué tiene en la mano?
4. ¿Qué necesita darle a ella la mujer que trabaja para Iberia?
5. ¿Qué hace el hombre con las maletas?
6. ¿Qué información se ve detrás de los agentes de Iberia?
7. ¿Qué está haciendo el hombre que lleva la cámara? ¿En qué sección del avión querrá sentarse?
8. ¿Quiénes son las señoritas que llevan uniformes? ¿Qué harán ellas en el avión?
9. ¿Quién es el hombre enfrente de ellas? ¿Adónde va?
10. ¿Qué dirección se toma para llegar a la sala de reclamación? ¿Qué hacemos allí?
11. ¿Qué están haciendo las personas enfrente de la ventana?

AeroPeru

TARJETA DE EMBARQUE
BOARDING PASS

DERECHO E BARQUE
US 12,50 $

Y

Nº VUELO Nº FLIGHT	696/06
DESTINO DESTINATION	lia
Nº ASIENTO Nº SEAT	7C
Nº PUERTA Nº GATE	2

EJERCICIO 2 Preguntas personales

Conteste en oraciones completas.

1. ¿Ha viajado usted en avión? ¿Adónde? ¿Cuánto tiempo se quedó allí?
2. ¿Le gusta a usted volar? ¿Tiene usted miedo a veces? ¿Cuándo?
3. ¿A qué partes del mundo quiere usted viajar? ¿al Oriente? ¿a África? ¿a Europa?
4. ¿Con qué línea aérea prefiere usted volar? ¿Por qué?
5. En su opinión, ¿cuál es un aeropuerto muy malo? ¿Por qué?
6. ¿Le gustaría a usted ser piloto? ¿Por qué? ¿y azafata o auxiliar de vuelo? ¿Por qué?
7. Generalmente, ¿qué hacen los auxiliares de vuelo o las azafatas?

8. En el avión, ¿prefiere su asiento en la sección de fumar o en la sección de no fumar?
9. Cuando usted viaja, ¿lleva usted una cámara? ¿Le gusta sacar fotos?
10. ¿Tiene usted un pasaporte? ¿A cuántos países ha viajado?

EJERCICIO 3 Asociación

¿Qué actividades asocia usted con las siguientes palabras?

> Modelo el pasaporte
> **conseguir**
> **recibir**
> etc.

1. la tarjeta de embarque
2. la escala
3. la agencia de viajes
4. el vuelo
5. la cámara
6. el equipaje
7. la puerta
8. la sala de espera
9. el cinturón
10. la aduana
11. la sala de reclamación de equipajes
12. el avión
13. la azafata

CONVERSACIÓN ▪

*Son las 9:18 de la mañana. El pasajero llega al **aeropuerto** muy tarde y, encontrando su **línea aérea,** busca algún **agente que pueda** ayudarlo.*

PASAJERO	Señorita, con permiso. ¿Ya ha salido el **vuelo** 501 para Caracas?
AGENTE	Está para salir, señor. **Es mejor** que usted **espere** hasta el **vuelo** de esta tarde.
PASAJERO	Tengo muchísima prisa. **Es urgente que llegue** a Caracas antes del mediodía. Tengo un asunto de negocios importantísimo.
AGENTE	Bueno. Le doy su **tarjeta de embarque tan pronto como fac-ture** su maleta.
PASAJERO	No **es necesario facturarla.** Me la llevo conmigo.

INSPECCION

| AGENTE | Bueno, pues, dése prisa, por favor. Llamo a la **puerta** 17 **para que** lo **esperen.** |
| PASAJERO | Mil gracias. ¡Se lo agradezco! |

It is 9:18 in the morning. The passenger arrives at the airport very late and, finding his airline, looks for an agent who can help him.

PASSENGER	*Miss, excuse me. Has flight 501 for Caracas already left?*
AGENT	*It's about to leave, sir. It's better if you wait until this afternoon's flight.*
PASSENGER	*I am really in a hurry. It's urgent that I arrive in Caracas before noon. I have a very important business matter to attend to.*
AGENT	*All right. I'll give you your boarding pass as soon as you check your suitcase through.*
PASSENGER	*It isn't necessary to check it through. I'll take it with me.*
AGENT	*Well, hurry please. I'll call gate 17, so that they will wait for you.*
PASSENGER	*Many thanks. I appreciate it! (I am grateful to you!)*

PREGUNTAS

Conteste en oraciones completas.

1. ¿Ha salido el vuelo para Caracas?
2. ¿Cuándo hay otro vuelo?
3. ¿Por qué necesita llegar el pasajero antes del mediodía?
4. ¿Qué le va a dar la agente?
5. ¿Quiere el pasajero que la agente facture su maleta?
6. ¿Por qué llama la agente a la puerta 17?

ACTIVIDAD   Conversaciones con los agentes de la línea aérea X

a. *Varios estudiantes hacen el papel de agentes de la línea aérea X.*
b. *Los otros estudiantes, pasajeros en la línea aérea, conversan con los agentes acerca de (about) sus varios problemas.*

Situaciones:

1. Usted llama a la línea aérea para confirmar su vuelo y encuentra que su nombre no está en la lista de pasajeros.
2. Usted llega tarde al aeropuerto y ha perdido su asiento en el avión.
3. Usted quiere llevar cuatro maletas pequeñas en el avión, pero sólo se permite que lleve dos.
4. Usted tiene siete maletas (las necesita todas urgentemente), pero sólo se permite que facture tres.
5. Usted llega tarde al aeropuerto y ha perdido su vuelo a X.
6. Usted ha perdido su tarjeta de embarque y el vuelo sale en cinco minutos.
7. Usted tiene que mostrar su pasaporte antes de recibir su tarjeta de embarque, pero no puede encontrarlo.
8. Está en un vuelo con una escala. Durante la escala encuentra que hay una demora de siete horas.
9. Usted va a la sala de reclamación de equipajes y encuentra que su equipaje no está allí.

ESTRUCTURA ▪

I. El subjuntivo con expresiones impersonales
The subjunctive with impersonal expressions

You can (1) express opinions, attitudes, doubts, uncertainties, etc., about the activities or actions of another person or thing, or (2) wish to influence someone by using impersonal expressions such as *it is a shame, it is possible, it is necessary,* etc., plus the subjunctive. Observe these uses of the impersonal expressions in the following sentences.

Es una lástima que no **puedas** venir.
It is a shame that you cannot come.

Es posible que el avión **llegue** tarde.
It is possible that the plane will arrive late.

Es necesario que llames al aeropuerto ahora.
It is necessary that you call the airport now.

> impersonal expression + **que** + subjunctive

Some frequently used impersonal expressions include:

es una lástima	*it is a pity, it is a shame*
es bueno	*it is good*
mejor	*better*
extraño	*strange*
es necesario	*it is necessary*
importante	*important*
urgente	*urgent*
es posible	*it is possible*
imposible	*impossible*
probable	*probable*
improbable	*improbable*
no es cierto (verdad)	*it is not true*

If there is no change of subject after the impersonal expression, the infinitive is used, not **que** + subjunctive.

Es necesario **salir** ahora.   *It is necessary to leave now.*
   vs.
Es necesario **que salgas.**   *It is necessary for you to leave.*

EJERCICIO 4   Es bueno . . .

*Imagínese que usted es un(a) abuelo(a). Dé consejos (advice) a sus nietos, indicándoles lo que **es bueno que hagan**. Siga el modelo.*

¿Podrán facturar todo ese equipaje? Aeropuerto, Puerto Vallarta, México.

Modelo   hacer la tarea todas las noches
Es bueno que hagan la tarea todas las noches.

1. acostarse temprano
2. dormir ocho horas todas las noches
3. levantarse temprano
4. comer bien
5. trabajar mucho
6. ahorrar su dinero
7. estudiar mucho
8. no mirar mucho la televisión
9. ser honestos
10. siempre decir la verdad
11. escuchar a sus padres
12. no ponerse impacientes

EJERCICIO 5   ¿Es posible?

*Indique si, en su opinión, **es posible** o **imposible**, es **probable** o **improbable** que le ocurran a usted las cosas indicadas.*

Modelo   recibir una ''C'' en español
Es (im)posible, etc., que yo reciba una "C" en español.

1. recibir una ''A'' en español
2. recibir una ''F'' en español
3. salir de la clase temprano hoy
4. ganar la lotería
5. viajar a la luna
6. casarse este año
7. comprometerse este año
8. encontrar un regalo en su cuarto
9. hacer un viaje a España este verano
10. comprar un coche nuevo este año
11. llamar a sus padres esta noche
12. ser un(a) profesor(a) de español

EJERCICIO 6   Situaciones

Complete las oraciones indicando una variedad de posibilidades, según la situación.

1. Su coche no funciona y usted se encuentra abandonado(a) en la carretera. ¿Qué debe hacer usted?
   Es urgente que . . .
2. Usted ha tenido un accidente serio en el coche nuevo de su padre.
   Es mejor que . . .
3. Usted va a salir con su novio(a) dentro de cinco minutos. ¿Qué necesita hacer usted?
   Es necesario que . . .
4. Usted está solo en una casa vieja y posiblemente encantada (*haunted*). Exprese lo que está ocurriendo.
   Es extraño que . . .
5. Su amigo(a) ha recibido una "F" en su examen de español. ¿Qué le recomienda usted?
   Es importante que . . .
6. Usted aprende que su mejor amigo(a) está muy enfermo(a). ¿Qué le dice usted?
   Es una lástima que . . .
7. El señor y la señora *X* son muy famosos en el mundo de negocios. ¿Por qué?
   Es posible (probable) que . . .
8. Su amigo(a) está en una fiesta y ha bebido demasiada cerveza. ¿Qué le dice usted?
   Es mejor que . . .

II. El subjuntivo con referencias a lo que es indefinido o inexistente
The subjunctive with references to what is indefinite or nonexistent

The subjunctive is used after a reference to persons or things that are indefinite (unidentified, hypothetical, unknown) or nonexistent in the mind of the speaker. If the reference is known, identified, or definitely exists in the mind of the speaker, the indicative is used. Compare the sample sentences below.

> ¿**Hay alguien** aquí que **pueda** ayudarme?
> (unidentified)   (subjunctive)
> Sí, **hay alguien** aquí que **puede** ayudarle—la señorita Torres.
> (identifiable)   (indicative)

> ¿**Conoce usted**[1] **una persona** que **quiera** comprar mi coche?
>   (unknown)   (subjunctive)
> Sí, **conozco a una persona** que **quiere** comprar su coche.
>   (known)   (indicative)

¿Has volado en la línea
aérea Aeropostal?
Mérida, Venezuela.

Pero **no hay nadie** aquí que **tenga** el dinero.
    (nonexistent)   (subjunctive)
Y no hay ningún banco que **esté** abierto ahora.
    (nonexistent)   (subjunctive)

reference to what is indefinite or nonexistent + **que** + subjunctive

NOTE 1:   When the direct-object noun refers to a hypothetical person,
the personal **a** is not used, except before **alguien, nadie, alguno,**
and **ninguno.**

refrán: **No hay mal que dure cien años.**

EJERCICIO 7   ¿Qué buscamos?

a. *Imagínese que usted es el (la) representante de una compañía muy grande
que necesita emplear a varios individuos de calificaciones (qualifications)
específicas. Hable con un(a) representante de una agencia de empleos.*

b. *Su compañero(a) de clase es el (la) representante de la agencia que, al
contestar, indica si tiene o no tiene personas con las calificaciones desig-
nadas.*

Modelo   entender el japonés
     (a) **Buscamos una persona que entienda el japonés.**
     (b) **Ah, sí. Conocemos a una persona que entiende el japonés.**

(o)

     (c) **Lo siento** (*I'm sorry*), **pero no conocemos a nadie que entienda el japonés.**

1. hablar ruso
2. saber escribir a máquina
3. ser muy responsable
4. llegar al trabajo a tiempo siempre
5. poder usar una computadora
6. tener un coche
7. querer viajar
8. ser bien educado
9. conocer bien el mundo de negocios

¿Es buena o no es buena la agencia de empleos?

EJERCICIO 8   Preguntas personales

Conteste para indicar si usted conoce a personas como las indicadas.

Modelo   ¿Conoce usted a alguien que tenga mucho dinero?
     Sí, conozco a alguien que tiene mucho dinero. (o)
     No, no conozco a nadie que tenga mucho dinero.

1. ¿Conoce usted a alguien que no beba cerveza? ¿que nunca use drogas? ¿que nunca fume?
2. ¿Tiene usted un(a) amigo(a) que hable chino? ¿que sepa volar? ¿que sepa esquiar? ¿que sea vegetariano? ¿que viva en Finlandia?
3. ¿Tiene usted un(a) compañero(a) de cuarto que entienda sus problemas? ¿que estudie mucho? ¿que limpie el cuarto?
4. ¿Conoce usted una persona que tenga diez hijos? ¿que tenga cuatro coches? ¿que viva en una mansión?

ACTIVIDAD   Anuncios en el periódico

Escriba anuncios para el periódico. Tanto como pueda, use las construcciones que usted acaba de estudiar.

1. Para la sección titulada (*titled*) "personales", indique el tipo de persona que usted es y el tipo de hombre o mujer que usted busca.
2. Para la sección titulada "empleos," indique el tipo de persona que usted busca para su compañía, las cosas que necesita saber hacer, etc.
3. Para la sección titulada "apartamentos", indique en detalle el tipo de apartamento que usted busca.

III. El subjuntivo después de conjunciones de finalidad y de condición
The subjunctive after conjunctions of purpose and condition or proviso

The subjunctive is used after conjunctions denoting purpose (*so that . . .*) and condition or proviso (*unless, provided that, in case . . .*). Such use indicates that the actions are contingent upon other actions and therefore considered to be indefinite in the mind of the speaker. Observe the use of the subjunctive after these conjunctions.

Voy a llamar a la puerta **para que** lo **esperen.**	*I am going to call to the gate, so that they will wait for you.*
Con tal que se **dé** prisa, llegará a tiempo.	*Provided that you hurry, you will arrive on time.*

Conjunctions denoting purpose and condition or proviso include:

para que	*so that, in order that*	**con tal que**	*provided that*
a menos que	*unless*	**en caso de que**	*in case*

> NOTE: When there is no change of subject, the conjunction **para que** most commonly becomes the preposition **para** + infinitive.

Volvamos a casa **para descansar.**
vs.
Volvamos a casa **para que** el niño **descanse.**

EJERCICIO 9   Siempre hay condiciones.

A. *Nos vamos a Sudamérica **con tal que** . . .*

Modelo   tenemos el dinero
Nos vamos con tal que tengamos el dinero.

1. recibimos los pasaportes
2. conseguimos las visas
3. podemos hacer las reservaciones
4. encontramos un hotel
5. hay un vuelo directo
6. no hay una catástrofe

B. *No nos vamos **a menos que** . . .*

Modelo   el vuelo es barato
No nos vamos a menos que el vuelo sea barato.

1. el cambio es bueno
2. ahorramos más dinero
3. podemos quedarnos con amigos
4. tenemos dos semanas de vacaciones
5. nuestra abuela se siente mejor
6. ella sale del hospital
7. aprendemos a hablar un poco de español
8. ganamos la lotería

EJERCICIO 10 Todo para mí

Sus padres van a Puerto Rico, ¿verdad? Y lo llevan para que usted tenga la oportunidad de hacer muchas cosas diferentes. Indique cuáles según el modelo.

> Modelo ¿Van para ver el bosque tropical?
> **Van para que yo vea el bosque tropical.**

1. ¿Van para nadar en el océano?
2. ¿Van para subir las montañas?
3. ¿Van para comer los mariscos?
4. ¿Van para beber el ron (*rum*)?
5. ¿Van para conocer la capital?
6. ¿Van para hablar en español?

EJERCICIO 11 Tú y yo: provisiones

*Usted y su compañero(a) van a Puerto Rico bien preparados para cualquier circunstancia. Háganse las preguntas y contéstense para saber por qué **llevan** las cosas indicadas.*

> Modelo el suéter
> (pregunta) **¿Por qué llevas el suéter?**
> (posible respuesta) **Lo llevo en caso de que haga frío.**

1. la chaqueta
2. el paraguas
3. el traje de baño
4. las gafas de sol
5. el sombrero
6. la tarjeta de crédito
7. la cámara
8. el diccionario español
9. la medicina
10. la aspirina
11. el Alka-Seltzer

IV. El subjuntivo después de conjunciones temporales
The subjunctive after conjunctions of time

The subjunctive is used in Spanish when the conjunction of time (*when . . . , until . . . , after . . .* , etc.) introduces an action or state of being that is pending or yet to occur, and therefore not an accomplished fact in the mind of the speaker. In contrast, if the action is habitual or completed, the indicative is used. Note the contrasts in the examples.

(action pending, yet to occur—subjunctive)
Cuando vuelvas a casa, tráeme un regalo.
When you return home, bring me a gift.

(action habitual—indicative)
Cuando mi tío **vuelve** a casa, siempre me trae un regalo.
When my uncle returns home, he always brings me a gift.

(action pending, yet to occur—subjunctive)
Me quedaré aquí **hasta que llegue**.
I will stay here until he arrives.

(action completed—indicative)
Me quedé aquí **hasta que él llegó**
I stayed here until he arrived.

Conjunctions of time include:

cuando	*when*	**hasta que**	*until*
antes de que[1]	*before*	**tan pronto como**	*as soon as*
después de que	*after*		

NOTE 1: The conjunction **antes de que,** because of its meaning (signaling an action yet to occur), is *always* followed by the subjunctive.

NOTE 2: When there is no change of subject, the conjunctions **hasta que, después de que,** and **antes de que** most commonly become the prepositions **hasta, después de,** and **antes de** + infinitive.

Voy a llamar a la agencia **antes de salir.**
vs.
Voy a llamar a la agencia **antes de que salgas.**

EJERCICIO 12   ¿Cuándo saldremos?

A. *Primero, estamos esperando al agente. Saldremos **tan pronto como** . . .*

> Modelo   llegar
> **Saldremos tan pronto como llegue.**

1. llamar
2. confirmar las reservaciones
3. mandar los boletos
4. darnos la información
5. traernos los pasaportes
6. conseguir los otros documentos

B. *Segundo, estamos esperando a Paquito. Nos quedaremos **hasta que** . . .*

> Modelo   despertarse
> **Nos quedaremos hasta que se despierte.**

1. levantarse
2. lavarse
3. cepillarse los dientes
4. peinarse
5. vestirse
6. hacer las maletas

EJERCICIO 13   Antes y después

*Complete para indicar lo que usted hará **antes** y **después** de las situaciones indicadas.*

1. Voy a limpiar mi cuarto antes de que mi madre . . .
2. Voy a comer toda la pizza antes de que mi compañero(a) de cuarto . . .
3. Voy a estudiar el capítulo antes de que la profesora . . .
4. Voy a terminar la tarea antes de que nosotros . . .
5. Compraré el regalo después de que mi padre . . .
6. Manejaré al centro después de que tú . . .
7. Prepararé la comida después de que tú . . .

EJERCICIO 14 Tú y yo: muchas excusas

*Imagínense que un estudiante es el novio y una estudiante es la novia. Pregúntense **cuándo** las actividades **van a** ocurrir. Contéstense usando la conjunción **cuando**.*

> Modelo   llevarme al cine; terminar este proyecto
> (pregunta) **¿Cuándo vas a llevarme al cine?**
> (respuesta) **Cuando termine este proyecto.**

1. llamarme; poder
2. visitarme; tener más tiempo
3. ayudarme con la tarea; terminar la mía
4. llevarme a la playa; reparar mi coche
5. comprarme un regalo; recibir mi cheque
6. darme tu foto; encontrarla
7. mostrarme tu computadora; conseguirla
8. prestarme tu radiograbadora; ir a tu casa
9. devolverme mis cosas; gustarme

¡Qué antipático!

EJERCICIO 15 Contentísimos

*Complete para indicar bajo qué circunstancias las personas estuvieron o estarán contentas. (Recuerde que, con una acción completada, se usa el indicativo después de **cuando,** etc.)*

1. (a) Mi compañero(a) de cuarto **estuvo** muy contento(a) cuando yo . . .
   (b) **Estaré** muy contento(a) cuando él (ella) . . .
2. (a) **Estuve** muy contento(a) cuando mi profesor(a) de español . . .
   (b) Mi profesor(a) de español **estará** muy contento(a) cuando yo . . .
3. (a) Mis padres **estuvieron** contentos cuando yo . . .
   (b) **Estaré** contento(a) cuando ellos . . .

EJERCICIO 16 En el pasado y en el futuro

Indique lo que usted hizo o lo que usted hará en las circunstancias mencionadas. Conteste con tantas variaciones como posible.

1. ¿Qué hizo usted tan pronto como llegó a su cuarto anoche?
2. ¿Qué hará usted tan pronto como llegue a su cuarto hoy?
3. ¿Qué hizo usted tan pronto como llegó a la casa de sus abuelos?
4. ¿Qué hará usted tan pronto como llegue al centro de la ciudad?
5. ¿Qué hizo usted cuando llegó a la playa?
6. ¿Qué hará usted cuando llegue a Europa?

EJERCICIO 17 Expresión personal

Complete para indicar cuándo o bajo qué condiciones usted hará las cosas indicadas.

1. ¿Me ayudarás? **Sí, tan pronto como** . . .
2. ¿Te quedarás aquí? **Sí, hasta que** . . .
3. ¿Volverás? **Sí, cuando** . . .
4. ¿Vas a visitar Sudamérica? **Sí, con tal que** . . .
5. ¿Vas a llevar el libro de español? **Sí, en caso de que** . . .

V. El presente perfecto de subjuntivo
The present perfect subjunctive

Observe the formation and use of the present perfect subjunctive in the sample sentences.

Espero que mis padres **hayan llegado.**	*I hope that my parents have arrived.*
Dudo que **hayan reclamado** las maletas.	*I doubt that they have claimed the suitcases.*
Es posible que alguien las **haya recogido.**	*It is possible that someone has (may have) picked them up.*

Formation:

the present subjunctive of **haber** (*to have*) + the past participle

Modelo **vender** *to sell*

Es bueno que lo **haya vendido.**	*that*	*I have sold it.*
hayas vendido.		*you have sold it.*
haya vendido.		*he has sold it.*
hayamos vendido.		*we have sold it.*
hayáis vendido.		*you have sold it.*
hayan vendido.		*they have sold it.*

EJERCICIO 18 ¿De qué se alegra?

*Imagínense que todos los estudiantes de esta clase van terminando un semestre de estudio en España. Después de escribir a su profesor(a), ustedes reciben una carta de él (ella). Según la carta, ¿de qué **se alegra** él (ella)?*

> Modelo yo/aprender mucho
> **Se alegra de que haya aprendido mucho.**

1. yo/visitar la Alhambra
2. nosotros/estudiar mucho
3. Ana/sacar muchas fotos
4. Lisa y Lupe/recibir buenas notas
5. vosotros/ver el Mediterráneo
6. Felipe/conocer a muchas chicas españolas
7. nosotros/hacer un viaje a Barcelona
8. nosotros/divertirse
9. nadie/tener problemas

EJERCICIO 19   Tú y yo: ¡declaraciones!

*Un(a) estudiante hace declaraciones indicando algo que **haya hecho**. Otro(a) estudiante indica si **cree** (indicativo) que la acción **ha ocurrido** o si **duda** que la acción **haya ocurrido**.*

> Modelo   comprar un Mercedes
> (estudiante #1) **He comprado un Mercedes.**
> (estudiante #2) **Dudo** (etc.) **que hayas comprado un Mercedes.**

1. recibir una A+ en mi examen de español
2. encontrar cien dólares
3. ganar mil dólares esta semana
4. ahorrar todo el dinero
5. gastar todo el dinero
6. pasar cuatro horas en la biblioteca hoy
7. viajar a Europa
8. esquiar en Suiza
9. cruzar el Océano Pacífico
10. besar a más de mil hombres (mujeres)

EJERCICIO 20   Situaciones

Complete las oraciones según la situación, indicando varias posibilidades de lo que haya pasado.

1. Mi abuela viajó a Panamá. **Espero que . . .**
2. Varios amigos venían de visita pero no han llegado. **Temo que . . .**

3. Algunos de mis amigos no vinieron a la clase hoy. **Es posible que . . .**
4. Alguien critica a su mejor amigo(a). Usted lo (la) defiende diciendo: **No es cierto (verdad) que . . .**

ACTIVIDAD

Usted quiere trabajar para una línea aérea internacional. Escríbale al (a la) director(a) de personal una carta breve en la cual usted:

1. se presenta;
2. presenta sus calificaciones y/o experiencia educacional;
3. explica por qué quiere trabajar para una línea aérea;
4. clarifica la clase de trabajo que espera;
5. afirma el sueldo (salario) que espera y bajo qué condiciones usted puede aceptar menos; e
6. indica cuándo estará libre para aceptar un empleo posible.

PANORAMA CULTURAL ▪

In this PANORAMA CULTURAL and that of Chapter 14, you will read materials as they appear in Spanish advertisements, brochures, and magazines. Glossed vocabulary has been omitted. Now you will see how well your accumulated knowledge benefits you. Don't worry if you do not understand every word. You're on your own! *¡Buen viaje!*

LA EXPOSICIÓN UNIVERSAL SEVILLA–92*
Un vuelo al futuro por el pasado

Si Ud., viajero, aterriza en Sevilla entre el 20 de abril y el 12 de octubre de 1992 podrá vivir una experiencia única: LA EXPOSICIÓN UNIVERSAL SE-VILLA–92. . . .

La ocasión es, asimismo, excepcional: en 1992, se cumplirán cinco siglos de un viaje cuyas consecuencias transformaron la realidad y la imagen de nuestro planeta. Tres naves españolas al mando de Cristóbal Colón, Almirante de Castilla, abrieron la ruta del "Nuevo Mundo". Quinientos años después, la comunidad internacional está convocada para "conmemorar"—recordar colectivamente—aquel hecho histórico. . . .

Si en 1992 visita Sevilla, podrá realizar un mágico viaje que le transportará, a través del "túnel del tiempo", a lo que era el mundo antes de 1492. . . . También le conducirá a "recrear"—a crear de nuevo—el viaje de las tres carabelas españolas en 1492 y los que le siguieron, hasta que el hombre pudo descubrir la propia identidad de la tierra y de la humanidad

*Tomado de "Viaje a la Expo '92 de Sevilla" por Manuel Olivencia, Comisario General de España para la Exposición Universal de Sevilla '92, *Ronda*, Iberia, Octubre 1987, Especial V Centenario, pp. 40–41.

En Sevilla podemos ver la Giralda, famosa torre construida por los moros. Sevilla, España.

que la poblaba. . . . En la Exposición, a través de ese "túnel", se podrá recorrer el flujo y reflujo de ideas que hicieron cambiar las lenguas y las religiones, las bellas artes, el derecho, la economía, la política . . . y hasta la filosofía y la teología.

Ud., viajero del tiempo en Sevilla, tendrá la ocasión única de vivir el prodigioso mestizaje que se produjo en la historia de la humanidad a consecuencia de la comunicación, el encuentro y el intercambio entre culturas, ideas, razas y productos que antes se ignoraban. . . .

Ese largo viaje le servirá para alumbrar, con la luz de la historia, el presente en que vivimos, para comprender cómo el mundo actual es consecuencia de aquellos hechos del pasado. . . . Pero, la Exposición le va a ofrecer, además, un maravilloso viaje al futuro. Pretende incentivar su imaginación, su ilusión y su esperanza en el porvenir de la humanidad. . . .

La Exposición, al conmemorar el "descubrimiento del Nuevo Mundo" quiere contribuir al "descubrimiento de un nuevo mundo" con un mensaje de paz y de humanismo, con un estímulo de cooperación entre las naciones, de comunicación entre los pueblos. El hombre, que conoció y dominó la naturaleza, debe conservarla como morada de felicidad. Ése es el mundo nuevo al que también le invitamos a viajar.

¡Volemos a Sevilla!

BIENVENIDO a bordo

Nuestros servicios a bordo han sido diseñados para que disfruten del máximo confort durante el vuelo. La Tripulación de este avión está formada

La hermosa ciudad de Sevilla, España, atrae a visitantes de todo el mundo.

por expertos profesionales que harán que su vuelo resulte lo más agradable y tranquilo posible.

VIAJE CÓMODO

Equipaje de Mano

Por razones de seguridad y comodidad a bordo, nos vemos obligados a limitar el equipaje de mano de nuestros pasajeros. . . . Ud. puede llevar en cabina: una maleta cuyas medidas no superen los 100 cm., un bolso, cartera o monedero; un abrigo o manta de viaje; un paraguas o bastón; una máquina fotográfica y lectura para el viaje. . . . Por últimos, les recomendamos que no incluyan en su equipaje de mano objetos como cuchillos, tijeras y armas de cualquier clase, ya que les serían retenidos por los controles de seguridad previos al embarque.

Equipaje facturado

La legislación internacional obliga a que cada maleta vaya identificada con su etiqueta correspondiente. . . . En los mostradores de facturación de IBERIA les proporcionarán todas las etiquetas que necesitan. Les recomendamos que las sitúen en el exterior y en el interior de las maletas y que éstas sean fuertes y puedan ser cerradas con llave.

Fumadores/no fumadores

Las zonas de no fumadores están debidamente señalizadas. No está permitido fumar en los lavabos. *Les rogamos se abstengan de fumar puros o en pipa.*

SEVILLA

credi vuelo

Desde 2.800 ptas.
al mes por persona
(mínimo 2 personas).

Fin de semana

- SALIDAS: Viernes.
- Viajes individuales.

El viaje:

Día 1.º.—Salida en **avión de línea regular**, clase turista, de la compañía IBERIA, con dirección a Sevilla. Llegada al hotel. **Alojamiento.**
Día 2.º: SEVILLA.—Desayuno y alojamiento en el hotel. Visita de la ciudad: El Alcázar (visita) antiguo palacio árabe de estilo mudéjar y residencia de los reyes cristianos; típico barrio de Santa Cruz, antiguo barrio judío, con sus tortuosas calles y blancas casas, balcones floridos y adornados pátios. Posteriormente se continuará por el Paseo de Cristóbal Colón hacia el antiguo puerto comercial. **Basílica de la Macarena**, donde se puede contemplar la imagen de Nuestra Señora de la Esperanza.
Día 3.º: SEVILLA.—Desayuno y alojamiento en el hotel. Día libre a su disposición.
Día 4.º.—Desayuno. Salida en **vuelo de línea regular**, clase turista, de la compañía IBERIA, con destino a la ciudad de origen. **Llegada y FIN DEL VIAJE.**

Los precios incluyen:

- Billete de avión, clase turista.
- Estancia en régimen de alojamiento y desayuno.
- Visita de la ciudad, medio día.
- Seguro turístico.

Su butaca

El avanzado diseño de las butacas instaladas en GRAN CLASE permite posiciones de extraordinaria comodidad para el reposo durante los vuelos de larga duración. . . . En el brazo de las butacas de nuestros aviones DC-10 y B-747 se encuentran los mandos del interruptor de luz individual, pulsador para llamar a la Tripulación Auxiliar, enchufe para auriculares, control de volumen de sonido y selector de canales de música.

Descanso a bordo

Nuestra Tripulación Auxiliar le proporcionará almohadas y mantas especialmente diseñadas para hacer más confortable su descanso nocturno. En los vuelos intercontinentales (América, África, Oriente Medio) le ofrecemos unas cómodas zapatillas.

Otros servicios y sugerencias

La Tripulación Auxiliar le informará gustosamente sobre los horarios de nuestra Compañía, conexiones nacionales e internacionales. Si desea hacer algún comentario o sugerencia, en relación con el servicio, puede solicitar a algún miembro de la Tripulación Auxiliar la carta establecida para este fin.

AVISO A NUESTROS PASAJEROS

Le recordamos que el pasajero debe reconfirmar su vuelo de continuación al llegar a cada ciudad de su itinerario. También recomendamos verificar el horario de salida del vuelo, para evitar así posibles inconvenientes.

Su récord de vuelos se encuentra en el computador de

___AEROPOSTAL___ bajo el localizador: _____ PD

Gracias y Feliz Viaje!!!

Favor estar en el Aeropuerto a las: 17:00pm

Panorama Tours
VIAJES Y TURISMO

PREGUNTAS   La Exposición Universal Sevilla-92

Conteste las preguntas para explorar esta experiencia única.

1. Aproximadamente, ¿cuántos meses es la Exposición?
2. ¿Cuál es la ocasión?
3. ¿Qué ruta abrieron las tres naves españolas?
4. ¿Para qué estará convocada la comunidad internacional?
5. ¿Cómo se puede realizar el "mágico viaje"?
6. ¿A qué mundo nos transportará primero el "túnel del tiempo"?
7. ¿Cómo se produjo el "mestizaje"?
8. La Exposición nos ofrece un viaje al pasado. ¿Qué más nos ofrece?
9. ¿Cómo quiere contribuir la Exposición al "descubrimiento de un nuevo mundo"?

¿CIERTO O FALSO?   ¡Volemos a Sevilla!

¿Es usted un pasajero bien informado? Escuche las declaraciones y diga si son ciertas o falsas.

_____ 1. La tripulación está formada por expertos profesionales.
_____ 2. No limitan el equipaje de mano de los pasajeros.
_____ 3. Se puede llevar en cabina una maleta grande.
_____ 4. Recomiendan que no incluyan cuchillos y armas en el equipaje.
_____ 5. La legislación internacional obliga a que cada maleta tenga identificación.
_____ 6. Se consiguen etiquetas de identificación donde se facturan las maletas.
_____ 7. Está permitido fumar en los lavabos.
_____ 8. Las butacas o los asientos en Gran Clase son muy confortables.
_____ 9. En los vuelos largos se distribuyen almohadas y mantas.

INTEGRACIÓN VISUAL: CAPÍTULO 13 ▪

EJERCICIO 13.1   Vocabulario, El aeropuerto

EJERCICIO 13.2   El subjuntivo con expresiones impersonales

Alfonso

Ejemplo   ¿Qué es necesario?
**Es necesario que
Alfonso se levante.**

Julia

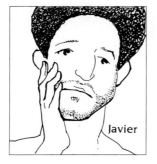
Javier

Ricardo

Rubén

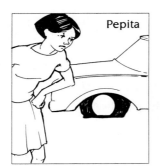
Pepita

Rosa

EJERCICIO 13.3   El subjuntivo después de conjunciones de condición

Mónica

Ejemplo   ¿Por qué lleva Mónica su
tarjeta de crédito?
**La lleva en caso de que
vaya de compras.**

EJERCICIO 13.4   El subjuntivo después de conjunciones temporales

la madre

Ejemplo   ¿Cuándo van a salir?
**Van a salir tan pronto
como la madre prepare
los sandwiches.**

la abuela

el padre

Juanito

Elena

¿TÍA ELISA?

la madre

el abuelo

EJERCICIO 13.5   El presente perfecto de subjuntivo

Esteban

Ejemplo   ¿De qué se alegra usted?

Me alegro de que Esteban haya recibido una "A".

Ricardo

Alfonso

Pepita

Javier

Paco

Julia

MI GATO RODOLFO

REPASO DE VOCABULARIO ▪

Sustantivos

la **aduana**	el **cinturón**	el **piloto**
el **aeropuerto**	la **documentación**	la **puerta**
la **agencia de viajes**	la **escala**	la **reservación**
el **asiento**	la **foto**	el **rollo de película**
el **auxiliar de vuelo**	la **línea aérea**	la **sala de espera**
el **avión**	el **mundo**	la **sala de reclamación de**
la **azafata**	el **pasajero**	**equipajes**
la **cámara**	el **pasaporte**	la **tarjeta de embarque**
		el **vuelo**

Verbos

abrocharse	**quedarse**
confirmar	**reclamar**
conseguir (i, i)	**recoger**
despedirse (de) (i, i)	**servir** (i, i)
facturar	**volar** (ue)

Expresiones

es bueno	**es mejor**	**es urgente**
es extraño	**es necesario**	**no es cierto**
es importante	**es posible**	**no es verdad**
es imposible	**es probable**	**por todas partes**
es improbable	**es una lástima**	**todo el mundo**

Conjunciones

a menos que	**cuando**	**hasta que**
antes de que	**después de que**	**para que**
con tal que	**en caso de que**	**tan pronto como**

AUTOEXAMEN Y REPASO #13 ▪

I. Vocabulario: El aeropuerto

¿Qué palabras asocia usted con las siguientes actividades?

1. hacer una reservación
2. volar
3. sacar fotos
4. facturar
5. conseguir
6. esperar

7. abrocharse
8. servir la comida
9. reclamar
10. mostrar documentación
11. quedarse
12. despedirse de

II. Expresiones impersonales

Responda a las declaraciones de su compañero(a) usando la expresión impersonal indicada.

Modelo   No llevo estas revistas en el avión.   Es mejor . . .
   Es mejor que no lleves estas revistas en el avión.

1. El avión *llega* tarde.   **Es una lástima . . .**
2. *Tengo* todo el equipaje.   **Es bueno . . .**
3. *Vamos* a la aduana.   **Es urgente . . .**
4. *Sé* el número del vuelo.   **Es importante . . .**
5. ¡No *puedo* encontrar el boleto!   **No es cierto . . .**
6. No *hay* azafatas.   **Es extraño . . .**
7. ¡No *hay* piloto!   **Es imposible . . .**

III. El subjuntivo después de los antecedentes indefinidos y negativos

Usted les indica a los agentes de bienes raíces qué tipo de casa busca. Un(a) agente no tiene lo que usted busca, y el (la) otro(a) sí.

Modelo   ser
   (usted) **Busco una casa que sea vieja.**
   (agente #1) **No tenemos una casa que sea vieja.**
   (agente #2) **Sí, ¡tenemos una casa que es vieja!**

1. estar cerca del mar
2. tener cuatro alcobas
3. no necesitar reparaciones
4. no costar mucho

IV. El subjuntivo después de conjunciones de finalidad, de condición y de tiempo

A. *Conjunciones de finalidad y de condición. Complete para explicar sus acciones.*

1. ¿Vas a Disneylandia? **Sí, para que mi hermano . . .**
2. ¿No vas a Miami? **No, a menos que . . .**
3. ¿Vas a México también? **Sí, con tal que . . .**
4. ¿Vas a llevar tu libro de español? **Sí, en caso de que . . .**

B. *Conjunciones de tiempo. Complete para indicar cuándo usted hizo o cuándo va a hacer las cosas indicadas.*

1. ¿Llamaste a la agencia? **Sí, cuando . . .**
2. ¿Vas a llamar al aeropuerto? **Sí, cuando . . .**
3. ¿Hiciste tus maletas? **Sí, tan pronto como . . .**
4. ¿Vas a hacer las mías? **Sí, tan pronto como . . .**
5. ¿Conseguiste los boletos? **Sí, después de que tú . . .**
6. ¿Vas a conseguir los pasaportes? **Sí, después de que tú . . .**

V. El presente perfecto de subjuntivo

¿Sientes o te alegras que las cosas siguientes hayan ocurrido?

Modelo mi amiga/salir
Siento que (me alegro de que) mi amiga haya salido.

1. mi amiga/venir a la universidad
2. mi amiga/traerme un regalo
3. mi amiga/tener un accidente
4. mis amigos/llamarme de larga distancia
5. mis amigos/darme malas noticias
6. tú/escribirme de Panamá
7. Elena y yo/recibir el paquete

VI. Repaso del Capítulo 13

A. *Conteste las preguntas dando la información necesaria según la situación. Use el subjuntivo.*

1. Es urgente (necesario, mejor, etc.) que su compañero(a) de cuarto haga ciertas cosas. ¿Cuáles?
2. Usted es el (la) presidente(a) de una compañía. ¿Qué tipo de empleados busca usted?
3. Usted invita a sus amigos a su casa. ¿Para qué?
4. Usted necesita escribir una carta a su familia. ¿Cuándo va a hacerlo?
5. Su amigo dijo que volvería a las ocho, y son las once. ¿Qué teme usted que haya pasado?

B. *Traduzca.*

1. María, do you know anyone who can translate this letter?
2. No, I don't know anyone who has studied Chinese.
3. Pablo, will you travel to the mountains this weekend?
4. Yes, provided that the weather is good.
5. We will have to leave before it begins to snow.
6. We will put our things in the car as soon as they have checked the oil.

VII. Repaso: Los mandatos tú; participios pasados irregulares

A. *Dígale a su amigo(a) que no haga las cosas indicadas **ahora** sino (but) que las haga* ***más tarde.***

Modelo recoger el equipaje
No recojas el equipaje ahora.
Recógelo más tarde.

1. facturar el equipaje
2. sacar las fotos
3. ir a la sala de espera
4. salir
5. despedirse

B. *Hablando de las actividades de su amigo(a), haga preguntas y respuestas según el modelo.*

Modelo   abrirlo/espero
          (pregunta) **¿Lo ha abierto?**
          (respuesta) **Espero que lo haya abierto.**

1. verlo/espero
2. devolverlo/no es cierto
3. escribirlo/es probable
4. hacerlo/es improbable
5. ponerlo en el coche/es posible
6. decirlo/me alegro
7. romperlo/temo

■CAPÍTULO■

14

Goals for communication
- Getting hotel accommodations
- Expressing reactions relevant to actions or events that occurred in the past
- Stating hypothetical situations

Cultural Exploration
- A resort hotel

VOCABULARIO EL HOTEL ■

Entramos en el **vestíbulo** del **hotel.**	*lobby; hotel*
En la **recepción** es posible	*front desk*
pedir una **habitación,**	*room*
registrarse,	*to register* (at a hotel)
pedir la **llave,**	*key*
la **información,**	*information*
el **recado,**	*message*
el **precio,**	*price*
la **cuenta**	*bill*
y el **recibo.**	*receipt*
¿Hay **impuesto**?	*tax*
¿Queremos un **cuarto doble** o	*double room*
un **cuarto sencillo**?	*single room*
¿una **cama de matrimonio** o	*double bed*
una **cama individual**?	*single bed*
¿**calefacción**?	*heating*
¿**aire acondicionado**?	*air conditioning*
¿y un **baño privado**?	*private bath*

¿Hay **servicio de cuartos**?	room service
¿y una **piscina**?	swimming pool

Estamos en la **planta baja**.	main floor
Usamos el **ascensor**	elevator
para subir al **primer**¹ piso.	first
segundo(a)	second
tercero(a)	third
cuarto(a)	fourth
quinto(a)	fifth
sexto(a)	sixth
séptimo(a)	seventh
octavo(a)	eighth
noveno(a)	ninth
décimo(a)	tenth

¿Quién está en el hotel?

el **botones**	bellboy
la **camarera**	waitress
el **camarero**	waiter
la **criada**	maid
el **huésped**	guest
el **portero**	doorman
el (la) **recepcionista**	receptionist

Otras palabras útiles:

la **almohada**	pillow
la **sábana**	sheet
la **manta**, la **cobija**	blanket
el **cubo de basura**	trash can
la **luna de miel**	honeymoon

desayunar	to have breakfast
almorzar (ue)	to have lunch
cenar	to dine, have dinner

bienvenido	welcome
felicitaciones	congratulations

NOTE 1: **Primero** and **tercero** become **primer** and **tercer** before a masculine singular noun.

NOTE 2: For ordinal numbers higher than **décimo,** the cardinal numbers (**once,** etc.) are used.

EJERCICIO I   En el hotel

Conteste las preguntas según el dibujo.

1. ¿En qué parte del hotel estamos?
2. ¿Está la recepción en la planta baja o en el primer piso?
3. ¿Ya se ha registrado el huésped?
4. Describa al huésped y a la recepcionista.
5. ¿Quién va a llevar el equipaje a la habitación?
6. ¿Quién abre la puerta del hotel?
7. ¿Cómo se llama el restaurante del hotel? ¿Quién es el señor que está allí? ¿Qué están haciendo las personas en el restaurante?
8. ¿Qué ve usted a la izquierda del camarero? ¿En qué piso está ahora?
9. ¿Qué está haciendo el hombre que está sentado en el sofá?

EJERCICIO 2   Preguntas generales

Conteste en oraciones completas.

1. ¿Qué preguntas puede usted hacerle al recepcionista al llegar a un hotel? ¿y al salir?
2. En un hotel elegante, ¿qué hace el botones? ¿y el portero? ¿y la criada? ¿y el camarero? ¿y el huésped?
3. Usted está en el ascensor. ¿Después de la planta baja, ¿a qué piso sube usted? ¿y después del tercero? ¿del quinto? ¿del séptimo? ¿del noveno?
4. ¿Cuáles son algunas características de un hotel muy elegante? ¿y de un hotel muy, muy económico?

EJERCICIO 3   Asociación de palabras

¿Qué asocia usted con las siguientes palabras del vocabulario?

1. desayunar
2. almorzar
3. cenar
4. registrarse
5. el vestíbulo
6. el ascensor
7. la recepción
8. la calefacción
9. el aire acondicionado
10. la cuenta
11. la sábana
12. la llave
13. la luna de miel
14. el recado

CONVERSACIÓN ■

*Alicia y Orlando están de **luna de miel**. Pasan por un pueblo pequeño donde deciden buscar una **habitación** en un **hotel** pintoresco.*

ORLANDO	Buenas tardes, señor. **Quisiéramos** saber si ustedes tienen una **habitación** para dos personas.
RECEPCIONISTA	Ah . . . ustedes tienen suerte. Hace unos minutos alguien **llamó pidiendo que** le **cancelara** las reservaciones.
ALICIA	¿Verdad? ¡Qué bueno! ¿Es posible que tengan una **habitación** con vista al mar? Estamos de **luna de miel** y preferimos un cuarto que sea muy especial.

La señorita se ha registrado y ahora recibe su llave. Calí, Colombia.

RECEPCIONISTA	¡Qué casualidad! ¡Tenemos la habitación perfecta para ustedes! Tiene un **baño privado, aire acondicionado** y . . . ¡vista al mar!
ORLANDO	¡Perfecto! **Si tuviéramos** más tiempo, **nos quedaríamos** aquí varios días; pero solamente tenemos el fin de semana.
RECEPCIONISTA	Está bien. La habitación está en el **tercer** piso. El **botones** tiene la **llave** y puede subir las maletas.
ALICIA	Muchísimas gracias, señor.
RECEPCIONISTA	De nada, y en caso de que necesiten algo, llamen en seguida. A propósito ¡**bienvenidos** y **felicitaciones!**

Alicia and Orlando are on their honeymoon. They are passing through a small town where they decide to look for a room in a quaint (picturesque) hotel.

ORLANDO	*Good afternoon, sir. We would like to know if you have a room for two persons.*
RECEPTIONIST	*Ah . . . you're in luck. A few minutes ago someone called asking that I cancel their reservations.*
ALICIA	*Really? Wonderful! Is it possible that you might have a room with a view of the sea? We are on our honeymoon and prefer a room that is very special.*
RECEPTIONIST	*What a coincidence! We have the perfect room for you! It has a private bath, air conditioning, and . . . the view of the sea!*
ORLANDO	*Perfect! If we had more time, we would stay here several days; but we only have the weekend.*
RECEPTIONIST	*That's fine. The room is on the third floor. The bellboy has the key, and he can bring up your suitcases.*
ALICIA	*Thank you so much, sir.*
RECEPTIONIST	*You're welcome, and in the event that you need something, call right away. By the way, welcome and congratulations!*

PREGUNTAS

Conteste en oraciones completas.

1. ¿Qué están celebrando Alicia y Orlando?
2. ¿Por qué necesitan preguntar si hay una habitación?
3. ¿Cómo es posible que haya una habitación?
4. ¿Qué tipo de cuarto desea Alicia?
5. ¿Cuánto tiempo van a quedarse?
6. ¿Dónde está la habitación?
7. ¿Qué hará el botones?
8. ¿Qué dice el recepcionista al final de la conversación?

ACTIVIDAD   En el hotel—dramas espontáneos

Algunos estudiantes hacen el papel de los (las) recepcionistas en un hotel grande. Los otros estudiantes, los huéspedes, van a la recepción para hablar de o quejarse de varios problemas urgentes que tienen. Los recepcionistas, claro, se defienden.

Problemas de los huéspedes:

1. Tarde por la noche usted entra en el hotel, el único (*only*) hotel en el pueblo. Usted quiere registrarse, pero al aprender el precio usted cree que es demasiado caro. Pida el precio e insista en que el (la) recepcionista baje el precio.
2. Usted, su esposo(a) y sus tres niños quieren registrarse en el hotel, en una habitación, por el precio de dos personas. Usted necesita convencer al (a la) recepcionista que se lo permita.
3. Usted entra en su habitación y encuentra que está en una condición desastrosa. Explíqueselo al (a la) recepcionista.
4. Usted entra en el baño privado de su cuarto y lo encuentra en una condición desastrosa y algunas cosas no funcionan. Explíqueselo al (a la) recepcionista.
5. Usted quiere comer, pero el restaurante del hotel está cerrado. Usted quiere nadar, pero la piscina está cerrada, etc. Explique por qué usted necesita/quiere hacer estas cosas. Insista en que el (la) recepcionista resuelva la situación.
6. El portero llevó sus maletas al cuarto e insistió en recibir una propina ENORME. Usted, furioso(a), explica las circunstancias al (a la) recepcionista. Insista en que resuelva la situación.
7. La criada lo (la) despertó a usted esta mañana a las 7:30, diciendo que necesitaba limpiar el cuarto. Era muy insolente en su actitud. Usted, furioso(a), le explica las circunstancias al (a la) recepcionista. Insista en que resuelva la situación.
8. Usted y sus amigos tuvieron una fiesta en su habitación anoche, y desgraciadamente (*unfortunately*) rompieron varias cosas. Explíqueselo muy específicamente al recepcionista.

9. Al salir del hotel usted indica que quiere pagar la cuenta, pero encuentra que ha perdido su dinero, tarjeta de crédito, libro de cheques, etc. Explique la situación al (a la) recepcionista.

10. Al recibir su cuenta antes de salir del hotel, usted nota que le han cobrado por servicios no usados. Resuelva la situación con el (la) recepcionista.

ESTRUCTURA ■

I. El imperfecto de subjuntivo
The imperfect (past) subjunctive

In Chapters 12 and 13 you studied many different concepts/uses of the subjunctive and practiced the **present subjunctive** (relating actions and events that *take place* in the present or in the future) and the **present perfect subjunctive** (relating actions and events that *have taken place* in the immediate past). The **imperfect** and **past perfect subjunctive** that are presented in this chapter relate, respectively, actions or events that *took place* in the past or *had taken place* prior to another past event.

A. Formación del imperfecto de subjuntivo

Observe the forms of the verbs in the sample sentences.

Quería que Carmen **llamara** al hotel.	*I wanted Carmen to call the hotel.*
Temía que no **pudiéramos** encontrar ninguna habitación.	*I was afraid we wouldn't be able to find any rooms.*
Dudaba que **tuvieran** una cancelación.	*I doubted that they would have a cancellation.*
Mamá te dijo que no **fueras** sin reservaciones.	*Mom told you not to go without reservations.*

The imperfect subjunctive of **-ar, -er,** or **-ir** verbs is formed by using the **ellos** form of the preterit tense indicative minus **-ron** and adding the endings indicated.

endings   Modelo **llamar**   *to call*

-ra	Mi tío quería que (yo) llama**ra**.
-ras	. . . que (tú) llama**ras**.
-ra	. . . que (ella) llama**ra**.
-´ramos	. . . que (nosotros) llamá**ramos**.
-rais	. . . que (vosotros) llama**rais**.
-ran	. . . que (ustedes) llama**ran**.

Otros modelos

comer	comie~~ron~~	comie**ra**, comie**ras**, comie**ra**, comié**ramos**, comie**rais**, comie**ran**
salir	salie~~ron~~	salie**ra**, salie**ras**, salie**ra**, salié**ramos**, salie**rais**, salie**ran**
andar	anduvie~~ron~~	anduvie**ra**, anduvie**ras**, anduvie**ra**, anduvié**ramos**, anduvie**rais**, anduvie**ran**
ser	fue~~ron~~	fue**ra**, fue**ras**, fue**ra**, fué**ramos**, fue**rais**, fue**ran**
pedir	pidie~~ron~~	pidie**ra**, pidie**ras**, pidie**ra**, pidié**ramos**, pidie**rais**, pidie**ran**

> NOTE: The past perfect subjunctive is formed by using the imperfect subjunctive of **haber** (**hubiera, hubieras, hubiera,** etc.) plus the past participle.

Temían que no **hubiéramos llegado** a tiempo.
They were afraid that we had not arrived on time.

B. La función del imperfecto de subjuntivo

Contrast the present and past time of the action in the pairs of sample sentences below.

Quiero que **vayas.**	*I want you to go.*
Quería que **fueras.**	*I wanted you to go.*
Temo que lo **pierda.**	*I am afraid that he will lose it.*
Temía que lo **perdiera.**	*I was afraid that he would lose it.*
No **hay** nadie que **pueda** hacerlo.	*There is no one who can do it.*
No **había** nadie que **pudiera** hacerlo.	*There was no one who could do it.*
Trae su paraguas en caso de que **llueva.**	*He is bringing his umbrella in case it rains.*
Trajo su paraguas en caso de que **lloviera.**	*He brought his umbrella in case it should rain.*

Referring to events in the past, the imperfect subjunctive functions under the same basic requirements as the present subjunctive:

1. in indirect (implied) commands;
2. with expressions of emotion;
3. with expressions of doubt, denial, and disbelief;
4. with references to what is indefinite or nonexistent;
5. after conjunctions of purpose and condition or proviso;
6. after conjunctions of time (because of its meaning, almost exclusively **antes de que**)

In such sentences if the verb in the independent clause is in a past tense, the imperfect subjunctive is used in the dependent clause.

NOTE: The imperfect subjunctive is translated like the imperfect indicative, although it also can have the meaning of *might* or *would* (since there is no conditional subjunctive).

EJERCICIO 4   Mis padres insistían

¿Qué insistían sus padres? Cambie las oraciones según el modelo.

Modelo   Insistían que trabajara. (tú)
Insistían que trabajaras.

1. Insistían que viviera en casa. (Francisco, tú, vosotros, nosotros)
2. Insistían que me quedara aquí. (tú, mis hermanos, Ana, nosotros)
3. Insistían que fuera a la iglesia. (nosotros, mis hermanos, tú, Lola)

EJERCICIO 5   ¿Qué más querían?

*Indique las otras cosas que sus padres **querían** que usted **hiciera**.*

Modelo   ¿Qué querían? decir la verdad
Querían que dijera la verdad.

¿Qué querían?

1. estudiar mucho
2. hacer la tarea
3. leer muchos libros
4. aprender español
5. conseguir un trabajo
6. ahorrar dinero
7. pagar las cuentas
8. limpiar el cuarto
9. poner las ropas en el ropero
10. lavar el coche
11. cortar la hierba
12. no salir demasiado
13. traer amigos a la casa
14. no fumar
15. no beber cerveza
16. dormir bastante
17. divertirse

EJERCICIO 6   Cuando tenía 16 años . . .

*¿Cuando tenía 16 años **quería** o **no quería** usted que sus padres **hicieran** las cosas indicadas?*

Modelo   ¿lavarle la ropa?
Sí, quería que me lavaran la ropa.

1. ¿prestarle el coche?
2. ¿comprarle un coche?
3. ¿besarlo (la) mucho?
4. ¿abrazarlo (la) mucho?
5. ¿mostrarle cariño?
6. ¿llevarlo (la) a Hawaii?
7. ¿llevarlo (la) al dentista?
8. ¿traerle regalos?
9. ¿darle dinero?
10. ¿dejarlo (la) solo(a) en la casa? la casa?

Vamos a cenar en el restaurante elegante del Hotel Mayaland, México.

EJERCICIO 7   Lugares diferentes

Exprese sus reacciones y esperanzas en las situaciones indicadas.

1. En la biblioteca, yo dudaba que los estudiantes . . .
2. En el restaurante, deseaba que el camarero . . .
3. En la peluquería, temía que el peluquero . . .
4. En el quiosco, quería que el vendedor . . .
5. En el banco, era necesario que la cajera . . .
6. En el almacén, sugerí que la dependienta . . .
7. En la estación de servicio, era urgente que el empleado . . .
8. En el aeropuerto, recomendaban que yo . . .
9. En el hotel, yo esperaba que el botones . . .
   esperaba que la criada . . .
   esperaba que el recepcionista . . .

EJERCICIO 8   Tú y yo, en la escuela secundaria

*Háganse preguntas y contéstense, pensando en los años cuando ustedes estaban en la escuela secundaria. Usen los verbos **querer** y **hacer** en las preguntas.*

Modelos   tus amigos/(tú)
          (pregunta)   **¿Qué querían tus amigos que hicieras?**
          (posible respuesta) **Querían que saliera con ellos,** etc.
          (tú)/tus amigos
          (pregunta)   **¿Qué querías que tus amigos hicieran?**
          (posible respuesta) **Quería que no fumaran,** etc.

1. los maestros (*teachers*)/(tú)
   (tú)/los maestros
2. tu novio(a)/(tú)
   (tú)/tu novio(a)
3. tu hermano(a)/(tú)
   (tú)/tu hermano(a)
4. tus padres/(tú)
   (tú)/tus padres
5. la azafata/(tú)
   (tú)/la azafata
6. el camarero/(tú)
   (tú)/el camarero

EJERCICIO 9   ¿Qué buscaba usted?

*Explique qué tipo o clase de cosa usted buscaba. Conteste con tantas varia-
ciones como posible.*

> Modelo   ¿Qué tipo de tienda buscaba usted?
> **Buscaba una tienda que vendiera muebles.**
> **. . . que aceptara mi tarjeta de crédito,** etc.

1. ¿Qué tipo de coche buscaba usted?
2. ¿Qué tipo de regalo buscaba usted?
3. ¿Qué tipo de apartamento buscaba usted?
4. ¿Qué tipo de restaurante buscaba usted?
5. ¿Qué tipo de compañero(a) de cuarto buscaba usted?

II. Cláusulas con si

If clauses

In the sample sentences below observe:

1. The use of the *past subjunctive* to express a condition that is contrary to
   fact or unlikely to occur, and
2. the use of the *conditional* to express the result.

> Si **tuviera** el dinero, **haría** el viaje.
> *If I had the money, I would take the trip.*
>   (contrary to fact)   (result)

> Si **hiciéramos** el viaje, **necesitaríamos** tres meses de vacaciones.
> *If we were to take the trip, we would need three months of vacation.*
>   (unlikely to occur)   (result)

> **Estaría** muy contento si **tuviéramos** tres meses de vacaciones.
> *I would be very happy if we were to take three months of vacation.*
>   (result)   (contrary to fact)
>   (unlikely to occur)

> if **(si)** + imperfect subjunctive + conditional
>   (contrary-to-fact-clause)   (result clause)

NOTE: When an *if* clause does not express a condition that is contrary to fact or unlikely to occur, the indicative is used.

Si estoy cansado, no estudio.   *If I am tired, I do not study.*

> refrán: **Si el mozo supiera
> y el viejo pudiera
> no habría cosa
> que no se hiciera.**

EJERCICIO 10   Si pudiera ...

*Indique lo que usted **haría si pudiera.***

> Modelo   tomar una siesta
> **Si pudiera, tomaría una siesta.**

1. comprar un coche
2. ir de compras
3. salir con mi novio(a)
4. hablar con el presidente
5. ayudar a la gente pobre
6. viajar por el mundo
7. subir el Aconcagua
8. vivir en una isla tropical
9. volar a la luna

EJERCICIO 11   Estaría muy contento(a) si ...

*Indique las condiciones bajo las cuales usted **estaría muy contento(a).***

> Modelo   recibir un paquete en el correo
> **Estaría muy contento(a) si recibiera un paquete en el correo.**

1. recibir una "A" en español
2. saber todas las respuestas
3. conseguir un coche
4. encontrar $100,00
5. ganar la lotería
6. hacer sol
7. poder ir a la playa
8. tener una tabla hawaiana (*surfboard*)

EJERCICIO 12   Preguntas personales

Conteste para indicar lo que usted haría en las circunstancias mencionadas.

1. Si no tuvieras que estudiar, ¿qué te gustaría hacer?
2. Si tuvieras un millón de dólares, ¿qué harías?
3. Si estuvieras en una tienda de ropa, ¿qué comprarías?
4. Si estuvieras en un restaurante elegante, ¿qué pedirías?
5. Si pudieras hacer un viaje, ¿adónde irías?
6. Si fueras profesor(a), ¿ qué harías?
7. Si pudieras, ¿a quién besarías?

Vamos a tomar el sol y nadar en la piscina. Hotel Camino Real, Ciudad de Guatemala.

EJERCICIO 13   Emociones y fantasías

A. *Exprese las posibles causas de sus sentimientos.*

1.   Estaría muy triste si . . .
2.   Estaría muy preocupado si . . .
3.   Estaría muy enojado si . . .
4.   Estaría muy sorprendido (*surprised*) si . . .
5.   Estaría muy contento si . . .

B. *Exprese lo que usted haría en los lugares indicados.*

6.   Si estuviera en España . . .
7.   Si estuviera en México . . .
8.   Si estuviera en el Perú . . .
9.   Si estuviera en Puerto Rico . . .
10.   Si estuviera en la luna . . .

ACTIVIDAD   Una cadena (*chain*) de posibilidades

En grupos, y con mucha imaginación, construyan una cadena larguísima (muy, muy larga) de condiciones y resultados según el modelo. Después lean sus "creaciones" a la clase.

Modelo   Si tuviera mil dólares . . .
            Si **tuviera** mil dólares, **haría** un viaje.
            Si **hiciera** un viaje, **iría** a México.
            Si **fuera** a México, **comería** muchas tortillas.
            Si **comiera** muchas tortillas, . . . etc.

1. Si tuviera un coche nuevo . . .
2. Si tuviera tiempo . . .
3. Si tuviera un novio (una novia) muy especial . . .
4. Si no estuviera aquí . . .
5. Si pudiera hablar ruso . . .
6. Si pudiera volar . . .
7. Si viviera en un castillo (*castle*) en España . . .
8. (originales) . . .

III. Correspondencia de los tiempos
Sequence of tenses

As you have observed, in Spanish the tense of the verb in the independent indicative clause dictates the tense of the verb in the dependent subjunctive clause. The most frequently used sequences of tenses are:

Independent clause	Dependent clause
present indicative future indicative command form	present subjunctive or present perfect subjunctive

Quiero que me **haga** una reservación.
Le **pediré** que me **haga** una reservación.
Dígale que me **haga** una reservación.
Espero que me **haya hecho** una reservación.

Independent clause	Dependent clause
imperfect indicative preterit indicative conditional	imperfect (past) subjunctive or past perfect subjunctive

Quería que me **hiciera** una reservación.
Le **pedí** que me **hiciera** una reservación.
Esperaba que me **hubiera hecho** una reservación.
Me **haría** una reservación si **tuviera** las fechas.

EJERCICIO 14   En camino al examen final

Lea la conversación y conteste las preguntas según la situación.

Ana y Roberto están hablando en camino al examen final de español.

ROBERTO   Ana, ¿sabes que después de que tomemos el examen final es probable que no nos veamos hasta septiembre?

ANA   Sí. ¿Por qué no hacemos planes para vernos durante el verano? Me gustaría que vinieras a visitarnos en nuestra casa que está en la playa.

ROBERTO   ¡Buena idea! Es necesario que yo trabaje casi (*almost*) todo el verano, pero es posible que tome una o dos semanas de vacaciones.

ANA   ¡Formidable! Escríbeme cuando llegues a casa para que podamos hacer los planes. Debo confesar, Roberto, que me alegro de que hayas estado en esta clase.

ROBERTO   Gracias, Ana, y ¡buena suerte en el examen!

1. ¿Qué era probable?
2. ¿Qué le gustaría a Ana?
3. ¿Qué decía Roberto que era necesario?
4. ¿Qué era posible?
5. ¿Por qué debía Roberto escribirle a Ana pronto?
6. ¿De qué se alegraba Ana?

IV. Perspectiva original: una síntesis

A. Mini-dramas

En grupos, preparen y presenten mini-dramas originales. Escojan (choose) uno de los siguientes tópicos:

1. en el restaurante
2. en la oficina del médico
3. en el almacén
4. en el banco
5. en la estación de ferrocarril
6. en la estación de servicio/coche
7. en el aeropuerto/avión
8. en el hotel

B. Presentaciones orales

Preparen uno de los siguientes tópicos para presentación oral:

Individual:

1. Usted, el (la) agente de viajes, narra y describe un lugar/país—
   a. ¿Dónde está?
   b. clima; ropa apropiada para llevar
   c. hoteles, comida, pasatiempos
   d. modos de transporte para llegar
   e. precios
2. Usted narra un incidente interesante/extraño (*strange*)/chistoso (*funny*)/o extraordinario que ocurrió en su vida o recientemente o hace algunos años.

En pares:

3. Para discutir (*debate*)—la vida del campo contra la vida de la ciudad
4. Para discutir—la vida en la residencia de estudiantes/universidad contra la vida en casa con familia
5. Para discutir—casarse joven contra casarse más tarde

6. Una conversación—
Es el primer día de clases y usted se sienta al lado de la persona más fascinante del mundo. Después de la clase ustedes conversan,
   a. saludándose y presentándose
   b. conociéndose (con muchas preguntas)
   c. haciendo planes para el futuro inmediato.

C. Expresión escrita

Exprese en forma escrita sus ideas sobre uno de los siguientes tópicos:

1. Si usted ganara la lotería, ¿cómo cambiaría su vida?
2. Si usted tuviera que pasar un año solo(a) en una isla remota,
   a. ¿qué cinco cosas llevaría usted y por qué decidiría llevar esas cosas?
   b. ¿Cómo sería su vida allí?
3. Reflexione (*reflect*) en cómo era su vida hace cinco años y cómo será, posiblemente, cinco años en el futuro.

PANORAMA CULTURAL ■

Vamos a viajar
De vacaciones en el hotel
(según un folleto turístico mexicano)

Sus vacaciones empiezan al aproximarse a la bahía de Acapulco a bordo de su jet. Su guía estará esperando para recibirle y llevarle a su confortable hotel, situado entre las flores y las palmeras de una sección remota de la playa, donde usted encontrará su espacioso búngalow con vista al mar. La belleza de Acapulco se ve por todas partes: las flores, las nubes, las puestas de sol, los pájaros, las montañas, la playa, el mar y la gente.

Nosotros, preocupados por los problemas diarios no nos damos el tiempo para ver y para participar en la vida. Ahora, por lo menos, durante el tiempo de vacaciones cambiemos de ritmo y divirtámonos.

¿Qué ofrecemos?

El alojamiento: Usted vivirá en unos búngalows que evocan el estilo de las bellas haciendas mexicanas, pero con todo el confort moderno: aire acondicionado, camas ''Queen-size'', baño-ducha, terraza privada, fondo musical F.M. y servicio telefónico directo.

Tarifas:	Plan	Sencillo	Doble (*pesos*)
	Americano	$150.000	$165.000*
	Europeo	$120.000	$150.000*

*Los menores de 12 años se benefician de una reducción del 20%.

El clima tropical, la bahía, las montañas y las palmeras nos invitan a Acapulco.

La comida: ¡Para la persona que no nos conoce, la comida es cosa de imaginarse! Primero, el desayuno: es fantástico encontrarse, vestido con traje de baño, entre la calma y la frescura de las grandes mesas adornadas de flores y frutas, dulces, pasteles sabrosos, jarras de yogurt, leche fresca, jugo, miel, mantequilla, chocolate, platillos de huevos frescos y jamón, quesos y mermeladas y el aroma del más delicioso té o café. El almuerzo: una mañana llena de actividades le abrirá el apetito para el almuerzo—un bufét donde se encuentra una fantástica selección de ensaladas, platillos preparados fríos o calientes, de pollo, carne, pescado, legumbres y deliciosos panes con mantequilla. También hay un grill donde podrá elegir su carne o pescado favorito, acompañado de deliciosos platillos típicos del país. ¡Hemos olvidado los postres—una avalancha de frutas, pasteles, tortas, almendras! La cena: ¡La cena es otra cosa! Es servida en mesas para dos o cuatro personas con música y luces de velas. Tendrán ustedes el placer de descubrir su menú con cinco platillos. Y el vino . . . cada día en la comida y la cena, grandes jarras de vino adornan las mesas. Podrá elegir entre el fresco y ligero vino rosado o el buen vino del país, rojo y delicioso.

Deportes: Podrá practicar los siguientes deportes, ya que todo está comprendido en el precio especial de vacaciones:

Vólibol Ping Pong — Buceo Libre — Tenis — Surf — Esquí Acuático — Buceo con Botellas — Yoga — Excursiones Paseos en el Mar — Vela — Piscina — Paseos a Caballo — Golf

Hay también actividades extraordinarias como las excursiones en barco, teatro, cursos de danza, noche de baile al son de una orquesta, grupos folklóricos, discoteca y conciertos de música clásica.

Clima: Temperatura media de 27 a 34 grados en verano y 22 a 27 en invierno.

						F (Fahrenheit)
32	50	68	86	98	122	212
0	10	20	30	37	50	100
						C (Celsius)

Ropa: Trajes de baño y sandalias son lo acostumbrado en el hotel. Pero para vestirse, como para todo lo demás, la libertad es absoluta.

Formalidades: Pasaportes y la visa de turista mexicana son obligatorios. La lengua oficial es el español. La moneda local es el peso.

SU VIAJE A ACAPULCO

Usted y su amigo(a) acaban de llegar al aeropuerto en Acapulco. Según el folleto turístico:

1. ¿Qué documentación debe usted tener al llegar al aeropuerto?
2. ¿Quién estará esperándoles?
3. ¿Dónde está situado el hotel?
4. ¿Qué plan prefieren ustedes? ¿Cuánto pagarán?
5. De la selección indicada, ¿qué desea usted tomar en el desayuno?
6. ¿Qué selección hará usted en el almuerzo? ¿Qué postre prefiere?
7. ¿Qué vino desea usted con la cena?
8. ¿Qué deportes practicará usted?
9. ¿Qué desea usted hacer por la noche?
10. ¿Qué ropa piensa usted llevar con más frecuencia?
11. ¿Sabe usted bastante español para comunicarse con los mexicanos?

INTEGRACIÓN VISUAL: CAPÍTULO 14 ■

EJERCICIO 14.1   Vocabulario, El hotel

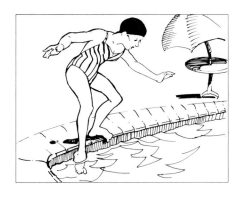

EJERCICIO 14.2 El imperfecto de subjuntivo

Rosa

Ejemplo ¿A quién era necesario escribir?
**Era necesario que Rosa escribiera
a la familia.**

EJERCICIO 14.3 Cláusulas con s<u>i</u>

Esteban

Ejemplo   Si estuviera allí . . .
**Si estuviera allí,
dormiría en una hamaca.**

REPASO DE VOCABULARIO ACTIVO ▪

Sustantivos

el **aire acondicionado**
la **almohada**
el **ascensor**
el **baño privado**
el **botones**
la **calefacción**
el (la) **camarero(a)**
la **cobija**
la **criada**
el **cuarto doble**
el **cuarto sencillo**

el **cubo de basura**
la **cuenta**
la **habitación**
el **hotel**
el **huésped**
la **información**
el **impuesto**
la **luna de miel**
la **llave**
la **manta**
la **piscina**

la **planta baja**
el **portero**
el **precio**
el **recado**
la **recepción**
el **recepcionista**
el **recibo**
la **sábana**
el **servicio de cuartos**
el **vestíbulo**

Verbos

almorzar (ue)
cenar
desayunar
registrarse

Números ordinales

primero(a)   **sexto(a)**
segundo(a)   **séptimo(a)**
tercero(a)   **octavo(a)**
cuarto (a)   **noveno(a)**
quinto(a)   **décimo(a)**

Expresiones

bienvenido
felicitaciones

AUTOEXAMEN Y REPASO #14 ▪

I. Vocabulario

Haga usted una definición para las siguientes palabras.

Modelo la llave
Lo que usamos para abrir la puerta.

1. el recepcionista
2. el botones
3. la criada
4. el camarero
5. el portero
6. la piscina
7. el servicio de cuartos
8. el ascensor
9. el cubo de basura
10. la manta, la cobija
11. el huésped
12. el recibo

II. El imperfecto de subjuntivo

Indique los deseos y las reacciones de usted y de algunos miembros de la familia.

Modelo ¿Qué querías? mi hermano/bañarse
Quería que mi hermano se bañara.

1. ¿Qué querías? mi hermano/cepillarse los dientes
   mi hermano/peinarse
   mi hermano/vestirse
2. ¿Qué esperaban los padres? los hermanos/no enojarse
   los hermanos/no quejarse
   los hermanos/no preocuparse
3. ¿Qué sugería el abuelo? tú/quedarte aquí
   tú/conseguir trabajo
   tú/ahorrar tu dinero
4. ¿De qué se alegraba la abuela? nosotros/comprometernos
   nosotros/casarnos
   nosotros/venir a visitarla

III. Cláusulas con si

Haga usted oraciones indicando la condición (si . . .) y el resultado.

Modelo conseguir un trabajo/ganar dinero
Si consiguiera un trabajo, ganaría dinero.

1. ganar dinero/ahorrarlo
2. ahorrarlo/tener mucho dinero
3. tener mucho dinero/comprar un carro
4. comprar un carro/hacer un viaje
5. hacer un viaje/ir a México
6. ir a México/quedarme allí dos meses
7. quedarme allí dos meses/perder mi trabajo
8. perder mi trabajo/no tener dinero
9. no tener dinero/. . .

IV. Repaso del Capítulo 14

A. *Conteste.*

1. El año pasado, ¿qué querías que tus padres te compraran?
2. ¿Para qué deseabas que te compraran un coche?
3. Para evitar (*avoid*) un conflicto entre tú y tu compañero(a) de cuarto [o entre tú y tu novio(a)], ¿qué era necesario que hicieran ustedes?
4. ¿Qué cosas harías si tuvieras mucho tiempo libre (*free*)?
5. Si estuvieras en la ciudad de Nueva York, ¿qué harías?

B. *Traduzca.*

1. If he were here, he would call her.
2. We were hoping that she would come.
3. She would be here if it were possible.
4. It was a shame that we didn't see her.
5. We left a message for her before he left.

V. Repaso: comparaciones; verbos en el indicativo y en el subjuntivo

A. *Hagamos comparaciones iguales entre* **este botones** *y* **ese botones.**

Modelo   Son amables.
          Sí. Este botones es tan amable como ése.

1. Son jóvenes.
2. Llevan muchas maletas.
3. Ayudan mucho.
4. Trabajan muchas horas.
5. Reciben mucho dinero.

B. *Hagamos comparaciones desiguales entre las cosas indicadas.*

Modelo   Este hotel es pequeño. (ése) (aquél)
          Ése es más pequeño que éste.
          Aquél es el más pequeño de los tres.

1. Este hotel es bueno. (ése) (aquél)
2. Esta habitación es cara. (ésa) (aquélla)
3. Este restaurante es malo. (ése) (aquél)
4. Esta piscina es grande. (ésa) (aquélla)

C. *Indique cuándo usted se despide de sus amigos según las referencias.*

depedirse de sus amigos

1. Hoy . . . **me despido de mis amigos.**
2. En este momento . . .
3. Ayer . . .
4. Al final de cada semestre . . .
5. La semana que viene . . .
6. Acabo de hacerlo. Ya . . .
7. Acababa de hacerlo. Cuando terminó el semestre ya . . .
8. Miguel no quiere . . .
9. Miguel no quería . . .

■ APPENDIX ■

I

Verbs

A. Conjugation of regular verbs

Infinitive

-ar	**-er**	**-ir**
hablar, *to speak*	comer, *to eat*	vivir, *to live*

Present Participle

hablando, *speaking*	comiendo, *eating*	viviendo, *living*

Past Participle

hablado, *spoken*	comido, *eaten*	vivido, *lived*

Indicative Mood

Present

I speak, do speak, am speaking, etc.	*I eat, do eat, am eating, etc.*	*I live, do live, am living, etc.*
hablo	como	vivo
hablas	comes	vives
habla	come	vive
hablamos	comemos	vivimos
habláis	coméis	vivís
hablan	comen	viven

Preterit

I spoke, did speak, etc.	*I ate, did eat, etc.*	*I lived, did live, etc.*
hablé	comí	viví
hablaste	comiste	viviste
habló	comió	vivió
hablamos	comimos	vivimos
hablasteis	comisteis	vivisteis
hablaron	comieron	vivieron

Imperfect

I was speaking, used to speak, spoke, etc.	*I was eating, used to eat, ate, etc.*	*I was living, used to live, lived, etc.*
hablaba	comía	vivía
hablabas	comías	vivías
hablaba	comía	vivía
hablábamos	comíamos	vivíamos
hablabais	comíais	vivíais
hablaban	comían	vivían

Future

I will speak, etc.	*I will eat, etc.*	*I will live, etc.*
hablaré	comeré	viviré
hablarás	comerás	vivirás
hablará	comerá	vivirá
hablaremos	comeremos	viviremos
hablaréis	comeréis	viviréis
hablarán	comerán	vivirán

Conditional

I would speak, etc.	*I would eat, etc.*	*I would live, etc.*
hablaría	comería	viviría
hablarías	comerías	vivirías
hablaría	comería	viviría
hablaríamos	comeríamos	viviríamos
hablaríais	comeríais	viviríais
hablarían	comerían	vivirían

Present Perfect

I have spoken, etc.	*I have eaten, etc.*	*I have lived, etc.*
he hablado	he comido	he vivido
has hablado	has comido	has vivido
ha hablado	ha comido	ha vivido
hemos hablado	hemos comido	hemos vivido
habéis hablado	habéis comido	habéis vivido
han hablado	han comido	han vivido

Past Perfect (Pluperfect)

I had spoken, etc.	*I had eaten, etc.*	*I had lived, etc.*
había hablado	había comido	había vivido
habías hablado	habías comido	habías vivido
había hablado	había comido	había vivido
habíamos hablado	habíamos comido	habíamos vivido
habíais hablado	habíais comido	habíais vivido
habían hablado	habían comido	habían vivido

Future Perfect

I will have spoken, etc.	*I will have eaten, etc.*	*I will have lived, etc.*
habré hablado	habré comido	habré vivido
habrás hablado	habrás comido	habrás vivido
habrá hablado	habrá comido	habrá vivido
habremos hablado	habremos comido	habremos vivido
habréis hablado	habréis comido	habréis vivido
habrán hablado	habrán comido	habrán vivido

Conditional Perfect

I would have spoken, etc.	*I would have eaten, etc.*	*I would have lived, etc.*
habría hablado	habría comido	habría vivido
habrías hablado	habrías comido	habrías vivido
habría hablado	habría comido	habría vivido
habríamos hablado	habríamos comido	habríamos vivido
habríais hablado	habríais comido	habríais vivido
habrían hablado	habrían comido	habrían vivido

Subjunctive Mood

Present Subjunctive

(that) I (may) speak, etc.	*(that) I (may) eat, etc.*	*(that) I (may) live, etc.*
hable	coma	viva
hables	comas	vivas
hable	coma	viva
hablemos	comamos	vivamos
habléis	comáis	viváis
hablen	coman	vivan

Imperfect Subjunctive

(that) I might speak, etc.	*(that) I might eat, etc.*	*(that) I might live, etc.*
hablara	comiera	viviera
hablaras	comieras	vivieras
hablara	comiera	viviera
habláramos	comiéramos	viviéramos
hablarais	comierais	vivierais
hablaran	comieran	vivieran

Present Perfect Subjunctive

(that) I (may) have spoken, etc.	(that) I (may) have eaten, etc.	(that) I (may) have lived, etc.
haya hablado	haya comido	haya vivido
hayas hablado	hayas comido	hayas vivido
haya hablado	haya comido	haya vivido
hayamos hablado	hayamos comido	hayamos vivido
hayáis hablado	hayáis comido	hayáis vivido
hayan hablado	hayan comido	hayan vivido

Past Perfect (Pluperfect) Subjunctive

(that) I might have spoken, etc.	(that) I might have eaten, etc.	(that) I might have lived, etc.
hubiera hablado	hubiera comido	hubiera vivido
hubieras hablado	hubieras comido	hubieras vivido
hubiera hablado	hubiera comido	hubiera vivido
hubiéramos hablado	hubiéramos comido	hubiéramos vivido
hubierais hablado	hubierais comido	hubierais vivido
hubieran hablado	hubieran comido	hubieran vivido

Command Forms

usted	hable	coma	viva
	no hable	no coma	no viva
ustedes	hablen	coman	vivan
	no hablen	no coman	no vivan
nosotros	hablemos	comamos	vivamos
	no hablemos	no comamos	no vivamos
tú	habla	come	vive
	no hables	no comas	no vivas
(vosotros)	[hablad]	[comed]	[vivid]
	[no habléis]	[no comáis]	[no viváis]

B. Stem-changing verbs

1. -ar and -er stem-changing verbs: e→ie and o→ue

pensar (ie)   *to think*

Present Indicative: pienso, piensas, piensa, pensamos, penséis, piensan
Present Subjunctive: piense, pienses, piense, pensemos, penséis, piensen
Commands: piense (usted), piensen (ustedes), pensemos (nosotros), piensa (tú), no pienses (tú), [pensad (vosotros), no penséis (vosotros)]

volver (ue)   *to return*

Present Indicative: vuelvo, vuelves, vuelve, volvemos, volvéis, vuelven
Present Subjunctive: vuelva, vuelvas, vuelva, volvamos, volváis, vuelvan
Commands: vuelva (usted), vuelvan (ustedes), volvamos (nosotros), vuelve (tú), no vuelvas (tú), [volved (vosotros), no volváis (vosotros)]

Other verbs of this type are:

cerrar (ie)	to close	**almorzar (ue)**	to have lunch
despertarse (ie)	to wake up	**contar (ue)**	to count, tell
empezar (ie)	to begin	**costar (ue)**	to cost
encender (ie)	to turn on (light)	**doler (ue)**	to hurt
entender (ie)	to understand	**encontrar (ue)**	to find
negar (ie)	to deny	**jugar (ue)**	to play
nevar (ie)	to snow	**llover (ue)**	to rain
perder (ie)	to lose	**mostrar (ue)**	to show
querer (ie)	to wish, want, love	**poder (ue)**	to be able, can
recomendar (ie)	to recommend	**recordar (ue)**	to remember
sentarse (ie)	to sit down	**sonar (ue)**	to sound, ring
acostarse (ue)	to go to bed		

2. -ir stem-changing verbs: e→ie and o→ue, u

preferir (ie, i) *to prefer*

Present Participle: prefiriendo
Present Indicative: prefiero, prefieres, prefiere, preferimos, preferís, prefieren
Preterit: preferí, preferiste, prefirió, preferimos, preferisteis, prefirieron
Present Subjunctive: prefiera, prefieras, prefiera, prefiramos, prefiráis, prefieran
Imperfect Subjunctive: prefiriera, prefirieras, prefiriera, prefiriéramos, prefirierais, prefirieran
Commands: prefiera (usted), prefieran (ustedes), prefiramos (nosotros), prefiere (tú), no prefieras (tú), [preferid (vosotros), no prefiráis (vosotros)]

dormir (ue, u) *to sleep*

Present Participle: durmiendo
Present Indicative: duermo, duermes, duerme, dormimos, dormís, duermen
Preterit: dormí, dormiste, durmió, dormimos, dormisteis, durmieron
Present Subjunctive: duerma, duermas, duerma, durmamos, durmáis, duerman
Imperfect Subjunctive: durmiera, durmieras, durmiera, durmiéramos, durmierais, durmieran
Commands: duerma (usted), duerman (ustedes), durmamos (nosotros), duerme (tú), no duermas (tú), [dormid (vosotros), no durmáis (vosotros)]

Other verbs of this type are:

divertirse (ie, i)	to have a good time
morir (ue, u)	to die
sentir (ie, i)	to be sorry, regret
sentirse (ie, i)	to feel
sugerir (ie, i)	to suggest

3. -ir stem-changing verbs: e→i, i

pedir (i, i) *to ask for*

Present Participle: pidiendo
Present Indicative: pido, pides, pide, pedimos, pedís, piden
Preterit: pedí, pediste, pidió, pedimos, pedisteis, pidieron
Present Subjunctive: pida, pidas, pida, pidamos, pidáis, pidan
Imperfect Subjunctive: pidiera, pidieras, pidiera, pidiéramos, pidierais, pidieran
Commands: pida (usted), pidan (ustedes), pidamos (nosotros), pide (tú), no pidas
  (tú), [pedid (vosotros), no pidáis (vosotros)]

Other verbs of this type are:

conseguir (i, i)	*to get, obtain*
despedirse de (i, i)	*to say good-bye*
repetir (i, i)	*to repeat*
servir (i, i)	*to serve*
seguir (i, i)	*to follow*
vestirse (i, i)	*to get dressed*

C. Verbs with orthographic changes

1. c→qu

tocar   *to play (instrument)*

Preterit: toqué, tocaste, tocó, tocamos, tocasteis, tocaron
Present Subjunctive: toque, toques, toque, toquemos, toquéis, toquen
Commands: toque (usted), toquen (ustedes), toquemos (nosotros), toca (tú), no
  toques (tú), [tocad (vosotros), no toquéis (vosotros)]

Like **tocar** are **buscar,** *to look for,* and **sacar,** *to take out.*

2. z→c

empezar (ie)   *to begin*

Preterit: empecé, empezaste, empezó, empezamos, empezasteis, empezaron
Present Subjunctive: empiece, empieces, empiece, empecemos, empecéis,
  empiecen
Commands: empiece (usted), empiecen (ustedes), empecemos (nosotros), empieza
  (tú), no empieces (tú) [empezad (vosotros, no empecéis (vosotros)]

Like **empezar** are **abrazar,** *to hug,* and **cruzar,** *to cross.*

3. g→gu

pagar   *to pay (for)*

Preterit: pagué, pagaste, pagó, pagamos, pagasteis, pagaron
Present Subjunctive: pague, pagues, pague, paguemos, paguéis, paguen
Commands: pague (usted), paguen (ustedes), paguemos (nosotros), paga (tú), no
  pagues (tú), [pagad (vosotros), no paguéis (vosotros)]

Like **pagar** are **llegar,** *to arrive;* **jugar (ue),** *to play;* **negar (ie),** *to deny;* **apagar,** *to turn off.*

4. gu→g

seguir(i, i)   *to follow, continue*

Present Indicative: sigo, sigues, sigue, seguimos, seguís, siguen
Present Subjunctive: siga, sigas, siga, sigamos, sigáis, sigan
Commands: siga (usted), sigan (ustedes), sigamos (nosotros), sigue (tú), no sigas
(tú), [seguid (vosotros), no sigáis (vosotros)]

5. g→j

recoger   *to pick up*

Present Indicative: recojo, recoges, recoge, recogemos, recogéis, recogen
Present Subjunctive: recoja, recojas, recoja, recojamos, recojáis, recojan
Commands: recoja (usted), recojan (ustedes), recojamos (nosotros), recoge (tú), no
recojas (tú), [recoged (vosotros), no recojáis (vosotros)]

6. i→y

leer   *to read*

Present Participle: leyendo
Preterit: leí, leíste, leyó, leímos, leísteis, leyeron

Like **leer** is **oír,** *to hear*; and in the present participle **traer,** *to bring*: **trayendo;** and
ir, *to go*: **yendo.**

D. Irregular Verbs

Only the tenses and commands that have irregular forms are given.

andar   *to walk, to go, to run (machinery)*

Preterit: anduve, anduviste, anduvo, anduvimos, anduvisteis, anduvieron
Imperfect Subjunctive: anduviera, anduvieras, anduviera, anduviéramos,
anduvierais, anduvieran

conocer   *to know, be acquainted with*

Present Indicative: conozco, conoces, conoce, conocemos, conocéis, conocen
Present Subjunctive: conozca, conozcas, conozca, conozcamos, conozcáis, conozcan

dar   *to give*

Present Indicative: doy, das, da, damos, dais, dan
Preterit: di, diste, dio, dimos, disteis, dieron
Present Subjunctive: dé, des, dé, demos, deis, den
Imperfect Subjunctive: diera, dieras, diera, diéramos, dierais, dieran

decir   *to say, tell*

Present Participle: diciendo
Past Participle: dicho

Present Indicative: digo, dices, dice, decimos, decís, dicen
Preterit: dije, dijiste, dijo, dijimos, dijisteis, dijeron
Present Subjunctive: diga, digas, diga, digamos, digáis, digan
Imperfect Subjunctive: dijera, dijeras, dijera, dijéramos, dijerais, dijeran
Future: diré, dirás, dirá, diremos, diréis, dirán
Conditional: diría, dirías, diría, diríamos, diríais, dirían
Affirmative *tú* command: di

estar *to be*

Present Indicative: estoy, estás, está, estamos, estáis, están
Preterit: estuve, estuviste, estuvo, estuvimos, estuvisteis, estuvieron
Present Subjunctive: esté, estés, esté, estemos, estéis, estén
Imperfect Subjunctive: estuviera, estuvieras, estuviera, estuviéramos, estuvierais, estuvieran

haber *to have*

Present Indicative: he, has, ha, hemos, habéis, han
Preterit: hube, hubiste, hubo, hubimos, hubisteis, hubieron
Present Subjunctive: haya, hayas, haya, hayamos, hayáis, hayan
Imperfect Subjunctive: hubiera, hubieras, hubiera, hubiéramos, hubierais, hubieran
Future: habré, habrás, habrá, habremos, habréis, habrán
Conditional: habría, habrías, habría, habríamos, habríais, habrían

hacer *to do, make*

Past Participle: hecho
Present Indicative: hago, haces, hace, hacemos, hacéis, hacen
Preterit: hice, hiciste, hizo, hicimos, hicisteis, hicieron
Present Subjunctive: haga, hagas, haga, hagamos, hagáis, hagan
Imperfect Subjunctive: hiciera, hicieras, hiciera, hiciéramos, hicierais, hicieran
Future: haré, harás, hará, haremos, haréis, harán
Conditional: haría, harías, haría, haríamos, haríais, harían
Affirmative *tú* command: haz

ir *to go*

Present Participle: yendo
Past Participle ido
Present Indicative: voy, vas, va, vamos, vais, van
Preterit: fui, fuiste, fue, fuimos, fuisteis, fueron
Imperfect: iba, ibas, iba, íbamos, ibais, iban
Present Subjunctive: vaya, vayas, vaya, vayamos, vayáis, vayan
Imperfect Subjunctive: fuera, fueras, fuera, fuéramos, fuerais, fueran
Affirmative *tú* command: ve
Affirmative *nosotros* command: vamos

oír *to hear*

Present Participle: oyendo
Past Participle: oído
Present Indicative: oigo, oyes, oye, oímos, oís, oyen
Preterit: oí, oíste, oyó, oímos, oísteis, oyeron
Present Subjunctive: oiga, oigas, oiga, oigamos, oigáis, oigan
Imperfect Subjunctive: oyera, oyeras, oyera, oyéramos, oyerais, oyeran

poder *to be able, can*

Present Participle: pudiendo
Present Indicative: puedo, puedes, puede, podemos, podéis, pueden
Preterit: pude, pudiste, pudo, pudimos, pudisteis, pudieron
Present Subjunctive: pueda, puedas, pueda, podamos, podáis, puedan
Imperfect Subjunctive: pudiera, pudieras, pudiera, pudiéramos, pudierais, pudieran
Future: podré, podrás, podrá, podremos, podréis, podrán
Conditional: podría, podrías, podría, podríamos, podríais, podrían

poner *to put, place*

Past Participle: puesto
Present Indicative: pongo, pones, pone, ponemos, ponéis, ponen
Preterit: puse, pusiste, puso, pusimos, pusisteis, pusieron
Present Subjunctive: ponga, pongas, ponga, pongamos, pongáis, pongan
Imperfect Subjunctive: pusiera, pusieras, pusiera, pusiéramos, pusierais, pusieran
Future: pondré, pondrás, pondrá, pondremos, pondréis, pondrán
Conditional: pondría, pondrías, pondría, pondríamos, pondrías, pondrían
Affirmative *tú* command: pon

querer *to wish, want*

Present Indicative: quiero, quieres, quiere, queremos, queréis, quieren
Preterit: quise, quisiste, quiso, quisimos, quisisteis, quisieron
Present Subjunctive: quiera, quieras, quiera, queramos, queráis, quieran
Imperfect Subjunctive: quisiera, quisieras, quisiera, quisiéramos, quisierais, quisieran
Future: querré, querrás, querrá, querremos, querréis, querrán
Conditional: querría, querrías, querría, querríamos, querríais, querrían

saber *to know*

Present Indicative: sé, sabes, sabe, sabemos, sabéis, saben
Preterit: supe, supiste, supo, supimos, supisteis, supieron
Present Subjunctive: sepa, sepas, sepa, sepamos, sepáis, sepan
Imperfect Subjunctive: supiera, supieras, supiera, supiéramos, supierais, supieran
Future: sabré, sabrás, sabrá, sabremos, sabréis, sabrán
Conditional: sabría, sabrías, sabría, sabríamos, sabríais, sabrían

salir *to go out, leave*

Present Indicative: salgo, sales, sale, salimos, salís, salen
Present Subjunctive: salga, salgas, salga, salgamos, salgáis, salgan

Future: saldré, saldrás, saldrá, saldremos, saldréis, saldrán
Conditional: saldría, saldrías, saldría, saldríamos, saldríais, saldrían
Affirmative *tú* command: sal

ser *to be*

Present Indicative: soy, eres, es, somos, sois, son
Preterit: fui, fuiste, fue, fuimos, fuisteis, fueron
Imperfect: era, eras, era, éramos, erais, eran
Present Subjunctive: sea, seas, sea, seamos, seáis, sean
Imperfect Subjunctive: fuera, fueras, fuera, fuéramos, fuerais, fueran
Affirmative *tú* command: sé

tener *to have*

Present Indicative: tengo, tienes, tiene, tenemos, tenéis, tienen
Preterit: tuve, tuviste, tuvo, tuvimos, tuvisteis, tuvieron
Present Subjunctive: tenga, tengas, tenga, tengamos, tengáis, tengan
Imperfect Subjunctive: tuviera, tuvieras, tuviera, tuviéramos, tuvierais, tuvieran
Future: tendré, tendrás, tendrá, tendremos, tendréis, tendrán
Conditional: tendría, tendrías, tendría, tendríamos, tendríais, tendrían
Affirmative *tú* command: ten

traducir *to translate*

Present Indicative: traduzco, traduces, traduce, traducimos, traducís, traducen
Preterit: traduje, tradujiste, tradujo, tradujimos, tradujisteis, tradujeron
Present Subjunctive: traduzca, traduzcas, traduzca, traduzcamos, traduzcáis, traduzcan
Imperfect Subjunctive: tradujera, tradujeras, tradujera, tradujéramos, tradujerais, tradujeran

traer *to bring*

Present Participle: trayendo
Past Participle: traído
Present Indicative: traigo, traes, trae, traemos, traéis, traen
Preterit: traje, trajiste, trajo, trajimos, trajisteis, trajeron
Present Subjunctive: traiga, traigas, traiga, traigamos, traigáis, traigan
Imperfect Subjunctive: trajera, trajeras, trajera, trajéramos, trajerais, trajeran

venir *to come*

Present Participle: viniendo
Present Indicative: vengo, vienes, viene, venimos, venís, vienen
Preterit: vine, viniste, vino, vinimos, vinisteis, vinieron
Present Subjunctive: venga, vengas, venga, vengamos, vengáis, vengan
Imperfect Subjunctive: viniera, vinieras, viniera, viniéramos, vinierais, vinieran
Future: vendré, vendrás, vendrá, vendremos, vendréis, vendrán
Conditional: vendría, vendrías, vendría, vendríamos, vendríais, vendrían
Affirmative *tú* command: ven

ver *to see*

Past Participle: visto
Present Indicative: veo, ves, ve, vemos, veis, ven
Preterit: vi, viste, vio, vimos, visteis, vieron
Imperfect: veía, veías, veía, veíamos, veías, veían
Present Subjunctive: vea, veas, vea, veamos, veais, vean
Imperfect Subjunctive: viera, vieras, viera, viéramos, vierais, vieran

APPENDIX II

Answers to Review Exercises

Autoexamen y repaso #1

I.
1. Buenas tardes (noches). Muy buenas.
2. ¿Cómo te llamas?
3. ¿Cómo se llama?
4. ¿Cómo está usted?
5. ¿Qué hay de nuevo?
6. Nada de particular. De nada.
7. Muy bien, gracias. Bastante bien, gracias.
8. Permítame presentar a (*name*).
9. El gusto es mío. Mucho gusto.
10. Hágame el favor de abrir la puerta.
11. Muchas gracias.
12. No hay de qué. ¿Qué tal? ¿Qué hay de nuevo?
13. Hasta luego.

II. A. 1. la pizarra 2. la pluma, el bolígrafo 3. el profesor/la profesora, la clase 4. la puerta 5. la mesa 6. la pregunta 7. el libro 8. el examen 9. el cuaderno, el lápiz, etc. 10. el (la) estudiante

B. 1. Cierre . . . , Abra . . . 2. Complete . . . 3. Vaya . . . 4. Conteste . . . 5. Escriba . . . , Repita . . . , etc. 6. Estudie . . . , Repita. . . .

III. A. 1. La alumna es americana. 2. La señora Linares es española. 3. La estudiante es inteligente. 4. La señora Gómez es una profesora superior.

B. 1. Las profesoras son inglesas. 2. Los estudiantes son alemanes. 3. Ana y Lupe son sentimentales. 4. Las clases son interesantes.

IV. 1. Los libros no son interesantes. 2. El profesor no es ridículo. 3. La pregunta no es importante. 4. Andrés no es un alumno extraordinario.

V. 1. ocho, diez, doce, catorce, diez y seis (dieciséis), diez y ocho (dieciocho)
2. siete, nueve, once, trece, quince, diez y siete (diecisiete)
3. miércoles, jueves, viernes, sábado

VI. 1. Es la una y cuarto (quince) de la tarde.
2. Son las nueve y media de la noche.
3. Son las cuatro menos veinte de la mañana.
4. Son las seis menos diez de la mañana.

VII. A. 1. Me llamo (*name*). 2. Muy bien, gracias. etc. 3. Nada de particular.
4. Hoy es (*día*). 5. Es la una (son las dos, etc.) y/menos veinte, etc. 6. Sí, la clase es fantástica. (No, la clase no es fantástica.)

B. 1. ¿A qué hora es el examen? 2. Es a las dos y veinte de la tarde. 3. ¿Cómo se llama el profesor (la profesora)? 4. Se llama la señora Pérez. 5. La señora Pérez es una profesora muy buena. 6. Los estudiantes en la clase de español no son americanos. (Ellos) son ingleses.

Autoexamen y repaso #2

I. 1. abuela 2. sobrino 3. prima 4. tío 5. nieta 6. novio 7. nene, bebé

II. 1. No soy tonto(a). Soy inteligente. 5. Carlos no es rubio. Es moreno.
2. No eres feo. Eres guapo. 6. No sois pobres. Sois ricos.
3. No somos débiles. Somos fuertes. 7. No es gorda. Es delgada (flaca).
4. No son altas. Son bajas. 8. Las clases no son difíciles. Son fáciles.

III. 1. No estoy triste. Estoy contento(a).
2. No estás enfermo. Estás bien.
3. No estamos mal. Estamos bien.
4. Mis hermanos no están en la ciudad. Están en el campo.
5. El coche no está aquí. Está allí.
6. Las puertas del coche no están abiertas. Están cerradas.

IV. 1. Su casa es grande. 6. La hija es muy simpática.
2. Su carro es viejo. 7. La familia está en la Florida.
3. Los padres son jóvenes. 8. Los tíos son de la Florida.
4. El padre es japonés. 9. Los niños están en la playa.
5. La madre es abogada. 10. La familia está muy contenta.

V. 1. Roberto y Pablo van a la escuela. 4. El profesor Martínez va a un restaurante.
2. Vamos a la universidad. 5. Voy a la cafetería.
3. Vas a la clase. 6. Vais a la residencia de estudiantes.

VI. A. 1. Soy inteligente, guapo(a), etc.
2. Mi madre es bonita, simpática, etc.
3. El presidente es viejo, etc.
4. Mis amigos son jóvenes, simpáticos, etc.
5. Estoy bien [mal, enfermo(a), cansado(a)].
6. Sí, estamos en la universidad.
7. No voy a la clase los sábados.
8. Sí, (No, no) vamos al centro de la ciudad con frecuencia.
9. No va a estar en la clase el domingo.

B. 1. Es rica, inteligente y hermosa.
2. Es la hija del profesor (de la profesora).

3. La puerta está abierta y los estudiantes están en la clase.
4. ¿Están cansados?
5. No, no estoy cansado(a). Estoy aburrido(a).
6. ¿Vas al campo el domingo?
7. Mis padres van a estar allí.

Autoexamen y repaso #3

I. 1. el vinagre 2. el azúcar, la crema 3. la leche, el desayuno 4. la langosta, los camarones, el pescado 5. la naranja, el limón 6. la sandía 7. el jamón, el tocino, la salchicha/el chorizo 8. la lechuga, el tomate, las cebollas, etc. 9. el jamón, el queso, la lechuga, etc. 10. la cerveza, el vino 11. el pastel de manzana 12. el helado.

II. 1. Necesita . . . Vende . . . Desea . . .
2. Preparan . . . Compran . . . Venden . . .
3. ¿Estudias . . . ? ¿Comes . . . ? ¿Vives . . . ?
4. Aprendo . . . Escribo . . . Preparo . . .
5. Estudiamos . . . Aprendemos . . . Escribimos . . .

III. 1. ¿Qué bebe? 2. ¿Dónde vive? 3. ¿De dónde es? 4. ¿Cuándo trabaja? 5. ¿Adónde va? 6. ¿Cuántos necesita? 7. ¿Cómo se llama? 8. ¿Cuál es su clase favorita?

IV. 1. Les gusta . . . Te gusta . . . Nos gusta . . .
2. Me gusta . . . (a Alberto) le gusta . . . Nos gusta . . .
3. No les gustan . . . No me gustan . . . No le gustan . . .
4. ¿Les gustan . . . ? ¿Os gustan . . . ? ¿Te gustan . . . ?

V. A. 1. Como huevos, pan tostado, cereal, etc.
2. Como pollo, arroz, ensalada, etc.
3. Mi bebida favorita es la leche, etc.
4. Mi postre favorito es el helado, etc.
5. Mi fruta favorita es la fresa, etc.
6. Soy de Chicago, etc.
7. Vivo en Richmond, etc.
8. Estudio por la noche, etc.
9. Sí, (No, no) llego a tiempo todos los días.
10. Sí, aprendemos el español. No aprendemos el ruso.
11. No, no escribimos todos los ejercicios.
12. Sí, me gustan los estudiantes de la clase de español.

B. 1. ¿Necesitas la crema y el azúcar?
2. Necesitan la sal y la pimienta.
3. Compramos frutas y legumbres en el mercado hoy.
4. ¿Adónde vas ahora?
5. ¿Por qué estudia (él) toda la noche?
6. ¿Cuántos libros venden (ellos)?
7. ¿Quién prepara la cena?
8. ¿Quieres comer aquí esta noche?
9. ¿Les gusta la comida mexicana?
10. Nos gusta el vino.

VI. A. 1. Voy a estudiar.
2. Mi hermano va a trabajar.
3. Teresa y Linda van a preparar la comida.
4. Vamos a comprar una pizza.
5. Vas a leer toda la novela.

B. 1. ¡Ah! ¡El café está caliente!
2. Camarero, la sopa está fría.
3. La torta es de chocolate, ¿verdad?
4. Camarero, ¿dónde está el helado?
5. No me gusta este restaurante. El servicio es horrible.

Autoexamen y repaso #4

I. 1. correr, caminar, bailar, etc.
2. abrazar, jugar al béisbol, etc.
3. besar, hablar, etc.
4. ver, mirar
5. oír, escuchar
6. comer
7. bailar, jugar al tenis, etc.
8. tocar el piano, pintar, etc.

II. 1. Veo a mi amigo. Veo la casa. Veo a los muchachos. 2. Conozco a la señorita. Conozco al señor Lorca. Conozco la ciudad de Nueva York.

III. 1. Oigo . . . Oyes . . . 2. Traigo . . . Trae . . . 3. No hago . . . No hacemos . . . 4. Pongo . . . Ponéis . . . 5. Veo . . . Ven . . . 6. Traduzco . . . Traduce . . . 7. Sé . . . Saben . . . 8. Salgo . . . Salimos . . . 9. Conozco . . . Conoces . . .

IV. 1. Carlos, ¿duermes . . . ? 2. ¿Repites . . . ? 3. ¿Entiendes . . . ? 4. ¿Quieres . . . ? 5. ¿Prefieres . . . ? 6. ¿Juegas . . . ? 7. ¿Puedes nadar . . . ? 8. ¿Vuelves . . . ?

V. 1. Yo digo . . . Nosotros decimos . . . Ellos dicen . . .
2. Yo tengo . . . Nosotros tenemos . . . Ustedes tienen . . .
3. Carmen viene . . . Yo vengo . . . Tú vienes . . .

VI. 1. treinta y tres 2. cuarenta y cuatro 3. cincuenta y cinco 4. sesenta y seis 5. setenta y siete 6. ochenta y ocho 7. noventa y nueve 8. cien.

VII. A. 1. Las partes de la cara son: los ojos, la nariz, la boca, etc.
2. Uso la cabeza, los hombros, los brazos, las piernas, los pies.
3. Salgo de la residencia de estudiantes a las ocho, etc.
4. Traigo libros, cuadernos, un lápiz, un bolígrafo, etc.
5. Sí, (No, no) vengo a clase a tiempo todos los días.
6. Preferimos los profesores fáciles (difíciles).
7. Conozco a (nombre) bien.
B. 1. Sé que está aquí. 2. ¿Sabe (él) nadar? 3. ¿Puede (ella) tocar el piano? 4. ¿Qué quieres hacer ahora? 5. Debemos ir a clase. 6. (Él) mira a María y busca una respuesta.

VIII. A. 1. ¿Cuándo vuelven? ¿Por qué no vuelven?
2. ¿Cuántos equipos no vienen? ¿Por qué no vienen?
3. ¿Quién puede manejar?
4. ¿Dónde están?
5. ¿Qué quieren hacer? ¿Adónde quieren ir? ¿Por qué no quieren ir?
B. 1. A mi hermano le gusta bailar.
2. A mis hermanas les gusta cantar.
3. No nos gusta limpiar la casa pero nos gusta cocinar.
4. Me gustan los deportes.
5. Eva, ¿te gustan las hamburguesas?

Autoexamen y repaso #5

I. 1. los guantes   2. los calcetines, los zapatos   3. la camisa, la blusa, el suéter, la chaqueta   4. los pantalones   5. el traje, el abrigo

II. 1. Tengo hambre.   2. Tengo sed.   3. Tienen sueño   4. Tiene miedo. 5. Tenemos calor.   6. Tenemos frío.   7. Tengo razón.   8. No tienes razón.

III. 1. junio, julio, agosto; hace calor, hace sol
2. septiembre, octubre, noviembre; hace fresco, hace viento, llueve
3. diciembre, enero, febrero; hace frío, nieva

IV. 1. El niño está durmiendo . . .   2. Estoy leyendo . . .
3. Están escribiendo . . .   4. Estamos comiendo . . .
5. Estás mirando . . .   6. Están escuchando . . .

V. 1. Es la niña del señor Martínez.   3. Es la novia de Felipe.
2. Es el esposo de Elena.   4. Es la prima de Carlota.

VI. 1. Sí, son mis gafas. Sí, son mías.   4. Sí, son nuestros suéteres. Sí, son
2. Sí, es su reloj. Sí, es suyo.   nuestros.
3. Sí, es su chaqueta. Sí, es suya.   5. Sí, son sus botas. Sí, son suyas.

VII. A. 1. Llevan un vestido, medias, etc. Llevan pantalones, una chaqueta, una camisa y una corbata.
2. Voy a llevar mi abrigo, mis suéteres, mis botas, etc. Voy a llevar mi traje de baño, mis camisetas, etc.
3. Las manzanas son rojas, verdes o amarillas. Las bananas son amarillas. Los guisantes son verdes. Las cebollas son blancas o amarillas.
4. Hace frío (calor) (fresco). Hace buen (mal) tiempo, etc.
5. Tengo que ir a las clases, etc.
6. Estoy estudiando, aprendiendo el español, etc.
7. Es el coche de mi familia. (Es mi coche.) (Es nuestro coche.)
8. Mis libros están en el escritorio.

B. 1. ¿Qué está haciendo (ella)?
2. Tengo mucha hambre.
3. Tengo ganas de comer una hamburguesa y papas fritas.
4. ¡Hace mucho frío hoy!
5. Voy a llevar mi abrigo largo, mis guantes y las botas de mi hermano.
6. Nuestros padres van de compras mañana.
8. Sus amigos(as) y un amigo nuestro (una amiga nuestra) llegan esta noche.

VIII. A. 1. Los calcetines están sucios. La blusa está sucia. Las panti-medias están sucias.
2. El suéter está limpio. La chaqueta está limpia. Los blujeans están limpios.
3. La ropa buena es cara. Las joyas son caras. Los abrigos de Inglaterra son caros.
4. Los zapatos de mi hermano son baratos. La corbata del profesor es barata. Las sandalias de Marta son baratas.
5. La falda es roja, blanca y azul. Las camisas son rojas, blancas y azules. Los sombreros son rojos, blancos y azules.

B. 1. Felipe dice . . . Está diciendo . . .
2. Mis hermanas duermen . . . Están durmiendo . . .
3. ¿Juegas . . . ? ¿Estás jugando . . . .?
4. Pido . . . Estoy pidiendo . . .
5. Mi madre cierra . . . Está cerrando . . .

Autoexamen y repaso #6

I. 1. biblioteca, librería   2. iglesia   3. autobús, taxi, metro   4. parada de autobús   5. museo, catedral   6. almacén, joyería   7. película, teatro

II. 1. Trabajé . . .   2. Salí . . .   3. Compraste . . .   4. Comiste . . .   5. Llevó . . .   6. Leyó . . .   7. Bailamos . . .   8. Bebimos . . .   9. Escuchasteis . . . 10. Abristeis . . .   11. Manejaron . . .   12. Volvieron . . .

III. 1. Ana, ¿pidió usted el arroz con pollo?
   Carlos y Felipe, ¿pidieron ustedes . . . ?
  2. Ana, ¿prefirió usted el helado de fresas?
   Carlos y Felipe, ¿prefirieron ustedes . . . ?
  3. Ana, ¿durmió usted bien?
   Carlos y Felipe, ¿durmieron ustedes . . . ?

IV. 1. No, no hay nada en el autobús.
  2. No, no hay nadie en el taxi.
  3. No, no hay ninguna persona en la catedral.
  4. No, no voy ni al museo ni al parque.
  5. No, nunca voy a la librería Galdós.
  6. No, no voy a la biblioteca tampoco.

V. 1. Necesito quinientos cincuenta dólares.
  2. Necesito seiscientos cuarenta dólares.
  3. Necesito trescientos setenta y cinco dólares.
  4. Necesito mil setecientos treinta dólares.
  5. Necesito novecientos ochenta dólares.

VI. A. 1. Sí, (No, no) estudié mucho anoche.
    2. Sí, (No, no) comí una pizza.
    3. Pedí langosta, etc.
    4. Sí, (No, no) bebimos todas las Coca-Colas.
    5. Sí, (No, no) visitamos la biblioteca.
    6. Dormimos seis, etc., horas.
    7. Hoy es el (número) de (mes) de mil novecientos . . .
  B. 1. No vieron la película.   2. ¿Llamaste anoche?   3. ¿Pidió alguien un taxi?   4. Compró algo interesante en el almacén.   5. La fecha de su cumpleaños es el ocho de octubre de mil novecientos cuarenta y tres.

VII. A. 1. Generalmente vuelve . . .   2. No entiende . . .   3. Pide . . .   4. No recuerda . . .   5. Prefiere . . .   6. No piensa . . .   7. No duerme . . .
  B. 1. . . . bailo bien; . . . estoy bailando bien; . . . bailé bien.   2. . . . aprendemos el vocabulario; . . . estamos aprendiendo el vocabulario; . . . aprendimos el vocabulario.   3. . . . escribe a la familia; . . . está escribiendo a la familia; . . . escribió a la familia.   4. . . . esperan el autobús; . . . están esperando el autobús; . . . esperaron el autobús.

Autoexamen y repaso #7

I. 1. el cerdo   2. la gallina   3. la vaca   4. el bosque   5. el mar   6. el lago, el río, el océano   7. las flores, la tierra   8. el mar, la arena   9. los árboles, las culebras, los insectos   10. el cielo   11. el pez, el pescado

II. 1. Vine . . . Vino . . .   2. No supe . . . No supieron . . .   3. No pudo . . . No pudimos . . .   4. Tuvisteis . . . Tuviste . . .   5. Anduve . . . Mi hermana anduvo . . .   6. Fuimos . . . Mis primos fueron . . .   7. Di . . . Mis padres dieron . . .

8. Carmen no estuvo . . . Mis amigos no estuvieron . . . 9. Quisimos . . .
Quisiste . . .

III. A. 1. Quiero vivir cerca de las montañas. 2. fuera de 3. encima del 4. detrás
del 5. después de

B. 1. . . . en vez de estudiar, etc.
2. . . . antes de salir, etc.
3. . . . después de hablar con mis padres, etc.
4. . . . sin dormir, etc.

C. 1. para 2. para 3. para 4. por 5. por 6. para 7. por

IV. A. 1. Sí (No, no) hice un viaje. Fui a . . .
Sí (No, no) me gustó.
2. Veo montañas, desiertos, valles, selvas, islas, etc.
3. Veo las nubes, la luna, el sol y las estrellas.
4. Estudié, comí, dormí, etc.
5. Dije "¡hola, buenos días!" etc.
6. Puse mi abrigo en la silla.
7. Después de comer voy a hacer la tarea, etc.
8. Sí, (No, no) quiero ir al cine contigo (con usted).
9. Estudio para aprender, para ser profesor(a), etc.
10. Voy a estar en la universidad por cuatro años.

B. 1. Cuando fuimos a Chile, viajamos por el desierto.
2. Pudimos ver los Andes y el Océano Pacífico.
3. Estuvimos allí por dos meses.
4. En vez de ir a restaurantes, compramos frutas y empanadas de los vendedores.
5. Un día caminamos al centro para comprar regalos.
6. Tengo algo interesante en casa para ti.

V. A. 1. Voy . . . 2. Tengo . . . 3. Vengo . . . 4. Traigo . . . 5. Pongo . . .
6. Doy . . . 7. Salgo . . . 8. Digo . . . 9. Voy . . . 10. Hago . . .

B. 1. La hacienda es nuestra. Es (la) nuestra.
2. Los gatos son suyos. Son sus gatos. Son (los) suyos.
3. ¿Son tuyos los caballos? ¿Son (los) tuyos?
4. La vaca es suya. Es su vaca. Es (la) suya.
5. Los animales son míos. Son (los) míos.

Autoexamen y repaso #8

I. 1. la cama, la cómoda, etc. 2. el sofá, el sillón, el televisor, etc. 3. la estufa,
el refrigerador, el fregadero, etc. 4. la mesa, las sillas, los platos, etc. 5. el
lavabo, la bañera, la ducha, etc.

II. 1. Abrazaba . . . 2. Corría . . . 3. Amabas . . . 4. Leías . . . 5. Pedía
. . . 6. Andaba . . . 7. Queríamos jugar . . . 8. Visitábamos . . . 9. Salíais
. . . 10. Caminabais . . . 11. Comían . . . 12. Hablaban . . .

III. 1. . . . fui a la playa. 2. . . . iba a una sección remota de la playa. 3. . . .
nadé en un lago. 4. . . . nadaba en el océano. 5. . . . corría en la playa.
6. . . . corrí por el pueblo. 7. . . . tuve una experiencia extraordinaria. 8. . . .
tenía experiencias interesantes. 9. . . . volvía a casa en agosto. 10. . . . volví
a casa en septiembre.

IV. A. 1. Hace dos semanas que trabajo aquí. 3. Hace un año que conozco
2. Hace tres meses que juego al tenis. a mi compañero de cuarto.

B. 1. Hablé con mis abuelos hace dos semanas.
2. Limpié mi cuarto hace tres días.
3. Vi una película hace un mes.

V. 1. Compré este sillón, ése y aquél.
2. Compré estas toallas, ésas y aquéllas.
3. Compré estos platos, ésos y aquéllos.
4. Compré esta lámpara, ésa y aquélla.

VI. A. 1. ¿Cuántas alcobas (recámaras) tiene? ¿Cuántos baños? ¿Tiene muebles?, etc.
2. Era grande y nuevo. Tenía una sala y tres alcobas, etc.
3. Hablaban, estudiaban, miraban la televisión, comían, etc.
4. Hace (_____ meses/años) que estudio en la universidad.
5. Hace (_____ meses/años) que llegué aquí.

B. 1. Era la medianoche.
2. Hacía mucho viento.
3. Las estrellas estaban en el cielo.
4. Dormía cuando alguien entró en la casa.
5. Llamé al policía a la una de la mañana.
6. Hace cinco horas que estoy en mi alcoba.
7. Salió hace cinco minutos.
8. ¡Esto es horrible!
9. Este sombrero y esos zapatos son suyos.

VII. A. 1. No, no había nadie en la cocina.
2. No, no había nada en la estufa.
3. No, no vi ningún insecto en el comedor.
4. No, no entré ni en la alcoba ni en el baño.
5. Nunca cierro la puerta al salir.
6. Tampoco cierro las ventanas.

B. 1. Tenía sed. 2. Tenía frío. 3. Tenía calor. 4. Tenía miedo. 5. Tenía sueño.

C. 1. Hacía mucho frío. 2. Nevaba. 3. Hacía calor. Hacía sol. 4. Hacía viento. 5. Llovía.

Autoexamen y repaso #9

I. 1. terminar, ganar, contestar, recibir, gastar, depositar, poner   2. la dirección
3. el buzón   4. el paquete   5. sellos   6. efectivo   7. prestar   8. devolver
9. la máquina de escribir, la computadora

II. A. 1. Antonio va a llevarme.   2. Va a llevarnos.   3. Va a llevarlos.   4. Va a llevarlas.   5. Va a llevarlos.   6. Va a llevarla.   7. Va a llevarte.   8. Va a llevarlo.

B. 1. Sí, las encontré.   2. Sí, los compré.   3. Sí, lo cambié.   4. Sí, las pagué.   5. Sí, la recibí.

III. 1. Ella acaba de escribirme.   2. Acaba de escribirles.   3. Acaba de escribirles.
4. Acaba de escribirte.   5. Acaba de escribirnos.

IV. 1. Sí, se la presté.
2. Sí, se los devolví.
3. Sí, se lo di.
4. Sí, te la traje.
5. Sí, te los mostré.
6. Sí, te los compré.
7. Sí, voy a dárselo (a ustedes).
8. Sí, voy a prestársela (a ustedes).
9. Sí, voy a devolvérselas (a ustedes).
10. Sí, me lo diste.
11. Sí, me la mostraste.
12. Sí, me lo devolviste.

V. 1. Lo hizo rápidamente. 2. Lo hizo profesionalmente.
3. Lo hizo frecuentemente. 4. Lo hizo recientemente.
VI. A. 1. Estoy tratando de estudiar, etc.
2. Acabo de terminar la tarea, etc.
3. Sí, (No, no) quiero prestártelo.
4. Sí, (No, no) voy a pedírselas (a ella).
5. Sí, (No, no) se la di (a él) (a ella).
6. Sí, (No, no) voy a mostrárselo (a él) (a ella).
B. 1. No me conoce bien. 2. Voy a escribirle mañana.
3. Nos mandó el paquete. 4. Tina, quiero mostrártelo.
5. David, ¿puedes prestárselo (a ellos)?
VII. A. 1. No. Está escribiéndola ahora.
2. No. Está haciéndola ahora.
3. No. Está devolviéndolos ahora.
4. No. Está leyéndola ahora.
5. No. Está terminándolo ahora.
B. 1. Me mandaba . . . 2. Me invitaba . . . 3. Me prestaba . . . 4. Me
mostraba . . . 5. Me leía . . . 6. Me decía . . . 7. Me quería . . .
C. 1. Le gustaron las catedrales.
2. Nos gustó la biblioteca.
3. Les gustaron los almacenes.
4. Te gustó el teatro.
5. Me gustaron los restaurantes.

Autoexamen y repaso #10

I. 1. sonar 2. secarse 3. sentarse 4. vestirse, ponerse 5. ponerse 6. peinarse
7. cepillarse 8. cortarse 9. afeitarse 10. lavarse, bañarse 11. acostarse,
dormirse 12. enamorarse, comprometerse, casarse 13. divertirse
14. preocuparse
II. 1. Mi compañera de cuarto se despierta. 2. Me levanto. 3. Te quitas los
pijamas. 4. Os vestís. 5. Nos preocupamos por el examen. 6. Ana y Susana se enojan. 7. Me voy. 8. Acabo de bañarme. 9. Felipe acaba de
secarse. 10. Acabas de lavarte la cara. 11. Acabamos de afeitarnos.
12. Acaban de cepillarse los dientes. 13. Acabo de peinarme. 14. Pedro
acaba de ponerse los calcetines.
III. 1. He caminado . . . 2. Hemos visitado . . . 3. Has sacado . . . 4. Ha ido
. . . 5. Habéis comprado . . . 6. Mis amigos han escrito . . . 7. Ha viajado
. . . 8. He subido . . . 9. Has visto . . . 10. Han conocido . . . 11. He
hecho . . . 12. Me he divertido. 13. Hemos vuelto . . .
IV. 1. El profesor lo había dicho. 2. Habíamos hecho . . . 3. Lupe y Cecilia
habían escrito . . . 4. Había estudiado . . . 5. ¿Los habías terminado?
6. ¿Ustedes habían leído . . . ?
V. 1. El cheque fue firmado por el abogado.
2. La dirección fue mandada por mi tío.
3. Los sellos fueron encontrados por mi hermano.
4. Los paquetes fueron recibidos por mi hermana.
5. Las cartas fueron escritas por la mujer.
VI. A. 1. Después de levantarme, me baño, me visto, me peino, etc.
2. Al levantarse, se lavó, se vistió, se cepilló los dientes, etc.
3. Se besaron, se abrazaron, etc.

4. Sí, nos queremos mucho. Sí, nos abrazamos mucho.

5. Se puede estudiar bien en la biblioteca. No se puede estudiar bien en el dormitorio/la residencia de estudiantes.

6. Se venden libros en la librería. Se vende comida en la cafetería, etc.

7. Me he levantado, me he vestido, he ido a las clases, etc.

8. Sí, nos hemos divertido.

B. 1. Tuve que acostarme temprano porque no me sentía bien.

2. Se enojó y se fue (salió).　　　4. Ana, ¿te habían llamado?

3. No la hemos visto recientemente.　5. La carta fue encontrada por la hija.

VII. A. 1. Sí. Estuve en España el año pasado.

2. Sí. Fui a Alaska . . .　　　　4. Sí. Anduve por la selva Amazonas . . .

3. Sí. Hice un viaje a Australia . . .　5. Sí. Tuve muchos problemas . . .

B. 1. La hice esta mañana.　2. Lo traje . . .　3. Lo traduje . . .　4. La puse en la computadora . . .　5. So lo dije . . .

C. 1. La navaja está encima de la toalla.　2. fuera de　3. cerca del　4. detrás de

D. 1. para　2. para　3. por　4. por　5. por　6. por　7. por　8. para　9. para

Autoexamen y repaso #11

I. 1. la salida, la llegada　2. el boleto/billete　3. de primera (segunda) clase, de ida y vuelta　4. las maletas, el equipaje, la propina　5. la revista, el periódico　6. las noticias, las caricaturas　7. de cobro revertido, de larga distancia, común, etc.　8. ocupada　9. la guía telefónica, el código de área.

II. 1. Juanita y Mario tendrán . . .　2. Alquilaré . . .　3. Mi esposo(a) y yo pasaremos . . .　4. Harás . . .　5. Volveréis . . .　6. Carlota irá . . .　7. Alberto será . . .　8. Podremos ir . . .　9. Trabajarán . . .

III. 1. Compraría . . .　2. Alicia daría . . .　3. Pepe pondría . . .　4. Viajaríamos . . .　5. Monica y Lupe saldrían . . .　6. Tendrías . . .　7. Comerían . . .

IV. 1. Los hombres son tan inteligentes como las mujeres.　2. Roberto es tan alto como Miguel.　3. Lisa es tan simpática como Rosario.　4. Los Gutiérrez tienen tanto dinero como los Gómez.　5. Los Gutiérrez tienen tantos coches como los Gómez.　6. Los Gutiérrez tienen tanta ropa como los Gómez.

V. 1. Mi hermano es más fuerte que yo. Mi primo es el más fuerte de los tres.

2. Tina es más bonita que Teresa. Nina es la más bonita de las tres.

3. La ensalada es mejor que la carne. El postre es el mejor de los tres.

4. Mis primos son peores que mis hermanos. Mis primas son las peores de los tres.

VI. A. 1. Limpia el cuarto.　2. Apaga la radio.　3. Haz la cama.　4. Pon la mesa.　5. Come las legumbres.　6. Sé bueno(a).　7. Córtate el pelo.　8. Acuéstate temprano.

B. 1. No bebas cerveza.　2. No vuelvas tarde a la casa.　3. No vayas a la fiesta.　4. No me digas mentiras.　5. No salgas con esos muchachos.　6. No seas insolente.　7. No te levantes tarde.　8. No te preocupes.　9. No te pongas impaciente.　10. No te enojes.

VII. A. 1. Dormiré, etc.　2. Nadaría en el océano, etc.　3. Sí, (No, no) soy tan inteligente como mi hermano(a).　4. Sí, (No, no) tengo tantas camisetas como mi hermano(a).　5. Sí, (No, no) trabajo tanto como mi hermano(a).

6. Soy más (menos) guapo(a) que mi hermano(a).   7. Soy mayor (menor) que mi hermano(a).   8. Mi padre, etc., es la persona más generosa de mi familia.

B.   1. Saldremos para la estación de ferrocarril a las diez.   2. ¿Quién comprará los boletos (billetes)?   3. (Él) dijo que llegaríamos a la medianoche. 4. Pepe, ¿podrías llevar mi equipaje?   5. Carmen tiene tantas maletas como yo.   6. Es tan divertida como su hermano.   7. Es más responsable que él.   8. Es la mejor estudiante de nuestra clase de español.   9. El tren ha llegado. ¡Ven aquí! ¡Corre!   10. ¡No dejes la revista en el banco!

VIII. A.   1. era   2. fue   3. esperaban   4. leían   5. compró   6. se sentó 7. estuvo   8. dormía   9. lo despertó   10. corrió   11. vio   12. había 13. subió   14. tuvo

B.   1. Sí, les escribiré.   2. Sí, las haré.   3. Sí, las traeré.   4. Sí, se lo mandaré.   5. Sí, se lo mostraré.   6. Sí, se la daré.

Autoexamen y repaso #12

I.   1. Puede revisar la batería, los frenos, el motor, las llantas, el aceite, etc. Llena el tanque. Limpia el parabrisas. Cambia el aceite y las llantas.
2. Digo ¡caramba! o ¡qué barbaridad!
Digo ¡lo siento mucho! o ¡qué lástima!
3. No debo estacionarme en los puentes, en la carretera, etc.
4. ¿Tiene usted su licencia de chófer? ¿Tiene usted seguro de automóvil? ¿A cuánta velocidad (millas por hora) viajaba?

II.   1. Espere un momento.   2. Tráigamelo mañana.   3. Siéntese aquí.   4. Muéstremelo.   5. Dígame lo que sabe.   6. Vuelvan a las diez.   7. No se vayan enojados.   8. Escríbame su respuesta.

III.   1. Hagámoslo otra vez. No lo hagamos.   2. Salgamos ahora mismo. No salgamos.   3. Vamos a la discoteca. No vayamos.   4. Parémonos aquí. No nos paremos.   5. Entremos en este restaurante. No entremos.

IV.   1. Me alegro que Juanita vaya.   2. Deseo que se divierta mucho.   3. Prefiero que viaje en tren.   4. Insisto en que lleve cheques de viajeros.   5. Espero que llegue a tiempo.   6. Temo que pierda las maletas.   7. No creo que encuentre el hotel fácilmente.   8. Dudo que quiera volver a casa.

V.   A.   1. Quieren que los estudiantes estudien, vengan a la clase a tiempo, etc. 2. Espero que me visiten, etc.   3. Dudo que mi compañero(a) de cuarto vaya a la biblioteca, etc.

B.   1. Doble a la derecha en la esquina.   2. Al llegar al semáforo, doble a la izquierda.   3. Siga recto (derecho) cuatro cuadras.   4. Llámenos de la estación de gasolina.   5. No se estacionen en el puente.   6. Parémonos aquí. 7. Juan, ¿sugieres que salgamos ahora mismo?   8. Me alegro que el coche tenga bastante gasolina.   9. No estoy seguro(a) que podamos encontrar la casa.

VI.   A.   1. Lo comprarán.   2. Lo harán.   3. Las traerán.   4. Saldrán.   5. Podrán llegar mañana. (Llegarán mañana.)   6. Tendrán cuidado.   7. Las entenderán.

B.   1. Repare este motor y ése.   2. Cambie estas llantas y ésas.   3. Revise esta batería y ésa.   4. Lave estos coches y ésos.   5. Arregle este camión y ése.   6. Revise esta motocicleta y ésa.

Autoexamen y repaso #13

I. 1. la agencia de viajes 2. el avión, etc. 3. la cámara, el rollo de película
4. el equipaje 5. los boletos, la tarjeta de embarque 6. la sala de espera
7. el cinturón 8. la azafata, el auxiliar de vuelo 9. el equipaje, la sala de
reclamación de equipajes 10. la aduana 11. la escala 12. los amigos, etc.

II. 1. Es una lástima que el avión llegue tarde. 2. Es bueno que tengas todo el
equipaje. 3. Es urgente que vayamos a la aduana. 4. Es importante que sepas
el número del vuelo. 5. No es cierto que no puedas encontrar el boleto. 6. Es
extraño que no haya azafatas. 7. ¡Es imposible que no haya piloto!

III. 1. Busco una casa que esté cerca del mar. No tenemos una casa que esté cerca
del mar. Sí, ¡tenemos una casa que está cerca del mar!
2. Busco una casa que tenga cuatro alcobas. No tenemos una casa que tenga
cuatro alcobas. Sí, ¡tenemos una casa que tiene cuatro alcobas!
3. Busco una casa que no necesite reparaciones. No tenemos una casa que no
necesite reparaciones. Sí, ¡tenemos una casa que no necesita reparaciones!
4. Busco una casa que no cueste mucho. No tenemos una casa que no cueste
mucho. Sí, ¡tenemos una casa que no cuesta mucho!

IV. A. 1. Sí, para que mi hermano se divierta, vea a "Mickey Mouse", etc. 2. No,
a menos que tenga tiempo, etc. 3. Sí, con tal que consiga la reservación,
etc. 4. Sí, en caso de que necesite encontrar una palabra, etc.
B. 1. Sí, cuando llegué a casa, etc. 2. Sí, cuando llegue a casa, etc. 3. Sí,
tan pronto como lavé la ropa, etc. 4. Sí, tan pronto como lave la ropa,
etc. 5. Sí, después de que tú me llamaste, etc. 6. Sí, después de que tú
me llames, etc.

V. 1. Me alegro (de) que mi amiga haya venido a la universidad. 2. Me alegro
(de) que mi amiga me haya traído un regalo. 3. Siento que mi amiga haya
tenido un accidente. 4. Me alegro (de) que mis amigos me hayan llamado de
larga distancia. 5. Siento que mis amigos me hayan dado malas noticias. 6. Me
alegro (de) que me hayas escrito de Panamá. 7. Me alegro (de) que Elena y yo
hayamos recibido el paquete.

VI. A. 1. Es urgente (necesario, mejor, etc.) que limpie el cuarto, etc. 2. Busco
empleados que sean inteligentes, etc. 3. Los invito para que podamos
hablar, etc. 4. Voy a hacerlo tan pronto como tenga tiempo, etc. 5. Temo
que haya tenido un accidente, etc.
B. 1. María, ¿conoces a alguien que pueda traducir esta carta? 2. No, no
conozco a nadie que haya estudiado chino. 3. Pablo, ¿viajarás a las
montañas este fin de semana? 4. Sí, con tal que haga buen tiempo.
5. Tendremos que salir antes de que empiece a nevar. 6. Pondremos
nuestras cosas en el coche tan pronto como hayan revisado el aceite.

VII. A. 1. No factures el equipaje ahora. Factúralo más tarde. 2. No saques las
fotos ahora. Sácalas más tarde. 3. No vayas a la sala de espera ahora. Ve
más tarde. 4. No salgas ahora. Sal más tarde. 5. No te despidas ahora.
Despídete más tarde.
B. 1. ¿Lo ha visto? Espero que lo haya visto. 2. ¿Lo ha devuelto? No es cierto
que lo haya devuelto. 3. ¿Lo ha escrito? Es probable que lo haya escrito.
4. ¿Lo ha hecho? Es improbable que lo haya hecho. 5. ¿Lo ha puesto en
el coche? Es posible que lo haya puesto en el coche. 6. ¿Lo ha dicho? Me
alegro de que lo haya dicho. 7. ¿Lo ha roto? Temo que lo haya roto.

Autoexamen y repaso #14

I. 1. La persona que trabaja en la recepción, hace las reservaciones, etc.
2. La persona que trabaja en el hotel, lleva las maletas de los huéspedes a las habitaciones, etc.
3. La persona que limpia las habitaciones, etc.
4. La persona que trabaja en el restaurante, sirve la comida, etc.
5. La persona que trabaja en el hotel, abre la puerta para los huéspedes, etc.
6. Donde nadamos.
7. Lo que llamamos cuando queremos que traigan comida, etc., a la habitación.
8. Lo que usamos para subir rápidamente de un piso a otro.
9. Donde ponemos los papeles, etc., que ya no necesitamos.
10. Lo que usamos en la cama, encima de las sábanas, cuando tenemos frío.
11. La persona que visita el hotel.
12. El papel que indica cuánto hemos pagado.

II. 1. Quería que mi hermano se cepillara los dientes. Quería que mi hermano se peinara. Quería que mi hermano se vistiera.
2. Esperaban que los hermanos no se enojaran. Esperaban que los hermanos no se quejaran. Esperaban que los hermanos no se preocuparan.
3. Sugería que te quedaras aquí. Sugería que consiguieras trabajo. Sugería que ahorraras tu dinero.
4. Se alegraba (de) que nos comprometiéramos. Se alegraba (de) que nos casáramos. Se alegraba (de) que viniéramos a visitarla.

III. 1. Si ganara dinero, lo ahorraría. 2. Si lo ahorrara, tendría mucho dinero. 3. Si tuviera mucho dinero, compraría un carro. 4. Si comprara un carro, haría un viaje. 5. Si hiciera un viaje, iría a México. 6. Si fuera a México, me quedaría allí dos meses. 7. Si me quedara allí dos meses, perdería mi trabajo. 8. Si perdiera mi trabajo, no tendría dinero. 9. Si no tuviera dinero, . . .

IV. A. 1. Quería que me compraran un coche, etc. 2. Deseaba que me compraran un coche para que pudiera manejar a la universidad, etc. 3. Era necesario que habláramos, que nos entendiéramos, etc. 4. Si tuviera mucho tiempo libre, descansaría, leería novelas, iría a la playa, etc. 5. Si estuviera en la ciudad de Nueva York, iría a los museos, etc.

B. 1. Si (él) estuviera aquí, la llamaría. 3. Estaría aquí si fuera posible.
2. Esperábamos que (ella) viniera. 4. Era una lástima que no la viéramos.
5. Dejamos un recado para ella antes de que (él) saliera.

V. A. 1. Sí. Este botones es tan joven como ése. 2. Sí. Este botones lleva tantas maletas como ése. 3. Sí. Este botones ayuda tanto como ése. 4. Sí. Este botones trabaja tantas horas como ése. 5. Sí. Este botones recibe tanto dinero como ése.

B. 1. Ése es mejor que éste. Aquél es el mejor de los tres. 2. Ésa es más cara que ésta. Aquélla es la más cara de las tres. 3. Ése es peor que éste. Aquél es el peor de los tres. 4. Ésa es más grande que ésta. Aquélla es la más grande de las tres.

C. 1. . . . me despido de mis amigos.
2. . . . estoy despidiéndome de mis amigos.
3. . . . me despedí de mis amigos.
4. . . . me despedía de mis amigos.
5. . . . me despediré de mis amigos.
6. . . . me he despedido de mis amigos.
7. . . . me había despedido de mis amigos.
8. . . . que me despida de mis amigos.
9. . . . que me despidiera de mis amigos.

■ VOCABULARIO ■

SPANISH-ENGLISH ■

The numbers refer to the lessons in which words are first introduced as active vocabulary.

A

a at, to, 2; **a causa de** be-cause of; **a comienzo** at the beginning; **a continuación** following; **a la vez** at the same time; **a lo largo de** along; **a menos que** unless, 13; **a partir de** beginning with; **a pesar de** in spite of; **a tiempo** on time, 3; **a veces** at times, 6

abierto open, 2
abogada f lawyer, 2
abogado m lawyer, 2
abrazar to hug, 4
abrazo m hug, 9
abrigo m coat, 5
abril April, 5
abrir to open, 3
abrocharse to fasten, 13
abrumador overwhelming
abuela f grandmother, 2
abuelo m grandfather, 2
aburrido bored, 2
a.C. (antes de Cristo) B.C.

acabar de to have just, 9
accidente m accident, 12
aceite m oil, 3
aceituna f olive, 3
acontecimiento m event
acostarse (ue) to go to bed, 10
actual present
adelante forward
además de besides
adiós good-bye, 1
adobar to marinate
¿adónde? (to) where?, 3
aduana f customs, 13
aéreo: correo aéreo m air-mail, 9; **línea aérea** f airline, 13
aeropuerto m airport, 13
afeitarse to shave, 10
agencia f agency, 13; **agencia de viajes** f travel agency, 13
agosto August, 5
agradecer to thank
agua f water, 3; **agua mineral** f mineral water, 3

aguacate m avocado
ahora now, 3; **ahora mismo** right now, 12
ahorrar to save, 9
aire m air, 12; **aire acondicio-nado** m air conditioning, 14
ajo m garlic, 3
al on, upon, 10; **al lado de** beside, 7
alcanzar to achieve
alcoba f bedroom, 8
alegrarse to be happy, glad, 12
alemán German, 1
alfombra f carpet, rug, 8
algo something, 6
algodón m cotton
alguien someone, somebody, 6
alguno someone (pron.), some (adj.), 6
alimento m food
allí there, 2
almacén m department store, 6
almendra f almond

454

almíbar *m* syrup
almohada *f* pillow, 14
almorzar (ue) to have lunch, 14
almuerzo *m* lunch, 3
alojamiento *m* lodging
alquilar to rent, 8
alto tall, high, 2; stop; **en voz alta** aloud, 1
altura *f* height, altitude
alumbrar to enlighten
alumna *f* student, 1
alumno *m* student, 1
alza *f* rise
amable kind, nice, amiable, 2
amante *m, f* lover
amar to love, 4
amarillo yellow, 5
ambos both
americano American, 1
amiga *f* friend, 2
amigo *m* friend, 2
amistad *f* friendship
analfabetismo *m* illiteracy
anaranjado orange (color), 5
andaluz Andalusian
andar to walk, to go, run (machinery), 6
andén *m* platform, track, 11
angustia *f* anguish
anillo *m* ring, 5
animal *m* animal, 7
anoche last night, 6
antes de before, 7; **antes de que** before (conj.), 13
antipático disagreeable, unpleasant (persons), 2
antitético antithetical
antiguo ancient
añadir to add
año *m* year, 6; **año pasado** last year, 6; **año que viene** next year, 10; **tener . . . años** to be . . . years old, 5
apagar to turn off, 8
apellido *m* surname
aprender to learn, 3
apresurar to hurry
aproximarse to approach
aquel *m* that, 8; **aquellos** *m* those, 8

aquella *f* that, 8; **aquellas** *f* those, 8
aquí here, 2
araña *f* spider, 7
árbol *m* tree, 7
arena *f* sand, 7
arete *m* earring, 5
arreglar to fix, 12
arroz *m* rice, 3
artesanía *f* artifact, craft
artículo *m* article
asado roasted, 3; roast *m*
ascendiente *m* ancestor
ascensor *m* elevator, 14
asegurar to assure
aseo *m* restroom, 11
así so, 1; thus
asiento *m* seat, 13
asimismo similarly
asunto *m* matter
atentamente attentively, 9
aterrizar to land
atrevimiento *m* daring
aun even
aún yet, still
auto *m* car, 2
autobús *m* bus, 6
auxiliar de vuelo *m* steward, 13
avasallar to enslave
avenida *f* avenue, 6
avión *m* airplane, 13
ayer yesterday, 6
ayudar to help, 11
azafata *f* stewardess, 13
azafrán *m* saffron
azúcar *m* sugar, 3
azul blue, 5

B

bahía *f* bay
bailar to dance, 4
bajar (de) to go down, get off, 8
bajo short, low, 2; under; **planta baja** *f* main floor, 14
banana *f* banana, 3
banco *m* bank, bench, 6
bañarse to bathe, take a bath, 10

bañera *f* bathtub, 8
baño *m* bath, bathroom, 8; **traje de baño** *m* bathing suit, 6
bar *m* bar, 6
barato cheap, 5
barco *m* boat, ship, 7
barrio *m* neighborhood
básquetbol *m* basketball, 4
bastante enough, quite, 11
basura *f* trash; **cubo de basura** *m* trash can, 14
bata *f* robe, 5
batalla *f* battle
batería *f* battery, 12
batir to beat
bebé *m* baby, 2
beber to drink, 3
bebida *f* drink, beverage, 3
béisbol *m* baseball, 4
belleza *f* beauty
bello beautiful
besar to kiss, 4
biblioteca *f* library, 6
bicicleta *f* bicycle, 6
bien well, fine, 1
bienvenido welcome, 14
billete *m* ticket, 11; bill (money)
bistec *m* steak, 3
blanco white, 5
blujeans *m* jeans, 5
blusa *f* blouse, 5
boca *f* mouth, 4
bocadillo *m* sandwich, 3
boletero(a) *m, f* ticket agent, 9
boleto *m* ticket, 11; **boleto de ida y vuelta** round-trip ticket, 11
bolígrafo *m* ballpoint pen, 1
bolsa *f* purse, bag, 5
bonito pretty, 2
bosque *m* forest, woods, 7
botas *f* boots, 5
botones *m* bellboy, 14
bragas *f* underpants, 5
brazo *m* arm, 4
buceo *m* diving (skin or scuba)
bueno good, 2
burro *m* donkey, 7

buscar to look for, 4
búsqueda *f* search
butaca *f* seat
buzón *m* mailbox, 9

C

caballería *f* chivalry
caballo *m* horse, 7
cabeza *f* head, 4
cacahuete *m* peanut
cada each, every, 11
café *m* coffee, 3; cafe, 6
caída *f* fall
calabaza *f* squash
calcetines *m* socks, 5
calculadora *f* calculator, 9
calefacción *f* heating, 14
calidad *f* quality
caliente hot, 3
calor *m* heat, 5; **hacer calor** to be hot (weather), 5; **tener calor** to be hot (person), 5
callar(se) to be quiet, 11
calle *f* street, 6
calzoncillos *m* undershorts, 5
cama *f* bed, 8
cámara *f* camera, 13
camarera *f* waitress, 14
camarero *m* waiter, 14
camarón *m* shrimp, 3
cambiar *m* to change, 9
cambio *m* change, 9
caminar to walk, 4
camino *m* road, 12
camión *m* truck, 12
camisa *f* shirt, 5; **camisa de dormir** nightgown, 5
camiseta *f* T-shirt, undershirt, 5
campo *m* country, field, 2
canción *f* song
canoso gray, white (hair)
cansado tired, 2
cantar to sing, 4
cara *f* face, 4
carabela *f* vessel
¡caramba! my goodness!, 12
caricatura *f* cartoon, 11
cariño *m* affection, 9
carne *f* meat, 3

caro expensive, 5
carretera *f* highway, 12
carro *m* car, 2
carta *f* letter, card, 9; menu
cartera *f* wallet, 5
casa *f* house, home, 2; **casa de correos** post office, 9
casarse (con) to get married, 10
casi almost
caso *m* case; **en caso de que** in case, 13
cassette *m* cassette, 8
castaño brown (hair)
casualidad *f* coincidence
catedral *f* cathedral, 6
católico Catholic
catorce fourteen, 1
cautivar capture
cebolla *f* onion, 3
cena *f* supper, dinner, 3
cenar to dine, have dinner (supper), 14
centro *m* center, downtown, 6; **centro comercial** *m* shopping center
cepillar(se) to brush, 10
cepillo *m* brush, 10; **de dientes** toothbrush, 10
cerca de near, 7
cerdo *m* pig, 7
cereal *m* cereal, 3
cereza *f* cherry, 3
cero zero, 1
cerrar (ie) to close, 4; **cerrado** closed, 2
certificado certified
cerveza *f* beer, 3
cielo *m* sky, 7
cien(to) one hundred, 4
cigarro *m* cigar
cine *m* movie theater, movies, 6
cinco five, 1
cincuenta fifty, 4
cinturón *m* belt, seatbelt, 13
ciudad *f* city, 2
ciudadano *m* citizen
¡claro! of course
clase *f* class, 1
cobarde *m* coward; cowardly
cobija *m* blanket, 14

cobrar to cash, charge, 9
cocina *f* kitchen, 8
cocinar to cook, 4
coche *m* car, 2
código de área *m* area code, 11
collar *m* necklace, 5
comedor *m* dining room, 8
comer to eat, 3
comerciante *m* merchant
comida *f* meal, food, 3
como as, 11; **¿cómo?** how?, 1; **¿cómo te va?** how's it going?, 1; **¡cómo no!** of course!
cómoda *f* chest of drawers (bureau), 8
compañero *m* companion; **compañero(a) de cuarto** roommate, 10
compañerismo *m* companionship
compendio *m* compendium
complejo complex
completar to complete
complemento *m* object (of an action)
comportamiento *m* behavior
comprar to buy, 3
compras: ir de compras to go shopping, 5
comprendido included
comprometer(se) con to get engaged to, 10
comprometido engaged, 10
computadora *f* computer, 9
con with, 7; **con permiso** excuse me, 1; **con tal que** provided that, 13
concierto *m* concert
concordancia *f* harmony
concreción *f* realization
confianza *f* confidence
confiar to trust
confirmar to confirm, 13
conjunto *m* totality
conmigo with me, 7
conocer to know, to be acquainted with (persons, places), 4
conocimiento *m* knowledge

consecuencia f result
conseguir (i, i) to get, obtain, 13
consejo m advice
consigo with himself, etc.
contar (ue) to count
contento happy, content, 2
contestar to answer, 9
contigo with you (fam.), 7
contra against
convocar to assemble
copa f glass, goblet
corazón m heart
corbata f tie, 5
cordillera f mountain range
correo m mail, 9; **correo aéreo** air mail, 9
correr to run, 4
corrida de toros f bullfight
corromper to corrupt
cortar(se) to cut (oneself), 10
cortina f curtain, 8
corto short, 5
cosa f thing, 5
costar (ue) to cost, 5
crear to create
crecer to grow
crecimiento m growth
crédito m credit; **tarjeta de crédito** f credit card, 9
creer to believe, 12
crema f cream, 3; **crema de afeitar** shaving cream, 10
criada f maid, 14
criollo m creole
cruzar to cross, 12
cuaderno m notebook, 1
cuadra f block, 12
cuadro m picture, painting, 8
cualquier any
¿cuál? which (one)?, 3; **¿cuáles?** which (ones)?, 3
cuando when, 3
¿cuándo? when?, 3
¿cuánto? how much?, 3; **¿cuántos?** how many?, 3
cuarenta forty, 4
cuarto m room, 8; fourth, 14; quarter, 1
cuatro four, 1

cuatrocientos four hundred, 6
cubierto covered
cubo de basura m trash can, 14
cuchara f spoon, 8
cuchillo m knife, 8
cuello m neck, 4
cuenta f bill, 14; **por cuenta de** responsibility of
cuerpo m body, 4
cuidado m care; **tener cuidado** to be careful, 12
cuidar to take care of
culebra snake, 7
cumpleaños m birthday, 6
cumplirse to realize
cuyo whose

CH

champú m shampoo, 10
chaqueta f jacket, 5
charlar to talk
cheque m check, 9; **cheque de viajero** traveler's check, 9
chica f girl, 2
chicle m chewing gum
chico m boy, 2
chimenea f chimney, fireplace, 8
chino Chinese, 1
chocar to collide
chorizo m sausage, 3
choza f hut, 7
chuleta f: **chuleta de cerdo** pork chop, 3
churro m Spanish-style donut

D

dar to give, 4; **darse prisa** to hurry up, 12
d.C. (después de Cristo) A.D.
de of, from, about, 2; **de nada** you are welcome, 1; **de prisa** hurriedly
debajo (de) beneath, under, 7
deber to owe, should, ought, 4
debidamente exactly
debido a because
débil weak, 2

decidir to decide
décimo tenth, 14
decir to say, tell, 4
dedo m finger, 4
dejar to leave behind, allow, let, 11
delante (de) in front (of), ahead, 7
deleitar to delight
delgado slender, 2
demasiado too, too much, 11
demora f delay, 11
dentro (de) inside, 7
dependienta f saleswoman, clerk
dependiente m salesman, clerk
deporte m sport, 4
depositar to deposit, 9
derecha f right (direction), 12
derecho m law; **derecho** (adv.) straight ahead, 12
derrotar to defeat
desarrollar to develop
desarrollo m development
desayunar to have breakfast, 14
desayuno m breakfast, 3
descansar to rest, 4
desde from
desear to desire, to wish, to want, 3
desgraciado unfortunate
desierto m desert, 7
desinflado flat, 12
despacio slowly, 12
despedirse (i, i) to say good-bye, 13
despertador m alarm clock, 10
despertarse (ie) to wake up, 10
despreciar to scorn
después (de) after, 7; **después de que** after, 13
desventaja f disadvantage
detrás (de) behind, 7
devolver (ue) to return (something), 9
devuelto returned, 10
día m day, 1; **buenos días** good morning, 1; **todo el día** all day, 3; **todos los días** everyday, 3

día festivo *m* holiday
diablo *m* devil
diario daily (adj.); newspaper (noun) *m*
diarrea *f* diarrhea
dibujo *m* drawing
diciembre December, 5
dicho said, 10
diente *m* tooth, 4
diez ten, 1
difícil difficult, 2
digestivo digestive
dinero *m* money, 6
Dios *m* God; **¡Dios mío!** My God!
dirrección *f* address, direction, 9
disco *m* phonograph record, 8
diseñar to design
disfrutar to enjoy
divertido amusing, funny, 2
divertirse (ie, i) to have a good time, 10
doblar to turn, 12
doble: cuarto doble *m* double room, 14
doce twelve, 1
documentación *f* documents, 13
dolor *m* pain, ache, 4; **dolor de cabeza** headache, 4; **dolor de estómago** stomach ache, 4; **dolor de garganta** sore throat, 4
dominar to dominate
domingo *m* Sunday, 1
don title of respect for men
¿dónde? where?, 3; **¿de dónde?** from where?, 3; **¿adónde?** (to) where?, 3
doña title of respect for women
dormir (ue, u) to sleep, 4; **dormirse** to fall asleep, to go to sleep, 10
dormitorio *m* dormitory, 10
dos two, 1
doscientos two hundred, 6
ducha *f* shower, 8
duda *f* doubt, 12
dudar to doubt, 12
dulces *m* sweets, candy
durante during, 7
durazno *m* peach, 3

E

e and (before *i*, *hi*)
echar to throw; **echar al correo** to mail, 9
edad *f* age
edificio *m* building, 6
efectivo *m* cash, 9
ejercer to exercise
ejercicio *m* exercise, 1
él he (subject), 2; him (obj. of prep.), 7
el the, 1
elegir to elect, choose
ella she (subject), 2; her (obj. of prep.), 7
ellas *f* they (subject), 2; them (obj. of prep.), 7
ellos *m* they (subject), 2; them (obj. of prep.), 7
embarazada pregnant
emparedado *m* sandwich
empeorar to deteriorate
empezar (ie) to begin, 9
empleado(a) *m, f* clerk
empleo *m* job, work, 4
en in, on, at, 1; **en caso de que** in case, 13; **en cuanto a** with respect to; **en el exterior** abroad; **en seguida** right away; **en vez de** instead of, 7
enamorado in love, 10
enamorar(se) to fall in love, 10
encantar to enchant
encargarse to be in charge
encender (ie) to turn on (lights), 8
encima (de) on top of, 7
encinta pregnant
encontrar (ue) to find, 9
encontrarse to meet
encubrir to conceal
enchiladas *f* regional dish from Mexico
enchufe *m* plug
endeudamiento *m* debt
enero January, 5
enfermero(a) *m, f* nurse, 2
enfermo sick, 2
enfrente de in front of, facing, opposite, 7
engaño *m* deception

enojado angry, 2
enojarse to get angry, 10
enorgullecer to fill with pride
ensalada *f* salad, 3
entender (ie) to understand, 4
entrar (en) to enter, to go in, 6
entre between, among, 7
equivocado wrong, 11
equipaje *m* luggage, 11
equipo *m* team, 4
esa *f* that, 8; **esas** *f* those, 8
escala *f* stopover (plane), 13
escalera *f* stairs, 8
escasear to be scarce
esconder to hide
escribir to write, 3; **escribir a máquina** to type, 9
escrito written, 10
escritorio *m* desk, 1
escuchar to listen (to), 4
escuela *f* school, 2
ese *m* that, 8; **esos** those, 8
esfuerzo *m* effort
eso that (neuter), 8
espalda *f* back, 4
español Spanish (adj.), 1; Spaniard (noun) *m*, 1
espejo *m* mirror, 8
esperanza *f* hope
esperar to wait, hope (for), 6
esposa *f* wife, 2
esposo *m* husband, 2
esquiar to ski, 4
esquina *f* corner, 12
esta *f* this, 8; **estas** *f* these, 8
estación *f* station, 11; season, 5; **estación de ferrocarril** railroad station, 11; **estación de servicio** service station, 12
estacionarse to park, 12
estado *m* state; **estado civil** marital status
estante *m* shelf, bookcase, 8
estar to be, 2
este *m* this, 8; **estos** *m* these, 8
este *m* east
estimado dear, 9
esto this (neuter), 8
estómago *m* stomach, 4
estrella *f* star, 7
estudiante *m, f* student, 1

estudiar to study, 3
estufa f stove, 8
etapa f period
ética f ethic
etiqueta f tag
examen m examination, test, 1
examinar to examine
exigir to demand
experimentar to experience
extranjero foreign
extraño strange, 13

F

fácil easy, 2
fácilmente easily, 7
facturar to check (baggage), 13
falda f skirt, 5
falta f lack
familia f family, 2
favor: por favor please, 1; **hágame el favor de . . .** please
. . . , 1
febrero February, 5
fecha f date, 6
felicitaciones f congratulations,
14
feliz merry, happy, 6
feo ugly, 2
ferrocarril m railroad, 11
fiebre fever, 4
fiel faithful
fila f line, 9; **hacer fila** to
stand in line, 9
fin m end; **fin de semana** m
weekend, 1; **por fin** finally
firma f signature, 9
firmar to sign, 9
flaco skinny, 2
flan m custard
flor f flower, 7
florecer to flourish
flujo m flow; **flujo y reflujo**
ebb and flow
fondo m depth; **al fondo**
deeper; **fondo musical** background music
fortaleza f fortress
foto f photo, 13
fracaso m failure
fractura f fracture, breakage

francés French (adj.), 1;
Frenchman, 2
frecuente frequent, 9
frecuentemente frequently, 9
fregadero m sink (kitchen), 8
freno m brake, 12
fresa f strawberry, 3
fresco cool, fresh, 5; **hacer
fresco** to be cool (weather), 5
frijol m bean, 3
frío m cold, 3; **hacer frío** to
be cold (weather), 5; **tener frío**
to be cold (person), 5
frito fried, 3
frontera f border, 12
fruta f fruit, 3
fuego m fire
fuera (de) outside, 7
fuerte strong, 2
fuerza f strength
fumar to smoke, 4
funcionar to work (machinery),
12
fútbol m football, soccer, 4

G

gafas f glasses, 5; **gafas de sol**
sunglasses, 5
galleta f cookie, 3
gallina f chicken, 7
ganado m cattle, livestock
ganar to earn, win, 9
ganas: tener ganas de to feel
like, 5
garaje m garage, 8
garbanzo m chickpea
garganta f throat, 4
gaseosa f soft drink, 3
gasolina f gasoline, 12
gastar to spend (money), 9
gato m cat, 7
gaucho m Argentine cowboy
general general, 9
generalmente generally, 9
gente f people, 6
gobierno m government
gordo fat, 2
gozar to enjoy
gracias thanks, 1
gran great

grande large, big, 2
gripe f flu
gris gray, 5
guantes m gloves, 5
guapo handsome, 2
guerra f war
guía m, f guide; **guía telefónica**
phone book, 11
guisante m pea, 3
gustar to like, to be pleasing, 3
gusto m pleasure, taste; **mucho
gusto** pleased to meet you, 1

H

haber (auxiliary verb) to have,
10
había there was, there were, 8
habichuelas f green beans, 3
habitación f (hotel) room, 14
hablar to speak, 3
hacendado m landowner
hacer to do, make, 4; **hacerse**
to become; **hacer buen (mal)
tiempo** to be good (bad)
weather, 5; **hacer calor** to be
hot, 5; **hacer fresco** to be
cool, 5; **hacer frío** to be
cold, 5; **hacer sol** to be
sunny, 5; **hacer viento** to be
windy, 5
hacienda f farm, ranch, 7
hallar to find
hambre f hunger, 5; **tener
hambre** to be hungry, 5
hamburguesa f hamburger, 3
harina f flour
hasta until; **hasta luego** see
you later, 1; **hasta mañana**
see you tomorrow, 1; **hasta
que** until (conj.), 13
hay there is, there are, 2; **no
hay de que** you are welcome, 1; **¿qué hay de nuevo?**
what's new?, 1
hecho m fact
hecho done, 10
helado m ice cream, 3
heredar to inherit
hermana f sister, 2
hermano m brother, 2

hermoso beautiful, 2
hielo *m* ice, 3
hierba *f* grass, 7
hierro *m* iron
higiene *f* sanitation
hija *f* daughter, 2
hijo *m* son, 2
hogar *m* home, 8
hola hello, hi, 1
hombre *m* man, 2; **hombre de negocios** *m* businessman, 2
hombro *m* shoulder, 4
hora *f* hour, time, 1
horario *m* schedule, 11
hornear to bake
hotel *m* hotel, 14
hoy today, 3; **hoy día** nowadays
huésped *m* guest, 14
huevo *m* egg, 3
humilde humble

I

ibérico Iberian
ida y vuelta round-trip, 11
iglesia *f* church, 6
igual same, equal
impaciente impatient, 11; **ponerse impaciente** to become impatient, 11
imperio *m* empire
impermeable *m* raincoat, 5
importante important, 13
importar to matter
imposible impossible, 13
impresionante impressive
improbable improbable, 13
impuesto *m* tax, 14
impunemente with impunity
información *f* information, 14
ingeniero(a) *m, f* engineer, 2
inglés English, 2
inodoro *m* toilet, 8
insecto *m* insect, 7
insistir (en) to insist (on), 12
inteligente intelligent, 2
interior: ropa interior *f* underclothing, 5
invierno *m* winter, 5

invitar to invite, 9
ir to go, 2; **irse** to go away, 10; **ir de compras** to go shopping, 5
irrespetuoso disrespectful
isla *f* island, 7
italiano Italian, 1
izquierda *f* left, 12

J

jabón *m* soap, 8
jamón *m* ham, 3
japonés Japanese, 2
jardín *m* garden, 8
jarra *f* pitcher
jefe *m* head, boss
joven young, 2
joyas *f* jewelry, 5
joyería *f* jewelry shop, 6
judías *f* green beans, 3
jueves *m* Thursday, 1
jugar (ue) to play (game), 4
jugo *m* juice, 3
julio July, 5
junio June, 5
junto together

K

kilómetro *m* kilometer (0.62 mile), 12

L

la *f* the, 1; you (sing.), her, it (dir. obj.), 9
labio *m* lip, 4
lado *m* side, edge; **al lado de** beside, 10
lago *m* lake, 7
lámpara *f* lamp, 8
langosta *f* lobster, 3
lápiz *m* pencil, 1
largo long, 5
las *f* the (pl.), 1; you (pl.), them (dir. obj.), 9
lástima *f* pity, shame, 13
lastimar to hurt

lavabo *m* sink, 8
lavarse to wash oneself, 10
le to him, to her, to you (ind. obj.), 9
lección *f* lesson, 1
leche *f* milk, 3
lechuga *f* lettuce, 3
leer to read, 4
legar to bequeath
legumbre *f* vegetable, 3
lejos (de) far (from), 7
lengua *f* tongue, language, 4
lentamente slowly, 9
lentes *m* (eye) glasses, 5
lento slow, 9
les to them, to you (ind. obj.), 9
levantarse to get up, 10
libertad *f* freedom, liberty
libre free
librería *f* bookstore, 6
libro *m* book, 1; **libro de cheques** checkbook, 9
licencia de chófer *f* driver's license, 12
líder *m* leader
liderazgo *m* leadership
ligero light
limón *m* lemon, 3
limpiaparabrisas *m* windshield wiper, 12
limpiar to clean, 4
limpio clean, 5
línea *f* line; **línea aérea** *f* airline, 13
lío: ¡qué lío! what a mess!, 12
lo *m* you (sing.), him, it (dir. obj.), 9; **lo que** that which, what, 3
los *m* the (pl.), 2; you (pl.), them (dir. obj.), 9
lucha *f* fight, struggle
luchar to fight
luego: hasta luego see you later, 1
lugar *m* place, 6
luna *f* moon, 7; **luna de miel** honeymoon, 14
lunes *m* Monday, 1
luz *f* light, 8

LL

llamada f call, 11; **común** station-to-station, 11; **de cobro revertido** collect, 11; **de larga distancia** long-distance, 11; **de persona a persona** person-to-person, 11

llamar to call, 4; **llamarse** to be called, named

llanta f tire, 12; **desinflada** flat tire, 12

llave f key, 14

llegada f arrival, 11

llegar to arrive, 3; **llegar a ser** to become

llenar to fill, 12

lleno full

llevar to carry, wear, take, 5

llover(ue) to rain, 5; **llueve** it's raining, 5

lluvia f rain, 5

M

madera f wood

madre f mother, 2

magnífico magnificent, terrific

maíz m corn, 3

mal bad, badly, 2

maleta f suitcase, 11; **hacer la maleta** to pack, 11

maletero m porter, 11

malo bad, 2

mandar to send, command, order, 9

manejar to drive, 4

manga f sleeve

maní m peanut

mano f hand, 4

manta f blanket, 14

mantener to maintain

mantequilla f butter, 3

manzana f apple, 3; block, 12

mañana f morning, 1; tomorrow (adv.), 3; **por la mañana** in the morning, 1

máquina f machine, 9; **máquina de afeitar** electric shaver, 10; **máquina de escribir** typewriter, 9

mar m sea, 7

marcar to dial, 11; to mark

mariscos m seafood, 3

martes m Tuesday, 1

marzo March, 5

más more, 11; plus

masa f dough

mayo May, 5

mayor older, 11; major; **el mayor** the oldest, 11

mayoría f majority

me me, to me, 9; myself, 10

mediados middle

medianoche f midnight, 1

medias f stockings, 5

médico(a) m, f doctor, 2

medio middle, half, 1

mediodía m noon, 1

mejor better, 11; **el mejor** the best, 11

mejorar to improve

melocotón m peach, 3

menor younger, 11; **el menor** the youngest, 11

menos less, 11; minus; **a menos que** unless, 13; **por lo menos** at least

mentira f lie, 4

mercado m market, 3

merienda f afternoon snack, 3

mermelada f jam, preserves, 3

mes m month, 5

mesa f table, 1

meseta f plateau

mestizo of mixed Indian and Spanish ancestry

metro m metro, subway, 6

mexicano Mexican, 1

mezcla f mixture

mezquita f mosque

mi my, 5

mí me (obj. of prep.), 7

miedo m fear, 5; **tener miedo** to be afraid, 5

miel f honey; **luna de miel** f honeymoon, 14

mientras while

miércoles m Wednesday, 1

mil thousand, 6

milla f mile, 12

millón m million, 6

mío mine, of mine, 5

mirar to look (at), 4

misa f mass

mismo same; **ahora mismo** right now, 12; **hoy mismo** this very day

moneda f coin, money, currency, 9

montaña f mountain, 2

morada f abode

morado purple, 5

moreno dark, brunette, 2

moro m Moor

morir (ue, u) to die, 6

mosca f fly, 7

mosquito m mosquito, 7

mostrador m counter

mostrar (ue) to show, 9

motocicleta f motorcycle, 6

motor m motor, 12

mozo m young man

muchacha f girl, 2

muchacho m boy, 2

mucho much, a lot, 3; **muchos** many, 1

muebles m furniture, 8

muerte f death

muerto dead, 10

mujer f woman, 2 **mujer de negocios** businesswoman, 2

multa f fine, 12

mundo m world, 13; **todo el mundo** everyone, 13

museo m museum, 6

musulmán Muslim

muy very, 1

N

nacer to be born

nada nothing, not anything, 6; **de nada** you are welcome, 1

nadar to swim, 4

nadie no one, nobody, 6

naranja f orange, 3

nariz f nose, 4

natación f swimming

natal native

navaja f razor, 10

Navidad *f* Christmas, 6
necesario necessary, 13
necesitar to need, 3
negar (ie) to deny, 12
negocios: hombre de negocios *m* businessman, 2; **mujer de negocios** businesswoman, 2
negro black, 5
nena *f* baby girl, 2
nene *m* baby boy, 2
nevar (ie) to snow, 5; **nieva** it's snowing, 5
ni . . . ni neither . . . nor, 6
nieta *f* granddaughter, 2
nieto *m* grandson, 2
nieve *f* snow, 5
ninguno not one, none, (pron.), 6; not one, not any (adj.), 6
niña *f* girl, 2
niño *m* boy, 2
nivel *m* level; **nivel de vida** *m* standard of living
no no, 1; **no hay de que** you are welcome, 1
noche *f* night, 1; **buenas noches** good evening, night, 1; **esta noche** tonight, 3; **por la noche** in the evening, 3
nombre *m* name, noun
norte *m* north
nos us, to us, 9; ourselves, 10
nosotros we, 2; us (obj. of prep.), 7
nota *f* grade, 1
noticia *f* news, 11
novecientos nine hundred, 6
noveno ninth, 14
noventa ninety, 4
novia *f* girlfriend, sweetheart, 2
noviembre November, 5
novio *m* boyfriend, sweetheart, 2
nube *f* cloud, 7
nuestro our, 5
nueve nine, 1
nuevo new, 2; **¿qué hay de nuevo?** what's new?, 1
número *m* number, 1
nunca never, 6

O

o or, 8
o . . . o either . . . or, 6
obra *f* work; **obra maestra** *f* masterpiece
océano *m* ocean, 7
ochenta eighty, 4
ocho eight, 1
ochocientos eight hundred, 6
octavo eighth, 14
octubre October, 5
ocupado busy, occupied, 11
oeste *m* west
oír to hear, 4
ojo *m* eye, 4
ola *f* wave
olvidar to forget, 11; **olivadarse (de)** to forget (about), 11
once eleven, 1
operador(a) operator, 11
oración *f* sentence, 1
oreja *f* ear, 4
orgullo *m* pride
orilla *f* edge, shore
oro *m* gold
os you, to you (fam. pl.), 9; yourselves, 10
otoño *m* autumn, 5
otro other, another, 5; **otra vez** again, 12
oveja sheep, 7

P

padre *m* father, 2
padres *m* parents, 2
paella *f* regional dish from Spain
pagar to pay (for), 9
página *f* page, 1
país *m* country, 11
paisaje *m* landscape
pájaro *m* bird, 7
palabra *f* word, 1
pampa *f* plain
pan *m* bread, 3; **pan tostado** *m* toast, 3
pantalones *m* pants, 5
papa *f* potato, 3

papel *m* paper, 1; **papel higiénico** toilet paper, 10
paquete *m* package, 9
para for, by, in order to, 7; **para que** so that, in order that, 13
parabrisas *m* windshield, 12
parada *f* stop; **de autobús** bus stop, 6
paraguas *m* umbrella, 5
parar(se) to stop, 12
pardo brown, 5
parecer to seem, 9
pared *f* wall, 8
pariente *m* relative, 2
parque *m* park, 6
parte *f* part; **por todas partes** everywhere, 13
parrilla (a la) grilled, 3
pasado *m* past
pasajero *m* passenger, 13
pasaporte *m* passport, 13
pasar to pass, spend (time), happen, 6
pascuas Christmas, Easter, 6
pasear to walk, stroll
paseo *m* ride; **paseos a caballo** horseback rides
paso *m* step
pasta: pasta de dientes toothpaste, 10
pastel *m* pastry, pie, 3
patata *f* potato, 3
patria *f* fatherland
pecho *m* chest, breast, 4
pedir (i, i) to ask (for), 4
peinarse to comb (one's hair), 10
peine *m* comb, 10
película *f* film, 6
pelirrojo red-haired, -headed
pelo *m* hair, 4
peluquería *f* hairdresser's, beauty shop, 6
pensar (ie) to think, intend, 6
peor worse, 11
pepino *m* cucumber
pequeño small, little, 2
pera *f* pear, 3

perder (ie) to lose, to miss (trains, etc.), 9

perdón pardon me, excuse me, 1

perfectamente perfectly, 9

perfecto perfect, 9

periódico *m* newspaper, 11

permiso *m* pardon; **con permiso** excuse me, 1

permitir to allow, to let; **permítame presentar a** . . . allow me to introduce . . . , 1

pero but, 2

perro *m* dog, 12

persona *f* person, 2

personaje *m* character

personal personal, 9

personalmente personally, 9

pescado *m* fish, 3

pescar to fish, 7

peseta *f* monetary unit of Spain

peso *m* monetary unit of Mexico, Argentina, Colombia, Uruguay, and Philippines

pez *m* fish, 7

pie *m* foot, 4

pierna *f* leg, 4

pijamas *m* pajamas, 5

piloto *m* pilot, 13

pimienta *f* pepper, 3

pintar to paint, 4

pintoresco picturesque

piña *f* pineapple, 3

piscina *f* pool, 14

piso *m* floor, story, 8

pizarra *f* blackboard, 1

plan *m* plan

plano flat

planta *f* plant; **planta baja** *f* main floor, 14

plata *f* silver

plátano *m* banana, 3

platillo *m* prepared dish

plato *m* plate, dish, 8

playa *f* beach, 2

plaza *f* square, 6

pluma *f* pen, 1;

población *f* population

poblador *m* inhabitant

poblar to inhabit

pobre poor, 2

pobreza *f* poverty

poco little (quantity), 3

poder (ue) to be able, can, 4; power *m*

policía *m* policeman, 12

pollo *m* chicken, 3

poner to put, place, 4; to turn on (lights, etc.), 8; **ponerse** to put on, 10; **ponerse impaciente** to become impatient, 11

por for, by, through, along, around, down, by way of, because of, on account of, on behalf of, in exchange for, per, 7; **por casualidad** by chance; **por eso** therefore; **por favor** please, 1; **por fin** finally; **por todas partes** everywhere, 13; **por lo menos** at least; **por medio de** by means of

por ciento percent

¿por qué? why?, 3

porque because, 3

portero *m* doorman, 14

porvenir *m* future

posible possible, 9

posiblemente possibly, 9

postre *m* dessert, 3

precio *m* price, 14

preferir (ie, i) to prefer, 4

pregunta *f* question, 1

preguntar to ask (question), 9

preocuparse (de) (por) to worry (about), 10

preparar to prepare, 3

presentar to present, introduce, 1

preso *m* prisoner

prestar to lend, 9

prima *f* cousin, 2

primavera *f* spring, 5

primero first, 11

primo *m* cousin, 2

privado private, 14

probable probable, 9

probablemente probably, 9

problema *m* problem

profesional professional, 9

profesionalmente professionally, 9

profesor *m* professor, teacher, 1

profesora *f* professor, teacher, 1

pronto soon, quickly, right away, 12; **hasta pronto** see you soon; **tan pronto como** as soon as, 13

propio own

propina *f* tip, 11

proporcionar to furnish

próspero prosperous, 6

próximo next

psicológico psychological

pueblo *m* village, town, people, 6

puente *m* bridge, 12

puerta *f* door, 1; gate (airport), 13

puerto *m* port

pues well

puesta del sol *f* sunset

puesto put, placed, 10

pulsera *f* bracelet, 5

pupitre *m* desk (school), 1

puro *m* cigar

Q

que that, who, which, 3; than, 7

¡qué! what!, what a . . . !; **¡Qué barbaridad!** How awful!, 12

¿qué? what?, 3; **¿qué tal?** how are you?, 1

quedarse to stay, remain, 13

quehacer *m* chore

quejarse to complain, 10

querer (ie) to wish, want, desire, love, 4; **querer decir** to mean

querido dear, 9

queso *m* cheese, 3

¿quién(es)? who?, 3

quince fifteen, 1

quinientos five hundred, 6

quinto fifth, 14

quiosco *m* newsstand, 11

quitar to take away;
  quitarse to take off, 10

R

raíz f root, stem; **bienes raíces** real estate
rápidamente rapidly, 9
rápido rapid, fast, 9
rascacielos m skyscraper, 6
rasgo m characteristic
razón f reason; **tener razón** to be right, 5; **no tener razón** to be wrong, 5
recámara f bedroom, 8
recado m message, 14
recepción f front desk, 14
recepcionista m, f receptionist, desk clerk, 14
recibir receive, 9
recibo m receipt, 14
reciente recent, 9
recientemente recently, 9
reclamar claim, 13
recoger to pick up, 13
recomendar (ie) to recommend, 12
recordar (ue) to remember, 6; remind
recto straight ahead, 12
recuerdo m remembrance
refresco m refreshment
refrigerador m refrigerator, 8
regalo m gift, present, 5
registrarse to register, 14
regresar to return
regular regular, fair, 1
rellenar to stuff
reloj m clock, watch, 5
reparar to repair, fix, 12
repasar to review
repaso m review
repetir (i, i) to repeat, 4
requesón m cottage cheese
reservación f reservation, 13
resfriado m cold, 4; **tener resfriado** to have a cold, 4
residencia f residence; **residencia de estudiantes** dormitory, 10
respuesta f reply, answer, 1

restaurante m restaurant, 6
resuelto resolved
resumen m summary, resume
retirar(se) to withdraw
retrete m toilet, 8
revisar to check, 12
revista f magazine, 11
revuelto scrambled, 3
rey m king
rico rich, 2; delicious
río m river, 7
riqueza f wealth
rojo red, 5
rollo de película m roll of film, 13
romper to break, tear, 10
ropa f clothing, 5; **ropa interior** underclothing, 5
ropero m closet, 8
rosado rosé, pink, 5
roto broken, torn, 10
rubio blonde, 2
ruido m noise, 10
ruso Russian, 1

S

sábado m Saturday, 1
sábana f sheet, 14
saber to know (how to), 4
sabio wise
sabor m flavor, taste
sabroso tasty
sacar to take out, 9
sal f salt, 3
sala f living room, 8; **sala de espera** waiting room, 13; **sala de reclamación de equipaje** baggage-claim room, 13
salchicha f sausage, 3
salida f exit, departure, 11
salir (de) to leave, go out of, 4
salud f health
saludo m greeting
sandía f watermelon, 3
sazonar to season
se himself, herself, yourself, themselves, yourselves, 10
secador m dryer; **secador de pelo** hair dryer, 10
secar(se) to dry, 10

secretario(a) m, f secretary, 2
secundaria secondary (school)
sed f thirst, 5; **tener sed** to be thirsty, 5
seguir (i, i) to follow, continue, 12
según according to
segundo second, 11
seguro sure, certain, 12; **seguro de automóvil** m car insurance, 12
seis six, 1
seiscientos six hundred, 6
sello m stamp, 9
selva f jungle, 7
semáforo m traffic light, 12
semana f week, 1; **semana pasada** last week, 6; **semana que viene** next week, 10; **fin de semana** m weekend, 1
sencillo simple; **cuarto sencillo** m single room, 14
sensible sensitive
sentarse (ie) to sit down, 10
sentir (ie, i) to regret, feel sorry, 12
sentirse (ie, i) to feel, 10
señalar to indicate
señor m man, gentleman, sir, Mr., 1
señora f ma'am, lady, Mrs., 1
señorita f lady, Miss, 1
septentrional northernmost
septiembre September, 5
séptimo seventh, 14
ser to be, 2
serio serious, 2
serpiente f snake, 7
servicio m service, 14; restroom, 11
servilleta f napkin, 8
servir (i, i) to serve, 13
sesenta sixty, 4
setecientos seven hundred, 6
setenta seventy, 4
sexto sixth, 14
si if, 14
sí yes, 1
siempre always, 6
siete seven, 1
siglo m century
siguiente following

silla *f* chair, 1

sillón *m* (easy) chair, 8

simpático nice (person), 2

sin without, 7; **sin embargo** nevertheless

sinfín *m* endless amount

singular unique

sino but

síntoma *m* symptom

sobre *m* envelope, 9; about, over; **sobre todo** above all, especially

sobremesa *f* after dinner

sobreponer to overcome

sobrevivir to survive

sobrina *f* niece, 2

sobrino *m* nephew, 2

¡socorro! help!, 12

sofá *m* sofa, 8

sol *m* sun, 7; **hacer sol** to be sunny, 5

solamente only

soledad *f* solitude

sombrero *m* hat, 5

sonar (ue) to ring, sound, 10

sonido *m* sound

sopa *f* soup, 3

sostén *m* bra, 4

sótano *m* basement, 8

su his, her, your, its, their, 5

subir (a) to climb, go up, get on, 8

sucio dirty, 5

sudoeste *m* southwest

suelo *m* floor, 8

sueño *m* dream; **tener sueño** to be sleepy, 5

suerte *f* luck; **tener suerte** to be lucky

suéter *m* sweater, 5

sugerencia *f* suggestion

sugerir (ie, i) to suggest, 12

sumamente extremely

superar to overcome

superpoblado overpopulated

sur *m* south

surgir to arise

suroeste *m* southwest

sustentar to support

suyo his, hers, its, theirs, yours, 5

T

tal such, like; **con tal que** provided that, 13; **¿qué tal?** how are you?, 1; **tal vez** perhaps

talla *f* size, 5

también also, too, 6

tambor *m* drum

tampoco neither, not either, 6

tan so, as, 11; **tan pronto como** as soon as, 13

tanque *m* tank, 12

tanto so much, as much, 11; **tantos** so many, as many, 11; **tanto como** as much as

tapa *f* appetizer

taquilla *f* ticket window, 11

tarde *f* afternoon, 1; late, 3; **buenas tardes** good afternoon, 1; **más tarde** later, 3; **por la tarde** in the afternoon, 3

tarea *f* task, homework, assignment, 1

tarjeta *f* card; **tarjeta de crédito** credit card, 9; **tarjeta de embarque** boarding pass, 13; **tarjeta postal** *f* post card, 9

taxi *m* taxi, 6

taza *f* cup, 8

té *m* tea, 3

te you, to you, 9; yourself, 10

teatro *m* theater, 6

telefonear to telephone, 11

teléfono *m* telephone, 9; **teléfono público** public telephone, 11

televisor *m* television set, 8

tema *m* theme

temer to fear, 12

templado mild, temperate

temprano early, 3

tenedor *m* fork, 8

tener to have, 4; **tener . . . años** to be . . . years old, 5; **tener cuidado** to be careful, 12; **tener ganas de** to feel like, 5; **tener que** to have to, 5; **tener razón** to be right, 5; **tener resfriado** to have a cold, 4; **tener sueño** to be sleepy, 5

tenis *m* tennis, 4

tercero third, 14

terminar to finish, 9

ti you (obj. of prep.), 7

tía *f* aunt, 2

tiempo *m* time, 8; weather, 5; tense (verb); **a tiempo** on time, 3

tienda *f* store, shop, 6

tierra *f* land, earth, 7

tijeras *f* scissors

tío *m* uncle, 2

título *m* degree

tizo *f* chalk, 1

toalla *f* towel, 8

tocadiscos *m* record player, 8

tocar to touch, to play (instrument), 4

tocino *m* bacon, 3

todavía yet, still

todo all, 3; **todo el día** all day, 3; **toda la noche** all night, 3; **todos los días** everyday, 3; **todo el mundo** everyone, 13

tomar to take, drink, eat, 3

tomate *m* tomato, 3

tonto dumb, stupid, silly, 2

toro *m* bull; **corrida de toros** *f* bullfight

torta *f* cake, 3

tortilla *f* flat cornmeal pancake (Mexico); omelet (Spain)

tos *f* cough, 4

trabajar to work, 3

trabajo *m* job, work, 9

traducir to translate, 4

traer to bring, 4

tráfico *m* traffic, 12

traje *m* suit, 5; **traje de baño** *m* bathing suit, 5

tránsito *m* traffic, 12

tratar de to try to, 9

trece thirteen, 1

treinta thirty, 4

tren *m* train, 11

tres three, 1

trescientos three hundred, 6

trigo *m* wheat

tripulación *f* crew

triste sad, 2
trono *m* throne
tú you, 2
tu your, 5
tuyo yours, of yours, 5

U

último last, ultimate
un a, an, 1
una a, an, one, 1
uno one, 1
unido united
unir to unite
universidad *f* university, 2
usar to use, 4
usted you, 2; **ustedes** you (pl.), 2
uva *f* grape, 3

V

vaca *f* cow, 7
valiente brave
valer to be worth
valle *m* valley, 7
vaso *m* glass, 8
vaqueros *m* jeans, 5
vecino *m* neighbor, 8

vegetal *m* vegetable, 3
veinte twenty, 1
vela *f* candle, sail
velocidad *f* speed, 12
vender to sell, 3
venir to come, 4
venta *f* sale
ventana *f* window, 1
ventanilla *f* cashier's window, 9
ver to see, 4; **a ver** let's see
verano *m* summer, 5
verdad *f* truth, 4; really
verde green, 5
vestíbulo *m* lobby, 14
vestido *m* dress, 5
vestirse (i,i) to dress, to get dressed, 10
vez *f* time, occasion; **a veces** at times, sometimes, 6; **en vez de** instead of, 7; **muchas veces** often, 8; **otra vez** again, 12; **una vez** once, 8
vía *f* route, way
viajar to travel, 7
viaje *m* trip, 7; **hacer un viaje** to take a trip, 7
viajero *m* traveler, 9
vida *f* life
viejo old, 2

viento *m* wind, 5; **hacer viento** to be windy, 5
viernes *m* Friday, 1
vinagre *m* vinegar, 3
vino *m* wine, 3
visitar to visit, 6
vista *f* view
visto seen, 10
vivir to live, 3
volar (ue) to fly, 13
volver (ue) to return, 4
vosotros you (familiar pl.), 2
voz *f* voice; **en voz alta** aloud, 1
vuelo *m* flight, 13
vuelta: ida y vuelta round-trip, 11
vuelto returned, 10
vuestro your, 5

Y

y and, 1; plus
ya already, 6; **ya que** since
yo I, 2

Z

zanahoria *f* carrot, 3
zapato *m* shoe, 5

ENGLISH-SPANISH ▪

A

a un, una, 1
able, to be poder (ue), 4
abode morada *f*
about de, 2; sobre
above encima de, 7
abroad en el exterior
accident accidente *m*, 12
according to según
ache dolor *m*, 4
achieve alcanzar
A.D. d.C. (después de Cristo)
add añadir
address dirección *f*, 9
advice consejo *m*

affection cariño *m*, 9
afraid, to be temer, 12; tener miedo, 5
after después de, 7; después de que, 13
afternoon tarde *f*, 1; **good afternoon** buenas tardes, 1; **in the afternoon** por la tarde, 3
again otra vez, 12
against contra
age edad *f*
air aire *m*, 12; **air conditioning** aire acondicionado, 14
airline línea aérea *f*, 13
airmail correo aéreo *m*, 9

airplane avión *m*, 13
airport aeropuerto *m*, 13
alarm clock despertador *m*, 10
all todo(s), 3
allow dejar, 11; permitir, 1
almond almendra *f*
almost casi
along por, 7; a lo largo de
already ya, 6
aloud alto; en voz alta, 1
also también, 6
altitude altura *f*
always siempre, 6
American americano, 1
amiable amable, 2
among entre, 7

amusing divertido, 2
ancestor ascendiente
ancient antiguo
Andalusian andaluz
and y, 1; e (before i, hi)
angry enojado, 2
angry, to get enojarse, 10
anguish angustia f
animal animal m, 7
another otro, 5
answer contestar, 9; respuesta f, 1
antithetical antitético
any cualquier
appetizer tapa f
apple manzana f, 3
approach aproximarse, acercarse
April abril, 5
area code código de área m, 11
arise surgir
arm brazo m, 4
around por, 7
arrival llegada f, 11
arrive llegar, 3
artifact artesanía f
as como, tan, 11; **as much (many) as** tanto(s) como, 11; **as soon as** tan pronto como, 13
ask preguntar, 9; **to ask for** pedir(i, i), 4
assemble convocar
assignment tarea f, 1
assure asegurar
at a, en, 2; **at least** por lo menos; **at the same time** a la vez
attentively atentamente, 9
August agosto, 5
aunt tía f, 2
autumn otoño m, 5
avenue avenida f, 6
avocado aguacate m
awful: how awful! ¡qué barbaridad!, 12

B

baby bebé m, 2; nena f, nene m, 2

back espalda f, 4
background fondo m
bacon tocino m, 3
bad malo, 2
badly mal, 2
bag bolsa f, 5
baggage equipaje m, 13; **baggage-claim room** sala de reclamación de equipaje f, 13
bake hornear
banana banana f, 3; plátano m, 3
bank banco m, 6
bar bar m, 6
baseball béisbol m, 4
basement sótano m, 8
basketball básquetbol m, 4
bath baño m, 8; **to take a bath** bañarse, 10
bathing suit traje de baño m, 5
bathroom baño m, 8
bathtub bañera f, 8
battery batería f, 12
battle batalla f
bay bahía f
B.C. a.C. (antes de Cristo)
be ser, estar, 2
beach playa f, 2
bean frijol m, 3
beat batir
beautiful hermoso, 2; bello
beauty belleza f, **beauty shop** peluquería, 6
because porque, 3; **because of** por, 7; debido a; a causa de
become llegar a ser; hacerse
bed cama f, 8
bedroom alcoba f, 8; recámara f, 8
beer cerveza f, 3
before antes de, 7; antes de que, 13
begin empezar (ie), 9
behavior comportamiento m
behind detrás de, 7
believe creer, 12
bellboy botones m, 14
bench banco m, 4
beneath debajo de, 7
bequeath legar
beside al lado de, 7

besides además de
best el mejor, 11
better mejor, 11
between entre, 7
beverage bebida f, 3
bicycle bicicleta f, 6
big grande, 2
bill cuenta f, 14
bird pájaro m, 7
birthday cumpleaños m, 6
black negro, 5
blackboard pizarra f, 1
blanket cobija f, 14
block cuadra f, 12; manzana f, 12
blond rubio, 2
blouse blusa f, 5
blue azul, 5
boarding pass tarjeta de embarque f, 13
boat barco m, 7
body cuerpo m, 4
book libro m, 1
bookcase estante m, 8
bookstore librería f, 6
boots botas f, 5
border frontera f, 12
bored aburrido, 2
born nacido; **be born** nacer
boss jefe m
both ambos
boy chico m, 2; muchacho m, 2
boyfriend novio m, 2
bra sostén m, 5
bracelet pulsera f, 5
brake freno m, 12
brave valiente
bread pan m, 3; **bread shop** panadería f
break romper, 10; fracturar
breakfast desayuno m, 3; **have breakfast** desayunar, 14
breast pecho m, 4
bridge puente m, 12
bring traer, 4
broken roto, 10
brother hermano m, 2
brown pardo, 5; castaño (hair)
brunette moreno, 2
brush cepillar(se), 10; cepillo m, 10

building edifico *m*, 6
bull toro *m*, **bullfight** corrida de toros *f*
bureau cómoda *f*, 8
bus autobús *m*, 6; **bus stop** parada de autobús *f*, 6
businessman hombre de negocios *m*, 2
businesswoman mujer de negocios *f*, 2
busy ocupado
but pero, 2
butter mantequilla *f*, 3
buy comprar, 3
by por, 7; para, 7; **by way of** por, 7; **by means of** por medio de; **by chance** por casualidad

C

cafe café *m*, 6
cake torta *f*, 3
call llamar, 4; llamada *f*, 11; **collect call** llamada de cobro revertido, 11; **long-distance call** llamada de larga distancia, 11; **person-to-person call** de persona a persona, 11; **station-to-station call** llamada común, 11
calculator calculadora *f*, 9
camera cámara *f*, 13
candle vela *f*
capture cautivar
car coche *m*, 2; carro *m*, 2; auto *m*, 2; **car insurance** seguro de automóvil *m*, 12
card tarjeta *f*; **credit card** tarjeta de crédito, 9
care cuidado *m*; **to be careful** tener cuidado, 12
carpet alfombra *f*, 8
carrot zanahoria *f*, 3
carry llevar, 5
cartoon caricatura *f*, 11
case caso *m*; **in case** en caso de que, 13
cash cobrar, 9; efectivo *m*, 9
cassette cassette *m*, 8

cat gato *m*, 7
cathedral catedral *f*, 6
Catholic católico
cattle ganado *m*
center centro *m*, 6
century siglo *m*
cereal cereal *m*, 3
certain (sure) seguro, 13
certified certificado
chair silla *f*, 1; **easy chair** sillón *m*, 8
chalk tiza *f*, 1
change cambiar, 9; cambio *m*, 9
characteristic rasgo *m*
charge, to be in encargarse
charge cobrar, 9; **charge card** tarjeta de crédito *f*
cheap barato, 5
check revisar, 12; (baggage) facturar, 13; cheque *m*, 9; **traveler's check** cheque de viajero *m*, 9
checkbook libro de cheques *m*, 9
cheese queso *m*, 3
cherry cereza *f*, 3
chest pecho *m*, 4; **chest of drawers** cómoda *f*, 8
chicken pollo *m*, 3; gallina *f*, 7
chickpea garbanzo *m*
child niño *m*, 2; niña *f*, 2
chimney chimenea *f*, 8
Chinese chino, 1
chivalry caballería *f*
choose elegir
chore quehacer *m*
Christmas Navidad *f*, 6; Pascuas *f*, 6
church iglesia *f*, 6
cigar puro *m*
citizen ciudadano *m*
city ciudad *f*, 2
claim reclamar, 13
class clase *f*, 1
clean limpiar, 4; limpio, 5
clerk dependiente(a), empleado(a) *m*, *f*
climb subir (a), 8
clock reloj *m*, 5

close cerrar (ie), 4; **closed** cerrado, 4
closet ropero *m*, 8
clothing ropa *f*, 5
cloud nube *f*, 7
coat abrigo *m*, 5
coffee café *m*, 3
coin moneda *f*, 9
coincidence casualidad *f*
cold frío, 3; resfriado *m*, 4; **be cold (persons)** tener frío, 5; **be cold (weather)** hacer frío, 5; **have a cold** tener resfriado, 4
collide chocar
comb peinarse, 10; peine *m*, 10
come venir, 4
command mandar, 9; mandato *m*
companionship compañerismo *m*
compendium compendio *m*
complain quejarse, 10
complete completar
complex complejo
computer computadora *f*, 9
concert concierto *m*
confidence confianza *f*
confirm confirmar, 13
congratulations felicitaciones *f*, 14
conquer vencer
continue seguir (i, i), 12; continuar
cook cocinar, 4
cookie galleta *f*, 3
cool fresco, 5; **be cool (weather)** hacer fresco, 5
corn maíz *m*, 3
corner esquina *f*, 12; rincón *m*
corrupt corromper
cost costar (ue), 5
cottage cheese requesón *m*
cotton algodón *m*
cough tos *f*, 4
count contar (ue)
counter mostrador *m*
country campo *m*, 2; país *m*, 11
course curso *m*; **of course** claro, 12
cousin primo *m*, 2; prima *f*, 2
covered cubierto

cow vaca *f,* 7
coward cobarde *m*
cowboy gaucho *m* (Argentina)
craft artesanía *f*
cream crema *f,* 3
create crear
credit card tarjeta de crédito, *f,* 9
creole criollo *m*
crew tripulación *f*
cross cruzar, 12
cucumber pepino *m*
cup taza *f,* 8
currency moneda *f,* 9
curtain cortina *f,* 8
custard flan *m*
customs aduana *f,* 13
cut cortar(se), 10

D

daily diario
dance bailar, 4; baile *m*
daring atrevimiento *m*
date fecha *f,* 6; cita *f*
daughter hija *f,* 2
day día *m,* 1; **all day** todo el día, 3; **everyday** todos los días, 3
dead muerto, 10
dear querido, estimado, 9
death muerte *f*
debt endeudamiento *m*
December diciembre, 5
deception engaño *m*
decide decidir
deeper al fondo
defeat derrotar, derrota *f*
degree título *m*
delay demora *f,* 11
delicious rico
delight deleitar
demand exigir
deny negar (ie), 12
department store almacén *m,* 6
departure salida *f,* 11
deposit depositar, 9
desert desierto *m,* 7
design diseñar

desire querer (ie), 4; desear, 3; deseo *m*
desk escritorio *m,* 1; **(school)** pupitre *m,* 1; **desk clerk** recepcionista *m, f,* 14; **front-desk** recepción *f,* 14
dessert postre *m,* 3
deteriorate empeorar
develop desarrollar
development desarrollo *m*
devil diablo *m*
dial marcar, 11
diarrhea diarrea *f*
die morir (ue, u), 7
died muerto, 11
difficult difícil, 2
digestive digestivo
dine cenar, 14
dining room comedor *m,* 8
dinner, to have cenar, 14; cena *f,* 3
dirty sucio, 5
disadvantage desventaja *f*
disagreeable (persons) antipático, 2
dish platillo *m;* plato *m,* 8
disrespectful irrespetuoso
diving (skin or scuba) buceo *m*
do hacer, 4
doctor médico *m,* 2; médica *f,* 2
documents documentación *f,* 13
dog perro *m,* 2
done hecho, 10
donkey burro *m,* 7
door puerta *f,* 1
doorman portero *m,* 14
dormitory dormitorio *m;* residencia de estudiantes *f,* 10
double doble, 14
doubt dudar, 12; duda *f*
dough masa *f*
down por, 7
downtown centro *m,* 6
drawing dibujo *m*
dress vestido *m,* 5; **get dressed** vestirse (i, i), 10
drink beber, 3; tomar, 3; bebida *f,* 3; **soft drink** gaseosa *f,* 3

drive manejar, 4
drum tambor *m*
dry secar(se), 10; seco
dumb tonto, 2
during durante, 7

E

each cada, 11
ear oreja *f,* 4
early temprano, 3
earn ganar, 9
earring arete *m,* 5
earth tierra *f,* 7
easily fácilmente, 9
Easter Pascuas *f*
easy fácil, 2
east este *m*
eat comer, 3; tomar, 3
edge orilla *f*
effort esfuerzo *m*
egg huevo *m,* 3
eight ocho, 1
eighteen diez y ocho, dieciocho, 1
eighth octavo, 14
eighty ochenta, 4
either . . . or o . . . o, 6
electric eléctrico; **electric shaver** máquina de afeitar *f,* 10
elevator ascensor *m,* 14
eleven once, 1
empire imperio *m*
enchant encantar
endless (amount) sinfín *m*
engaged comprometido, 10; **to get engaged to** comprometerse con, 10
engineer ingeniero(a) *m, f,* 2
engineering ingeniería *f*
English inglés, 2
enjoy gozar; disfrutar
enlighten alumbrar
enough bastante, 11
enslave avasallar
enter entrar (en), 6
envelope sobre *m,* 9
equal igual
especially sobre todo
ethic ética *f*

even aun

evening noche *f*, 13; **good evening** buenas noches, 1

event acontecimiento *m*

every todo(s), 3; cada, 11; **everyday** todos los días, 3; **everyone** todo el mundo, 13; **everywhere** por todas partes, 13

exactly debidamente, exactamente

exam examen *m*, 1

examine examinar

exchange cambio *m*, 9; **in exchange for** por, 7

excuse me perdón; con permiso, 1

exercise ejercer

exercise ejercicio *m*, 1

exit salida *f*, 11

expensive caro, 5

experience experimentar

extremely sumamente

eye ojo *m*, 4

F

face cara *f*, 4

fact hecho *m*

failure fracaso *m*

fair regular

faithful fiel

fall: to fall in love enamorar(se), 10

fall caída *f*

family familia *f*, 2

far lejos, 7

farm hacienda *f*, 7

fast rápido, 9

fasten abrocharse, 13

fat gordo, 2

father padre *m*, 2

fatherland patria *f*

fear miedo *m*, 4; temer, 12; tener miedo, 5

February febrero, 5

feel sentir (ie, i), 13; sentirse (ie, 1), 10; **to feel like** tener ganas de, 5

fever fiebre *f*, 4

field campo *m*, 2

fifteen quince, 1

fifth quinto, 14

fifty cincuenta, 4

fight luchar; lucha *f*

fill llenar, 12

film película *f*, 6

finally por fin

find encontrar (ue), 9; hallar

fine bien, 2; multa *f*, 12

finger dedo *m*, 4

finish terminar, 9

fire fuego *m*

fireplace chimenea *f*, 8

first primero, 11

fish pescar, 7; pescado *m*, 3; pez *m*, 7

five cinco, 1

fix arreglar, 12; reparar, 12

flat desinflado, 12; **flat tire** llanta desinflada *f*, 12

flat plano

flight vuelo *m*, 13

floor (story) piso *m*, 8; suelo *m*, 8; **main floor** planta baja *f*, 14

flour harina *f*

flourish florecer

flower flor *f*, 7

flu gripe *f*

fly volar (ue), 13; mosca *f*, 7

follow seguir (i, i), 12

following siguiente; a continuación

food comida *f*, 3; alimento *m*

foot pie *m*, 4

football fútbol *m*, 4

for por, 7; para, 7

foreign extranjero

forest bosque *m*, 7

forget olvidar, 11; **to forget (about)** olvidarse de, 11

fork tenedor *m*, 8

fortress fortaleza *f*

forty cuarenta, 4

forward adelante

four cuatro, 1

fracture fractura *f*

free libre

freedom libertad *f*

French francés, 1

frequent frecuente, 9

frequently frecuentemente, 9

fresh fresco, 4; frescura *f*

Friday viernes *m*, 1

fried frito, 3

friend amigo(a) *m, f*, 2; compañero(a) *m, f*

friendship amistad *f*

from de, 2; desde

fruit fruta *f*, 3

full lleno

funny divertido, 2

furniture muebles *m*, 8

future porvenir *m*

G

garage garaje *m*, 8

garden jardín *m*, 8

garlic ajo *m*, 3

gasoline gasolina *f*, 12

gate (airport) puerta *f*, 13

general general, 9

generally generalmente, 9

German alemán, 1

gerund gerundio *m*

get (obtain) conseguir (i, i), 13; obtener; **(receive)** recibir, 9; **get angry** enojarse, 10; **get dressed** vestirse (i, i), 10; **get engaged** comprometerse, 10; **get married** casarse, 10; **get off** bajar (de), 8; **get on** subir (a), 8; **get up** levantarse, 10

gift regalo *m*, 5

girl chica *f*, 2; muchacha *f*, 2

girlfriend novia *f*, 2

give dar, 4

glad, to be alegrarse, 12

glass (drinking) vaso *m*, 8; copa *f*, 8; vidrio *m*

glasses gafas *f*, 5; lentes *m*, 5

gloves guantes *m*, 5

go ir, 2; **go away** irse, 10; **go down** bajar de, 8; **go out** salir, 4; **go shopping** ir de compras, 5; **go to bed** acostarse (ue), 10; **go to sleep** dormirse (ue, u), 10; **go up** subir a, 8

goblet copa *f*, 8
God Dios
gold oro *m*
good bueno, 2; **my goodness!** ¡caramba!, 12
good-bye adiós, 1; **to say good-bye** despedirse (i, i), 13
grade nota *f*, 1
granddaughter nieta *f*, 2
grandfather abuelo *m*, 2
grandmother abuela *f*, 2
grandson nieto *m*, 2
grape uva *f*, 3
grass hierba *f*, 7
gray gris, 5; **(hair)** canoso
great grande, 2; gran
green verde, 5; **green beans** habichuelas *f*, 3; judías *f*, 3
greeting saludo *m*
grilled a la parrilla, 3
grow crecer
growth crecimiento *m*
guest huésped *m*, 14
guide guía *m*, *f*
gum chicle *m*

H

hair pelo *m*, 4
hairdresser's peluquería *f*, 6
hair dryer secador de pelo *m*, 10
half medio, 1
ham jamón *m*, 3
hamburger hamburguesa *f*, 3
hand mano *f*, 4
handsome guapo, 2
happen pasar, 6
happy contento, 2; alegre; **to be happy** alegrarse, 12
hard difícil, 2
harmony concordancia *f*
hat sombrero *m*, 5
have tener, 4; haber, 10; **have a good time** divertirse (ie, i), 10; **have just** acabar de, 9; **have to** tener que, 5
he él, 2
head cabeza *f*, 4; **headache** dolor de cabeza *m*, 4
health salud *f*

hear oír, 4
heart corazón *m*
heat calor *m*
heating calefacción *f*, 14
height altura *f*
hello hola, 1
help ayudar, 11
hen gallina *f*, 7
her su (poss.), 5; ella (obj. of prep.), 7; la (dir. obj.), 9; le (ind. obj.), 9
here aquí, 2
hers suyo (de ella), 5
herself se, 10
hi! ¡hola!, 1
hide esconder
high alto, 2; **high school** escuela secundaria *f*
highway carretera *f*, 12
him lo (dir. obj.), 9; él (obj. of prep.), 7; le (ind. obj.), 9
himself se, 10
his su, 5; suyo (de él), 5
holiday día festivo *m*
home casa *f*, 2; hogar *m*, 8
honey miel *f*; **honeymoon** luna de miel *f*, 14
hope esperar, 13; esperanza *f*
horse caballo *m*, 7
hot caliente, 3; **be hot (persons)** tener calor, 5; **be hot (weather)** hacer calor, 5
hotel hotel *m*, 14
hour hora *f*, 4
house casa *f*, 2
how ¿cómo?, 1; **how are you? how's it going?** ¿qué tal?, 1; ¿cómo está?, 1; ¿cómo te va?, 1
how many ¿cúantos?, 3
how much ¿cuánto?, 3
hug abrazar, 4; abrazo *m*, 4
humble humilde
hundred cien, 4
hunger hambre *m*, 5, **to be hungry** tener hambre, 5
hurriedly de prisa
hurry darse prisa, 12; apresurar
hurt lastimar
husband esposo *m*, 2
hut choza *f*, 7

I

I yo, 2
Iberian ibérico
ice hielo *m*, 3
ice cream helado *m*, 3
if si, 14
illiteracy analfabetismo *m*
impatient impaciente; **to become impatient** ponerse impaciente, 11
important importante, 13
impossible imposible, 13
impressive impresionante
improbable improbable, 13
improve mejorar
in en, 7; **in case** en caso de que, 13; **in exchange for** por, 7; **in front of** delante de, 7; enfrente de, 7; **in order that** para que, 13; **in order to** para, 7; **in spite of** a pesar de
indicate señalar
information información *f*, 14
inhabit poblar
inhabitant poblador *m*
inherit heredar
insect insecto *m*, 7
inside dentro de, 7
insist insistir (en), 12
instead of en vez de, 7
intelligent inteligente, 2
intend pensar (ie), 6
introduce presentar, 1
invite invitar, 9
iron hierro *m*
island isla *f*, 7
Italian italiano, 1

J

jacket chaqueta *f*, 5
jam mermelada *f*, 3
January enero, 5
Japanese japonés, 2
jeans blujeans *m*, 5; vaqueros *m*, 5
jewelry joyas *f*, 5; **jewelry shop** joyería *f*, 6
job empleo *m*, 9; trabajo *m*, 9
juice jugo *m*, 3

July   julio, 5
June   junio, 5
jungle   selva *f*, 7

K

key   llave *f*, 14
kilometer   kilómetro *m* (0.62 mile), 12
kind   amable, 2
king   rey *m*
kiss   besar, 4
kitchen   cocina *f*, 8
knife   cuchillo *m*, 8
know (facts, skills)   saber, 4; **(persons, places)**   conocer, 4
knowledge   conocimiento *m*

L

lack   falta *f*
lady   señora *f*, 1; señorita *f*, 1
lake   lago *m*, 7
lamp   lámpara *f*, 8
land   aterrizar; tierra *f*, 7; terrestre (adj.)
landowner   hacendado *m*
landscape   paisaje *m*
language   lengua *f*
large   grande, 2
last   último; **last night**   anoche, 6; **last week**   semana pasada *f*, 6; **last year**   año pasado *m*, 6
late   tarde, 3; **later**   más tarde, 3
law   derecho *m*
lawyer   abogado *m*, 2; abogada *f*, 2
leader   líder *m*
leadership   liderazgo *m*
learn   aprender, 3
leave   salir, 4; **(leave behind)**   dejar, 11
left   izquierda, 12
leg   pierna *f*, 4
lemon   limón *m*, 3
lend   prestar, 9
less   menos, 11
lesson   lección *f*, 1

let   dejar, 11
letter   carta *f*, 9
lettuce   lechuga *f*, 3
level   nivel *m*
library   biblioteca *f*, 6
licence   (driver's) licencia de chófer *f*, 12
lie   mentira *f*, 4
life   vida *f*
light   luz *f*, 8; ligero
like   gustar, 3; querer(ie), 5
line   fila *f*, línea *f*, 11; **stand in line**   hacer fila, 9
lip   labio *m*, 4
listen   escuchar, 4
little (size)   pequeño 2; **(quantity)**   poco, 3
live   vivir, 3
living room   sala *f*, 8
lobby   vestíbulo *m*, 14
lobster   langosta *f*, 3
lodging   alojamiento *m*
long   largo, 5
look at   mirar, 4
look for   buscar, 4
lose   perder (ie), 9
love   amar, 4; querer (ie), 4; **be in love**   estar enamorado, 10
lover   amante *m*, *f*
low   bajo, 2
luck   suerte *f*
luggage   equipaje *m*, 11
lunch   almuerzo *m*, 3; **have lunch**   almorzar (ue), 14

M

ma'am   señora, 1
machine   máquina *f*, 9
made   hecho, 11
magazine   revista *f*, 11
magnificent   magnífico
maid   criada *f*, 14
mail   correo *m*, 9; echar al correo, 9
mailbox   buzón *m*, 9
maintain   mantener
majority   mayoría *f*
make   hacer, 4
man   hombre *m*, 2

many   muchos, 1; **so many**   tantos, 11
March   marzo, 5
marinate   adobar
market   mercado *m*, 3
marry   casarse (con), 10
mass   misa *f*
masterpiece   obra maestra *f*
matter   importar; asunto *m*
May   mayo, 5
me   mí (obj. of prep.), 7; me (dir. obj. or ind. obj.), 9
meal   comida *f*, 3
mean   querer decir
meat   carne *f*, 3
meet   reunir; conocer, 4; encontrarse
merchant   comerciante *m*, *f*
merry   feliz, 6
mess   lío *m*, 12
message   recado *m*, 14
metro   metro *m*, 6
Mexican   mexicano, 1
middle   mediados
midnight   medianoche *f*, 1
mile   milla *f*, 12
milk   leche *f*, 3
million   millón *m*, 6
mine   mío, 5
mineral water   agua mineral *f*, 3
mirror   espejo *m*, 8
miss   señorita, 1; **miss trains, etc.**   perder (ie), 9
mixture   mezcla *f*
Monday   lunes *m*, 1
money   dinero *m*, 6; moneda *f*
month   mes *m*, 5
moon   luna *f*, 7
Moor   moro *m*
more   más, 11
morning   mañana *f*, 3; **good morning**   buenos días, 1; **in the morning**   por la mañana, 3
Muslim   musulmán
mosque   mezquita *f*
mosquito   mosquito *m*, 7
mother   madre *f*, 2
motor   motor *m*, 12
motorcycle   motocicleta *f*, 6

mountain montaña *f*, 2; **mountain range** sierra *f*, cordillera *f*
mouth boca *f*, 4
movies cine *m*, 6
movie theater cine *m*, 6
Mr. señor, 1
Mrs. señora, 1
much mucho, 3; **so much** tanto, 11
museum museo *m*, 6
my mi, 5
myself me, 10

N

napkin servilleta *f*, 8
native natal
near cerca de, 7
necessary necesario, 13
neck cuello *m*, 4
need necesitar, 3
neighbor vecino *m*, 8
neither tampoco, 6
neither . . . nor ni . . . ni, 6
necklace collar *m*, 5
neighborhood barrio *m*
nephew sobrino, 2
never nunca, 6
nevertheless sin embargo
new nuevo, 2; **what's new** ¿qué hay de nuevo?, 1
news noticia *f*, 11
newspaper periódico *m*, 11; diario *m*
newsstand quiosco *m*, 11
next próximo; **next week** la semana que viene, 10; **next year** el año que viene, 10
nice simpático, 2; amable, 2
niece sobrina *f*, 2
night noche *f*, 3; **all night** toda la noche, 3; **in the evening** por la noche, 3
nightgown camisa de dormir *f*, 5
nine nueve, 1
nineteen diez y nueve, diecinueve, 1
ninety noventa, 4
ninth noveno, 14

nobody nadie, 8
noise ruido *m*, 10
none ninguno, 6
noon mediodía *m*, 1
no one nadie, 6; ninguno, 6
north norte *m*
northernmost septentrional
nose nariz *f*, 4
notebook cuaderno *m*, 1
nothing nada, 6
noun nombre *m*, 1, sustantivo *m*
November noviembre, 5
now ahora, 3
nowadays hoy día
number número *m*, 1
nurse enfermero(a) *m*, *f*, 2

O

obtain conseguir (i, i), 13; obtener
occupied ocupado, 11
ocean océano *m*, 7
October octubre, 5
of de, 2
often muchas veces, 8
oil aceite *m*, 3
old viejo, 2
older mayor, 11
oldest el mayor, 11
olive aceituna *f*, 3
on en, 7; **on account of** por, 7; **on behalf of** por, 7; **on top of** encima de, 7
once una vez, 8
one uno, 1
onion cebolla *f*, 3
only solamente
open abierto, 2, abrir, 3
operator operador(a) *m*, *f*, 11
opposite enfrente de, 7
or o, 8; **either . . . or** o . . . o, 8
orange naranja *f*, 3; **(color)** anaranjado, 5
other otro, 5
ought deber, 4
our nuestro, 5; **ours** nuestro, 5

ourselves nos, 10
outside fuera de, 7
over sobre
overcoat abrigo *m*, 5
overcome superar; sobreponer
overpopulated superpoblado
overwhelming abrumador
owe deber, 4
own propio

P

pack hacer la maleta, 11
package paquete *m*, 9; bulto *m*
page página *f*, 1
pain dolor *m*, 4
paint pintar, 4
painting cuadro *m*, 8; pintura *f*
pajamas pijamas *f*, 5
pants pantalones *m*, 5
paper papel *m*, 1
pardon me perdón, 1; con permiso, 1
parents padres *m*, 2
park parque *m*, 6; estacionarse, 12
pass pasar, 6
passenger pasajero *m*, 13
passport pasaporte *m*, 13
pastry pastel *m*, 3
pay (for) pagar, 9
peach durazno *m*, 3; melocotón *m*, 3
peanut cacahuete *m*
pear pera *f*, 3
peas guisantes *m*, 3
pen pluma *f*, 1; **(ballpoint)** bolígrafo *m*, 1
pencil lápiz *m*, 1
people gente *f*, 6; personas *f*, 6; pueblo *m*, 6
pepper pimienta *f*, 3
per por, 7
percent por ciento
perfect perfecto, 9
perfectly perfectamente, 9
perhaps tal vez
period etapa *f*
person persona *f*, 2
personal personal, 9

personally   personalmente, 9
photo   foto *f*, 13
pick up   recoger, 13
picture   cuadro *m*, 8
picturesque   pintoresco
pie   pastel *m*, 3
pig   cerdo *m*, 7
pillow   almohada *f*, 14
pilot   piloto *m*, 13
pineapple   piña *f*, 3
pink   rosado, 5
pitcher   jarra *f*
pity   lástima *f*, 13
place   poner, 4; lugar *m*, 6; sitio *m*
placed   puesto, 10
plan   plan *m*
plate   plato *m*, 8
plateau   meseta *f*
platform (train)   andén *m*, 11
play (game)   jugar (ue), 4; **(instrument)**   tocar, 4
please   por favor, 1; hágame el favor de . . . , 1
pleasure   placer *m*, gusto *m*
plug   enchufe *m*
policeman   policía *m*, *f*, 12
pool   piscina *f*, 14
poor   pobre, 2
population   población *f*
pork: pork chop   chuleta de cerdo, 3
port   puerto *m*
porter   maletero *m*, 11
possible   posible, 9
possibly   posiblemente, 9
postcard   tarjeta postal *f*, 9
post office   casa de correos *f*, 9
potato   patata *f*, 3; papa *f*, 3
poverty   pobreza *f*
power   poder *m*
prefer   preferir (ie, i), 4
pregnant   embarazada, encinta
prepare   preparar, 3
present (current)   actual
present   presentar, 1
preserves   mermelada *f*, 3
pretty   bonito, 2; lindo
price   precio *m*, 14

pride   orgullo *m*, **fill with pride**   enorgullecer
prisoner   preso *m*
private   privado, 14
probable   probable, 9
probably   probablemente, 9
problem   problema *m*
profesional   profesional, 9
professionally   profesionalmente 9
professor   profesor *m*, 1; profesora *f*, 2
provided that   con tal que, 13
psychological   psicológico
purple   morado, 5
purse   bolsa *f*, 5
put   poner, 4; **put on** ponerse, 10

Q

quality   calidad *f*
quarter   cuarto, 1
question   pregunta *f*, 1
quiet: to be quiet   callarse, 11
quite   bastante, 11

R

railroad   ferrocarril *m*, 11
rain   lluvia *f*, 5; llover (ue), 5; **it's raining**   llueve, 5
raincoat   impermeable *m*, 5
ranch   hacienda *f*, 7
rapid   rápido, 9
rapidly   rápidamente, 9
razor   navaja *f*, 10
read   leer, 4
real estate   bienes raíces
realize   cumplirse
receipt   recibo *m*, 14
receive   recibir, 9
recent   reciente, 9
recently   recientemente, 9
recommend   recomendar, 12
record (phonograph)   disco *m*, 8
record player   tocadiscos *m*, 8
red   rojo, 5; **red-haired, -headed**   pelirrojo

refreshment   refresco *m*
refrigerator   refrigerador *m*, 8
register   registrarse, 14
regret   sentir (ie, i), 12
relative   pariente *m*, *f*, 2
rely on   contar con
remain   quedarse, 13
remember   recordar (ue), 6
remembrance   recuerdo *m*
rent   alquilar, 8
repair   reparar, 12
repeat   repetir (i, i), 4
reply   respuesta *f*, 1
reservation   reservación *f*, 13
resolved   resuelto
rest   descansar, 4
restaurant   restaurante *m*, 6
restroom   servicio *m*, 11; aseo *m*, 11
result   consecuencia *f*
return   volver (ue), 4; **(something)**   devolver (ue), 9
returned   vuelto, devuelto, 10
review   repaso *m*; repasar
rice   arroz *m*, 3
rich   rico, 2
right (direction)   derecha *f*, 12; **(legal)**   derecho *m*; **be right**   tener razón, 5; **right away** pronto, 12; **right now** ahora mismo, 12
ring   sonar (ue), 10; anillo *m*, 3
rise   alza *f*; levantarse, 10
river   río *m*, 7
road   camino *m*, 12
roast   asado *m*; **roasted**   asado, 3
robe   bata *f*, 5
roll of film   rollo de película *m*, 13
room   cuarto *m*, 8; habitación *f*, 14
roommate   compañero(a) de cuarto *m*, *f*, 10
root   raíz *f*
route   ruta *f*, vía *f*
rug   alfombra *f*, 8
run   correr, 4; **(machinery)**   andar, 6; funcionar, 12
Russian   ruso, 1

S

sad triste, 2
saffron azafrán *m*
said dicho, 10
salad ensalada *f*, 3
sale venta *f*
salesman dependiente *m*
saleswoman dependienta *f*
salt sal *f*, 3
same igual
sand arena *f*, 7
sandwich bocadillo *m*, 3; sandwich *m*, 3
sanitation higiene *f*
Saturday sábado, 1
sausage salchicha *f*, 3; chorizo *m*, 3
save ahorrar, 9
say decir, 4
scarce, to be escasear
schedule horario *m*, 11
school escuela *f*, 2
scrambled revuelto, 3
sea mar *m*, 7
seafood marisco *m*, 3
search búsqueda *f*
season sazonar; estación *f*, 5
seat asiento *m*, 13
seatbelt cinturón *m*, 13
second segundo, 11
secondary (school) secundaria
secretary secretario(a) *m, f*, 2
see ver, 4; **see you later** hasta luego, 1; **see you tomorrow** hasta mañana, 1
seem parecer, 9
seen visto, 10
sell vender, 3
send mandar, 9
sensitive sensible
sentence oración *f*, 1
September septiembre, 5
serious serio, 2
serve servir (i,i), 13
service servicio *m*, 14
service station estación de servicio *f*, 12
seven siete, 1
seventeen diez y siete, diecisiete, 1

seventh séptimo, 14
seventy setenta, 4
shame lástima *f*, 13
shampoo champú *m*, 10
shave afeitarse, 10
shaving cream crema de afeitar *f*, 10
she ella, 2
sheep oveja *f*, 7
sheet sábana *f*, 14
shelf estante *m*, 8
shirt camisa *f*, 5
shoe zapato *m*, 5
shopping, to go ir de compras, 5
short (height) bajo, 2; **(length)** corto, 5
should deber, 4
shoulder hombro *m*, 4
show mostrar (ue), 9
shower ducha *f*, 8
shrimp camarón *m*, 3
sick enfermo, 2
sign firmar, 9
signature firma *f*, 9
silly tonto, 2
silver plata *f*
sing cantar, 4
single (room) cuarto sencillo *m*, 14
sink lavabo *m*, 8; fregadero *m*, 8
sir señor *m*, 1
sister hermana *f*, 2
sit down sentarse (ie), 10
six seis, 1
sixteen diez y seis, dieciseis, 1
sixth sexto, 14
sixty sesenta, 4
size talla *f*, 5
ski esquiar, 4
skinny flaco, 2
skirt falda *f*, 5
sky cielo *m*, 7
skyscraper rascacielos *m*, 6
sleep dormir(ue, u), 4; **go to sleep** dormirse, 10; sueño *m*, 4; **be sleepy** tener sueño, 5
slender delgado, 2
slow lento, 9
slowly lentamente, 9; despacio, 12

small pequeño, 2
smoke fumar, 4
snack (afternoon) merienda, 3
snake culebra *f*, 7; serpiente *f*, 7
snow nevar (ie), 5; nieve *f*, 5; **it's snowing** nieva, 5
so así, 1; **so that** para que, 13
soap jabón *m*, 8
socks calcetines *m*, 5
sofa sofá *m*, 7
some alguno, 6
someone alguien, 6
something algo, 6
sometimes a veces, 6
son hijo *m*, 2
song canción *f*
soon pronto; **as soon as** tan pronto como, 13
sorry, to be sentir (ie, i), 12
sound sonar (ue), 10
soup sopa *f*, 3
Spaniard español *m*, 1
Spanish español, 1
speak hablar, 3
speed velocidad *f*, 12
spend (money) gastar, 9; **(time)** pasar, 6
spider araña *f*, 7
spoon cuchara *f*, 8
sport deporte *m*, 4
spring primavera *f*, 5
square plaza *f*, 6
squash calabaza *f*
stairs escalera *f*, 8
stamp sello *m*, 9
standard of living nivel de vida *m*
star estrella *f*, 7
station estación *f*, 11; **railroad station** estación de ferrocarril, 11
stay quedarse, 13
steak bistec *m*, 3
step paso *m*
steward auxiliar de vuelo *m*, 13
stewardess azafata *f*, 13
still todavía
stockings medias *f*, 5

stomach estómago *m*, 4; **stomach ache** dolor de estómago *m*, 4
stop parar, 12
stopover (plane) escala *f*, 13
store tienda *f*, 6
stove estufa *f*, 8
straight ahead recto, 12; derecho, 12
strange extraño, 13
strawberry fresa *f*, 3
street calle *f*, 6
strength fuerza *f*
strong fuerte, 2
student estudiante *m, f*, 1; alumno *m*, alumna *f*, 1
study estudiar, 3; estudio *m*
subway metro *m*, 6
sugar azúcar *m*, 3
suggest sugerir, 12
suit traje *m*, 5
suitcase maleta *f*, 11
summary resumen *m*
summer verano *m*, 5
sun sol *m*, 7; **be sunny** hacer sol, 5
Sunday domingo *m*, 1
sunglasses gafas de sol *f*, 5
sunset puesta del sol *f*
supper cena *f*, 3
support sustentar
sure seguro, 13
sweater suéter *m*, 5
swim nadar, 4
swimming natación *f*
symptom síntoma *m*
syrup almíbar *m*

T

table mesa *f*, 1
tag etiqueta *f*
take (carry) llevar, 5; tomar, 3; **take a bath** bañarse, 10; **take off** quitarse, 10; **take out** sacar, 9; **take care of** cuidar
talk charlar; hablar, 3
tall alto, 2
tank tanque *m*, 12
taste gusto *m*; sabor *m*
tasty sabroso

tax impuesto *m*, 14
taxi taxi *m*, 6
tea té *m*, 6
teacher profesor *m*, profesora *f*, 1
team equipo *m*, 4
telephone teléfono *m*, 11; telefonear, 11; **telephone book** guía telefónica *f*, 11; **public telephone** teléfono público *m*, 11
tell decir, 4
teller cajero(a) *m, f*, 9
temperate templado
ten diez, 1
tennis tenis *m*, 4
tense (verb) tiempo *m*
tenth décimo, 14
test examen *m*, 1
than que, 11
thank agradecer
thanks gracias, 1
that ese *m*, 8; esa *f*, 8; eso (*neuter*), 8; aquel *m*, 8; aquella *f*, 8; que, 3; **that which** lo que, 3
the el, la, los, las, 1
theater teatro *m*, 6
their su(s), 5
theirs suyo, 5
them las, los (dir. obj.), 9; les (ind. obj.), 9; ellos, ellas (obj. of prep.), 7
theme tema *m*
themselves se, 10
there allí, 2
therefore por eso
there is (are) hay, 2; **there was (were)** había, 8
these estos *m*, 8; estas *f*, 2
thing cosa, 5
think pensar (ie), 6; creer, 13
third tercero, 14
thirst sed *f*, 5; **be thirsty** tener sed, 5
thirteen trece, 1
thirty treinta, 4
this este *m*, 8; esta *f*, 8; esto (*neuter*), 8
those esos *m*, 8; esas *f*, 8; aquellos *m*, 8; aquellas *f*, 8

thousand mil, 6
three tres, 1
throat garganta *f*, 4; **sore throat** dolor de garganta *m*, 4
throne trono *m*
through por, 7
throw echar, 9
Thursday jueves *m*, 1
ticket boleto *m*, 11; billete *m*, 11; **round-trip ticket** boleto de ida y vuelta, 11; **ticket window** taquilla *f*, 11
tie corbata *f*, 5
time hora *f*, 1; tiempo *m*, 7; vez *f*; **on time** a tiempo, 3
tip propina *f*, 11
tire llanta *f*, 12; **flat tire** llanta desinflada *f*, 12
tired cansado, 2
to a, 2
toast pan tostado *m*, 3
today hoy, 3
together junto
toilet inodoro *m*, 8; retrete *m*, 8; **toilet paper** papel higiénico *m*, 10
told dicho, 11
tomato tomate *m*, 3
tomorrow mañana, 3
tongue lengua *f*, 4
tonight esta noche, 3
too también, 8; demasiado, 11; **too much** demasiado, 11
tooth diente *m*, 4
toothbrush cepillo de dientes *m*, 10
toothpaste pasta de dientes *f*, 10
torn roto, 10
totality conjunto *m*
touch tocar, 4
toward para, 11
towel toalla *f*, 8
town pueblo *m*, 6
track (train) andén *m*, 11
traffic tránsito *m*, 12; tráfico *m*, 12; **traffic light** semáforo *m*, 12
train tren *m*, 11
translate traducir, 4
trash basura *f*; **trash can** cubo de basura *m*, 14

travel viajar, 7; **travel agency** agencia de viajes *f*, 13; **traveler's check** cheque de viajero *m*, 9

traveler viajero *m*, 9

tree árbol *m*, 7

trip viaje *m*, 7; **take a trip** hacer un viaje, 7

truck camión *m*, 12

trust confiar; confianza *f*

truth verdad *f*, 4

try to tratar de, 9

T-shirt camiseta *f*, 5

Tuesday martes *m*, 1

turn doblar, 12; **turn off** apagar, 8; **turn on** encender (ie), 8; poner, 8

twelve doce, 1

twenty veinte, 1

two dos, 1

type escribir a máquina, 9

typewriter máquina de escribir *f*, 9

U

ugly feo, 2

umbrella paraguas *m*, 5

uncle tío *m*, 2

under debajo de, 7; bajo

underpants bragas *f*, 5

undershirt camiseta *f*, 5

undershorts calzoncillos *m*, 5

understand entender (ie), 4

underwear ropa interior *f*, 5

unfortunate desgraciado

unique singular

unite unir

united unido

university universidad *f*, 2

unless a menos que, 13

unpleasant (persons) antipático, 2

until hasta, 13; hasta que, 13; **until later (see you later)** hasta luego, 1

upon al, 7

V

valley valle *m*, 7

vegetable legumbre *f*, 3; vegetal *m*, 3

very muy, 1

vessel carabela *f*

village pueblo *m*, 6

vinegar vinagre *m*, 3

visit visitar, 6

W

watermelon sandía *f*, 3

wave ola *f*

we nosotros(as), 2

weak débil, 2

wealth riqueza *f*

wear llevar, 5

weather tiempo *m*, 5

Wednesday miércoles *m*, 1

week semana *f*, 1; **weekend** fin de semana *m*, 1; **last week** la semana pasada, 6; **next week** la semana que viene, 10

welcome (you are) de nada, 1; no hay de qué, 1; **welcome** bienvenido, 14

well bien, 1; pues

west oeste *m*

what ¿qué?, 3; **what (that which)** lo que, 3; **what a . . . !** ¡qué . . . !

wheat trigo *m*

when cuando, 3; ¿cuándo?, 3

where ¿dónde?, 3; **(to) where** ¿adónde?, 3; **from where** ¿de dónde?, 3

which ¿cuál(es)?, 3; que, 3

while mientras

white blanco, 5

who ¿quién(es)?, 3; que, 3

whom ¿a quién(es)?, 3

whose cuyo

why ¿por qué?, 3

wife esposa *f*, 2

win ganar, 9

wind viento *m*, 5; **be windy** hacer viento, 5

windshield wiper limpiaparabrisas *m*, 12

window ventana *f*, 1; **cashier's window** ventanilla *f*, 9

windshield parabrisas *m*, 12

wine vino *m*, 3

winter invierno *m*, 5

wise sabio

wish querer (ie), 4; desear, 3

with con, 7; **with me** conmigo, 7; **with you** contigo, 7; **with them** consigo

withdraw retirarse

without sin, 7

woman mujer *f*, 2

wood madera *f*

woods bosque *m*, 7

word palabra *f*, 1

work trabajar, 3; empleo *m*, 9; trabajo *m*, 9; **(machinery)** andar, 6, funcionar, 12; obra *f*

world mundo *m*, 13

worry (about) preocuparse (de) (por), 10

worse peor, 11

worst el peor, 11

worth (be) valer

write escribir, 3

written escrito, 10

wrong (to be) no tener razón, 5; **wrong** equivocado, 11

Y

year año *m*, 5; **last year** el año pasado, 6; **next year** el año que viene, 10; **to be . . . years old** tener . . . años, 5

yellow amarillo, 5

yes sí, 1

yesterday ayer, 6

you tú (fam.), 2; usted (formal), 2; vosotros (fam. pl.), 2; ustedes (formal pl.), 2; ti (obj. of prep.), 7; te (dir. obj.), 9; lo, la, los, las (dir. obj.), 9; le, les (indir. obj.), 9; os (fam. pl.), 9

young joven, 2

younger menor, 11

youngest el menor, 11

your tu (fam.), 5; su (formal), 5; vuestro (fam. pl.), 5

yours tuyo (fam.), 5; suyo (formal), 5; vuestro (fam. pl.), 5

yourself te (fam.), 9; se (formal), 10

yourselves se, 10

Z

zero cero, 1

PHOTO CREDITS

INDEX